# To the thirsty land

## (Autobiograpy of a patriot)

God bless!

Author.

April 2005

# To the thirsty land

## (Autobiograpy of a patriot)

### Emmanuel Evans-Anfom

Africa Christian Press
2003

**ISBN: 9964-87-717-X**

*Typesetting / inside illustration: Kwadwo Osei-Safo*

Africa Christian Press

## TRADE ORDERS

**KENYA:**
Keswick Bookshop
P. O. Box 10242, Nairobi
E-mail: keswick@swiftkenya.com

**SOUTH AFRICA:**
New Africa Books
201 Werdmuller Centre, Newry Street
Claremont 7708, RSA
P. O. Box 23317
Claremont 7735, RSA
Tel: +27 21 674 4136
Fax: +21 674 2920
E-mail: newafrica@naep.co.za

**U. K:**
Africa Books Collective
The Jam Factory
27 park End Street
Oxford Ox1 1HU
U.K.
Tel: +44 0 1865 726686
Fax: +44 0 1865 793298
E-mail: abc@africanbookscollective.com

**U.S.A:**
ACP, USA
130 N. Bloomingdale
Suite 101
Bloomingdale, IL 60108 1035
Tel: 001 630 893 1977
Fax: 001 630 893 1141
E-mail: MAI_LittWorld@compuserve.com

**ZIMBABWE:**
Prestige Books
13 Belgrave House
21 Aberdeen Road
Avondale, Harare
Zimbabwe
Tel: 263 4 335105
Fax: 263 4 335105
E-mail: mccs@africaonline.co.zw

**All Other Orders to:**
Africa Christian Press
P. O. Box AH 30, Achimota
Ghana, West Africa.
Tel: +233 21 244147 / 8
Fax: +233 21 220271
E-mail: acpbooks@ghana.com

*Dr. Emmanuel Evans-Anfom*

# *DEDICATION*

*Dedicated to the memory*
*of*
**MY PARENTS**

*through whom God gave me Life*

*and to*

*my dear* **LEONORA**

*who brought meaning to that Life*

# CONTENTS

ix

# PREFACE

*I was thirsty and you gave me drink (Mt. 25:35)*

Shortly before I retired from the Public Service, at the instance of some friends, I promised that I would one day publish the story of my life. A quarter of a century later, this book comes to fulfil that promise. Although the idea was put on the back burner it was never abandoned. Over the years I made notes in preparation but hesitated in deciding on what form the book should take. Finally, I decided that it would be an autobiography, to write it myself and not to be written by anyone else.

Two years ago I embarked on a journey down memory lane, prepared to go as far as my mind would take me and reaching as far back as the age of four. The story therefore covers a period of four score years and is captured on 31 audiotapes of 90 minutes each!!

The title was inspired by the last line of the Achimota School Prayer which exhorts the sons and daughters of that great school to go forth as "Living water to a thirsty land: - " what may be regarded as the Achimota Commission analogous to the Great Commission in Mat. 28. The cover design attempts to depict the book's message in pictorial form. Our homeland Ghana, thirsts for the living water found in the knowledge and skills of the products of our educational institutions applied in her service. Sadly much living water from Ghana continues to be wasted on distant thirst-quenched lands."

# PREFACE

# ACKNOWLEDGEMENTS

When I started recording the story I began to have doubts about the value of what I was doing, for which reason I nearly gave up. I wondered why anyone should be interested in where and when I was born, how I grew up, etc. However, after reading a few chapters of the early transcripts, my wife Elise prevailed on me to continue, as she found it most interesting. Without her encouragement and sustained support this work would never have seen the light of day. I am indeed eternally grateful to her for her timely intervention.

Others to whom I owe many thanks include Rev. Dr. Chris Hesse, Mr. E. O. Attoh, a young author friend, my children, Nii Okai, Rachel, Charlie and Nii Teiko, my son-in-law, Dr. Henry Baddoo, Mr. Raymond Codjoe, Mr. Kwesi Sam-Woode, Dr. Timothy Awuku Asabre, Mr. K. B. Asante, Prof. J.S. Djangmah, Prof. Silas Dodu and my brother in law, Mr. Luther Henkel. All these people read the manuscript either in full or in part and offered useful suggestions. Mr. Vincent Okunor graciously did the major editing prior to handing over the manuscript to the publishers. The cover design I am proud to say was by my son, Nii Teiko.

Ms. Irene Ablosso for the past two years was an integral part of the project. Not only did she transcribe the majority of the audiotapes but she also worked through the various stages of editing right to the final stage. I owe her a great debt of gratitude for her dedication to the project.

Ms. Edwige Dessein, bi-lingual secretary, came to the rescue by transcribing the last six audiotapes to enable us to meet the deadline given by the publishers. I thank her also for helping with the selection of the pictures.

I thank my respected friend and colleague, Prof. Alex Kwapong, Chairman of the Council of State, for doing me the honour of writing the foreword for the book. Lastly, my sincere thanks go to my publishers, the Africa Christian Press, for their co-orperation and for working hard to outdoor the book in the shortest possible time. I need hardly add that I take full responsibly for any factual errors in the book.

Dr. Emmanuel Evans-Anfom
Leonora Lodge, Osu
September, 2003

# FOREWORD

Dr. Emmanuel Evans-Anfom is, undoubtedly, one of Ghana's living legends. He has been one of the great pioneers of the medical profession in this country and an outstanding university Vice-Chancellor. A gentleman of many parts and varied accomplishments, Dr. Evans-Anfom has indeed lived a rich and fulfilling life. A brilliant surgeon, a talented artist and an outstanding hockey player during his youth and middle age, Evans-Anfom in his later years brought to Ghanaian higher education a wealth of experience, vision and leadership amply recognized in the many local and international positions of honour and distinction that have come his way within his original profession of medicine and the general field of education since his retirement as Vice Chancellor of the Kwame Nkrumah University of Science and Technology, Kumasi.

His life-time of eighty four years has spanned the heyday and end of colonial Gold Coast and four and a half decades of independent Ghana and it is thus no wonder that his memoirs have been eagerly awaited by all and sundry, for Evans-Anfom has indeed touched the lives of many people in this country and abroad in the course of his long and distinguished life.

Old and young readers alike should, therefore, very much welcome the timely publication of this book, **To the thirsty land** (Autobiography of a Patriot), by Dr. Emmanuel Evans-Anfom; and they will find much to interest them in it. Old Achimotans-Akoras, as they are known – will, of course, readily recognize in the title of this book a direct reference to the central mandate given to all students of Achimota to go forth from the School "as living water to the thirsty land:" of Ghana. The "Patriotism" mentioned in the subtitle will become more fully comprehensible to all who complete reading the book and see how well the author has served his nation, Ghana.

Dr. Evans-Anfom's many recollections in his autobiography will no doubt bring much pleasure and nostalgia to his contemporaries, professional colleagues and friends. To the generality of younger readers and most Ghanaians, however, I believe that the story that Dr. Evans-Anfom tells in these pages about his early upbringing James Town and Osu Salem during the 1920's, the seminal impact of Achimota College on his education and career, and his medical training at Edinburgh University in wartime Britain will make the history of a bygone age in Colonial Gold Coast and the early years of independent Ghana come truly alive and provide them with a valuable insight into the true reality of the times and institutions so well chronicled by Dr. Evans-Anfom.

The younger generation of present day doctors today in brain drain – ravaged Ghana and, in particular, today's Ghanaian medical students will, I am certain, find Dr. Evans-Anfom's description of the early years of medical practice and health conditions in Colonial Gold Coast when he started working, not only fascinating but also instructive and inspirational and, one hopes, full of lessons and examples worthy of emulation, such as the high level of commitment and dedicated service that the early Ghanaian medical pioneers gave towards the well being and development of this country.

In this regard, I cannot resist drawing attention to a story that Dr. Evans-Anfom tells against himself. Within the eight years after he started working for the Gold Coast medical service, he was posted at short notice to six different locations in various parts of the country. On one occasion when, as a young surgeon, he had just returned to Accra on leave with his wife and two young children, he was suddenly ordered to interrupt his leave and to proceed to Tamale within four days! When he went to protest to the Director of Medical Services, Dr. Eustace Akwei, about the inconvenience of the transfer and that Tamale was too far away and the latter asked him, "Too far away from where?" he immediately realized the folly of his complaint, Tamale hospital, Dr. Akwei pointed out to him, was facing a crisis, without any qualified surgeon and with only an inexperienced expatriate, i.e. white, doctor who was from faraway Denmark at post. In the circumstances he shamefacedly gave up his protest and proceeded as ordered to Tamale, where he duly provided the professional surgical and other services to the hospital and patients in the Northern Region.

At the peak of his professional career as one of the leading surgeons of the country when he was also a Senior Lecturer at the new University of Ghana Medical School at Korle Bu, Dr. Evans-Anfom accepted an invitation from the council of the Kwame Nkrumah University of Science and Technology to become the second Vice-Chancellor of the University in succession to Dr. R.P. Baffour. There were some dissenting voices at the time of his appointment about this career change of his from the profession of surgery to university administration, especially of a technogical university and at a time when the county was so short of surgeons. Anfom well describes this and other challenges he faced during his six and a half years tenure as the Vice-Chancellor at KNUST.

As the Vice-Chancellor of the University of Ghana at the time (the other Vice-Chancellor in the country being the late Professor Amanor Boateng at Cape Coast, who was Anfom's classmate at Achimota), I can bear unsolicited testimony to the excellent contribution he made to the academic and administrative development of that great university and to higher education in the country as a whole. He was an excellent, loyal and dependable colleague. That he made a wise and good decision to enter the field of higher education in particular and education in general is borne out by the numerous positions of high responsibility and distinction he has held since he retired from KNUST and the chairmanship of the National Council for Higher Education in the 1970's. All these honours are duly reviewed in the latter part of his memoirs and will be better known to readers of this autobiography.

In conclusion, one must mention two important strands in Evans-Anfom's autobiography. One is the poignant, human story of his love and marriage to his talented first American wife, Leonora, who played such an intrinsic part in Evans-Anfom's success as surgeon, Vice-Chancellor and great educationist and the impact of her untimely death on him and his four children. The second strand tells the story of his good fortune in finding his second wife, Elise. He rightly pays tribute to the calming and comforting role that Elise has played in the resolution of his tragic loss and in sustaining his life in his later years, thereby enabling him to write these memoirs! There can also be no question of the fundamental support that he has derived from his solid Presbyterian upbringing and discipline and his firm roots in Ga culture. Have these memoirs then lived up to their title? For my part, the answer is yes.

Professor Alexander A. Kwapong
Accra 12th October, 2003

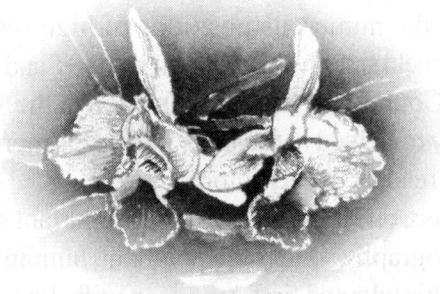

# INTRODUCTION

Amongst my earliest childhood recollections is my grandpa, William Timothy Evans, sitting in his rocking chair with five of his grand-children, all boys, gathered around him to listen to Bible stories. We took turns to sit on his lap: a most comfortable position. I remember on one occasion I found the stories so interesting that, as I happened to be sitting on his lap that day, I lingered on as the others left after the story telling session. Suddenly, grandpa asked me, " Emmanuel, do you know the meaning of your name?" "No, Grandpa." "It means, God with us." "But Grandpa, you told us that God is everywhere, therefore if He is with all of us, why single out some people and call them Emmanuel?" "The Lord does not want you ever to forget that He is with you, and that is why He has, through your parents, given you that name. This means that some others may forget, but you are not to ever forget that God is always with you."

This simple information given me by my grandpa when I was just about 4 years old has had a great impact on me. Throughout my life, I have kept this information in mind, the knowledge that God is with me. Indeed, the story of my life is ample testimony that the Lord has always been by my side. My grandpa was a dominant figure in my life right from the beginning. He had worked for the Basel Mission for many years as a tutor at the Seminary and as a catechist at Akropong Akuapem and, even though he was not a pastor, he was known as "Osofo Evans" or "Owura Evans" all along the Akuapem ridge. I made up my mind right form the beginning that I would one day be like Grandpa. He himself looked like a Basel missionary. He had a luxuriant white beard which we irreverently used to stroke playfully. My ambition was one day to become a teacher, and a catechist and even to go further to become a pastor of the Presbyterian Church.

When I was privileged to attend school at Osu Salem, where the foundations of my training were laid, I continued with Bible study, more of the stories from the Bible which Grandpa had initiated from our childhood. There are certain verses and passages in the Bible which I found attractive the most important and most memorable being the verse inscribed on my Confirmation Certificate before I left middle school. The bible verse was taken from 2Tim 1, 6, "I charge you therefore to rekindle God's gift that is in you." I was always impressed by this verse because it reminded me, as we have always been told, that all men are endowed with some God-given talents. There may be one, there may be several, but the important thing required of each of us is to develop those talents and use them in the service of God. Another verse which I found attractive was "Let your light so shine before men that they may see your good deeds and glorify your Lord in heaven." Other sayings were "Brighten the corner where you are", and also the Golden Rule, "Do unto others what you would want them to do unto you." We were introduced to the Ten Commandments with their dos and don'ts. Later on, I came across the cherished saying of Abraham Lincoln, "As I would not be a slave, neither would I be a master."

All these sayings, either from the Bible or elsewhere, stuck in my mind and reinforced the character foundation that I had at Osu Salem and was topped up at Achimota College. I had the opportunity to practise the virtues required of a good person for, I found that all the training that I was getting was designed to make me a good human being, good to myself and good to society, a useful member of society. Right from the beginning, I took all these things seriously. I tried to obey all the rules and regulations and to conform, and always to be a law-abiding, hard-working member of any community in which I have found myself.

Throughout the period of my formal education and training, I had the opportunity to study the Bible. In particular I am very thankful that I had the privilege to be a member of the Student Christian Movement, which helped in the formative years of my life, to supply spiritual support in my life. It was very good for me to have the opportunity to be part of a Bible study group, and to take part in Retreats and Conferences of the Student Christian Movement, to the extent that throughout my life the Bible has been my point of reference in any situation in which I find myself. The Bible says there is a time for everything. There are times of joy and times of sorrow. Whatever the situation, I have always found solace in some word in the Scriptures.

As the reader may find later on, the economic circumstances of my family were very modest and I consider myself extremely fortunate that by the Grace of God, I have managed through various scholarships to further my education, without which I would not be who I am today! I have given a lot of space to Achimota College because, following the strong character foundation that I had at Osu Salem it was at Achimota that I began to blossom. Those were important formative years in my life and, looking back now, I find that it was at Achimota that I formed the lifelong friendships that I have been privileged to enjoy in my life. At Achimota, certain pertinent questions cropped up. Biology confronted me with Darwin's Theory of Evolution and the Origin of the Species. How could I, a Christian, reconcile that theory with the story of Creation in the Bible? I must say that at first it was a matter that agitated my mind considerably and to which I could find no ready answer. But as time went on, the experience, especially at university, and also further knowledge of the intricacies of science, the complexity of the laws of science and all the wonders of nature conspired to consolidate my belief in the Bible and in the Creation. I came to terms with the fact that, above everything that exists in creation, there is a Force which brought all into being. I found that the more knowledge I acquired, the stronger my Christian faith became. There are those who say there is no God, or that they do not believe in God. That affirmation itself betrays the fact that they acknowledge that there is something or somebody somewhere called God!

Later on at the University of Edinburgh, I was introduced, through reading and through interaction with my mates, to socialist ideology. In actual fact, during a period of flirtation with Socialism I read as widely as I could about Socialism. I must say that I was attracted by the theory underlying the ideology, even to the extent of my believing that Communism (the extreme form of Socialism) at the end of the day could be the answer to all the social problems that we have in this world and that Communism would help to rectify the injustices and inequity that exist in society. I believe many young men and women, at some time or the other, have been drawn momentarily in that direction. However, as I have matured in life and come face to face with the practicalities of life, real life situations, I have come to believe more in a liberal society than a socialist society, which tends to promise utopia, a situation which, in practical terms is impossible to attain.

Capitalism in its naked form certainly represents an ideology of exploitation. Therefore the solution of our social problems must lie somewhere in between these ideologies which occupy the opposite ends of the ideological spectrum. I feel that, as a christian, Liberalism fits in better with my religious beliefs and coincides with the system which I believe is best suited to our circumstances, especially in a developing country like Ghana.

Throughout the narrative, the reader will notice that I have singled out my teachers, at various levels, for special mention. This is in acknowledgment of the help which they gave me. First, the knowledge and guidance that they gave to me and for their counselling when it came to the choice of a career. I believe strongly that we should all be eternally grateful to our teachers. These are the people who helped to impart the kind of knowledge which has helped us, by adding value to any qualities which we possess and helped us to develop. I certainly am grateful to all my teachers, from the very first year at school, through all the levels of my education ending with my university professors!

It is a matter of regret that throughout the world teachers are not given the remuneration commensurate with the work that they do. On the other hand, I believe that the teaching profession must be one of the most satisfying in the world. Before going abroad to study medicine, I taught science for one year at Achimota College and it is interesting that to this day, some of the students that I taught, who are now men and women of substance, important people in society, continue to refer to me as "Teacher." I dare say that teachers get some sort of compensation or intangible rewards in a number of ways. First of all, there is the satisfaction of knowing that someone you taught in the primary school has now become the Chief Justice or the President of Ghana something which must give any teacher a measure of great pride and satisfaction. There are little favours that teachers get from their former students at unexpected places and times, but I feel that teachers deserve far more recognition and reward in society than they do now.

I owe so much to my mother, a debt which I could never repay! First of all for bringing me up in the knowledge and fear of God and for all the support she gave me at a very difficult time when World War II was raging in Europe and there was uncertainty about the future. I wondered then whether I could ever go abroad to study medicine. She was the one who stood firmly by me and counselled patience in spite of side attractions which in the end could have diverted me from my purpose. I am glad that I was able to leave her for almost 8 years and came back for her to enjoy me, if I may put it that way, for another 11 years before she was called. My father did a lot for me at the early stages of my education, but reasons of poor health and also bad economic circumstances prevented him from doing more for me later. But he gave me every moral support and I regret very much that he died at an early age before I finished my secondary schooling, and that he did not live long enough to see and enjoy at least some of the fruits of his labours.

It is very interesting how one's horizon shifts and recedes as one gets on in life. In the elementary school, my horizon was just the outskirts of Accra. At Achimota College, my horizon receded and became the boundaries of the Gold Coast. Why? Because then I met Gold Coast boys and girls from all parts of the country. Then later in Edinburgh, my horizon shifted to the international scene, specifically to Great Britain, for the duration of the War. After the War, it shifted to Europe and, subsequently, during my working life in my travels around the world and meeting all sorts of people, visiting many countries, my horizon really became the geographical end of the world! Mentally therefore, I moved from the village to the town, to the country, to a continent, and then to the world. Now, what has that meant in my life? It has naturally made it possible for me to meet people from different backgrounds, of different races, colours, religions and political beliefs, and to come to realize that, at the end of the day, human beings are all the same. I have learnt to appreciate the qualities of individual human beings and accept them as they are. In short, I would say that from being a citizen of Accra, my outlook, activities, encounters, and interactions have made me a citizen of the world!

Without the taxpayer's money, I could never have had a chance to go abroad to study medicine. Therefore, the least I could do was to come back and serve my country. This is what I have done over the past 53 years since I returned home from my studies abroad as a doctor. It has been an eventful and interesting life, and quite exciting. Before I went abroad to study during World War II, I knew very little of my own country, the Gold Coast, as it was then. I knew Accra, Sekondi and Kumasi, and a few towns in the Eastern Region. Beyond that I knew very little. However, during the time I spent in Britain, I came to know practically every corner of the British Isles!

After coming back home, through service in different parts of the country, I can boast now that I know practically every corner of our country. I have met so many people from different backgrounds. I have made so many friends and I feel quite satisfied that the little professional and other services that I have been able to provide have been appreciated. I draw much satisfaction from the knowledge that everywhere I go in the country I meet former patients, students, professional colleagues in medicine and education and fellow workers in the Lord's vineyard. As the reader may find out, my public service has fallen into two main eras: the first twenty years of service were devoted to active medical service in different parts of the country. Subsequently I switched to education, starting from medical education at the Ghana Medical School as a foundation teacher, and then for almost 7 years, as Vice-Chancellor of the University of Science and Technology and subsequently as Commissioner for Education and Chairman of the Education Commission. All that I am trying to say is that the second part of my career has been focused on education. This is quite interesting because, as the reader may find out later, my first inclination was to train as a teacher after leaving elementary school. My first job was as a teacher at Achimota College. So it looks as if I have gone full circle. My interest in education has always been there. I started with education and I cannot really say I am ending with education, because I am still a doctor. That is my profession. Now I have added education to it and I am in a position now to express an opinion, to give advice and counselling in the field of education also.

As a Christian, one of my favourite passages in the Bible is "Do not be hearers of the word only, but doers also." I believe very strongly that Christianity is a way of life. As Christians, we should expect people to follow the example of our lives and not just tell them what they should do! We should practise what we preach. By doing so, we are more likely to win souls for Christ than if we preached and did not practice. St Paul says, "Faith without works is dead." I believe in that, and it seems to me that it should be impossible to have real faith and not show it with works. Whereas faith without works is dead, it is possible to show good works and yet not have faith. For true christians, we must have both. This is my philosophy of life. I spent years and years studying the Bible and it is still my reference point for any answers which I may need. I, therefore, believe that far more important, and I found this in my life, is to do what the word says. *Apart from the Lord, I am the only one who can testify to what I have gone through every moment of my life.*

I have had opportunities in the past to leave Ghana and go to what is now termed "greener pastures". But I believe that Ghana, has to be built by Ghanaians and the building has to be in Ghana, although I admit that from time to time it may be necessary for a Ghanaian to go abroad and acquire knowledge, skills and experience and then come back and use that experience in helping to develop the country, as some important people are doing at the present time.

This then is the philosophy of my life and I now invite the reader to come with me as we go through memory lane, starting from the very beginning. I hope that the reader will find it an interesting journey!

# CHAPTER 1

# EARLY CHILDHOOD YEARS AND PRESCHOOL

I was born on October 7, 1919 at the Evans Family House, High Street, Accra. The house is situated at the point where Salaga Market Street joins High Street and continues past the lighthouse towards Korle Gonno. My father was William Quarshie Anfom of Accra, Shai, and partly of Nzema origin. Of my paternal grandfather I know very little except that he was at one time a public officer, precisely, a customs and immigration officer stationed at Ada. He later went back home, and my efforts at tracing my roots have usually ended in a cul-de-sac. My mother was Mary Emma Anfom (née Evans), daughter of William Timothy Evans, a well known catechist of the Basel Mission Church, son of a Welsh trader and one time headmaster of the famous Basel Mission Middle School, otherwise known as Osu Salem; he subsequently became a tutor and house father at the Basel Mission Seminary, Akropong, Akuapem.

My paternal grandmother, Mami Akweley, a one-time successful trader in textiles and Aggrey Beads at Ada and Akuse, lived at Dodowa. She was the elder of twin sisters and they built twin houses at Dodowa at the bank of the Dodowa stream as one crossed towards the Zongo and Salem areas. My maternal grandmother, Emma Evans, who came from the Reindorf family died at child-birth in the year 1900 at Akropong.

The Evans Family House where I was born became my main base before I started school. At that time my father was a produce cocoa buyer and he worked for a few years at Mangoase and Pakro, places where I spent short periods with my parents and my elder brother, Joe. When my grandfather retired in the year 1912, he settled at Mampong Akuapem. The house he built was called Beula, situated on a hill at the outskirts of Mampong as one approached the town from Tutu. It is a six-acre property and, during that early period of my life, I spent most of the time shuttling between the family house at Accra and Beula at Mampong. On occasion also, I visited my grandmother at Dodowa. So this period was a very exciting one in my life. I was not stationary; I was moving around and enjoying the freedom and curiosity of life. Needless to say, at that time, Accra was a much smaller place. It was really a town and, as I recollect, the boundary was located somewhere near Tudu and Victoriaborg where the Government printing office was situated; westwards it ended just beyond the Korle Lagoon at Korle Gonno.

Osu, Adabraka, and La were then small satellite townships. Adabraka especially was like a small village where new developments were about to take place. High Street was the main commercial centre of the town, where all the important shops and commercial houses were situated, and it is interesting to note that all the small trading companies which subsequently amalgamated to form the United Africa Company were situated on High Street at the time. I recall Miller Brothers Ltd, F&A Swanzy, John Walkden and a number of other companies, mainly British.

Accra was a harbour town at that time and the port was just a stone's throw from my family house. Important Government offices were situated on the High Street. The Headquarters of the Customs Department was just a stone's throw from my house. There were also important banks and major Government buildings like the Secretariat. At that time, there were very few buildings in that area apart from Government bungalows occupied by British Government officials and also managers of the commercial concerns that I have already mentioned. There weren't many indigenous African houses between Victoriaborg and Christiansborg.

Vehicular traffic was small, and the very few cars were mainly official cars and a handful owned by successful African businessmen and a few professionals like lawyers and doctors. Much of the haulage within the town was done by horse and cart and donkey. There was no universal pipe-borne water and almost every important household had a well. As I recall, there was a major one situated near the Rowe Road Government Boys School, Kinbu School, as we now know it. Indeed, the word *'Kinbu'* is Ga for "the King's well." With the advent of pipe-borne water supply, most of these wells were closed, but in very old family houses in Accra there will be, at this time, remains of these wells.

Just a few years ago there was a tragedy involving some pupils at Akoto Lante School when apparently the concrete slabs covering one of these used wells caved in and many pupils lost their lives.

Sociologically, the population of Accra was homogeneous, with a high percentage of people of GaDangme origin but, as is natural in the scheme of things, over the years, being the capital of the country, where much development physically, economically, politically and in all spheres of life has taken place, Accra has now become highly cosmopolitan, and it isn't surprising that in the metropolis of Accra itself, the indigenous people are now in the minority. This is the lot of any people whose land is selected to become the capital of any country.

As Accra was then a small place there was easy interaction at the social level. Everybody knew more about other people than it is at this time when, with the rapid expansion and growth of the city, transport and communication has become more difficult, although in recent years telecommunications have improved, making interaction between those who have access to the facility easier. As a port at the time, ships anchored off Accra, and it was very interesting for us watching the ships come and go. One had to use surf boats to get to the ships, and I remember on one occasion we had the privilege of visiting a ship. We went by a surf boat and, at the side of the ship, there was what they called a "mammy chair" which was lowered into the boat. After we sat in it we were hauled up unto the deck of the ship. We had an exciting time going round the ship and it was a wonderful experience.

Before I started school, visits to the Evans family house at Mampong Akuapem, where our Grandpa lived, were occasions which we really looked forward to - my elder brother, Joe, and my cousins, Thomas, Willie and Alfred Evans. It was quite clear that the old man looked forward to our visits and, looking back now, I know how very troublesome we must have been to him, but the old man took it all in his stride. What we loved best was sitting on his lap in a rocking chair on the outside verandah overlooking the main road which went from Tutu to Akropong. The estate itself, about a six-acre plot of land, was like an orchard; the old man made sure that almost every important fruit tree was planted there. There were such fruit trees as avocado, guava, orange, plantain, pineapple, together with some exotic spices like cinnamon, nutmeg and coffee. In addition to this, the old man kept some sheep, goats, and poultry. In a sense, one had the feeling that the place was self-sufficient.

Grandpa also bought some farm lands dotted around Mampong, and on these there were cocoa plantations and also food crops, for example, cassava, cocoyam and maize. It was really like an oasis of self-reliance. For breakfast we had goat's milk in our tea, and I recall that my mother and her younger sister, Auntie Lizzy, liked to flavour their tea with cinnamon instead of milk.

Visits to Beula, Mampong, were occasions which we looked forward to with great eagerness. On his part, Grandpa doted on us and took time to tell us interesting stories from the Bible. Of course, being who he was, he had very important friends coming to visit, especially high ranking ministers of the Basel Mission Church, professionals, businessmen and other very important people, not only from the Akuapem range but also from Accra. Nothing pleased him more than showing us off. He used to line us up when we had these important visitors and ask us questions from the Bible, a sort of Bible quiz, knowing very well that we would all acquit ourselves with credit. In a way, this had an early influence on me and, right from the beginning, I decided that one day, after leaving school, I would like to train as a teacher at the Akropong Seminary and eventually become a priest. Of course, subsequent events altered these plans as I will narrate later, but in all, I feel that becoming a doctor rather than a priest has not made much difference to the contributions which, by His Grace, I have been able to make towards the development of this country.

One important visit that stands out clearly in my mind was when Nana Akuapemhene, Nana Akuffo, called. He did not come in majestic splendour. He came with just a couple of attendants, and it was quite clear to us children, from the preparations made for the visit, that this was a very important personality. Indeed, he was the first citizen of Akuapem. He did not have any elaborate gear. He was clothed simply, just a simple man with two attendants, but, as children, we were very much intrigued by this visit. Peeping from our hiding place, we saw with what respect he addressed our Grandpa, who, obviously, had been a long time friend and someone whose opinion he valued strongly. There were other people who visited. There was an important Koforidua businessman, Mr. Sarkodie-Addo, who was a friend of my uncle, Willie (W. T. Evans II), who was a frequent visitor to the house. His grandson, Julius, (Dr. Sarkodie-Addo) is currently a nephew-in-law, being married to my niece, Thelma (née Evans-Lutterodt).

Arriving at Beula was one thing, but getting there was quite another story. We usually went up the steep and dangerous Aburi hill by a Reo lorry owned by my uncle, Willie. It was a laterite road which demanded careful driving and a mechanically sound vehicle. It was quite a task to make the uphill journey from Ayi Mensah to Aburi and then to Mampong; and I recall that we had to make several stops on the way. The driver's mate had a wooden chock. At this time, all the adults had to come down leaving the children in the vehicle with the driver. As the vehicle crept slowly up it was chocked practically every few yards, so that the journey from Ayi Mensah to Mampong took a rather long time. We found it very irritating, as children, but, of course, with Beula as our destination, we were quite prepared to undergo the ordeal and any inconvenience caused by the journey itself. Needless to say, because of the risks involved, both in going up and down the hill, accidents to vehicles, especially those driven by drivers who were not so experienced, were quite frequent, so that in a way the journey to Mampong was quite hazardous.

Before I started school, I paid visits also to my paternal grandmother, Mami Akweley, at Dodowa. These visits were also very enjoyable. It was easier to get to Dodowa. There were no hills to climb, and the old lady, as all grandmothers do, doted on all of us. She found me particularly interesting because of the inquisitive questions that I used to ask. On these occasions also, we met other relatives from my paternal family : my cousins, daughters of my aunt, Mrs. Mercy Olympio, who were at school at the Keta Catholic Convent and who came on visits to Dodowa during the vacation, and also by my cousin, Comfort, daughter of my father's youngest sister, who was married to the son of Nene Doryumu of Doryumu, Shai. My grandmother had roots in Accra and Doryumu, Shai, and indeed, my father was buried at Doryumu in 1938. His tomb which I visit occasionally still stands at the cemetery there.

At this time also, daddy was a produce buyer (that is, a cocoa buyer) based at Mangoase and Pakro and I went there on short visits. The houses in which we stayed were close by the railway line, and I recollect a few occasions running to meet daddy on the platform of the railway station as he returned home from trips along the railway line. At that time there were no reliable, motorable access roads to both Pakro and Mangoase. At Pakro, I remember a Mr. Lokko, who lived next door, and who had an extensive coffee plantation. The Lokko family come from Osu, and for many years there was on the market coffee produced from the Lokko coffee plantation at Pakro. Alas, that business has died over the years, an example of the way in which some of our fathers and grandfathers had the foresight to start agro-businesses in a small way and how, without much encouragement, the businesses just folded up. Clearly, it looks as if for these small-scale businesses to thrive they need a favourable soil and climate in many areas - economically, socially, politically and otherwise. It is my hope that examples like the Lokko coffee, which once flourished in other parts of the country, would be resuscitated as we strive towards economic recovery. It is rather disappointing that Dodowa, Mangoase, and Pakro, all places which I once knew as flourishing commercial centres have now become dying towns. Clearly, there is a lot of work for us to do!

# CHAPTER 2

# ELEMENTARY SCHOOL
## Primary School – James Town Government Boys' School

My cousin, Willie, and I turned five in the year 1924. My elder brother, Joe, and my cousin, Thomas Evans, were already in school, the Government Junior Boys School, James Town, right across the road from the family house. We envied them and looked forward to joining them after our fifth birthday. Meanwhile, we decided that we would see them off every morning when they were going to school. We were really fascinated by the brass band music of the school, and we also watched the whole school parade in front of the school building every morning when they were doing physical training. This was something we really envied and we looked forward impatiently to the day when we would also be registered to start school.

In January 1925, at last the opportunity came, and Willie and I were registered at the Government Junior Boys' School in James Town. What a thrill that was! Our first day at school was memorable. We were wearing our school uniforms and collecting exercise books and writing materials, joining our elder brothers and meeting boys from other places, mostly from James Town. Officially, we were also to start our formal education. The duration of early school at that time was three years - Class One, Class Two, and Class Three. Class One, right at the bottom was called "ABC." This was where we started learning the English alphabet. We also learnt to count. Of course, we had the advantage of having some informal tuition by our elder brothers before we started school and therefore, had a bit of an advantage.

The school uniform was brown khaki, top and bottom, khaki shorts and short-sleeve shirts, most appropriate colour for children of our age, and our parents really had a tough time trying to keep our uniforms clean. By the time we came back home from school our clothes were ready for the laundry and for a change. As we stayed so close to the school, and it took us just less than half a minute to cross the street, we usually waited to hear the school bell ringing in the morning before we ran across the street. Always a close shave, because those who went in late ran the risk of getting some lashes on their backs. I must say, however, that on the whole, we managed to escape punishment.

The headmaster at the school was Mr. I. S. Lamptey, a small man physically but very affable and fatherly. My first class one teacher was a young man called Mr. Aquandah. Like the headmaster, he was short but much younger. A very pleasant person who got on very well with the young. As a master of the wolf cubs he also had very good rapport with us and made his classes very interesting. At that time it was the practice for the class teacher to teach all the subjects and, of course, at that young age, the important thing was to introduce us to the rudiments of the three Rs – Reading, 'Riting and 'Rithmetic. Mr. Aquandah did his best to lay a solid foundation for us. Other teachers in the school, as I recall, were Mr. Kojo Thompson, also young, but someone who obviously, was using teaching as a stepping stone to higher things. Rumour went round that his father was to send him abroad to study one of the professions (medicine I think) and indeed, he soon left us. Unfortunately, he died abroad in the early stages of his studies.

Another teacher, a young man who came straight from the Training College, was Adjei Schandorf, an athletic, handsome man, and an excellent footballer. I think he played for one of the two rival teams in Accra at the time, Standfast, of which he was a regular player. He, like Thompson, also left for further studies abroad after a couple of years with the school. Interestingly, very many years later, I met him in New York on my first visit to that city in 1955. He was then a qualified doctor working at a hospital in Queen's, one of the Boroughs of New York. The interesting thing about Schandorf was that, despite his long absence from home, and this was well over two decades, he remembered most things and he even remembered my name. Schandorf was a contemporary of Nkrumah at Lincoln University in the United States. At Ghana's independence, Nkrumah persuaded him to come back home to settle, which he did.

The other teacher who was very popular with the pupils was Mr. Lamptey. Mr. Lamptey was a good musician, a band master at the school who was also in charge of physical training. He was an active scout master and we looked up to him as a role model. Because of his interest in music, Teacher Lamptey, as he was popularly called not only in the school but in town, became the leader of the Accra Orchestra, one of the musical groups founded in those days and which played on special occasions outside the school.

At that young age, of course, we were more interested in play than in work, and eagerly awaited the day when we would participate in games like football, and engage in physical training and also participate in the activities of the Wolf Cubs, which is a junior version of the Boys' Scout. Teachers Lamptey and Aquandah were the two in charge of the Wolf Cubs section of the school, and we looked forward to camping at various sites on the beaches of Accra, especially the camping headquarters situated near the beach somewhere near where the Baiden Powell Memorial Hall presently stands.

During the year 1927, which was the third year of my starting school, my father got a job at Akuse as a cashier of the Basel Mission Factory and my mother had to join him. My brother, Joseph, and I therefore stayed with our Aunt, Mrs. Ellen Buckle at Belmont House that year. This was one of the buildings which housed Accra Academy when it was founded in 1931. Auntie Ellen's two daughters, Thelma and Elizabeth, were then at the Wesley Mission Girls' School which was a boarding school and was situated at the site where the Bank of Ghana now stands. It was an enjoyable year for us but we knew - my brother and I – that it was a temporary arrangement and that sooner or later we would move to the Senior School at Rowe Road, at the school presently called Kinbu School. In December of the year 1927 we completed studies at the James Town Junior Boys' School and said good-bye to the school.

## Rowe Road Government Boys' School

The following month, January 1928, we were promoted to the Senior School. We entered the Government Senior Boys' School at Rowe Road in Standard One. At that time the Senior School had seven classes, from Standard One to Standard Seven. It was at Standard Seven that one had to take the Standard Seven School Leaving Certificate Examination. The final destination of most children who entered the formal education system was Standard Seven. In the same month that we started school at the Government Senior Boys' School, my brother and I were moved from Accra to Osu. Our parents had decided that the time had come for us to really start laying the foundation of discipline and character building and we were, therefore, ushered into what I may call the Basel Mission/Presbyterian atmosphere. I was entrusted to the care of the Rev. and Mrs. Ludwig Lawrence Richter, the District Priest at Osu at the time (who later became Moderator of the Presbyterian Church of Gold Coast). My brother, Joe, was entrusted to the care of Mr. and Mrs. E. Max Dodu. Mr. Max Dodu was at the time headmaster of the Presbyterian Middle School. I stayed with the Richters, but continued to attend the school at Rowe Road for another two years. Incidentally, my brother, Joe, also continued at the Government School until he got admission to the boarding school, after one year.

I must now say a word about the Government Senior School. As there were seven classes ranging from Standard One to Standard Seven, the age range was also quite wide. The Headmaster of the School at that time was Mr. H. M. Grant, a stern disciplinarian. The teachers that I remember were Mr. V. C. Welbeck, a very friendly character who was very good with the boys and we all liked him. Mr. Abeashie-Mensah was also very outgoing and clearly one who cared for the welfare of the boys. Mr. Bruce-Tagoe was a pleasant and affable gentleman, very courteous in manners and in speech, and even at our tender age he treated us with much deference. Incidentally, all these teachers lived beyond the ripe old age of 80. Mr. Bruce-Tagoe died just a few years ago in his late 80s. I also remember a young well-dressed, pleasant and polished young man who was the Standard Seven teacher, Mr. William Van Lare. He later on went overseas to study law, and, on his return home, after a brief law practice, subsequently joined the Bench and became one of the outstanding judges of the country. Indeed, he was one of the three judges who, under the chairmanship of the then Chief Justice, Sir Arku Korsah, were dismissed by the first president of the Republic, Dr. Kwame Nkrumah, because of a judgment of the Supreme Court which Nkrumah did not like.

## Presbyterian Primary School – Osu

In 1930 we were able to secure places in the schools at Osu. I joined the Standard Three class of the Lower School, ironically called "Boarding" even though it was, and still is, a day institution, in contrast to Osu Salem, the Senior School, which rather was residential. The headmaster of the Lower School was Mr. John Teye (later Rev. John Teye) whose name has been immortalized by his son, Lawrence, in founding the Rev. John Teye Memorial School, named after this very illustrious son of Ghana. Rev. John Teye was a very interesting personality. He was a great lover of music, always humming different melodies to himself as he walked along. Needless to say, he taught the School many songs: choral music, a wide range of songs and, under his tutelage and baton, the school performed as a choir, during Sunday church services, and on other occasions won many laurels. Mr. John Teye was a great disciplinarian and one who could not be accused of sparing the rod whenever it was necessary. However eccentric his manners he was greatly loved by his pupils.

The Richter Family is a well established family at Osu and was of Danish origin, going back a few generations. Originally, perhaps traders, the family has established a reputation and made its mark in education and in missionary circles. Many members of the Richter family have distinguished themselves as educators or ministers of the Presbyterian Church.

Barely a month after I had arrived, one of Rev. Richter's sons, Mr. Vincent Richter, a 20-year old who left school three years previously and was a clerk at the Barclays Bank, High Street, Accra, paid a visit to his parents. When he saw me he immediately took a liking to me. The feeling was mutual and when he asked whether I would like to come and stay with him as his house boy, I had no objection. Indeed, it was for me a welcome idea and his parents, Rev. and Mrs. Richter, also did not object. So I went and stayed with the young man, thus starting a friendship and a relationship which was to last throughout Mr. Richter's life until his death in 1983. I owe so much to this gentleman. He himself was a product of the strict Basel Mission discipline and all the virtues that went with it - hard work, honesty, integrity, and the knowledge and fear of God. At that time, he was attending night classes somewhere near the Rowe Road School, at the Accra Technical School, next door. The classes were on banking, and sometimes after work he went to these classes and came back quite late at night. I would then be left all alone. However, this gave me the opportunity to do a lot of reading and I could tell that he was very grateful that I did not fuss much about being left alone. In all ways he was extremely kind to me and even when I had entered the Osu Salem Boarding School and later Achimota College, he continued to show interest in my progress and welfare. Whenever he could, he supplemented in whatever way he could, any provision made for me. When I was abroad for my medical studies, we kept corresponding regularly in spite of difficulties of the war years with delayed correspondence and censorship.

I am glad to say that his hard work, honesty and integrity bore rich fruits later when, on the establishment of the Ghana Commercial Bank, he became one of the foundation members of staff and rose rapidly to become the Managing Director of the Bank. Regretfully, Barclays Bank, which he had served for a quarter of a century or more, did little in appreciation of his long service. Whatever end of service benefits due him were very meagre and I know that this was one of his major regrets in life. Indeed, when the invitation came for him to join the new national bank, the Ghana Commercial Bank, he was torn between his loyalty to Barclays Bank and the call to, what I may term, national duty. I am glad to say that in keeping with his training and his attitude to life, he chose the latter path and did a lot to help establish the new bank.

There were several positive features of the School at Osu which strongly appealed to me. First of all, the education offered was holistic in the sense that whilst academic work was not neglected, there was also emphasis on the vocational and character building aspects of one's education. Secondly, there was more emphasis on the teaching of Ga. This I shall refer to later on. Then too, the system was co-educational. From Standard One to Standard Three, there were girls as well as boys, so one had the opportunity to mix freely with the girls. Lastly, the emphasis on religious studies, Bible Study or Religious Instruction was quite keen and, of course, this could only have a beneficial influence on one's character training.

There was, of course, a certain amount of teaching of Ga in the Government Schools, although the teachers who were teaching Ga themselves were not well grounded in the language. In contrast, the Basel Mission or the Presbyterian Mission philosophy of evangelization was based on the use of the mother tongue, and that was the reason the Basel missionaries were in the forefront of the translation of the Bible into Twi and Ga. Moreover there were Twi and Ga Hymn Books. Reading through the words of these hymns, one could see that every hymn is based on some passage of the Bible. I found myself greatly handicapped in reading Ga and, I must say that I was the source of amusement and entertainment to my classmates when I joined the class. When I was asked to read passages from the Bible I made howlers in my pronunciation. Ga is a highly tonal language, and speaking it is quite different from reading it. I, therefore, found myself pronouncing words well known to me in ways which were almost unrecognizable.

One thing which I found rather irritating but looking back now, quite amusing, was the fact that my classmates compiled a list of Ga words which I had mispronounced, and whenever they wanted to make fun of me, they started reciting these words, much to my discomfiture. One person who stood out in teasing was Joseph Andrew Ayettey. He was the foremost teaser but, after teasing me, taught me the correct pronunciation. Thus began a friendship which was to last the rest of his life. Our two families became close and I recall that my wife, Leonora, used to say that "Emman, if Joe had been a woman, he would have been my greatest rival!" Such was the intimacy of our friendship. We shared our joys and sorrows. Incidentally, the late Mr. Joe Ayettey was the father of Rev. Prof. Seth Ayettey, current Provost of the School of Health Sciences of the University of Ghana!

In my opinion, Joe was a really great man. He was simple, highly generous, and very approachable. He was really a pillar of the extended family. I learnt so much from Joe during his lifetime : the manner in which he handled people, his integrity and his reliability. If I wanted something done for me whilst I was at the Kumasi University, and I entrusted it to Joe, I knew it would be done. Joe was not just a friend, he was a brother. Joe and I started the Union of classmates who graduated from Osu Salem in the year 1934. Even though the girls at that time parted with us after Standard Three and went to schools like Government Girls' School, Accra Royal School or Wesley Girls' School in Accra, we considered them as members of 1934 Osu Salem Class. Joe's house was where the members of the Union met from time to time, especially when planning special anniversaries. To mark the 40th Anniversary of our leaving school, we donated the mosaic pulpit to the Osu Ebenezer Presbyterian Chapel to replace the wooden one donated very many years previously. Again, I recall that Joe and I visited the First Trade Fair held in 1967 and were able to identify a Hammond Electronic Organ which we felt the Church badly needed to replace its old organ. We quickly got together a handful of members of the congregation and encouraged them without much arm twisting to donate towards the purchase of the organ.

There is an interesting story about how we managed to secure the organ for the congregation. At that time there was great competition from various congregations around the country for this one Hammond organ. As fate would have it, we managed to secure the top position because the Osu Ebenezer Session at that time gave us a loan, so we were in a financial position to pay for the organ immediately. Secondly, the Chief Exhibitor of the Hammond organ appliances became my patient.

When I consider that there are many well-educated Ghanaians in all walks of life – professors, professionals, politicians - who are unable to read or write their own mother tongue as well as they do English, I consider myself extremely lucky that at that period of my life I was able to get a really thorough grounding in the Ga language. Because of the fun that was made of me I had to learn to read and write Ga as a second language to the extent that by the time we got to the middle school, I was in a position to win a prize in Ga on occasion. Later on also, I was able to offer Ga as a subject for my Cambridge School Leaving Certificate. So my ability to read and write and speak Ga well is one of the most priceless features of my education, for which I am eternally grateful.

Among our teachers at the Junior School at this time, was Mr. Robert Richter Bannerman, a very interesting character. Mr. Bannerman was something of a maverick in the way he related to pupils. He was a great sportsman; a cricketer, and a tennis player becoming the tennis champion of the Gold Coast at that time for a couple of years. At that time, the backbone of Ghana Cricket comprised gentlemen from Osu. Apart from Mr. Robert Bannerman, names which come to mind are M. L. Augustt, Mingle, Omaboe, Fleischer, Darko and others. These were the people who played regularly in the international matches which were held annually against Nigeria. I recall that the Nigerians would come over in one year and in the next year the Gold Coast Team would travel to Nigeria.

Teacher Bannerman was a member of the Bannerman family from Amanfon, Osu, his father being a well known goldsmith. Another member of the family, Mr. Charles James Bannerman, became an outstanding educationist, headmaster of Abuakwa Secondary School and later a Senior Deputy Registrar of the Cape Coast University from which post he retired. Until his death, he was a staunch member of the Osu Ebenezer Congregation and a one time Presbyter. Mr. C. J. Bannerman also ran the "Ebenezer Newsletter" which for a few years operated on a shoe-string budget, cyclostyled sheets which contained valuable information and which became defunct owing to lack of financial and other support. Fortunately, the paper has been recently resuscitated under the name "The Ebenezer Voice" which enjoys some support and which, unlike its predecessor, is very well produced. Hopefully, it will get the necessary readership support and the contribution of topical and useful articles and provide a forum for the development of journalistic talent among members of the congregation.

At the Junior School, one was also introduced to the dignity of labour. In those days there was expansive, virgin land around the Chapel, where the Church Hall and the Girls' School presently stand. This is an area where, under the supervision of the headmaster and other teachers, the pupils of the school helped in clearing land and growing vegetables like tomatoes and other produce, thus helping the students to become familiar with the use of the hands and not looking on agriculture as a punishment but rather as a worthwhile occupation.

One thing which I found very helpful, especially in the area of Bible Study and Bible Knowledge was the practice of memorizing important passages from the Bible and the Ga Hymnbook. Those who went through this experience, I am sure, would agree that it was a practice which helped to anchor in the minds of young Christians the passages in the Bible which they could fall back on and which would facilitate the understanding of the Bible and help in the Bible study. Concerning the Hymnbook there are hymns for all occasions and also those which one can resort to according to the occasion, for example, in times of sorrow, or times of joy. I have found that especially in times of frustration and despair, one could fall back on the words of some of these hymns from the Ga hymnbook and through that, to the relevant portions of the Bible as sources of comfort.

Whatever happened in the Junior School, was really a preparation for what lay ahead. At the end of every year from 1930 a special examination was held for entrance to the middle school, Standard Four, of that great institution, Osu Salem, the Basel Mission Middle Boys Boarding School which has the pride of place for being the first middle school to be established by the Basel Mission in the year 1863. This was followed by other middle schools at Akropong, Abokobi, Aburi, Bana Hill, Nsabaa, Begoro, Abetifi, Amejope and Anum. The Middle School was essentially a four-year school covering the classes from Standard 4 to Standard Seven. At that time, Standard Seven was the terminal point of what one might call basic education. After that the choices were a few secondary schools such as Achimota, Mfantsipim, Adisadel, Accra Academy and Accra High School and the Teacher Training Colleges, the notable ones being the Basel Mission Theological Seminary, now the Presbyterian Teacher Training College at Akropong and Wesley College, Kumasi. The Middle School was sandwiched between the junior school, which ended in Standard 3, and the post-middle school such as the teacher training colleges and secondary schools.

Before entering such a school there would have been preparations at the lower levels aimed at building a sound foundation of character training. The aim of this character training was based on the biblical injunction that "if you teach a child the way he should go, he will not depart from it in latter life." The training in the middle school was somewhat puritanical, and as the name implies, residential, so that the pupil, for four years, was in residence except during the school holidays when he visited home. The discipline in the middle school was so strict that it was compared with discipline in the army. Indeed, there have been examples of pupils who could not easily withstand the spartan discipline of the middle school and who subsequently joined the army, found it comparatively easy-going and made a success of their military career!

Whatever it is, it.cannot be denied that the Basel Mission Middle Schools (now Presbyterian Middle Schools), throughout the country over the years have produced distinguished citizens of this soil. Osu Salem, in particular, has produced eminent jurists, members of different professions, doctors, lawyers, entrepreneurs, great teachers and ministers of the gospel. Names that readily come to mind are those of Sir Emmanuel Quist, an eminent jurist and the first Speaker of the Legislative Assembly of Ghana, Mr. Justice Nii Amaa Ollenu, also a distinguished jurist and also a Speaker of Parliament, Rev. E. Max Dodu, an outstanding teacher and minister of the Gospel and one of the distinguished Ghanaian Moderators of the Presbyterian Church of Ghana, Dr. C. E. Reindorf, one of the pioneer medical doctors of the Gold Coast, Professor Charles Odamtten Easmon, first Ghanaian qualified surgeon and first Dean of the University of Ghana Medical School, Prof Fred Sai and a host of others. Those of us who were fortunate to have had the privilege of going through the walls of that institution look back with some nostalgia on our days there. However rigid the discipline, we realized in later life that it made a big difference to whatever contributions we have been able to make to the life and development of our country.

# CHAPTER 3

# OSU SALEM

After weeks of eager anticipation, at long last, the day arrived for me to enter the walls of Osu Salem. To this day, I remember my reaction on arrival. Even though I arrived in the company of friends from the lower classes at Osu, it was quite obvious from the beginning that the atmosphere over the next four years was going to be quite different. Frankly, I had a feeling of uneasiness for sometime, but as soon as I was settled in the dormitory, I found a quiet corner of the school and cried for about half an hour. After that I felt much better. I felt as though a process of catharsis had taken place and I was ready for whatever was in store for me. And there was plenty.

The organization at school was hierarchical. Boys in Standard Four were looked upon as the lowest form of animal life and indeed the appellation said so quite openly. The word "odonkpo" in Ga refers to a certain species of rodent which had some negative destructive qualities, and every Standard 4 boy was expected, indeed was obliged, to repeat loudly on certain occasions the phrase "*Odonkpo kronkron ji mi*", meaning "I am a holy rodent." The word "holy" in that context was rather sarcastic as it really meant "I am really the lowest form of animal life" and expect to be treated as such! So restrictions gave way to privileges as one climbed the ladder from Standard 4 through Standards 5 and 6 to Standard Seven. Of course, the Standard Seven boys were supposed to be the overlords and they enjoyed all the privileges that went with their seniority. They made sure that these privileges were well observed! They also enforced the restrictions and regulations on the lower forms. For example, the pupils in Standard 4 were not expected to have a part in their hair and if you were caught disobeying this rule, you ran the risk of being given a nasty hair cut, so that you looked a sorry sight when they finished with you.

The pupils in Standard 4 were supposed to have corresponding masters in Standard Seven whilst those in Standard 5 had their masters in Standard 6. You were supposed to be a fag of your master and you rendered a variety of services, the most notable being to go out twice a day to fetch food from whoever was the caterer for your master, and this went on for as long as you remained his fag. Other services you rendered were walking half a mile or so to the public stand pipe to fetch water for your master for his bath and he might even ask you to wash his clothes and press them.

The beauty of the system was that as long as you were in the lower form, you had to conform. But then as you climbed the ladder, you also started enjoying the privileges and, instead of serving, *you* in turn were assigned a fag who saw to your needs and served you. At that time one felt that it was an oppressive system and indeed, some senior boys could be quite cruel in the way they took advantage of their superior status. On the whole, looking back now, I can say that it helped me to recognize and accept my status in a given situation in life; to appreciate that there is time for everything, a time when you serve, and a time when you are served.

One important aspect of the training was to instill in the pupil the dignity of labour and not to be afraid of soiling one's hands whether in doing the laundry, in sweeping the school compound, in working in the garden, in fetching water for yourself or for someone else, or whether you were pressing clothes. The system, really taught you to learn to do things for yourself. To learn to use your hands. To learn to use your head and your heart. If you were able to go through that system then you felt prepared for many situations in life. The very strict regime made sure that you became accustomed to face difficult situations in life, rising early in the morning, sweeping, doing all sorts of difficult chores. In other words, the regulations made sure to encourage the pupil to tow the line and to instill in him a certain measure of self-discipline. It taught the pupil that without this self-discipline, it would be difficult to expect others to be disciplined themselves. As one climbed the ladder and assumed greater responsibilities, a certain measure of concern for people and situations in life was built into one's character and also appreciating the importance of leadership not only by word but also by example. At this stage I think I cannot do better than to quote the observations made by certain important people in connection with the objects and aims of the training in the school. A manager of one of the middle schools at the celebration of the golden jubilee of the school had this to say, "The object was and is to educate the youth for education's sake, to train them to gain will power, reason power, perceptiveness and last but by no means the least, to bring them up as Christian people. We want to educate the mind and the soul to impart knowledge and to train the boys in morals and principles which will guide them aright in later life". The distinguished General President of the Basel Mission, Rev G. Surker, also had this to say, "We do not go in for show and ostentation, we believe in thorough education, to attach importance to the secular subjects but we attach equal importance to moral and spiritual training. We enforce strict discipline and religious training but the great number of the boys who pass through this school, appreciate in later years the worth of our training and write to thank us".

Throughout my four years at Osu Salem, every day started with morning devotion and ended with devotion at night. The devotion took place in the assembly hall. The senior students had the privilege of conducting the devotion : reading passages from the Bible, singing hymns and saying a word of prayer so that each pupil during the four years, had many occasions on which he was responsible for conducting the devotion for the whole school. Because much attention was paid to extra curricula activities of the school and as a boarding school, the headmaster and all the teachers at the school were given live-in quarters in the school and they were assigned responsibilities for the pupils who went to them with any problems they might have. Problems ranging from class work to their personal problems. In a nutshell, the headmaster and the teachers were *in loco parentis,* they were in place of the parents and there was much that they could do to help the pupils. This in a way gave to the school the atmosphere of a family, a family of elders who had a number of children entrusted to their care.

At the time that I was at Osu Salem, the District Priest of the Osu Ebenezer Presbyterian Church was also manager of the School. There was no Church Choir, therefore, the school as a whole sang at services held on Sundays in the church. For this reason much time was spent in learning many anthems and other choral music which the school rendered during church services. In those days, also, there were frequent singing competitions among the various schools in Accra, and I am glad to say that on many occasions, our school, Osu Salem, won first place, thanks to the effort made by the headmasters in teaching us music. It is interesting that at that time, all the class teachers at Osu Salem, and also, in many other Basel Mission boys middle boarding schools in the country knew some music and were able to teach their classes the rudiments of the theory of music, and indeed, some of the teachers were very good instrumentalists. For example, at Osu Salem, Mr. Wilkens Engmann (later Rev. Wilkens Engmann) who was the first headmaster of the Presbyterian Secondary School at Odumase in later years, was an outstanding musician in the sense that he played the organ very well. Every classroom had a small harmonium with pedals and every pupil was encouraged to learn to play the harmonium so that the time was evenly allocated; I believe it was twenty minutes per pupil per week and a very elaborate roster was made to make sure that everybody had the opportunity to practise playing the harmonium outside working hours.

Despite this wonderful opportunity many pupils who were not really bothered about learning to play the harmonium were prepared to sell their time to other students. By paying one penny, you could have the privilege of playing and practising for twenty extra minutes. A handful of us who were interested in music took advantage of this and paid for time to practise. Other people saw it as a business and sold their time, so that at the end of the day, several years after, only a few of us could play the harmonium to the envy and regret of some of our mates. Personally, I regret not having had a qualified music teacher to teach me how to play the piano or the organ and have, therefore, had to build on my own on the foundation laid by amateurs. Whatever I can do on the keyboard at the moment is, therefore, largely self-taught as I have never been able to afford fees for piano lessons either at Achimota or subsequently.

At Osu Salem, we had some very good teachers competent in their work and highly dedicated. In Standards 4 and 5, we had Mr. Gershon Nehemiah Kuma, a soft-spoken, gentle, courteous and highly competent teacher, highly principled who in spite of the external façade of softness, was firm when necessary and on the whole I would say he managed to get a lot out of us. We were very happy that he taught us in Standard 4 and continued with us to Standard 5. So we had the benefit of his rich experience for two years. Subsequently, he became Reverend Kuma. After Salem he served at many Presbyterian Stations. It was a great joy to us when, on the occasion of the 40th Anniversary of our leaving school, he preached the sermon at the Osu Ebenezer Church and we had a good time together after the service. He was very pleased to learn of the achievements of his former pupils and we were very happy that he made a success of his mission in life as a Priest of the Presbyterian Church of Ghana.

In Standard 6 we had Mr. Anim as our class teacher. Quite a different personality, a sharp contrast between him and Mr. Kuma. Mr. Anim was an extrovert, he spoke quite a lot, but mercifully spoke a lot of sense and we learned a lot from him in the sense that he was able to draw us out of our shells, those who were normally shy. On the whole we were satisfied with what he had to teach us. At the end of the year he was transferred to another school.

Now in Standard Seven we had a young man fresh from Training College, Mr. E. K. Anum. We were the first class that he taught. Mr. Anum was a very hardworking and studious gentleman and it was quite clear to some of us from the beginning that he was not going to be satisfied with just teaching at the middle school and that he would want to carry on to gain further academic laurels. As it turned out, years later, he went to Achimota College as a mature student and, after a couple of years, sat for the Cambridge School Certificate, subsequently pursuing further higher studies towards the intermediate BA qualification with the view to teaching at the newly founded Presbyterian Secondary School at Odumase of which Mr. Wilkens Engmann was the first headmaster. Mr. E. K. Anum was a very interesting character, diminutive in size and proverbially short in temper. He could not withstand the pranks and practical jokes of the naughty boys of the class and we enjoyed the altercations between him and some of the bigger boys who enjoyed teasing him. I must say that for a young man fresh from training college, Mr. E. K. Anum really gave us a lot of information, imparted a lot of knowledge to us. He was a very keen, meticulous teacher who helped some of us to get better results than we would otherwise have contemplated.

As a matter of interest, when Mr. Anum came to Achimota college as a mature student, I had already completed the Secondary School and was in the Intermediate Classes reading for the Intermediate BSc. Therefore, I had the privilege of helping my former teacher with some of his lessons, especially in Mathematics.

In keeping with the vision and mission of the Basel mission on education, the training at Osu Salem was holistic and the non-academic aspect of one's training was given special attention. So we looked forward to the extra-curricula activities like games and sports - football, tourniquoit and athletics. We looked forward to ceremonial occasions when there was school competition in Accra in which our school was involved.

At that time the areas now covering Osu RE, Ringway Estates, the road leading to Cantonments where Morning Star School now stands and Rangoon Avenue (Tito Avenue) were all virgin bush and there were sizeable cassava farms and many mango and cashew-nut trees. The boys from Osu Salem School used to frequent these places, stealing from peoples' farms and coming away with cassava, mango and cashew nuts. Quite often, they were chased by the irate owners when they were seen and had to run for dear life. This, coupled with the fact that there were lots of rabbits in the area as well which the boys chased with the view to getting some bush meat, gave them much practice in sprinting. No wonder, therefore, that the boys from Osu Salem Middle School won prizes regularly in the sprint events during the Accra Schools' Competitions!

As I have already stated, the Osu Ebenezer Church had no choir. The school as a whole took the place of a choir. Therefore, once a year, the School was involved in a special event called "Anniversary Celebration." Now the Anniversary really was to mark the anniversaries of the date that the missionaries stepped ashore at Osu, and also to commemorate the expansion of the work of the Basel Mission in the country. This took place once a year at various stations over a weekend. It could be Osu, Teshie or any other station, and I recall that on two occasions we had to go out of Osu to spend the weekend. We had to walk all the way to Abokobi on a Saturday to take part in the Church Service on Sunday and then back to Osu on the Monday. And on another occasion we went to Teshie but we came back on the same day. On both occasions, we had to walk. We did not go by any vehicular transport. Though interesting, it was very tiring.

Whilst at Abokobi we were the guests of the congregation and the school and we made friends with the boys at Abokobi Middle Boys' School. This was something which, I think, many old boys of Osu Salem will always look back on with some amount of nostalgia. These days, the celebrations are low key and are no more called anniversary celebrations. They are called Church Extension Celebrations, and whatever happens takes place within the District. There is, of course, a certain amount of movement but certainly not the pomp, pageantry and fanfare which accompanied this event of old.

Speech and Prize Giving Days were days that we looked forward to at the School. It was an open day when parents, guardians and old boys of the school visited and went round to see the handiwork of the pupils: carpentry, metal work, weaving and, especially art work, painting and drawing, and even some of the class work, looking through the exercise books. It was a matter of pride for the teachers to display some of the works of the top pupils of the school. At this time of my life, I discovered I had the talent for drawing. I had shown early signs of this in my childhood, especially when I started school in the Government Boys' School in James Town. But at Salem, there was more opportunity to develop this talent further and I recall that every Sunday there was on the wall of the lobby of the school a huge blackboard and pupils with the gift of drawing were called upon from time to time to display this talent. On many occasions, I was given the opportunity to do chalk designs in various colours on the board. As art nearly became my career, I will defer the discussion of this matter to a later time during this narrative.

I personally looked forward to the Prize-Giving Day. The old boys at that time were very generous and donated book prizes on various subjects. I made quite a few friends among the old boys, especially and those who noticed that I was the winner of the prizes which they gave. Notable among these were the late Mr. E. T. Odoteye and Mr. E. W. Adjaye who worked at the Cable Office, Mr. M. L. Augustt, Mr. C. D. K. Lokko and interestingly, it was the sportsmen that I have mentioned before, the cricketers, Mr. Fleischer and Mr. Omaboe. Very many years after when I became a doctor and a surgeon, I had the greatest pleasure to attend to Mr. Fleischer then in his late middle age. Someone who had been my sporting idol in my childhood.

During my stay at Salem, I believe in the year 1932, when I was in Standard 5, I had the misfortune of contracting a very intractable scalp condition which necessitated my going home, away from school, to Akuse to my parents for treatment. All my hair was shaved most of the time. They tried various remedies, including traditional remedies which I detested and abhorred because it included the fumigation with some objectionable, foul-smelling smoke from leaves being burnt and my head was covered. I had to inhale these wretched fumes. I must say it made little difference to my condition. Eventually, I had to come back to Accra. My uncle, the late Dr. C. E. Reindorf, treated me with a barrage of injections and some very pungent ointments and lotions. Eventually, after about six weeks I recovered fully and rejoined the class. Whilst at home my father helped me with my lessons. I must say that I lost quite a bit of time but did not lose my position in the order of merit in the class.

During my four years at Osu Salem, we had two headmasters in succession. The first, Mr. E. Max Dodu, was the headmaster when I was in Standards 4 and 5, that is, in the years 1931 and 1932. He was followed by Mr. Carl Henry Clerk, headmaster for the next two years. Both men made much impact on me because of the force of their personalities and their attitude to their work.

Mr. Max Dodu was tall, with a commanding presence and an authoritative voice. His wife, Mrs. Margaret Lovering Dodu, became my own "mother" and died just last year (2000) at the age of 99. I have already indicated that my elder brother , Joe, was entrusted to the care of Mr. and Mrs. Dodu, when my parents worked at Akuse. Joe was, therefore, their ward. So long before I entered the middle school I had been visiting the Dodu's house and was regarded as a member of the family. Mr. Dodu, was a product of the Basel Mission Seminary, Akropong where my maternal grandfather was a tutor when he was a student at the Seminary. Therefore, my mother who was born and brought up at Akropong had known Mr. Dodu since those days. Mr. Dodu thus treated us not really as strangers who had been brought to his care but as family. For this reason, he took a special interest in my welfare and I was also on my best behaviour. So for the two years that Mr. Dodu was the headmaster, I had the benefit of a fatherly influence. Mr. Dodu was a strict disciplinarian and very firm in his ways. He was highly-principled and disciplined and he expected the highest standard of behaviour, not only from his pupils, but also his staff. With him as headmaster, the tone of discipline in the School, Osu Salem, was really of the highest. He was an excellent teacher and had a great command of the Ga language. He was, I think, one of the finest exponents of the language that I have known. He spoke flawless Ga and made sure that he set a good example to all of us so that we did not handle our mother tongue carelessly and in the end adulterate it with non-Ga words, especially English.

The school at that time being the choir for the church, Mr. Dodu spared no pains in teaching good choral music from great classical works. I did not realize this then. I knew the music was good but I did not know that the anthems were from great classical works of the great masters. At a later time when I went to Edinburgh University and I attended my very first concert and heard some of this music being sung by top-notch choirs and orchestras, I realized what treasures Mr. Dodu had bestowed on us. As a lover of music myself, I always cherished this - well, one may call it – endowment which I had from Mr. Dodu.

The relationship that was forged between me and the Dodu family lasted throughout his life, and long after I had lost my parents, I adopted the Dodus as my parents until the time of his death and subsequently mama's death also. This bond grew stronger with the years. Mr Dodu, was the father of one of Ghana's finest physicians. Professor Silas Dodu, first Professor of Medicine of the University of Ghana Medical School and subsequently the second Dean of the School in succession to the late Professor Charles Odamtten-Easmon.

At the end of the School Year in 1932, Mr. Dodu was transferred from Osu Salem to Teshie Middle School. He was succeeded by Mr. Carl Henry Clerk. Mr. Clerk was the offspring of the Clerks who together with other West Indian Missionaries were brought to the Gold Coast by the Basel Mission to demonstrate to the people of the Gold Coast, especially Nana Akuapemhene who had asked to see black Christians before he could recommend to his people conversion to Christianity. Mr. Clerk, therefore, had this very interesting and relevant antecedent.

Having returned from the United States of America, Mr. Clerk had a large repertoire of Negro Spirituals. Therefore, the gear changed from the highly classical pieces to basically gospel music and some of the well-known Negro Spirituals. Mr. Clerk maintained the disciplinary tone of the school, except that the pupils found him rather rigid and not as flexible as the previous headmaster. My personal relations with Mr. Clerk were very interesting. He must have discovered at an early stage that I was somebody he could use. I have the flair for drawing and for art. In many ways, I think Mr. Clerk saw in me someone who had a promising potential for the future. In short, I think Mr. Clerk thought more of me than I did of myself. What I know is that I was used extensively by him in copying volumes of music, different types of music especially the Negro Spirituals which he had cyclostyled and which he used in his teaching. At other times, he made me copy highly confidential material for him. To crown it all and in order not to dwell too much on this, something happened which I shall never forget. Getting to the end of the 1934 school year, round about September, at a time when I had aspirations of going to Akropong Seminary and Training College, after leaving School, I saw an advertisement in the newspaper for a Cadbury Scholarship to Achimota College in which I became interested. Indeed, Mr. Clerk, the headmaster, called me and asked whether I would like to try and win it. I replied that I was almost at the point of deciding to go to Akropong to train as a teacher, but I'd think about it. So I went to see him the following morning and he explained to me the advantages of obtaining a secondary school education, the vistas, avenues and doors that would open before me, if I were to win the scholarship and go to Achimota instead of going to Akropong. With the explanation that he gave I agreed and decided to apply; and I filled the form right there in his office. There was a portion for him to sign which he duly signed. I left it with him as he said that he would make sure that the application got to Achimota.

About a week later, I saw another advertisement for another secondary school. I assumed he would talk to me about this one too so I took the paper to him and said, "Sir, there is this advertisement in the paper and I would like to apply and also to sit for the examination." To my utter surprise, the headmaster told me that he was not going to sign the form. I was surprised and asked him why. "Anfom, do you not have any confidence in yourself? I think you should have more confidence than you do. You have great talents, a great potential and I do not want you to divide your energies between two applications. So I urge you to go and sit for the scholarship examination for Achimota and put all your energies in it and I know that you will win." So the rightful person to sign the application form for me declined to do so!

I was really flabbergasted; since I thought the headmaster had my interest at heart and that he would do everything to make sure that I succeeded. Surely, it was not wise to put all my eggs into one basket! The best idea, I felt, was, to have a number of options, and to me it was far better to sit for two scholarship examinations, Achimota and another school, rather than concentrate on one. But in spite of my pleadings the headmaster refused to budge. I, therefore, had to make the best out of what I considered a bad situation. When I look back now, it must have been that the headmaster had so much confidence in me that he thought I should not dissipate my energies sitting for too many examinations and that by concentrating on the Achimota Scholarship Examination, I would make sure that I won the scholarship. In any case, it is past and gone and one can only look back on it with a certain amount of nostalgia.

At about the same time, the Standard Seven School Leaving Examination, was just round the corner. The Standard Seven Certificate was a very important passport to employment or further education. For those who passed the examination and wished to enter the Civil Service, (it was then very prestigious to be employed in the Civil Service) there was a special nationwide examination called the Civil Service Examination, or CS for short, and those who were able to pass it were considered really good academically. In my case I did not even think about it because I had already made up my mind to go to Akropong to become a teacher. Besides, there was this new development, having to go to sit for a scholarship examination for Achimota College. I must say something about the Standard Seven Certificate. The previous year a new Certificate was introduced. It was a blue certificate called the Distinction Certificate; it was awarded to those who did exceptionally well in the examination. I believe those who got 70% aggregate and above of this very competitive examination were considered worthy of winning the distinction certificate. To me, with a possible scholarship to Achimota in view, I did not really think much about the Standard Seven Examination. I did not think I would have any problem passing it and, well, if by chance I made a distinction, so much the better.

Incidentally, one of the conditions of the award of the Cadbury Scholarship was that one should pass the Standard Seven Examination also so that it was not a matter that could be left out of consideration. But I did not think much about it because I thought I would not have any problem with it. I believe it was the Standard Seven Examination for which we sat first, and of course, the results took a long time to come; being released even after the scholarship examination results! On the day of the scholarship examination, I thought the headmaster's behaviour was rather odd. He made sure that I was up in time, and also that I got transportation to take me to Achimota village. The examination was fixed for 8 o'clock in the morning, so I had to leave the school before 6 o'clock.

On coming down at Achimota village, there were a number of other boys who were also making their way up the hill, a distance of a mile or so, to the College, some of whom were obviously also going to take part in the examination. I found myself walking along side a young lad, of about my age, from Kibi. We introduced ourselves. He was E. K. Twum from Kibi Presbyterian Middle School and he told me that he was going up the hill to sit for the examination, and of course, he had concluded that I was after the same objective, so we walked up the hill comparing notes on both Presbyterian Schools and the sort of life we had in our middle schools. Now, it was a four-hour examination which comprised Engligh, written and oral, Arithmetic and General Knowledge and by 12 o'clock the examination was over. The oral examination was conducted by an Englishman whom I got to know subsequently as Mr. Gillet. He was in charge of teaching agriculture in the College. The name of the Scholarship was Cadbury Agricultural Scholarship and though there were no strings attached, it was the expectation that winners of the Scholarship would opt for an agricultural career or take at least an agricultural course.

After the examination, I found my way back home quite easily. I was quite pleased with myself, and thought I had done well, but of course, I did not underestimate the competition at all. A week passed and nothing happened. When the school vacation came I went home to Evans House, James Town. The day after I got home, I went over with my brother to a café run by Kingsway Stores called "Soda Fountain." That particular building, I think stood at the place just behind the present Standard Chartered Bank adjacent to the West African Drug Company and facing the present Accra Metropolitan Council Offices. I was sitting with my brother and enjoying ice cream when I saw two Europeans at the counter of the café. One of them beckoned to me and as I drew nearer I discovered that it was the gentleman who interviewed me at Achimota, at the examination, Mr. Gillet. "You are Anfom, aren't you?" I said "Yes, Sir. How did you know my name, Sir?" He said, "You were at Achimota recently." "Yes", I said. "Have you got your letter?" "What letter, Sir,?" He said, "Well, you will be getting a letter through the post". We hope to see you at Achimota next term." I must say that I was really pleasantly surprised. I cannot describe the feeling. Here I was being informed at a café, almost in a casual manner, that I had won a scholarship to this prestigious institution, Achimota College!

We did not finish the ice cream! We just walked quickly home and broke the news to my mother and all the relatives at home. The following morning, I went over to the school as I knew that any communication to me would come through the mail and would come to the school address. I walked straight to the headmaster's office, and when he saw me, he got up from his chair, walked up to me and shook my hands vehemently and said to me, "Anfom, I told you, you could do it . Congratulations!" He had the letter in his hand and he read it to me. You can just imagine the joy that I felt. I did not know what went through the headmaster's head at the time but I had the feeling that perhaps he was even more delighted than myself. I would too if I had been in his shoes because he really stuck his neck out and I am sure that from time to time he must have had some misgiving about placing so much confidence in me. But, well, everything worked out for good and now I had to cope, assemble my thoughts and look to the future. This scholarship to Achimota School, the result of a decision taken on the spur of the moment, had transformed my whole outlook and vision. As the headmaster told me from the beginning, a course at Achimota College would open a variety of avenues and doors to me through which I could pass to a great future.

I could see that the headmaster's delight knew no bounds. Unfortunately, it was school vacation and so he could not, as I am sure he would have wished, assemble all the school in the assembly hall and make the announcement. However, he managed to get together in his office a few of the teachers who were around and announced the wonderful news to them. There was general jubilation and they all thought that after so many years I had really brought honour and credit to the school. After having a lengthy discussion with the headmaster about what I was going to do next, he took the opportunity to advise me with words of encouragement. After that, I took the letter and ran downstairs. Just as I got to the Salem Road, a young lad rushed on a bicycle from a distance and then stopped abruptly and shouted, "Anfom, Anfom, Emman, wait!" So I looked round. It was my classmate and friend, Kwakwei Quartey, who was working with Cadbury and Fry Ltd. There he got the news of the scholarship and he had come all the way to the school to inform me, thinking he would be the first to give me the news. But I already had the letter in my hand! He was so delighted that he promised to spread the news among our classmates. Kwakwei Quartey was a very good friend and, years after, when I was in Edinburgh studying medicine during the war, we had frequent correspondence. Unfortunately, he died during my absence. I really missed him when I came back.

The Headmaster Mr. C. H. Clerk, was the father of Reverend Dr. Nicholas Clerk of the Presbyterian Church and one time Director of GIMPA and later member of the Public Services Commission, presently attached to the Headquarters of the Presbyterian Church in Accra. Before I finish what I have to say about Mr. Clerk, I want to note that during his

time he taught us many Negro spirituals and there is one in particular
which I liked very much titled "MY TASK" which I quote below.

> *"To love someone more dearly every day,*
> *To help a wandering child to find his way,*
> *To ponder o'er a noble thought and pray,*
> *and smile when evening falls.*
> *This is my task.*
>
> *To follow truth as blind men long for light,*
> *To do my best from dawn of day till night*
> *To keep my heart fit for His Holy sight,*
> *And answer when He calls.*
> *This is my task.*
>
> *Then my Saviour by and by to meet*
> *When faith has made our task on earth complete.*
> *To lay my homage at the Master's feet,*
> *Within the Jasper walls,*
> *This crowns my task."*

One of the most important events that takes place during the last
half of ones' final year in a Presbyterian school  is the Church
confirmation.  All members of the  Standard Seven class are given
confirmation lessons and are confirmed and registered as full members
of the Presbyterian Church, after which they could participate at the
Sacrament of the Holy Communion.  In our case, this took place in June
1934. The Rev. Paul Djoleto, then District Priest at Osu confirmed us.
On each of the confirmation certificates, there is an inscription of a biblical
text.  Mine was taken from 2 Timothy, 1:6 which goes: "Therefore I
charge you to rekindle the gift that God has given you".

After confirmation day in  June 1934, I became a full member of
the Osu Ebenezer Presbyterian Church and have to this day kept my
membership there, except for long periods when I was away from Osu,
at Achimota, in Edinburgh and even when I started practising medicine
on my return and was posted to various stations, I always made sure
that I attended the Presbyterian Churches in those places.  Incidentally,

I may say that when finally the results of the Standard Seven Examination came, I had won a distinction certificate. By then, the news was something of an anti-climax, having been superceded by the most exhilarating news - winning a scholarship to Achimota College. In all, I spent seven years at Osu - from the 1st of January 1928 to December 1934. Soon I was about to leave Osu and say good-bye to the very many friends that I had made from among some outstanding families at Osu. Looking back now, I find that I have maintained contact with almost all of these families: the Richters who really were directly responsible for me, the Hesses, the Engmanns, the Swanikers, the Reindorfs, the Quists, the Lokkos, the Dowuonas, the Cochranes, the Wulffs, the Adumuahs and a host of others.

I had many friends also among the old boys of Osu Salem School who were then important members of society, working either for Government or for some commercial organizations. As I look back now, I can safely say that it was at Osu that the foundations of my character were well and truly laid. The Christian tradition at Osu really helped to mould my character. When I came to Osu, I was only nine years old, carefree, happy-go-lucky, and without any particular focus in life, although I would say that I was not exactly like a ship tossing aimlessly on the wild seas without a rudder, as my family upbringing at Evans House tempered by the Basel Mission influence through my grandfather and my mother had prepared soil upon which a firm foundation could be laid. Therefore the Teutonic life and the rigorous discipline at Osu Salem helped to shape my conduct and attitude to life in such a way that I can say that after seven years I had been taught to be independent.

I could do things for myself. I could walk a mile or two to fetch water and carry it on my head. I could wash my own clothes and iron them. I could till the soil. I could do all sorts of practical, handy things. In short, after Salem, I was not afraid to use my hands to do anything. After Salem I did not feel lazy when there was work to do. After Salem, I learnt to be obedient not only to my parents but also, in keeping with our own Ghanaian tradition and the Christian up-bringing, to those who were older than myself, and therefore, more experienced. I learnt to be humble. I learnt to be honest in whatever I did. I learnt to tell the truth whatever the outcome might be. I also learnt to function as a member of any team in which I found myself. I learnt to undergo stresses and strains and also to see the bright side of things. We had been taught at school to brighten the corner where we were, wherever we might be. Throughout my life, this is precisely what I have tried to do.

I began to contemplate both my impending farewell to Osu and my vision for the future, starting with my next stop, Achimota College. I had been to Achimota on just one occasion, to sit for an examination for a scholarship, and had even then taken in the splendour of the campus. Everything was spick and span, in contrast to the poorly-endowed old Basel Mission Presbyterian School. I was about to be translated or transformed to an entirely new environment. I wondered really what this would mean in my life. Would the standards of morality be the same at Achimota? Would Achimota really build upon the solid character foundation that I had acquired at Osu? Or would something happen to ruffle or disturb the spiritual course on which I was set? All these were matters for the future.

The prospect of going to Achimota encouraged me to read as much as I could about the College. I knew that the College was a Government-endowed College with its own Council. On his visit to the Gold Coast, in 1925, the Prince of Wales had consented to the institution being named after him. So that the full name of the Institution was Prince of Wales College, Achimota. I also knew that there were different departments spanning several levels from kindergarten right up to the early years of university work, and that I would be going to the secondary department of the school. I really looked forward, in a way, to meeting new friends. Friends who had started their formal education at Achimota, the kindergarten section, and climbed the ladder steadily and whose up-bringing could be quite different from mine.

I had been brought up on a shoestring budget, whilst a number of these pupils would have been brought up in relative luxury. However, I was consoled in the fact that the motto of the College "Ut Omnes Unum Sint" ("That They All May Be One") was also the motto of the Presbyterian Church to which I belong. So in a way, I looked forward to continuing in the same vein, from one Ut Omnes Unum Sint to another Ut Omnes Unum Sint, headed by the great Rev. A. G. Fraser, a Scotsman, an outstanding educationist of international fame, who had seen service in Asia and East Africa and who, together with Guggisberg and Aggrey, formed the great Triumvirate of founders of Achimota College. That Triumvirate was a forward looking group and the vision that they had for the College was one which would really help to produce people who would make great contributions to the development of our country.

Before I finish the story of Osu, I must say something about one individual who really made a profound impression on me, Mr. Emmanuel Adumuah, a Basel Mission trained teacher, who like Mr. Dodu, Mr. Clerk and Mr. John Teye, had been students of my grandfather at the Basel Mission Seminary at Akropong, and therefore, was well known to my parents. Mr. Emmanuel Adumuah took a personal interest in me when I was at Osu Salem. He always encouraged me and gave me words of advice. So we struck up good friendship. With the name Emmanuel, he called me "Name Sake". There were many occasions when I went to him for advice, especially during my early days at Achimota. He was the founder of Osu Progress School, and he was the one who gave a first employment to my elder brother, Joe, when he finished middle school in the year 1932.

One interesting thing about Mr. Adumuah was that he kept a daily diary throughout the time that I knew him until the time of his death. Now that I am in the middle of writing my autobiography, I wish I had done so. How much easier it would have been for me to recall events that happened many, many years ago! So the year 1934 ended and a new year began, and it was during that year that I entered Achimota College, the next stage of my journey through life. Though I left Osu many, many years ago, I have kept my contact with Osu, and upon retirement, I bought a house at Osu at the Ringway Estates, where I now live.

# CHAPTER 4

# SECONDARY EDUCATION
## Achimota College

On the second Friday of January 1935, I was admitted at Achimota College to Form 3 of the Secondary Department. It was an important day in my life. The previous night, I could not sleep, as I was contemplating the change that was about to take place. Going to what I considered a completely new world! Because of the importance of the change, my mother accompanied me herself. The previous day, we went to say good-bye to my uncle, Dr. C. E. Reindorf who very kindly offered to put one of his cars at my disposal. I, therefore, went to Achimota in grand style. As we drove up the hill from Achimota Village, I recalled the day that I had walked up the hill to go and sit for the Cadbury Scholarship Examination. As we entered the College compound, I requested the driver to spend about 10 minutes driving around the compound. I thought this was a splendid opportunity for me to see the whole of the campus. Achimota College was then just a few years old and the buildings looked in a really good condition. Nicely painted. The lawns were well kept and green even at that time of year; the season was harmattan. Everywhere one looked, the view was exquisite.

At the end of our drive around, we went to the Administration Block where a number of students had already assembled. We arrived at the College at about 9 o'clock in the morning. I went to the office and was duly registered. Then I had to undergo a medical examination by Dr. Griffiths, the medical doctor of the College. After completing the registration, we went to see Mr. Brakatu Ateko, a senior member of staff whom my mother had known ever since he was a student at the Basel Mission Training College. He had been brought to Achimota by the Principal to teach Twi. His bungalow was the last before one left the compound to enter the sports field. Mr. Ateko was very pleased to see my mother. It was an unexpected surprise because he hadn't seen her for very many years and he was very pleased to know that I was to become a student at the College. We were very well received, and as I recall, Mr. Ateko gave us an impromptu lunch. I must say that at that point, I was very relieved. At least here was someone in a senior position at the College whom my mother knew and who was very likely to take a personal interest in me. Needless to say, my mother and Mr. Ateko, engaged in long reminiscences of the Basel Mission Training College at Akropong, especially of my grand-father, the late Mr. W. T. Evans. Mr. Ateko told me many things about the old man which I did not know. In any case, it was clear to me that he held him in very high esteem, almost to the point of reverence, and that was a double assurance to me that here was somebody who was likely, taking account of what benefits he got from the old man, to extend the same courtesies to me while I was at Achimota.

There was a very interesting development whilst we were at Mr. Ateko's residence, a development which was to have a profound effect on my life in Achimota. Outside in the garden, pottering around and working among the flowers was Mr. Ateko's nephew, Kofi Atiemo, who as it turned out, was already a student at Achimota. As a matter of fact, he had all his education at Achimota, having started at the kindergarten classes many years before then. Kofi Ateimo was also entering the secondary department and we were both to be in Form 3 as classmates. Furthermore, he was assigned to Livingstone House, the House to which I had also been assigned. As fate would have it, Kofi Atiemo and I were to become lifelong friends. This was really a stroke of luck for me, to have somebody who had been in Achomota for many years and knew everything, one might say, about Achimota. Kofi Atiemo, as it turned out, was a great sportsman. I will say more about our relationship as sportsmen later.

After lunch, we bade good-bye to Mr. Ateko and Kofi took us to Livingstone House, where he had already been registered and settled, and helped me to go through the formalities to be registered at the House, and to meet the Housemaster, Mr. D. Herbert, (who was, very many years later, to inherit the title Lord Hemingford). Our Assistant Housemaster was Mr. Attoh Okine, a great sportsman and a great footballer whom I had not met personally but had seen in action playing football for the Accra XI. In those days, there were annual international matches between Accra and Lagos. Attoh Okine earned a reputation as a goal king as he was a very sharp striker and scored many goals against the Lagos team. Mr. Attoh Okine was from James Town, and he knew my family well, so it did not take long for us to become friends, and I must say that it was another reassurance for me that here as my Housemaster was somebody from Jamestown to whom I could go with any problems.

The House Prefect was A. K. Seku, a Teacher Training student in Form 6. He was the very friendly type and one who was mature in his dealings with young students, although a strict disciplinarian. He was not harsh but kept us all in check. My dormitory monitor was Mr. Enoch Okoh, also in the Sixth Form of the secondary department. I was to discover later that Mr. Okoh's father knew my father quite well. I met him in Accra on one occasion when I was on exeat and when he learnt that I was the son of Mr. William Quashie Anfom whom he had known many years before, during their cocoa buying days, he made known this fact to me. Mr. Enoch Okoh was very friendly and very efficient and I personally learnt a lot from him. He was also a quiet disciplinarian, soft-spoken, but a senior student full of wisdom. Mr. Enoch Okoh, became an outstanding civil servant and rose to become Secretary to the Cabinet of the Government of President Nkrumah.

My dormitory mate on the bed next to me was William Tamakloe from Keta. He was a T4 student, that is to say, a student in Form 4 of the Teacher Training Department. Willie was a very out-going person, a very friendly type. He spoke Ga fluently and knew quite a lot. He had been in the College for some time and from that day on, he and Kofi Atiemo took me in hand and showed me the ropes; the do's and don't''s in the House, the do's and don't's in the College, the idiosyncrasies of our housemasters, and even some of our class teachers. Willie Tamakloe was a great tonsorial artist. Of course, I was then much younger and had plenty of hair, and he and I serviced each other regularly. Twice a month on a Saturday or Sunday afternoon he would give me a hair cut and I would reciprocate. Later on, after leaving College, Willie, being a gifted artist, came back – after teaching for some years – to undergo a Special Art Course and became an outstanding artist and a great teacher. He taught for many years at the Specialist Training College, Winneba.

Years after leaving school, when I returned from my studies abroad in 1950, at our first meeting, Willie noticed that I had lost quite a bit of hair and he commented liberally on it, looking back at the time when I had plenty of hair. I assured him that there was more traffic now inside my head than outside! To which he responded with a hearty laugh.

By a quarter past six, on the opening day, most of the students had arrived on campus and we went for supper in the dining-hall. It was a very interesting occasion. The returnees, the old students were patting each other on the back and exchanging pleasantries. When they saw new faces, they made disparaging remarks. Remarks which were to translate into action about a week later at a ceremony which we had not expected, and did not know about before we arrived. The ceremony of being initiated into the fraternity on the campus. Many of the things that were done were rather childish in my view but they were done all the same. Imagine after having been in residence for a week, coming back to your dormitory and finding that all your things had been packed and taken outside on the insistence that you had not been properly admitted and that you had to pass, what they called *a nino's* examination before you would be properly admitted! The examination consisted of a long list of questions, some bordering on the ridiculous. All this was done to the amusement of the students who were already in residence and to the discomfiture of the new ones. In any case, all this was done in jest, but those who had never experienced this sort of *ninoing* before felt it very much. They took what in reality was a joke very seriously and some of the younger students were known to have wept bitterly thinking that everything was real and that they might be sent back home. For me, coming as I did, from the Teutonic regime of a Presbyterian School, Osu Salem, and having endured four years of the spartan system, all this was child's play and I took it in my stride. In any case, by the end of one week, I had stalwarts, like Kitson-Mills otherwise known as *Agreemo*, a tall, well-built student of Aggrey House and son of the legendary Kitson-Mills who founded Accra Royal School. Kitson-Mills was a boxer and had an intimidating presence and a very powerful voice. He was from Jaméstown and he became my unofficial bodyguard. That was the experience we had during the first week or so on the campus. The initiation rites over, one felt that one had at last been accepted to the Achimota fraternity.

My first day at the College ended with a roll call in Livingstone House, my House, at 9 o'clock in the common room, followed by evening prayers and lights out at 9.30. At the roll call, the housemaster, Mr. Herbert, welcomed all the newcomers to the House and hoped that we would all be happy on the campus; that we would learn all the rules and regulations and that as long as we lived within the law, there would not be any problem. He outlined some of the things we were expected to do in the House, especially keeping the environment clean, keeping our dormitories clean and taking part fully in gardening or ground work as it was known at that time. He stressed the point that Achimota was a happy family and that we would see that in the Livingstone House community students came from all four corners of the Gold Coast living the Achimota motto: "*Ut Omnes Unum Sint*" meaning, "That They All May Be One." We should always remember and treat each other as members of one big family without thinking of our ethnic background. As long as we were in Achimota, we were members of Livingstone House and members of the College. This was the only way by which when we went out after Achimota, we would become leaders and give leadership for a united country, a united nation. It was a long day for me, and even though I was tired, I remember having a dream, a strange dream. I dreamt that I was back at Osu Salem. I suppose this was really to take me back, and refresh my memory about my life during the previous four years and to compare with my new life. I woke up to find that I was in Livingstone House, in Achimota College! Strange new surroundings, but to me, it was a welcome change. I looked back on the previous day and all the friendly people that I had met, the welcome that I had had.

The following morning, I was up with the lark! At 5.30 prompt. After spending some time in the garden, I had my bath and went for breakfast in the dining hall at a quarter past seven. After breakfast we came back for morning prayers in the common room and then went to our dormitories for general cleaning. Saturdays, of course, were days for general cleaning and every Saturday, there was a competition among the dormitories and the housemasters' inspection. The winners would be announced and it would be in order of merit. The mere fact that you were winners was a prize enough to be coveted and every dormitory did its best to make sure that it won the cleaning competition. In those days, cleaning materials were in abundance and the parquet floors in the dormitories had to be nicely scrubbed and polished to give them a shine. The brass handles on the metal windows had to be nicely polished and the windows themselves and the window panes nicely dusted. Everything had to be scrupulously dusted and cleaned because no one knew where the probing fingers of the housemaster would reach! The housemaster's inspection was very thorough and it included not only the dormitories but the box rooms, and also rooms where the chop boxes were kept. I recall one occasion the housemaster, Mr. Herbert, who was something of a poet, on inspecting a chop box of one of the students, found a cockroach. Flabbergasted, he shouted, "Take away that creature and keep it clean in future!"

The garden, which was apportioned among the various dormitories, was also inspected. I must say that we all looked forward to the cleaning up. The competition element really inspired us to work hard so that our dormitory would be first every Saturday. The Saturday general cleaning also instilled in us students the dignity of labour. We were not afraid to use our hands to do any type of cleaning. We were not afraid to till the soil in the garden and we made sure that the flowers and flower-beds were properly kept. On the whole, this was one aspect of the training at Achimota which I found very useful.

That first Saturday of the term we spent part of the time going to the matron's office to make sure that we had all our kit – our uniform, and other things we needed. We also visited the bookshop to get our exercise books and books which needed to be supplied by the school for academic work. That first Saturday was a memorable day for me. At lunch, I was introduced to a new dish called "rice and beans" R and B. I had never really eaten rice treated in that way before and I must say that from the word go, I fell in love with rice and beans. Throughout my stay at Achimota College, whenever this dish was served in the dining-hall, I became very happy and it made a big difference to my attitude the whole day. In a way, I think rice and beans did much for my physical development. When I entered Achimota, I was rather short and rotund in physique but in no time I had started shooting up, to the amazement of my family when I came home. I ascribe this partly to R&B. Whenever "rice and beans" was to be served for lunch, although I was physically present in the classroom, my mind really was not there. My mind was in the dining-hall, great expectations, rice and beans! So it may well be that whereas that particular dish did much for my physical development, perhaps it affected my academic development to some extent. In any case, as we had a holistic education and we needed a sound body to have a sound mind, I do not think I missed much. That first Saturday, there was no official programme for sporting activities, but, unofficially, some of the students, the old students, went to the sports field and played all sorts of games. On that day, Kofi Atiemo and I took a stroll to the sports field and I must say that I was really impressed by the facilities that Achimota offered and I promised myself that I would take the fullest advantage as long as I was there

The following day, Sunday, was a free day and it was an opportunity for us to make acquaintance with friends both old and new : new students and mates with whom we were admitted on the same day, but who were in other Houses, to compare notes. It was also an opportunity for us to do a little bit of exploration, to get to know the various places and also who and who were in those places. In the evening, after supper, we attended our first Sunday Evening Service. At that time, the College occupied two campuses: the main compound for the boys, and the girls' compound at another location where the kindergarten and lower primary sections were also accommodated. The Sunday Evening Services were held in the girls' dining-hall. The boys had to walk all the way to the girls' dining-hall. That Sunday, apart from being the first Sunday of the year, the Principal had the opportunity to address the whole student body. Principal Fraser also preached the sermon. The occasion was rather solemn as it also turned out to be a Service to honour the memory of Elison Dogbatse.

Elison Dogbatse was a student of the College who in November of the previous year died on the sports field as he was about to finish a cross-country race. It was an inter-college competition in which other institutions, namely, the Wesley College, the Presbyterian Training College, Akropong Mfantsipim School and Adisadel Schools were involved. The Principal was full of emotion as he described the supreme sacrifice Dogbatse made. The sacrifice which every Christian is called upon to make to give up his life for a worthy cause. The Chief (Principal) reminded us that as Christians we were all running the race of life and we should be steadfast in our resolution and run the race and finish well.

At the beginning of term, two commemorative lamps were unveiled in honour of Dogbatse at the entrance to the Administration Block on either side of the stairs leading to the block. They will constantly remind all Old Achimotans of the example of sacrifice which Dogbatse made as a student at the College.

At the end of my first weekend at Achimota, it became quite clear that I was in an entirely new world. Achimota was a special institution born out of the vision of Sir Gordon Guggisberg then Governor of the Gold Coast. A vision to build a model school which would train future leaders for the Gold Coast. The atmosphere was to be highly liberal, it was to be co-educational, where male and female were educated together in order to demonstrate the equal capabilities, intellectual and otherwise, of girls with boys. The institution was to pay attention to the cultural barriers of the country and which, whilst emphasizing the academic aspect, ensured that not only the mind was trained but also the hand and the heart. The institution was to pay attention to the development of the physical body, a sound body being necessary for ensuring a soundness of mind.

At Achimota, there was to be no discrimination in any form whatsoever. There was to be no class distinction among the students. All students and staff were to feel a sense of equality! There was to be no distinction of race, colour, creed, or anything else. From my very first day of arrival, I felt that this was a place where any student arriving was accorded equal acknowledgement, equal recognition, no preferential treatment for anybody, whatever your status in life, economic or social. Everybody was treated as equals. In fulfilling his dream for Achimota, Governor Guggisberg had managed to enlist the services of Rev. Alexander Garden Fraser, an outstanding educationist of international repute who had been headmaster of the Trinity College, Candy, Ceylon, (now known as Sri Lanka) and Fraser in turn managed to prevail upon Dr. James Emmanuel Kwegyir Aggrey, that brilliant son of the Gold Coast and Africa who had been educated in the United States and was at that time teaching in one of the black universities of the United States, to come back home to help. So together, Guggisberg, Fraser and Aggrey, the Great Triumvirate, became the acknowledged founders of Achimota College.

My very first impressions of the College were very positive. I felt thoroughly excited and looked forward to spending at least the next four years in the climate of liberalism, where I would be free to take advantage of the many opportunities that the College offered for my self-development. As compared to the strict puritanical training of the past few years at Osu Salem, I had the feeling of a chicken who had been tied up and now let loose, given free rein! At this point, of course, it was a matter of great expectations. Whether these expectations would be fulfilled or not remained to be seen, although I told myself there and then that a lot would depend on me. The opportunities were there, the facilities were there, and it was really up to me to make the most of the time that I would spend there. It was up to me to go and grab these opportunities and make sure that at the end of the first four years, there would be a noticeable change in me, a change for the better!

After the Church Service all the boys strolled back to their compound and I noticed that some of the boys were accompanied by girlfriends who saw them off at the gate separating the girls' compound from the boys.' Lights out was at 9.30 pm and that night I lay awake thinking of the future. I must say that I felt really good with myself and slept soundly. I woke up early in the morning at the sound of the wake-up bell at 5.30. Of course for many years at Osu Salem we had been used to getting up early and the only difference here was that, unlike Osu Salem, I did not have to walk about 500 meters to fetch water from the public stand pipe for my bath. All I had to do was to turn on the tap and, hey presto, the water came and I had a nice shower and got ready for classes.

It was Monday, the first day of classes, and we were to start academic work. Naturally, not much work was done that morning. We made sure that we had all the prescribed books and spent time getting acquainted with each other and with the subject teachers who came that day. At Osu Salem, of course, each class had one teacher who taught everything. But here, we had subject masters. We had a form master who collated all the information about us. It was a new experience for me. I was introduced to a new subject, Latin. Latin as we know is a dead language. It was a language spoken by the Romans and some of the Romanic or Latinic tribes in ancient times; but it had survived, not as a living language but as a dead language which, nevertheless, found expression in documents and other areas of communication and activity. I must say that I thought that it was an absolute waste of time, learning a language, a dead language, which was not being spoken by any people, anywhere. However, I soon discovered that, whether dead or not, Latin was a very useful subject to learn because it made it easy to acquire or build up a vocabulary in English as many English words stem from Latin. A knowledge of Latin, therefore made it easier to understand words which you had not come across before. Not only that, but for me, many years later, I found the knowledge of Latin very useful in my medical studies, especially the study of human anatomy where many parts of the human body derive their names from Latin as they describe the function of a given part. For example, *adductor magnus* means the large muscle mass which causes the movement of the limb inwards *towards* the body. Whereas *abdactor* means that the muscle has a function of moving the limb *away* from the body. There are so many other parts of the human body whose names were really Latin names. To the extent that orthodox medicine is international, it made for easier communication. So it doesn't really matter whether you are studying medicine in Russia, or in France or in Britain, the anatomical names are standard Latin derivatives.

Whereas in the Elementary School, one studied Arithmetic, (i.e addition, subtraction, multiplication and division) at the secondary level, Algebra and Geometry were introduced. Added to the arithmetic the whole subject became known as Mathematics! The wide meaning and the scope of study made it highly interesting and this was very welcome. Nature Study, also became more interesting because of the way in which it was taught; not just being confined to the classroom, but also visiting the arboretum or even the farm and other interesting places to observe nature in different forms : insects, flowers, plants etc. Nature Study was made more interesting and the scientific basis of the way in which nature worked was made clear. Other subjects studied were Geography, History and Religious Instruction or Bible Knowledge.

I may explain once more that being a college, Achimota had a number of departments ranging from the Kindergarten, Primary, Middle School, the Secondary Department, Post-Middle Teacher Training Department to the Post-Secondary Department or Tertiary Department. Here one normally spent two years after obtaining the School Leaving Certificate and continued to higher education to pursue a course leading to an Intermediate Bachelor of Arts Degree certificate or Intermediate Bachelor of Science Degree. At that time too it was possible to pursue a whole four-year degree course of Bachelor of Science, Engineering. It was not until many years later that Achimota College, following dismemberment by loss of all other departments, became a secondary school only. The teacher training department moved to the Kumasi College of Technology, leaving the primary school or the preparatory school which persisted as the only preparatory department; the pre-secondary department which is still in existence. The post-secondary department moved to become the nucleus of the University College of the Gold Coast in 1948 marking the beginning of the University of Ghana, now known as the University of Ghana, Legon.

It is easy to understand, therefore, that the secondary department to which I was admitted was fed from two main sources : first of all, there were the students who had completed the middle school at Achimota and were continuing to the Secondary Department, or to the Teacher Training Department. Then there were outsiders, like myself, who had completed the middle school course in various other schools -

government schools, mission schools, etc. In my case, I came from Osu Salem Middle Boys' School. The qualification for entering the secondary school was a pass in the Standard Seven School Leaving Certificate. Some students entered Achimota under their own steam (that is to say, their parents paid their fees) and others through various scholarships. The Principal, for example, had scholarships which he could award. Then there was the Government scholarship based on performance in the country-wide Standard Seven School Leaving Examination. Then there were other scholarships like the Cadbury Agricultural Scholarship, on which I came to Achimota.

It is interesting to note that my companion on that day, walking up the Achimota Hill to sit for the scholarship, E. K. Twum, also won a Cadbury Scholarship. So we found ourselves in the same class. We were placed in Form 3, not Form 1, because the four year secondary course, started in Form 3 and continued through to Form 6. So it was in Form 6 that one sat for the Cambridge School Leaving Examination. This was a long time before the establishment of the West African Examinations Council and the subsequent introduction of the West African Secondary School Certificate.

The outsiders coming to Achimota to enter Form Three had to fight hard to prove themselves as most of the staff at Achimota were expatriates and were only used to the students and pupils who started from the lower rungs of the educational ladder at Achimota, at either the primary or middle level. They had been taught how to speak English properly with the correct phonetics, whereas the outsiders usually could be spotted immediately they opened their mouths, since they did not have the anglicized pronunciation. For some reason, the expatriate staff especially seemed to equate ability to speak English well with academic or intellectual capacity; therefore those of us who came from outside had to work very hard to be recognized by people like Mr. Henry Neill who was very partial to the pupils who came from the primary and middle sections of Achimota. As time went on it became clear that the products of the lower/pre-secondary classes of Achimota did not have the monopoly of academic ability and that the outsiders were as good and in some cases even better! Given time, of course, they too learned to speak English properly. Certainly, their grammar was not bad, all they required was fluency in speaking English with the proper accent. A situation like this, of course, gave rise to healthy rivalry among the students, and I think at the end of the day, it was a good thing for all of us because it helped to maintain our academic standards at a pretty high level.

As it turned out, my class at Achimota was full of very bright students and you can, therefore, imagine the keenness of the competition. Unfortunately, there was only one girl in a class of about forty, a percentage which by modern standards is very, very low. I do not know what the percentage is now, but I would not be surprised if it is now at leasty fifty percent! Classmates whose acquaintance I made during the first few days were, Kofi Atiemo, who I met on the first day of arrival and who was also in Livingstone House, E. K. Twum, my fellow Cadbury Scholarship holder, Ernest Amano Boateng, the son of a Presbyterian School headmaster, Lawrence Ofosu-Appiah from Akropong and coming also from a Presbyterian background.

Now a word or two about our teachers. The first was Mr. P. D. Quartey Jnr, the son of Mr. P. D. Quartey Snr., who was headteacher of the James Town Government Boys' School when I was in the lower primary stages in the Government School in Accra. Mr. P. D. Quartey Jnr was the junior housemaster of Gyamfi House. He took us through the first steps in Latin. Apart from teaching Latin, Mr. P. D. Quartey was an all round sportsman who coached students of Gyamfi House and the College teams in cricket, football and hockey. I found Mr. P. D. Quartey a very sympathetic person. He understood very well the problems of those of us who came from schools outside Achimota and did everything to encourage us to settle and to regain whatever confidence we might have lost in ourselves. At a later stage, Mr. Henry Neill took over the teaching of Latin. A very stern personality, a strict disciplinarian and one who shamelessly showed his bias in favour of the products of the Achimota junior levels, we had to work hard to satisfy him. Apart from Latin, he also taught English and he was a stickler for phonetics. Even though he was very strict with us, at the end of the day we all realized that he was really helping us to fall in line with the standards at Achimota.

Later on, in Form 6, Mr. Jack Marshall took over the teaching of Latin. That was our School Certificate year, and he prepared us for the School Certificate Examination. It was a joy to listen to Jack Marshall's teaching. He took us through Latin prose and poetry and somehow, at least to me, he made the subject very interesting. Jack Marshall, was also an outstanding pianist and, as I recall, throughout my years at Achimota, he was the one who accompanied on the piano the performance of the operattas of Gilbert and Sullivan and other musicals like Chu Chin Chow.

For English we had "Abrewa" or Miss Colbatch Clark. At that time, she must have been in her late fifties and we were really very surprised at her agility. As young students, to us she looked very old and yet, in spite of that, I can picture her now, on her bicycle, cycling up the hill every morning towards the administration block and the classrooms to teach. She made the subject of English very interesting. Her area was poetry and we found her a very inspiring teacher. For English language and also prose, we had Mrs. Kingsley Williams, wife of the Assistant Vice-Principal, the Rev. Kingsley Williams, Mrs. Kingsley Williams had a very lovely voice with a beautiful accent and we just loved to hear her speak. Apart from that, she was a very good teacher from whom we learnt a lot. Our Geography teacher in the first year was Captain Lawford, a retired army captain. His field was physical geography which personally, I found extremely boring. But my friend Amano Boateng, who obviously had a great interest in geography, enjoyed it thoroughly. Many years later, Boateng was to become Professor of Geography at the University of Ghana, Legon. The following year, our teacher was Mr. Daniel Chapman, a young Gold Coaster who had studied in Oxford on Achimota College scholarship, and had graduated with honours in Geography. A very active and handsome young man, he really made Geography a fascinating subject because he dealt with the area of regional geography and it was exciting to hear him talk about the peoples in the various lands we had to learn about. Later on he changed his name to Chapman-Nyaho and after spending some years in the Diplomatic Service, became the first African headmaster of Achimota School.

Our first History teacher was Mr. Miguel Ribeiro., who came to Achimota from Mfantsipim. He also, like Daniel Chapman, was an excellent teacher. He made the teaching of History very interesting. He too joined the Diplomatic Service, served as Ambassador to various countries and later as the Second Chancellor of the University of Cape Coast.

Our History Master for the senior classes was that great historian, Mr. W. E. F. Ward, author of the book "History of the Gold Coast", and many other history books. Mr. Ward died a few years ago, at the ripe old age 90 plus. Mr. Ward was an interesting character. He narrated the historical events as if he was there when they all happened. I must say that I enjoyed Mr Ward's History lessons very much.

Mr. A. G. Fraser Jnr., son of the Principal, was our first Mathematics teacher. He was popularly called "Sandy" or "Gallut", nicknames given him by the students. A very enthusiastic teacher, his mathematics teaching was rather dry. Mercifully, he interspersed his teaching with anecdotes here and there and that relieved us of the tedium. In the senior classes, Mr. B. A. Brown, a former teacher at Wesley College, took over. I found Mr. B. A. Brown quite a good teacher. What I did not like about him was that he thought Mathematics was the only subject on the curriculum and, therefore, he gave numerous pages of homework. Needless to say, I was naughty from time to time and I just selected a few examples out of the Mathematics book and did those only, much to his annoyance. Incidentally, Mr. Brown was to play a very important role in my life in later years, especially the final year of my secondary education, something which I will narrate later on.

Our Bible Knowledge teacher, was Mr. C. T. Shaw. an anthropologist. He was the curator of the Museum and a very good teacher of the Bible. Years after, I met him at the University of Ibadan where he was professor of Anthropology. Rev Bardsley also taught us Bible Knowledge. Rather a dull teacher, despite the fact that he was an Anglican priest. I found Mr. C. T. Shaw far more interesting.

Our Agricultural Science teacher was Dr. Fred Irvine. He was an excellent teacher on the field, but rather uncomfortable in the classroom. He wrote an interesting book "Woody plants of the Gold Coast" and also a book on agricultural science. For our practical teaching there was also Mr. Gillett. Mr. Gillett was the one who informed me at the Soda Fountain in Accra that I had won a scholarship and, of course, he was one of the interviewers at the scholarship examination. He was a highly practical man. I remember that he took our class out during the vacation to the Bunso Agricultural Station. Later on in subsequent years, he took us to Asuantsi Agricultural School where we spent a week of practical training. One thing which reminds me of that visit was that through the carelessness of one of the students, a barn, containing, I believe maize which was being stored, got burnt. It was a highly embarrassing incident for all of us, and I could well imagine the strain on Mr. Gillett's relations with the authorities of the Agricultural Department of the Gold Coast as a result.

For General Science or Elementary Science, we had teachers in the subdivisions. For Nature Study, as it was called, we had Miss Plumtree. Miss Plumtree was partially deaf and had to wear a hearing aid. Despite her handicap we found her a very good teacher, a good illustrator, on the blackboard and very active out on the field chasing butterflies and examining flowers and vegetation and pointing out the ecological arrangements of the environment. Miss Plumtree married Mr. A. H. R. Joseph who was the Senior Sports Master of the College. Mr. A. H. R. Joseph, a Ceylonese, was a first class cricketter and a good batsman. I recall that he played for the Accra Cricket Team. The Nigerians found him quite a hard nut to crack and it was almost impossible to get him out when he was batting. Cricket was his main sport but he also played tennis and coached hockey. Mr. Joseph stayed in this country for a long time. He became the Secretary to the National Sports Council and ended up as a Sports Master of the Kumasi College of Technology when it was established. Unfortunately he died in a tragic motor accident whilst he was at the University. The Paa Joe Sports Stadium of the University of Science and Technology is a memorial to the contributions which he made to sports in the country and to the University in particular.

Our Chemistry teacher was Mr. F. E. Joselyn. I found Mr. Joselyn a very good teacher. I liked the tricks he played in the laboratory, mixing compounds to change colour to look like a magical display. Mr. Joselyn incidentally, was the master of the College who accompanied us as chaperon of the contingent of students, including myself, who were going abroad to study in the year 1942. He happened to be going on his home leave in the U.K. and I was proceeding to study medicine.

For Physics, our subject master was George Hood. He was a great actor and whatever he taught he made very enjoyable with all sorts of anecdotes and illustrations. Apart from his teaching duties, George Hood was more or less the unofficial producer of all the important plays and musical shows and operattas performed in the College. I came to know George Hood quite well because at that time I was very much interested in art (drawing), and he used me in illustrating costumes he wanted to use for the various plays and operas. I remember drawing dozens of costumes for the *Pirates of Penzance* and the *Yeomen of the Guard* and others of the Gilbert and Sullivan operas. George Hood was a jolly good fellow. I never saw him flustered and he was always ready to come up with a joke. When you walked into the laboratory and George Hood was there teaching, it was really difficult to differentiate between the teacher and his students. For him, there was no generation gap – and he conversed freely with us. We all liked him. He was a popular housemaster for Lugard House. One would not call George Hood a serious minded person, but, in his own happy-go-lucky way, he made a tremendous impact on many students all of whom learnt a lot from his teaching. Coming from George Hood's class one always came away with something!

The foregoing were some of the academic teaching staff we had. Our class was a very strong one and in later years we were joined by students from other schools, some even from Nigeria. In our third year, we were joined by a student from Nigeria, Kenneth Dike, a quiet, well-behaved student. At that time, he was not outstanding, although a good student. After leaving Achimota School, however, he went to Furrah Bay College for his first degree and continued to Aberdeen where he did a masters degree in History. He later proceeded to Oxford for his PhD. When the University of Ibadan started, he went back to become one of the founding African members of staff of the History Department and rose up the ladder first as professor to become the very first Nigerian Vice-Chancellor of the University of Ibadan!

Our class produced some very outstanding people in various fields; a number of professors, Fellows of the Ghana Academy of Arts and Sciences, professionals, for example, lawyers, engineers, doctors, businessmen, and also traditional rulers. We had very good results at the Cambridge School Certificate Examination and it was quite clear, as they say, that future events cast their shadows and one could even tell at that time that the members of the class were destined for great achievements. I am glad to say that, until recently, we kept together as the Old Achimotan 1938 Year Group. At the time of writing the average age of the class would be perhaps hovering around 80. As the years roll by, there has been rapid attrition, and now there is just a handful of us.

Despite the keen competition and the variety of extra curricula activities I managed to keep my head above water to keep a fairly good academic record and, as I recall, I was able to secure one of the four form prizes each year during the course. Occasionally, I got a prize in Art or Ga Language. I do not recall getting a prize in any of the other important subjects like English, Mathematics, or whatever, but I was sure to get a prize in Art or Ga where I always scored high marks. I suspect that it was really Ga and Art which boosted my average and made it possible for me to secure form prizes during that period. At that time, we chose our examination subjects in Form Five. In my case, even at that stage I was still not decided on what I wanted to do, although the ambition I had haboured, from my childhood - to become a teacher – was always lurking somewhere. With a secondary education, it was reasonable to hope that it should end in a tertiary education and a degree of some sort. I must say that there were indications that I might be enticed to take Art seriously as l had a natural flair for drawing. Successive art masters, Mr. Pippet, first, and now the new art master Mr. Meyrowitz, had tried to woo me to the subject. Mr. Meyrowitz was certainly interested in me. So in a way, as far as the choice of a career went, I was really undecided. I felt like a floating voter with nowhere to cast my vote. However, this was soon to be rectified in a way, which to me, was nothing short of a miracle. Apart from the purely academic subjects, during the first two years, there were also practical non-examinable subjects which one could choose as a hobby. All of us were required to acquire some skills in woodwork and metalwork. Others chose book-binding or different types of weaving.

The College had a good library. In our fourth year, that is, our School Certificate Year, Mr. Marshall, who was the librarian, selected a number of us, from the Sixth Form to help in the library. Our duties were to make sure that the shelves were kept clean, the books were well arranged and, generally speaking, to assist the librarian in keeping the library clean and orderly. There were magazines and newspapers also available for us to read. The library was accessible to every student and there was a system of borrowing books from the library. From the point of view of those of us who were selected to assist the librarian, we found it very useful for our studies. In this connection, I recall my very good friend, Ernest Amano Boateng, and I were responsible for adjacent bookshelves for books on English Literature and Fiction. We took advantage of the opportunity to do as much reading as we could and Ernest and I arranged a competition to find out by the end of the year, who read the most books. I am very thankful to him for introducing me to important works of English Literature, especially the great authors. He also reluctantly read books on fiction which he did not like so much.

All in all, I gained tremendously. Not only did I read much fiction but also I read extensively from English Literature. This was to stand me in good stead in subsequent years during my medical studies abroad, because the life of a medical student is not an easy one; so much to do in the classroom, in the laboratories and on the wards which left one very little time to read much outside one's medical books. So, for me, having read a fair amount of English Literature whilst in secondary school, I did not really feel the need to do much extra medical reading, I am eternally grateful for the opportunity I had during my last year in secondary school to do this reading.

In keeping with Fraser's vision of making Achimota a truly Christian School, bringing up the boys and girls along Christian lines, much attention was paid to daily worship. The day started with prayers. During the weekdays after breakfast we went straight on to prayers in the School Chapel which at that time was right at the top floor of the Administration Building. Because our numbers were then small the Chapel could accommodate practically the whole school. At night we had evening prayers in the common rooms of our Houses. Prayers were conducted by the housemaster or the assistant housemaster in turn, or occasionally by the prefects and monitors. On Sunday evenings, regularly, we attended service for the whole school. Apart from Muslims and Catholics and those who were not inclined to attend church on a given day, the whole school walked to the Western Compound for service in the girls' dining-hall, which was quite spacious.

There was also the opportunity to join the Student Christian Movement. There weren't many of us, but the few who joined the Movement were privileged to be given daily reading material which we used during quiet time in the morning and also during the day when we were expected to rest. Fraser chose his staff well, and he made sure that all of them were good role models for us. Some of them even helped with our Bible study.

## Student Activities

The system of student governance provided for a Senior Prefect for the boys and a Senior Prefect for the girls. There was a Prefect for each House and a Games Prefect for the school as a whole. Then there were Debating Societies (for example the Plato Club) of which a few of us were members. All these clubs were mixed clubs. As much as possible, the boys and girls did things together, in order to emphasize that girls had the same capacity as boys to engage in any activity. Girls were not barred by physical considerations. Entertainment was well catered for. On Saturday evenings, the whole School gathered in the boys' dining hall and the various Houses took turns to stage plays or variety concerts. Kitson-Mills, whom I have referred to already as my bodyguard when I first entered the College, was a sort of amateur magician, who went by the name *Professor Agremokline* and he entertained the whole school from time to time to magical displays. There was another student called, Bob Lamptey, who also was some sort of lesser magician !

I have already referred to the Gilbert and Sulivan Operattas. During my days at Achimota, *the Pirates of Penzance, the Mikado, and the Yeomen of the Guard* were three which were performed. Both staff and students participated. At that time, most of the senior staff were expatriates. The accompaniment was piano music which was played by Mr. Jack Marshall, an excellent pianist. The plays were produced by George Hood. Other plays which were staged included *Chu Chin Chow* (which is a musical play, based on the story of Ali Baba and the Forty Thieves). I played the part of Nur.al Huda, son of Ali Baba. My leading lady was Miss Naomi Mitchual, who, after school, got married to my good friend Kwesi Appiah. There was also one of Shakespeare's Plays which our class had to study for the School Certificate Examination - *"A Mid-Summer Night's Dream."* In order to facilitate the study and for a better understanding, we staged it as a play and I recall taking the part of *Theseus*, the mythological king, and my queen, Hypolita, was played by Miss Katherine Konuah, who later became Mrs. Katherine Dowuona, wife of Dr. Modjaben Dowuona, who was then a senior member of staff.

Another very important form of entertainment for us was tribal drumming which took place on some Saturdays. We were grouped according to tribes, and the students who had some knowledge of cultural drumming and dancing, especially those who had links with a royal family or were actual royals themselves, were very helpful in playing leadership roles. For the Gas, I recall, a student called Ayibonte, the son of the occupant of the Gbese Stool of Accra, taught the Gas many dances and songs; he also taught the skilful and enterprising members of the Ga tribe different varieties of drumming. There were others also who knew and understood the drum language although, I must say, not many of us took this very seriously. We were more interested in singing and dancing around on Saturday nights.

## Sports

Achimota College was very famous for sports and invariably came first in the inter-colleges competition, whether in athletics or football, or cricket or hockey. Much attention was paid to sports, and the facilities provided were really first class : extensive and well kept playing fields and adequate sports equipment. Then, of course, among the staff were some who were very good sportsmen themselves and who acted as coaches for the various school teams. I have already mentioned A. H. R. Joseph, the senior sports master, brought by Chief Fraser from Trinity College, Candy, in Ceylon of which Fraser was head before he came to Achimota. "Paa Joe," as Joseph was affectionately called, was a great organizer and was ably assisted by outstanding sportsmen like P. D. Quartey Jnr., and Attoh-Okine, whom I have already mentioned as a great footballer, was also an excellent cricketer and hockey player. Then, of course, for hockey, there was Jaipal Singh. He was an Indian who was also on the staff of Fraser's former college in Ceylon. Jaipal Singh was an international hockey player. He was an Oxford Blue and a member of the All India Hockey Team. At that time, India were the world champions in hockey and had, if I may put it in Ghanaian parlance, "no challenger." They occupied this foremost place in world hockey for many, many years. So Achimota College was very lucky to have Jaipal Singh on the school staff. I cannot remember which academic subjects he taught, but certainly he was the number-one hockey coach and he did a lot to bring the Achimota hockey team up to a very high standard. There were other expatriate teachers like Charles Woodhouse and Henry Neill who were also good hockey players and who also contributed to raising the standard of hockey at Achimota. Cricket, was Joseph's domain, while Attoh Okine handled football.

P. D. Quartey handled athletics, assisted by some of the members of the junior staff. In the inter-college competitions' sprinting events, Wesley College always came first. For many years, at least for four consecutive years, Wesley College swept all the medals in the sprint events : the 100yards, the 200yards and the 440yards. The star of these events was a student called I. Boye-Doe. Boye-Doe also held the national records for these events which were broken only in the fifties, I think. Fortunately for Achimota, whenever Boye-Doe came first; Achimota was second and third in these races, thereby equalling the points awarded. During our time, the star sprinter at Achimota was a student from the North (Navrongo, I believe) and a member of our year group. He was in the Teacher Training Department. His name was Adda. Adda was to become the father of Brigadier Adda of the Ghana Armed Forces. In fact, I have learnt from authentic sources that he is still alive. If so, he must be well in his mid or late 80s!

Now, to come back to my own interests. When I was at Osu Salem, I played football and volley ball. There was no cricket and no hockey. I continued to play football at Achimota and improved my skills somewhat. At least I was adjudged to be good enough to play for my House. I got introduced to cricket which I quite liked because I like games in which you hit the ball, and I believe that if I had paid more attention to cricket I could have really developed into a fairly good cricketer. I was not a regular player for Livingstone House, but I was always on the reserve list. Occasionally, I got the chance to play.

With hockey, it was a different matter. My friend, Kofi Atiemo, was an all-round sportsman despite his short physical stature, Kofi must have been 5ft 6in tall but was really muscular and physically fit. He was a great cricketer who also played football. In hockey, however, he was almost a genius. His ball control was superb. Indeed, in my opinion, Kofi Atiemo, in his time, was easily the best attacker among all the hockey players in the schools and colleges of the Gold Coast. When Kofi realized that I could handle the hockey stick with some facility, he took me under his wing and he and I really spent a lot of time practising on the lawn in front of Livingstone House. We were so madly in love with the game that sometimes we even missed going to have our meals. We would play around, just the two of us, he attacking, and I trying to stop him. The result was that Kofi trained me to become a very competent player and an efficient stopper. He once said that I was the only one who could stop him when he was on the rampage! This was, of course, not surprising because he taught me and I knew all his tricks. He found it not so easy to by-pass me on the field.

Now if I could stop Kofi then I could stop anyone else because Kofi was incomparable. Thus it was that I settled on hockey. I decided to specialize in playing hockey, and in my second year, started playing hockey for the House. In my third and fourth years, I played for the College and earned my full colours. Well, you can imagine the impact that Kofi and I had on the Livingstone House Hockey team. We were able to build around us such a formidable team that for two successive years (1937, 1938) Livingstone House were the College champions.

I recall that in the year 1937, the year that I joined the College Team, we made a trip up north to Kumasi as guests of Wesley College. It was a very tough match. However, at that time the Achimota College team was made up of 11 very smart young lads, well trained, cohesive, formidable and, although I do not remember the exact score, I remember that we beat Wesley College on home ground. We had quite a number of old Achimotans resident in Kumasi - teachers, civil servants, and others both male and female - who came to cheer us on. That was my very first trip to Kumasi. It was then a small town but very beautiful and, of course, Wesley College at that time was fairly new with very lovely grounds. We enjoyed our week-end stay in Kumasi very much. The road to Kumasi, at that time, was not so good. It was not all tarred and we also had more or less to go through thick forest. There were then huge trees right by the side of the road, and not that severe deforestation which one witnesses today. Travelling through the forest at that time could be quite a risky business because occasionally, there could be huge tree trunks suddenly falling across the road and causing a great inconvenience and delaying the journey for hours until the villagers or other authority came to saw the trunks and push them out of the way.

In keeping with its motto *"Ut Omnes Unum Sint"* (That they all may be one), students came to Achimota from all corners of the Gold Coast. I was very fortunate in the friendships that I made at Achimota. In my second year at Achimota a couple of young men from Tamale who came to Achimota to pursue the Teacher Training course were assigned to Livingstone House. They were Ebenezer Adam (who still lives in Tamale and whom I see occasionally on my visits there) and the late Edmund Alhassan who became the first student from the North to obtain a university degree. After studying at Cambridge he came back as an Education Officer. Alas he died a tragic death whilst he was stationed at Bekwai–Ashanti. He was the husband of the late Mrs. Susan Alhassan, who became the first woman Minister in the government of Osagyefo Dr. Kwame Nkrumah. Ebenezer Adam, Edmund Alhasssan and I became very close friends. Both of them were sportsmen and Ali, as we fondly called him, was a very good cricketer and hockey player. I got to know him well because he and I played the full back positions in the Livingstone House hockey team. He had eyes like a hawk and he could hit the ball as nobody else could. I remember on one occasion when our goal mouth was threatened and finally he had to clear the ball, he hit it so hard that it went all the way past the goalkeeper on the other side and right into the goal! Occasionally, I used to jokingly ask him to have mercy on the ball! In subsequent years, Imoru Egala also came to Achimota and joined us in Livingstone House. Egala, was clearly much older and I believe he had been working before he came to the College. What I remember about Egala was that he was a good long distance runner and a footballer too. He also became a good friend.

At about the same time, we had a couple of students from Nigeria in the House. These two boys, Abdul Mumuni and Abdul Azizi Atta came to Achimota in 1937. They were sons of one of the important rulers from the north of Nigeria. It was not only the boys who came, they had younger sisters, Rakiya and Katsina, who were in the lower middle school. But Abdul Mumuni and Azizi and I became very good friends and from time to time when I was going on exeat, I took them home and they became well known to my family. Years after, when I was abroad in Edinburgh studying medicine, Abdul Mumuni also came to Edinburgh. Before coming, he went and said good-bye to my mother who sent some goodies through him. I shall say more about Abdul Mumuni later because throughout his stay in Edinburgh and even after, we became very close. Abdul is currently a well respected retired medical doctor in Kaduna in Nigeria. Azizi, a bright boy, went to Oxford. I believe he studied Economics. On his return home he joined the Civil Service and rose through the ranks to become Principal Secretary. Alas, he died at quite an early age. In Livingstone House, there were also students from different parts of Africa. There were students from Uganda who came to Achimota to pursue secondary courses.

Incidentally, Mr. Herbert, who was housemaster for Livingstone House, on leaving Achimota went to Kings College, Budo, Uganda, I believe, to be headmaster of that school. He came back later to the Gold Coast to head the Teacher Training Section of the Achimota College. By this time, he had inherited his father's title and had become Lord Hemmingford. Despite that, he still came back to work in the Gold Coast. The Teacher Training Department at Achimota was moved to the Kumasi College of Technology when that institution was established and became one of the founding departments of the College.

In sporting circles, I made friends who were not members of Livingstone House, and I think the most intimate friend I had was Toufeek Majdoub, as he was then, (now known as Toufeek Bedwei). He was in Aggrey House, but since we were classmates and also members of the College Hockey team we became friendly. I had great admiration for

Toufeek as he was also a first class cricketer, a top batsman so that even whilst he was a student, he and Kofi Atiemo were selected to play for the Gold Coast National team. We moved together so closely that some students nicknamed us the "College twins." To this day, I have a photograph on my desk, taken on the hockey field, of Toufeek and I wearing Achimota College hockey jerseys. Toufeek lives in Kumasi and whenever I am in Kumasi and time permits, I make it a point to visit him.

Other students whom I met at Achimota who became good friends of mine were E. L. Quartey (otherwise known as Nii Quartey), son of Father B. T. Quartey of the Anglican Church. Nii and I became very good friends, and also classmates. He joined Achimota at the lower primary section, so he was already at Achimota when I got there. He was among those who used to make fun of the "bush people" coming from outside Achimota to join the secondary department. They thought our pronunciation of English words was atrocious. We had no phonetics at all. We spoke grammatically correctly but with no phonetics. Our English needed polishing. Well, we admitted this and by the end of the first year, most of us had learnt to pronounce English words properly. Nii Quartey remained a very close friend, especially after we finished secondary school and proceeded to the tertiary department of the College. He and I shared some really interesting times together, which I shall narrate in due course.

Now, I have been talking about the facilities and opportunities which Achimota offered. Looking back now, I remember Achimota as a great big family: a levelling ground for everybody, socially, economically, culturally and so on. At Achimota everybody was regarded as equal, equal in the sense of equal rights and privileges. Your rights were respected and your privileges guaranteed. In turn you were expected to discharge your responsibilities diligently. Chief Fraser had a hand in choosing his own staff. He, therefore, made sure that he selected people who would provide the needed leadership for the students. Many members of staff were role models for the students. They provided leadership by example by the way they lived and comported themselves and by the way they dressed. In spite of their academic accomplishments, there was a certain humility, a certain modesty and an eagerness on their part to help students to discover their talents, to encourage and to counsel them so that after four years at Achimota, there was a marked change in ones' attitude and outlook. I would say that the sort of strict puritanical

foundation that I had at Osu Salem - respect for authority, all the attributes which were built into the foundation at Osu Salem - were tempered by the liberal atmosphere of Achimota. The opportunities that Achimota provided enabled me to understand and appreciate a cardinal aim of the College; namely, to help to make one a good human being! I acquired knowledge, I was given good moral training, I developed a sense of responsibility, I imbibed a certain spirit which I call the "Achimota Spirit" a spirit of brotherhood, to treat all men and women, from whatever background, with respect.

In the middle of the school year in 1935, Principal Fraser left Achimota on retirement after eight and a half years as the founding Principal of the College. Fraser enjoyed considerable freedom and independence which enabled him to implement in a large measure the vision of the founding fathers. Certainly, he laid the foundation on which his successors, over the years, managed to build Achimota into that widely acclaimed and prestigious educational institution of international repute. Fraser had the freedom to chose his own staff and by so doing, he was enabled, first of all, to assess the type of person he was appointing to the staff and to make sure that the person shared both in the philosophy of Achimota and the aims and objectives of the School and that the person was someone who had the necessary or required commitment to the work which had to be done. At the time that he was leaving, therefore, I believe that Fraser himself was quite satisfied with the foundation which he had laid. He was satisfied with the commitment and devotion to duty of the staff whom he had appointed, and he was also satisfied with the contributions which the first products of the College were making to the development of the country. They were living up to the expectations of the founding fathers. Fraser, I am sure, believed that his hope that the products of Achimota College would go out as living water to the thirsty land of the Gold Coast was being fulfilled graciously. Although Fraser left Achimota on retirement, he was not really tired. His work in the tropics had gone on for long enough and the time had come for him to go back home to enjoy the benefits of a temperate climate.

Indefatigable Fraser went on to become Warden of Newbattle Abbey in Edinburgh, Scotland and subsequently, a teacher and then headmaster of the famous boys' school in the west of Scotland – Gordonstoun School, famous for the type of boys who went there and their notable contributions to British national life - one of the most famous products of the school being the Duke of Edinburgh. Years afterwards when I was in the medical school, in Edinburgh, we the old Achimotans in Edinburgh, were able to organize yearly reunions, some of which Fraser gladly attended. This enabled us to know him better. I dare say that at that point in his life, the hopes with which he left Achimota were further heightened by the achievements of the products of Achimota because at that time there was quite a number of us on Gold Coast Government Scholarship in Scotland and the UK generally studying to become medical doctors, engineers, architects, and what have you!

Fraser was succeeded by Reverend Canon H. M. Grace, an Anglican priest. Grace was a fatherly, kindly, scholarly, soft-spoken gentleman. He had the sort of mien which inspired confidence. He was not as outgoing as Fraser but in his quiet way, he achieved results. Certainly, during the five years that he was at Achimota, he managed to consolidate and build upon the achievements of Fraser. I may say that he was the Principal whom I came to know best, because his years at Achimota coincided with my own at Achimota, and during my final year in the secondary school, I got to know him quite well as I was one of the House Prefects with whom the Principal from time to time interacted. At a personal level, he played a very vital role in furthering my education when I finally decided to take up medicine as a profession.

## Student Governance

The four-year secondary course, comprised 3rd, 4th, 5th and 6th forms. The 6th form, the last year, was the examination year, the Cambridge Schools Certificate Examination. In my case, it was in 1938, very many years before the West African Examinations Council was established. The prefects for the School were selected from the 6th form, and the student governance of the school was upon their shoulders. They were appointed by a committee consisting of the senior housemaster and all the housemasters meeting together. They chose the prefects for the various Houses. The Senior Prefect, according to custom, was elected by the out-going 6th Form members. In our year, the honour of becoming Senior Prefect fell on a very good friend, the late S. S. Newlands. He had no direct responsibility for any House but had an overall responsibility for all the Houses and presided over the Council of Prefects which met on regular basis to compare notes and consider matters relating to students' welfare.

In my first year at Achimota, the Senior Prefect was Seth Anthony. Seth Anthony became famous as the very first Gold Coaster to become an Officer in the West African Frontier Force during World War II. He saw action in the Far East and rose to become a Major of the Army. I feel sure that if he had so wished and continued to make a military career, he would have become the first General of the Ghana Army. Seth Anthony is still alive and now in his late eighties and lives in Accra.

The Senior Prefect for 1936 was A. E. Ofori-Atta, who after a career in education became a diplomat and served in various countries after the Gold Coast had become independent. In 1937, the Senior Prefect was D. A. Brown, a quiet but strict disciplinarian. He became a teacher of Mathematics and rose through the ranks in the Department of Education to become Chief Education Officer and then Principal Secretary of the Ministry of Education. The Senior Prefect for 1938, S. S. Newlands, was among the first to pursue a secondary-commercial course at Achimota. He became a manager of the United African Company (UAC) and later the Ghana National Trading Company (GNTC). He retired to his hometown in Denu and died just a few years ago.

Sometime in early December 1938, I was called by Mr. Attoh Okine, then Acting Housemaster of Livingstone House in the absence of Mr. Herbert, the housemaster. Mr. Okine informed me that it had been decided to appoint me a House Prefect. However, I wasn't to be prefect of Livingstone House, but prefect of House Six. House Six was a junior house as the boys there were young, mostly from the middle school section and a few who were in the secondary department but who were considered too small to be in a senior house. The other point about my prefectship was that as the inhabitants were troublesome young boys, House Six required two prefects. For that reason, I was a bit hesitant at first, but Mr. Okine told me that Mr. Charles Woodhouse, the housemaster of House Six, especially asked for me to become one of the Prefects of the House.

I must say here that I got to know Mr. Woodhouse quite well since he was a good sportsman; our initial contacts were on the hockey field where we had quite a few encounters. I did not know, at that time, that he was evaluating me, but from what Mr. Okine said, he must have had a high opinion of me. For a couple of years I had been captain of the Livingstone House Hockey Team and I suppose he must have been quite impressed with my performance. So I felt quite flattered and,

˜therefore, decided to accept and endeavour to do my best as joint Prefect of House Six. Interestingly, my partner in that endeavour was Modesto Apaloo whom I had got to know quite well and who was my personal friend also. Modesto was a teacher training student. He was a highly articulate young man with very pleasant manners and I really looked forward to working with him. I was quite pleased to learn that on hearing that I was to be his partner in the joint enterprise he too welcomed the idea.

Needless to say, for the one year that we were joint prefects, we enjoyed a very good and cordial relationship. We did not allow the young boys to drive a wedge between us as some of the mischievous boys tried to do from time to time. We shared our responsibilities and made sure that no one took advantage of our joint position. Mr. Woodhouse impressed upon us that there was no question of one person being the captain of the ship. We were mature enough to be able to share our responsibilities. Provided we did so there would not be any problem. I may say that being a sportsman myself, and quite a good hockey player at that I interacted more closely with the boys on the hockey field and there was the tendency for them to come to me with their problems rather than go to Modesto even when it was clearly his responsibility. We found a way of nipping this quickly in the bud and everything went on smoothly thereafter.

Modesto and I drew much inspiration from Mr. Charles Woodhouse who at that time was just about to get married. For many years he had been with the boys, and had a really uncanny way of dealing with even the most mischievous and getting them to tow the line. It was quite clear that the boys had great affection for him even when he was dispensing unpleasant doses of punishment. Altogether, I found that one year of my prefectship and joint responsibility with Modesto, and our relationship with the housemaster very fruitful. The useful experience I had in dealing with boys stood me in good stead in later years when I had to deal with groups of students very much younger than myself, especially at the time that I was Vice-Chancellor of the University of Science and Technology in Kumasi.

House Six, at the time, had some very lively and brilliant boys with a great potential. Of the dormitory monitors, I recall distinctly the late Victor Owusu, who became an outstanding lawyer, a politician, and a presidential aspirant, and then Silas Dodu, the son of my former headmaster at Osu Salem, a brilliant boy who went on to become an outstanding physician and the first Professor of Medicine of the University of Ghana Medical School and the second Dean of the School. Silas is retired now and lives in Accra. Victor, as we know, passed away recently after a very full and eventful life, a life during which he really made immense contributions to various aspects of life in Ghana. Then there was Peter Renner, a mischievous boy at the time, later to become Assistant Headmaster of the School. There was Mark Cofie, or Kofi Agbo, as he was called at the time, who, apart from becoming a very important traditional Chief of Tsito, studied engineering and set up a very flourishing automobile engineering business in Accra. Sadly, he died a few years ago, but right from his boyhood, one could see that he was a go-getter, full of action, and it was no surprise that he made such a success of the business enterprise which he founded. Other very lively and brilliant boys with a very bright future included K. B. Asante, who later on became a renowned civil servant and a diplomat, Kingley Nyinah who became an eminent jurist and R. S. Amegashie who also became a distinguished industralist with tremendous drive and resourcefulness.

It is quite interesting how seniors at school, maybe prefects or monitors or even teachers, are given nicknames by pupils or students which may go for years without their knowing. Years after my leaving Achimota, and when the late Peter Renner was Assistant Headmaster at Achimota School and I was visiting the School, he told me that whilst I was Prefect of House Six, the students gave me a nickname, *"Amale Sweat"*, meaning sweat induced by lies! I was quite taken aback when he described the occasion and the origin of that nickname. It happened that there was a minor crisis, I cannot quite recall, whether it had something to do with lights out or some sort of demand which the students had made. In any case, it was a promise which had not been fulfilled, and on this particular day, I came back from the sports field, sweating, perspiring all over, to meet a situation which I had to deal with before it turned nasty. So I had to go to the Common Room to address the students. I tried in every possible way to assure them that what was promised would be fulfilled, not knowing that all along, they were rather skeptical about the promise being fulfilled and even though that particular promise was later fulfilled, the skeptics among the students coined the name *"Amale Sweat"*, *sweat from lies*. A nickname which stuck over the years and one which was unknown to me until Peter Renner told me on my visit to Achimota some 30 years later! I must say, though, that in my relationship with the students, nothing ever happened to indicate that they thought of me as somebody who would deceive them or that I was a dishonourable person. On the contrary, over the years I found that all these former young boys of House Six have treated me with the greatest respect and I hope some of them have even looked upon me as a role model.

Apart from the immense interest which I took in sports, especially hockey, I was also very much involved with the Red Cross Society. The Red Cross group visited Anumle, Achimota and Dome villages around to advise the villagers and to help them in sanitation matters and also to attend to the children with sores. It may well be that my decision to become a doctor was influenced by my contact and other interaction with the villagers and the environmental circumstances that one saw at that time.

## Choosing A Career

I have already mentioned my interest in Art and the natural gift which I had for drawing. As the time approached for us to choose our subjects for the school certificate examination, pressure was brought to bear on me, especially by Mr. Meyerowitz, the new Art Master, to offer Art as one of my subjects. From that time on, I became closely involved with a number of situations chief among which was my relationship with Dr. Irvine, the teacher of Agriculture and Botany. He did extensive field work; he collected and classified plants and animals, especially flowering plants and fishes. At that time, Legon was virgin bush, and I recall that he and I made a few trips to Legon for me to draw orchids and various flowering plants. He was also interested in classifying fishes and we made several trips to beaches in Accra and places like La, Osu, Teshie and Korle Gonno. When the fishermen brought in the catch, Dr. Irvine selected some fish for me to draw. I must have drawn hundreds of different types of fishes, these were mostly line drawings. With regard to the flowering plants, I recall that there was a young lady teacher, Theresa Detrich, a teacher from one of the schools in Accra, who also came on some of these trips. Dr. Irvine later published a number of books and some of our drawings found their way as illustrations into some of these books. I looked forward very much to those trips out of the College with Dr. Irvine, outside of school hours. Needless to say that a strong bond of friendship developed between Dr. Irvine and me which out-lasted our Achimota days and which we continued subsequently in the United Kingdom when I was studying medicine.

Mr. Meyerowitz was a very dynamic person quite unlike his predecessor, Mr. Pippet, who was just interested in getting students to draw still life and to paint landscape using only water colour and did not really go beyond this sort of activity. He did not make any effort to teach us anything about the history of Art or various Art forms and did nothing to arouse any dormant creative talents which we might have. Mr. Meyerowitz was quite different. A few months after he arrived at Achimota he invited me to tea in his house and put it quite bluntly to me that he wanted me, after finishing my secondary course, to come back to Achimota to take a Special Art Course which he was planning to introduce, with a view to my becoming an Art Teacher; perhaps even going abroad to do a degree in Art and coming back to succeed him after he had left Achimota. This was a very interesting proposition to me because he told me that he was prepared to prevail on the Principal to make it easy for me to come back. There would be a scholarship and some fringe benefits so that the fact that after gaining my school certificate I could get employment or proceed to do other things might become irrelevant, as I would be financially quite well off to enable me to concentrate on Art. On the basis of this proposal, I entered Art as one of my School Certificate subjects. Of course, at this point, Mr. Meyrowitz was confidently thinking aloud! These were plans that he was formulating. He still had to discuss the plan with the Principal and the Special Art Course still had to be introduced, maybe the following year, which was to be my School Certificate year.

At this point, therefore, we had some sort of gentleman's agreement. This agreement was reinforced the following year when the Special Art Course was introduced with three foundation students. They were teachers who had been teaching for some time and they came to take the three year Special Art Course. There was Asihene, who later became Professor of Art at the University of Science and Technology; Yeboah, who for some time continued as a teacher of Art and later Assistant Education Officer and Asante. Sadly, one of the latter two died in a tragic motor accident. These three were really the foundation students of the Special Art Course. This course over the years has produced artists of international repute. Before the end of his first year at Achimota, Mr. Meyrowitz had done a bit of trekking in the country, visiting a number of schools. It was on one of these visits that he discovered Kofi Antubam, I believe in a middle school, somewhere in the Western Region, and managed to get a scholarship for him to come to Achimota to complete his middle school education and then to continue with Teacher Training and, of course, the Special Art Course. Kofi Antubam, as we know, went on to become an outstanding Artist and Sculptor and one of the best known Artists in Ghana. His major art works are to be found adorning public places not only in Ghana, for example the Community Centre in Accra but also international buildings such as the United Nations and other places. Sadly, Kofi Antubam died in his prime. His death was a great loss to Ghana.

As soon as circumstances permitted, Mr. Meyrowitz also went to Nigeria, to Benin and brought to Achimota one of the distinguished brass workers of Benin to teach brass work at Achimota College. I shall say a little more about Mr. Ineh, the brass worker, later on.

By the beginning of 1938, plans for Mr. Meyrowitz to establish his Special Art School had been finalized and the course started with the three students to whom I have already referred. He was also able to finalize with the Principal the arrangements for my coming to continue with the Special Art Course after my School Certificate Examination at the end of that year. As I recall, all the fees were to be paid and, in addition, any books and materials that I would require would be provided; I would also be given an allowance of £20 a year. Considering that graduates of the Cambridge School Certificate at that time on entering the Public Service or Civil Service were paid £48 a year, to take care of everything, I thought these terms were excellent. The plan would enable me at least to make some savings. In any case, as a bachelor, I would be better off than most working people. So I agreed to these terms although, to this day, I do not recall that I actually signed any document accepting it. It was more or less a "gentleman's agreement", and it was just as well that it was not an executed contract, because of what happened later.

I was so much absorbed with the whole question of becoming an artist and an Art teacher, or rather making Art a career that I did not really bother much about my choice of subjects for the School Certificate Examination. As I recall, my seven subjects were English, Mathematics, Latin, Bible Knowledge, Agricultural Science, Art and Ga, the minimum number required. So we settled down to working hard towards the School Certificate Examination which I was confident of passing at the end of the year. I spent a lot of time on extra curricula activities. I did not really devote as much time as I should have to my academic subjects because of my obsession with Art. I may add here that my daddy was then at Akuse but his health had been failing for some time and he was finally obliged to stop work at the age of 52 after which he settled at Akuse.

My mother lived in Accra and was then earning a living through baking bread and cakes and other confectioneries together with her younger sister, Auntie Lizzy, Mrs. Chinery. They became specialists in a product called "Sweet bad", which was really a rock bun fried in oil and which was a big favourite of the school children and students at Achimota, to the extent that throughout my student days, I was selling *sweet bad* on the side. Strictly speaking, it was against the regulations, but what are regulations when prefects and monitors are ready to turn a blind eye in order to benefit from a very popular confectionery? *Sweet bad* was in high demand, especially round about nine o'clock after evening studies, that is, about half an hour before lights out. Everybody was hungry and just wanted something to allay their hunger, and *sweet bad* came as a godsend. So with what one might call, "official" backing, I was able to bend the rules, and, since no one was hurt by so doing, it looked as if the net effect was more positive than negative. Sweet bad found a ready market and I was able, in a way, to help to support or improve the economic conditions at home. I say all this in reference to the terms of the scholarship that Mr. Meyrowitz managed to arrange for me whilst doing the Special Art Course: £20 a year in addition to everything! To get full board and all the rest really would make it possible for me to increase my mother's pocket money. Sadly, in the middle of that School year, 1938, 13th June, my daddy died at Akuse and, in the absence of my two elder brothers, I had to support my mother at the funeral at Doryumu, where he was buried. My paternal great grandmother originally came from Doryumu, so to this day, my father's tomb is at Doryumu and I pay occasional visits to it.

## The Turning Point

I would say then that during the latter half of the year that I completed my secondary school course, I felt quite at peace with myself knowing that at least for three years after leaving school I would have something to fall back on by doing further studies to improve on my artistic skills and also be comfortable economically. So it was that somewhere in November that year and about six weeks before the Cambridge School

Certificate Examination, on a Saturday morning, I was strolling past the junior staff houses, towards the sports field where something was happening in which I was interested, that I heard my name shouted from one of the bungalows, "Anfom, Anfom!" Looking round, I thought I recognized the voice. Yes, it was that of Mr. B. A. Brown, our Mathematics teacher. He beckoned. He said he wanted to have a word with me, so I went in. He offered me a chair to make me as comfortable as possible. I have already indicated that Mr. Brown as a maths teacher was quite a hard task master. On this occasion, he was very friendly and enquired about the forthcoming School Certificate Examination and how I felt about it. He was particularly interested in what I intended to do after the results came from Cambridge.

I may say here that at that time, his younger brother, Nii Moi Brown, had been awarded a Gold Coast Government Scholarship to go abroad to study Dentistry. He, together with a G. K. Brown, who originally went to Mfanstipim School but who later came to Achimota to continue with the Intermediate BSc Degree course, had been awarded scholarships for Dentistry. Mr. Brown felt that, maybe, if I worked hard I might be able to get a scholarship to go abroad. Therefore I told him, as he did not appear to know, about the scholarship for a Special Art Course which Mr. Meyerowitz had arranged for me and I thought he would be pleased about it. On the contrary, he thought that I needed to give it a second thought because in his opinion I could always continue with Art as a hobby, but not as a profession. He thought I would be wasting my talents; because according to him, I was always in the top bracket of the class and had the ability and capacity to do whatever I wanted to. Certainly, he did not think that Art was the thing to do at that time, especially teaching Art. He also felt that the cultural appreciation by the population at that time was not high enough for an artist to make a living. So he advised that I should give the matter a second thought. He told me quite frankly that he would prefer that I changed my mind about it since I would not lose much. I could always, as he stressed, continue with Art as a hobby, whatever profession I might decide to choose. I thanked him most sincerely for his kind advice and I promise that I would think about it carefully.

I may say that this sudden intervention by Mr. Brown, if I may call it so, took me off my guard and caused me to think very seriously about what I was planning to do. For that reason, it created a moment of confusion. I abandoned my going to the sports field and went to think, or brood, over it and to pray about it because this was going to be a turning around, as I had given my word, a gentleman's agreement, that I would be doing the Special Art Course. What would Mr. Meyerowitz think of me? What would the Principal think of me, if at this late hour I changed my mind? So, it was a day full of anxiety and perplexity, and it was a problem I did not really want to saddle anybody else with. There was no one whom I thought I could share this with. Not even the housemaster. So throughout the day I just prayed about it. I could not run home to discuss it with my mother who knew all about the plans, so I just had to think very carefully about it and give myself time. I had no appetite for lunch. In the afternoon I rested in my cubicle. Then round about four o'clock that day I had a brainwave. Although it came as a thought, I even wondered whether it was not premature. All the same, I thought even though a brainwave, I should act on it.

In the evening, after supper, at about half past seven I took a chance. Without any appointment or prior notice, I just walked straight to the Principal's bungalow. My first intention was to discuss this new development with him, to ask his advice as to what to do, and not to ask for any favours. I just wanted – I thought of the Principal as a father - and I just wanted to discuss my personal problem with him. The Principal knew me as one of the prefects. He knew who I was, and moreover in the negotiations about this Special Art Scholarship, he had been involved and had taken the decision in consultation with me. My fear was that he would, just on hearing what I had to say, insist that I was bound by a contractual obligation to take up the offer.

I got to the Principal's house at about a quarter-to-eight. Fortunately, he had already had supper. He and Mrs. Grace were conversing in the sitting room. I timidly knocked on the door and he walked up the door and ushered me in. "Anfom, what are you doing here? What can I do for you at this time? Are you in some trouble?" "No, Sir," I said ", but I have a problem and I think, Sir, you're the only one who can advise me and help me. I'm extremely sorry that I came here without any appointment. Perhaps I should have waited till Monday to come to the office to see you through the normal channels. But this is Saturday and it is a matter which is weighing heavily on my mind, so I thought I needed to have it resolved over the week-end as quickly as possible, and this is the reason for my coming here so unceremoniously I'm extremely sorry, really, to inconvenience you." "Oh, no. Not at all! Mrs. Grace and I were just relaxing and having some coffee. Would you like to have some coffee or some orange juice? Come and sit down and make yourself comfortable and don't look so miserable." That was round number one. I was completely disarmed. I was put completely at ease and it made it easier for me later on when we came to discuss my problem, to feel more confident and relaxed. After I sat down and Mrs. Grace asked me, "Well, Anfom, you have just a few weeks for your examination and then you will be leaving us. What are your plans for the future? Have you …?" She just continued with a barrage of questions. "Have you enjoyed your years at Achimota College?" "How do you find Achimota College?" She went on and on, but they were very friendly questions, all designed to put my mind at rest, I answered her as best I could.

After about ten minutes, the Principal said to his wife, "Would you please excuse us? Anfom and I will have a chat in the study." So he ushered me to the study, sat me down and then said, " Well, well, well. What problem have you? I did not think someone like you would have a problem. You always look happy and relaxed." "Well, Sir, I think I'll come straight to the point. You know the pains that Mr. Meyrowitz has taken to arrange the Art Scholarship for me, to come back to do the Special Art Course and to become an Art teacher in future. I've been thinking about it throughout the day. I've been considering other options. I've looked back on my life, especially my years at this College, the opportunities that I've had, not only in the College but in the extra-curricula work that we've been doing. I'm a member of the Red Cross and we've been working in the villages, and from time to time I've asked myself whether there wasn't something that I could do which would provide the opportunity for me to show other talents or gifts that I have, especially in service to humanity in the alleviation of suffering. I wondered whether I should not switch to do a medical course and to become a doctor in future. In short I wanted to let you know this feeling that I have now before changing to a medical career. I know Art will always be my love, but I can always pursue Art as a hobby. I really do feel that I need something which is more permanent and more durable that I can hold on to, and perhaps in the end provide wider service to more people. So I've come, really, to ask your advice and also to ask what you would think about this business of changing my mind about the Art course."

I expected a completely different reaction from the Principal. I thought that he would say to me, "Well, Anfom, you've led us all this time up the garden path and now you come at this eleventh hour, changing your mind and, in a way, breaking faith with us. You know, Mr. Meyrowitz has great faith in you, has high hopes in you and now you want to let him down and let the side down." This was the sort of reaction I expected from the Principal. But, Rev. Canon Grace, the Principal, was a wise, fatherly figure and one who really inspired confidence. I could see that he really understood the predicament in which I was. So his first question to me was, "Have you discussed this with Mr. Meyrowitz?" I said " No, Sir. I wanted to know your feelings about it first before seeing him." Thereupon, he said, "Let me see your hands." I just wondered what he was driving at. I stretched out both hands and he looked at them and said very casually, "Well, I suppose you'll make a good surgeon." Those were his very words. Then he proceeded, "You know, if you're a doctor you'll be called at night, at all times of the day. There'll be much inconvenience, and a good deal of sacrifice. You know, medicine is not just another job. It's a calling. Have you thought about all these things?" So I replied, "Yes, Sir. Throughout the day I've been brooding over this, and just praying about it, and it's because I'm very convinced that I'd be able to answer that call that I've come to see you." "How do you feel about your forthcoming examination?" "Well, I don't anticipate any problem with it." "You have to pass with a distinction and an exemption from London Matriculation before you can proceed, you know." "Yes, Sir." "Well, okay. If you're able to pass your examination and pass it well, then I can help you. I've known you all these years and I know that you have the temperament and the personal qualities required in a doctor, I can promise you that I can arrange for you to get a medical scholarship."

"But, Sir, the nearest science subject I'm taking is Agricultural Science". "That may pose a bit of a problem. But you know, this coming year, in January, we're starting a six-month crash programme to be called 'Inter-Prelim,' and it's really designed for those who want to be admitted to the intermediate science course, like a revision course. We know that some of our students come from other schools which are not as well endowed as Achimota and, therefore, do not have good laboratory facilities. Mfanstipim, for instance, is a very good school but it has not really had these facilities. Some students from these schools will come and take this revision course, six months before they start the real Intermediate BSc. Course. Will you be able to cover the course and reach the required standard within six months? If you're able to do that, then the promise I made you can stand. Meanwhile I'll leave you to go and sort things out with Mr. Meyrowitz. In spite of everything, Mr. Meyrowitz is a very considerate gentleman, and, provided you explain things to him well, he'll understand. You should sort these things out, to enable him, as soon as possible, to look for somebody else to replace you."

I thanked the Principal profusely. That episode really marked an important turning point in my life. After that things started moving fast. When we got in to say good-bye to Mrs. Grace, the Principal said to her, "You know, Anfom came here looking sort of glum, but he's going back with a smile on his face. Don't you think I've done well?" So Mrs. Grace just laughed. I thanked both of them and went off. I had a very sound sleep that night, although there was still one important hurdle before me, an encounter with my good friend, Mr. Meyrowitz.

The following day was a Sunday, and I thought to myself, "Well, I might as well strike while the iron's hot", so I didn't waste much time. I knew I'd find Mr Meyrowitz at home on Sunday morning because I didn't think he was a church-goer. In any case, the College Services were held in the evening. So I went to his bungalow around 11 o'clock. He greeted me warmly and offered me a chair. I went straight to the point. "Mr. Meyrowitz, I've come to see you about a very important matter. I don't know how you'll take it, but I hope you'll understand me when I've finished." His face fell. He did not know what I was going to say, so I went over all that had happened : all the arrangements that had been made for me to come back after the school certificate course to do the Special Art Course and all the fringe benefits, my change of mind and my chat with the Principal, and now I had come to him to have a heart-to-heart talk with him. To my surprise, he did not resist. He told me that he liked me very much. He hoped that I would always love Art, that I should continue to build on the foundations that he had laid for me, and that whatever I did I should not desert Art. We should always remain friends and he would continue to be in my corner. He knew I would make a good doctor and who knows, maybe one day, he might become one of my patients! So we sat down for some fruit juice and talked about other things. By the Grace of God all that happened did not sour our relationship.

Mr. Meyrowitz remained cordial for the remaining weeks of the year and he helped me tremendously with my dissertation for the Art examination. I recall that my dissertation was on the fishing canoes used by both inland and marine fishermen. It was a very interesting exercise and it involved my visiting some of the fishing villages in and around Accra. Looking back now, I sometimes wonder whether I took the right decision. But on the whole, I do not regret for one moment that I decided to become a doctor because I firmly believe that over the years, I have made a reasonable contribution to the development of my country, a contribution which I could not really have made as a professional Artist or even an Art teacher.

My interest in Art has persisted. I realized, long after I had taken my decision that, at the time, I wasn't really a creative artist, although I dare say that I had the potential which Mr. Meyrowitz could have helped me to develop. I was reasonably good at still life drawing and copying things, but I do not think one would really classify that sort of thing as Art. For me, without the creative element, the whole thing loses its flavour. This is something which, seeing that I changed my mind about pursuing an Art career, I would never know. Of course, whatever gift I had in Art helped me through my studies, especially in my biology and anatomy courses as a medical student. For my part, I have encouraged others who had the gift to continue with Art. I noticed that at least two of my children also have this gift. They did not become Artists but chose Architecture. Architecture is really a relation of Art and the gift of Art, at least theoritically speaking, should help an architect in his work. All too soon, the examinations came and about mid-December I sat for the Cambridge School Leaving Certificate Examination. The results of the examination did not come for several months after, but in January 1939 on the basis of my anticipated success in the examination, I was allowed to enrol in the Inter-Preliminary course of Science which the Principal had introduced.

# CHAPTER 5

# TERTIARY EDUCATION
## Inter-Prelim Course

I must at this stage point out that even though Agricultural Science and perhaps Mathematics were the nearest subjects to Science which I offered for the Cambridge School Certificate Examination, I was not entirely new to Science, because in the lower forms, we had done General Science and I had studied Elementary Chemistry and Physics. Of course, the gap between the standard attained at that level and the requirements for passing the Cambridge School Leaving Certificate Examination with a distinction that would exempt one from the London Matriculation, was very wide. For entering the university courses, the little knowledge which I had was very useful to me. As soon as I made the decision to switch over to medicine, I spent the few remaining weeks reading up chemistry and physics by way of revision and laying the foundation for what I was to do during the six months prior to entering the Intermediate Course.

The end of the year 1938 also signified the parting of the ways with my fellow travellers of the past four years, of both the secondary and the teacher training courses. At that point in time I knew practically all of them. There were about sixty. Those who finished the teacher training course we knew were going out to be posted to various schools in different parts of the country. With the students of the secondary course, it all depended on the results of the examination. There were those who would just be contented with a pass and would seek employment, usually in the Civil Service. There were others who would want to continue to do a post-secondary course either in the Arts or in the Sciences, and there were those who would opt to do Engineering and even continue to a full BSc degree in Engineering, which would take them four years. R. P. Baffour, three years previously, had been the first product of the

Engineering Course and there were others being trained. Names that come to mind are de Graft Johnson, Lawrence Apaloo, J. S. Annan and J. O'baka Torto. There were others also who went into private business. Then there was a handful, of course, who were aiming for a distinction in the School Certificate Examination and an exemption from London Matriculation, and who could then continue in the Intermediate Prelim six months' course. I may say that apart from me, all those who were in this pioneer course had offered science subjects for the school certificate examination. So you can imagine the amount of work I had to do in six months to be able to catch up. The Principal told me that at the end of the six months I would have to undergo an examination to assess my suitability or the standard I would have reached, and for a decision to be taken as to whether I could continue. Of course, this was a pre-condition for being awarded a medical scholarship to go abroad to study.

It is very interesting, and this is an illustration of the warm relations which existed between Mr. Meyrowitz and myself, that Mr. Meyrowitz arranged for me to teach Mr. Ineh, the brassworker from Benin, English, and my allowance was 10 shillings a month. The teaching was not full time. It was for a couple of hours a week, and my job was to try within six months to teach him enough English for him to be able to understand what was said and also to communicate with the students. There were some memorable incidents that happened with Mr. Ineh. As you can imagine, the time-table for his lessons depended on my own time-table for the various classes that I had to attend and, as an experimental course, the time-table was not rigid. From time to time, there were unexpected rearrangements which necessitated my postponing the lessons with Ineh. He did not understand this at all at first and used to be quite furious. But when he was able to understand a little bit of English and to communicate, it was easier then for him to know that the time that I had for him depended on the time-table for my own classes. One of these incidents stands out clearly in my mind.

One afternoon, as arranged, Ineh came to my cubicle for his lessons. On arrival, I told him that unfortunately, I had to attend some lectures in Physics at the same hour so, regretfully I had to rearrange his schedule or postpone our lesson to another hour. That wasn't the first time. But this time, he felt so frustrated that he shouted, "Oh, Mr. Anfom, why you suffer me so?" "I'm sorry, Mr. Ineh." "Oh, do not sorry," he responded. This was in my cubicle. The dormitory itself had been divided into ten cubicles, so these exchanges were being heard by my neighbours.

I recall that the late A. B. B. Kofi and my good friend, the late Henry Bannerman, were so amused that Kofi burst out into laughter. He just could not contain himself and rushed out of the cubicle laughing uncontrollably. Bannerman constantly referred to this incident in later years.

I must say I really enjoyed teaching Ineh and I think I was able to accomplish the mission, to get him to communicate intelligently in English in six months. As a footnote, years later (and this was just about eight years ago) when, as Chairman of the West African Examinations Council, I was visiting the Council's offices in various parts of Nigeria, and we got to Benin, I made enquiries about Ineh. Of course, at the time he came to Achimota he was in his forties so at the time that I was enquiring of him in Benin, he would have been over 90 years old. Unfortunately, he had passed away sometime before, but I met his eldest son who was carrying on the brass work business. He was highly interested to know that I had known his father in the late 30s and early 40s when he was teaching at Achimota.

## Medical Scholarship

The period January 1939 to 30th June 1939 was one of the busiest in my educational career. I had to cover a lot of ground in Physics, Chemistry, Botany and Zoology. This left me very little time, so teaching Mr. Ineh provided an outlet, a little bit of relaxation for me, a change. Of course, I made sure I continued playing hockey but, educationally, from the point of view of studying, I haven't worked harder in my life than I did during those six months. My future depended on it. If I was not able to make the grade then, at least, immediately I could not enter the intermediate BSc class to prepare for the intermediate BSc Examination or, as it turned out later, the first MB Examination of London University, and, therefore, no hope of my getting a medical scholarship that year. By the Grace of God, I was able, at the end of it all, to make the grade in the subjects to start the intermediate BSc Course in July 1939. It was to be a two-year course leading to the Intermediate BSc degree.

For those of us who were to pursue a medical course, we attended classes in Physics and Chemistry, with the Pure Science students but, in Biology we had to do a combined subject. Instead of Botany and Zoology, separately, we had to do Biology with a slant to medicine –

Biology for Medical Students. For the examination, one had to choose three subjects. For medicine it was standard: Physics, Chemistry and Biology. With the Pure Science student one could choose a combination of three : Physics, Chemistry, Botany, Zoology and Mathematics. The Engineering students were all obliged to do Mathematics. It was during this period, the latter half of 1939 and early 1940, that I was awarded a medical scholarship, so that my course, like that of other medical students, followed the requirements for the pre-medical - the first MB Examination of London University. At the end of two years, therefore, I sat for the first MB Examination of London University, which I passed in 1941.

## World War II Erupts

In September 1939, precisely 3rd September 1939, the Second World War started and of course, it was clear that there was going to be some interruption in my progress. The background to the War is well known. Over the years, Hitler had been stockpiling arms, building up a war machine. Hitler, of course, was never happy about the Treaty of Versailles, and felt that Germany had been cheated as the world looked on. First of all, he came to power in Germany and then started building up his war machine. The next thing was to annex one territory after another. After years of appeasement by the European powers, his cup became full. Despite being warned that if he invaded Poland there would be war, he felt all-powerful and all-conquering and treated the warning with contempt. The response of the allies, that is, Great Britain, and France, was to declare war on Germany. Of course, the allies were not as prepared for war as Hitler was, and in the words of Mr. Henry Neill, one of the masters at Achimota College, it was inevitable that that war would take place. After all, after piling up and building up the war machine, Hitler had to use the force behind it in an attempt to get what he wanted. Needless to say, the Allies suffered major reverses at the beginning of the war. It is not for me to recount the history of the war. Suffice it to say that the first few years of the war were very gloomy indeed and at one point, there was some doubt whether the war would end in good time so that those of us who had to go abroad to continue our studies, both medical and other students, would be able to go at all. The outlook was grim. So that it was under the shadow of World War II that we of the Intermediate classes at Achimota had to study.

The War also disrupted arrangements at Achimota in the sense that the headquarters of the West African Command was based in the Western Compound or the girls' compound of the College, commandeered for this purpose. The girls had to move to the boys compound and there were all sorts of rearrangements. The students doing the intermediate courses were given quarters at Anumle village.

In 1939, Principal Grace left and a new Principal, Rev. R. W. Stopford, took over at Achimota. For various reasons the academic standards at Achimota had begun to fall. There were quite a few students who did not pay much attention to academic work and concentrated more on sports and other things. So the arrival of Stopford marked a turning point. Stopford was a very strict disciplinarian and he demanded high academic standards. The term "*stopfordize*" was applied to students who, on failing examinations, were dismissed from Achimota College. By so doing, the academic standards of Achimota were restored somewhat.

I think at this point, it is important to say a word or two about the masters who helped in the teaching of the post-secondary courses. I recall Mr. Kenneth Whitaker who joined the Achimota staff in 1936 immediately after graduating from Oxford. Mr. Whitaker was in charge of Physics. When the Kumasi College of Technology started, he was transferred there and when the College became a University he was appointed Professor of Physics. Then there was George Hood whom I have mentioned already. He taught in the secondary classes but he also taught some practical courses at the post-secondary classes. The Biology classes were taken by Ms Veronica Foote who taught principally Zoology. Dr. Fred Irvine also helped with Botany. The Chemistry lectures were by Mr. F. E. Joycelyn. Mr. Amishadai Adu, an old Achimotan and an honours Chemistry graduate from Cambridge, also helped with the teaching. There was W. E. F. Ward for History and Daniel Chapman, later Daniel Chapman Nyaho, for Geography. Some of the teaching staff of the Secondary Department who were ajudged suitable for teaching at the post-secondary level were all roped in to teach at the post-secondary level. They did a very good job generally speaking, as the results of the Intermediate BSc and BA examinations were quite good.

# CHAPTER 6

# SUSPENSE
## Temporary Science Master – Achimota College

Most of us who completed the courses and passed our examinations in the middle of 1941 were left at a loose end. Some of us were immediately roped in to teach at the College. I was appointed a temporary member of staff to teach Biology, Physics and Mathematics, in the junior forms of the secondary department. I can, therefore, say that I started my career as a pupil teacher at Achimota College! I recall that some of my students at that time were Gloria Addae, now Dr. (Mrs.) Gloria Nikoi, an eminent economist and an outstanding lady of achievement, Osei Ahenkora, a very bright boy who later became Auditor General of Ghana, Frances Quarshie-Idun (now Mrs. Ademola), Hilda Vardon, (later Mrs. Ayensu), Letitia Asihene (now Dr. (Mrs.) Obeng) and, of course, some of the boys who had been in House Six when I was Prefect and who were now in the Secondary Department. As a temporary member of staff I lived in a detached house in Anumle village and used to walk up and down to the College.

I must say that I enjoyed teaching and the fact that I continued at Achimota after the secondary course and did a post–secondary course and was now a member of staff meant that my stay at Achimota was quite long. I continued to enjoy the facilities of the College : the Library, the sporting facilities, involvement in extra-curricula activities such as the Red Cross work and the Debating Societies. Generally speaking, I continued to be more involved with Achimota, which had then become a second home to me.

My starting salary on appointment to the staff was £4 a month or £48 per annum, pending the results of the first MB examination. When the results came a few months later, the salary was increased to £6 a month. I had my meals in the College dining-hall, £6 a month at that time was quite a good salary. Good in comparison with what one would earn in other places. In my case, I was able to save £1 every month, which I kept in the Post Office Savings Bank. I gave my mother £2 and the other £3 I used as pocket money to buy the things that I needed. The purchasing power of the pound was then quite high. The Gold Coast pound was at par with the British pound.

Now at this time, the fortunes of the war were still in favour of Hitler and the Gold Coast Government began to get anxious about what to do with those of us who were on medical scholarship. At that point in time there were four of us. There was Reginald Quarshie, Henry Bannerman, Matthew Barnor and myself. For my part, several things happened to me, including tempting offers to go and do other things. To start with, shortly after the exam results were received, the Acting Principal at the time, Vice Principal, Rev. R. C. Blumer, one Sunday morning called the four of us to his bungalow and informed us that the Gold Coast Government was thinking of sending us to Witwatersrand University in Johannesburg, South Africa, as it looked as if the war would drag on for many years, and they thought it would be one way of saving time. They wanted to know what we thought about it. As we had all read a lot and knew much about what was happening in South Africa we indicated that we were not interested in going to South Africa because of the conditions there. Rev. Blumer understood and said he was going to inform the Government that there was no way in which we could be enticed to go to South Africa to study under the unhappy conditions prevailing in that country.

Then sometime in November of that same year, 1941, Mr. S. T. Dunstan, the senior housemaster at Achimota, acted as Principal. He called me to his office one day and had a long chat with me. Mr. Dunstan and I had been good friends ever since the days that I was a Prefect of House Six and we had meetings with the Senior Housemaster. He made a proposal to me which was rather tempting and which nevertheless in the end I had to turn down. Briefly, he informed me that he had been asked to recommend someone for appointment as Assistant Town Clerk of Accra. Someone who would understudy the substantive Town Clerk, Mr. Dugal. The idea was for the gentleman to understudy Dugal for a few years and ultimately for him to take over as Town Clerk when Dugal finally left the country. The most tempting aspect of this offer was that I was to draw a salary of £11.6.8 month whilst occupying that post, and of course, when I became Town Clerk I would get £400 per annum, which was the standard starting point for Europeans at that time and also for all Africans occupying what was popularly known as European posts. Now at that time, I was getting £6 a month and the prospect of my salary doubling almost overnight seemed very tempting. Of course, I did not give my answer straight away. I told Mr. Dunstan that I had to think about this since it would mark a major turn in my career. Whatever the immediate advantages were, I had to think of the long term effects of this.

That evening I went home and discussed it with my mother. At that time, my mother was not enjoying the best of health and really could not do much in the way of baking bread and cakes which she relied upon for her living and this was one of my major anxieties. Even the idea of having to go abroad for some years and leaving her was something that weighed on my mind and I thought when she heard that I would be getting almost double my salary, she would just jump at it and say, "Emmanuel, you go on and take it." To my surprise, well I can't say really that I was surprised, because my mother was a very shrewd, wise woman, very far sighted, she replied, " No, no, no, no!" Why should I think about her? She was getting on in years, yes. I had my own life to live and she wanted the best for me. She felt very strongly that it was the will of God that I should become a doctor. If God willed I would go and come to meet her and nothing would please her more, so I should forget about the immediate advantages that I would be getting. The stand that she took promptly solved my problem. After all, the one whom I cared for most would not support any such move. The following morning, I went to see Mr. Dunstan and told him that I thanked him very much for the confidence that he had shown in me because the people who asked him to find somebody did not know me. He was the one who knew me and had to make the recommendation. I appreciated it very much, but, taking a long-term view of the situation, I believed that my best option was to stick to my original plan and wait to see what the Lord would do.

Mr. Dunstan was very pleased with the position I took. He agreed with me, but at the same time he thought that before making the offer to anybody else he would tell me first. Now, later on, a couple of years later, the offer was made to somebody else. I think it was another old Achimotan who took up this position, but I am not sure whether he ever became Town Clerk although he was sent abroad for training to become one. In any case, I merely mentioned this as an illustration of some of the events which occurred during the waiting period and the temptations which, without being resolute, one could easily have fallen for. I am very happy that the Lord helped me to stick to my decision to become a doctor for which I am very thankful.

## Life in the Senior Houses – 2 and 4

Now I must go back a bit to say a word or two about the period during which I was undergoing the course towards the first MB examination. At the post-secondary level all students were housed in two senior houses, House Two and House Four. When I say post-secondary it was, generally speaking, post-secondary students, but there were some who were secondary students, that is, they were doing secondary courses towards the Cambridge School Certificate. They were, however, mature students. Some of them had been teachers for many years.

During the two years that I was in the senior house, two Presbyterian School teachers were there doing the course. One of them, Mr. E. K. Anum, whom I have mentioned previously, was my Standard Seven teacher. He had come to take a course towards the school certificate examination, as he had been earmarked for teaching at the newly established Presbyterian Secondary School at Odumase. Then there was Mr. E. J. Klufio, who had also come from the Odumase Secondary School. Mr. E. J. Klufio, as I recall, had already passed the Cambridge School Certificate examination and was working towards the Intermediate BA examination. Both of them had been known to me but Mr. Anum who was my Standard Seven teacher was closer and I must say I was really privileged to help him with some of the subjects. It is rather interesting. Here was someone who taught me in Standard Seven and who really helped me and now I was in a position to pay back in a fitting manner some of the debt which I owed him. Mr. Klufio, later Rev. E. J. Klufio, became the second headmaster of the Presbyterian Secondary School, (PRESEC), then housed at Odumase, long before the school moved to Legon. Of course, at the time of writing there is another, a second secondary school at Odumase which also belongs to the Presbyterian Church. It is a secondary school for girls.

For me as a young member of staff, however temporary, my tenure was a rare privilege to rub shoulders with the greats, the intellectuals at the time. Certainly, I valued my interaction with Mr. Ephraim Amu, and I recall on many occasions the great man gathering some of us young members of staff of both sexes to his bungalow and teaching us some of his songs. Without his doing that I might never have become as familiar with his songs and the background to their composition. Mr. Amu emphasized the importance of our culture and of making sure that whatever we did, we did not forget how to speak and write our own mother tongue. Throughout his life, whenever we met, Mr. Amu never spoke to me in English. He would always start a conversation in Twi or Ga, which might end up in English when he detected my difficulty in communicating in Twi. His Ga was passable but we might still end up communicating in English. As I write now this is one of my great concerns about the educated Ghanaian. It seems to me that by literacy, we are really just paying premium to how well one can speak or write the English language. The fact that some outstanding professors and other academics and professionals are not able even to communicate properly or even to give a public address in their own mother tongue as well as they do in English bothers me, and I hope that one day we would all wake up to the realization that if care is not taken, we may lose the facility of speaking, reading and writing our own mother tongue. However much English may be important as a national and international language for communication, we still need to conserve our mother-tongue for national identity.

I also learnt to admire the modesty, the commitment and devotion of Gold Coast teachers like Mr. Brakatu Ateko, whom I first met on my first day at Achimota, the late Modjaben Dowuorna, Daniel Chapman and Miguel Reibeiro. These were great men who provided leadership by example. Also they were scholars in their own right. They did everything to make sure that there was no generation gap between them and the younger ones like ourselves. Of course, when we were students they appeared remote. As a member of staff, and a young colleague of these men, I got nearer to them and learnt a lot from them. I think the best lesson I learnt was the need for excellence, in whatever one did, integrity, hard work, commitment, loyalty to whatever one did, modesty, and humility. These are qualities which these great men exhibited, not only when they were at Achimota but throughout their lives. We looked upon them as role models who really influenced us. Regrettably, the nation in my view did not appreciate these heroes and they were not accorded the honours which they so richly deserved.

At the end of it all, by the time I left Achimota, I could say that Osu Salem had laid for me a strong foundation of character, morality, hard work and fear of God, and Achimota had built on that foundation. The liberal atmosphere at Achimota, the facilities that I had for wide reading, broadening my mind and widening my horizon, coming into contact with great men, though modest, really instilled in me, or rather prepared me for my subsequent life and all the various situations in which I would find myself and the responsibilities that I have been called upon to shoulder. They really became a point of reference for me in whatever I have done in my life later, whether in my professional life, my sporting life, my church life, or in my life as a public servant. Needless to say, by the time I came to say good-bye to Achimota. I had friends from all over the country, students of various tribes, religious persuasion, colour, and of different social and economic statuses. I think it was a tapestry of human life which really enriched my own vision of life.

## Earthquake

Before continuing, there is one incident that I must recount. During my two-year first MB course, almost right at the beginning of the course, in June 1939, one evening, my roommate, the late E. L. Quartey, and I were reading and at 8 o'clock in the evening, suddenly, both of us felt a very violent tremor, shaking of the furniture and desks. The books on the bookshelves started falling down and we found ourselves lying on the floor. Shortly afterwards, there was a big commotion within the House, people running helter skelter and out of their cubicles. We also followed. Again, a violent and sustained tremor. Naturally, we all ran outside onto the lawn. The interesting thing about the noise was that it started on a low note and increased to a very violent crescendo and then tailed off into a diminuendo and then silence after a few minutes. Although the duration must have been quite short, perhaps minutes, it seemed like eternity.

This was the Earthquake which hit the Gold Coast in 1939. It was a very violent quake, and all of us just stood outside dumbfounded, not knowing what to do. After brief intervals, the tremor recurred with lesser intensity. However, it went on throughout the night and, indeed, for a whole fortnight. Naturally, all of us stood around helplessly speculating what would happen. As the tremor came on with lesser intensity at fairly regular intervals one of our main concerns was whether it would be safe after some time to go back inside. The Geography students among us started propounding all sorts of theories, even the possibility of there being a rift in the earth which might swallow us! This put a certain measure of fear into some of us. One was really put in a position between the devil and the deep blue sea. Should one chance going back to sleep in the building with the probable risk of the building collapsing and one being buried under the rubble, or spending the night outside on the lawn and the earth opening its jaws and swallowing one. On the whole, we decided that the probability of the latter happening was very remote indeed, and, therefore, we chose to spend the night on the lawn rather than go back to our rooms. For the next fortnight, we had minor tremors at varying intervals which really did not amount to much, but one always felt that there was a distinct possibility of a major tremor occurring again; so whenever we heard a tremor we just ran out of our cubicles and sometimes onto the lawn until the tremor died down.

A very interesting thing happened during this period. My friends, E. L. Quartey, A. J. Addison and myself decided that perhaps we could play a practical joke on the members of House 4 by "manufacturing" an earthquake. The plan was quite simple; I was to stay in the cubicle and the other two were to go to the landing in between the dormitories, and at a given time just stamp their feet and run violently on the spot. Then when the vibration or the noise they made started I was to advertise the earthquake by running out of my cubicle and this would cause the others also to run out automatically. What happened usually was that we all came out from the dormitories and met on the landing. This plan was carried out by Quartey and Addison who "manufactured" the earthquake and I advertised it. As expected, all the members of the House in different cubicles came out onto the landing. The peculiar thing about this particular earthquake was that the tremor seized abruptly. Normally, the tremor started with a low intensity and then worked up to a crescendo and then tailed off. It was noticed also that this particular earthquake did not occur in other Houses nearby Everybody went back to his room. The question was, how did this happen? Who were the culprits? Of course, the plan was so neatly executed that the culprits were never found out. Our good friend, Obaka Torto, Snr., an Engineering student, who started a private enquiry on his own, went round asking leading questions of people whom he suspected and ended up with the nickname "Sherlock Holmes".

I narrate this story to illustrate the extent to which students, even at post-secondary level, would go with practical jokes which might inconvenience other people. All the three authors of that earthquake in later life became responsible members of distinguished professions. E. L. Quartey became Chief Executive of the Volta River Authority, Addison Head of the Post and Telecommunications Department for many years and, of course, yours truly became a surgeon and subsequently Vice-Chancellor of UST, Kumasi!

Fortunately for Achimota, the buildings were so solidly erected that none was damaged. There might have been a few cracks here and there in some of the lesser buildings but there was no damage to any important structure. On the other hand, in the city of Accra, there was much damage and some loss of life. More than 20 people were killed, especially in the James Town area, in the old part of Accra. Here there were mainly old buildings mostly built with swish and stones; and some of these were just razed to the ground. In my own family house, two members of the extended family lost their lives through falling masonry from damaged buildings. The result of this was that the Government established the new estates at Korle Gonno, Kaneshie, Osu and La for the displaced families. Of course, prior to that, it had been very difficult to persuade some of the people in the slum areas to move out to the outskirts of Accra. Now this natural disaster forced people to move out and the Gold Coast Government at that time really came to their rescue and made it possible for some people to be compensated with new houses in the new estates. I believe that many of them were given the opportunity to pay very low rents over a period towards owning their new houses.

My one year as member of staff of Achimota School was also really a waiting period before going abroad. The Second World War was raging and, as we know in the initial years of the war, Hitler simply swept across all Europe and just fell short of invading the United Kingdom. The saddest moment of the war, as I recall, was the day that France fell, and Churchill, as Prime Minister, then had to announce this on radio. At that time, radios and private wireless sets were not common and we had to rely on the re-diffusion boxes from station ZOY, Accra. Occasionally, we were able to listen to some of these speeches from private wirelesses. Some members of the Achimota staff owned wirelesses. Mr. Woodhouse at House 6 had one and I recall that when

King Edward VIII abdicated we were able to listen directly to the short speech of abdication.

My one-year teaching spell at Achimota was not only a period of waiting but also one of suspense. Suspense in the sense that I did not really know or have any idea whether I would ever go abroad or not, as everything depended on the fortunes of the war which at the beginning of 1941 were clearly in favour of Adolf Hitler. At that point in time, the war could have gone either way. The only thing that brought some hope was when Japan suddenly attacked the United States of America at Pearl Harbour and the United States was forced to come into the war officially on the side of Britain and her Allies. Prior to that the United States had been giving support in the form of equipment and other material to aid the war effort. The attack on Pearl Harbour was really the straw which broke the camel's back and America had to enter the war. The might of America coming on the side of the Allies brought hope and it was hope founded on reality because of the vast resources of the United States, so that by the end of 1941, it was clear that the tide of war was beginning to change in favour of the Allies. At that point in time, of course, Hitler had not only "finished" with Europe but had also come to North Africa and swept eastwards from Casablanca, and was knocking on the doors of Egypt. It was there that his advance was halted by Generals Wavel, Alexander, and Montgomery at a time when the German General Rommel appeared to be invincible. From then on, gradually the Germans were chased all the way back to Casablanca and America's entry into North Africa guaranteed a complete defeat of the Germans.

At the beginning of 1942, the ban which had been placed on travel to Europe was lifted to allow travel by students who had to go abroad for further studies. After the ban was lifted, the way became clear and for us medical students, places were secured at the University of Edinburgh, Scotland, for the 1942/43 Academic Year. We now knew we would be going abroad and this made a big difference to our spirits. However, it was easier said than done. Whilst the ban was in force, we knew there was no way we could travel abroad. After the ban was lifted, one had to decide again because, apart from everything else, it was still a risky business. One had to travel by sea and the ocean was infested with German submarines and torpedo boats. Occasionally, one heard news of a boat which had been sunk, especially in the Atlantic. The Germans were so brazen that at one time, a ship anchored off the port of Accra was sunk. The ship "Sangara" was sunk right under our very noses in Accra, so that really gave an indication how risky travel by boat could be. Of course, when the time came for us to travel the risk was not as great as earlier on; but the danger was still there. One therefore had to decide whether one was ready to take the risk or to wait until the end of the war. This called for a good deal of soul searching and, above all, prayers to seek God's guidance for what one should do. Given the stand taken by my mother, it was not too difficult for me to decide. I was prepared to take the risk.

At this time, I had been away from home for 12 whole years in boarding schools, first at Osu Salem, then at Achimota College with just occasional visits for holidays, short holidays. Therefore I did not really know some members of my extended family well. My mother thought that during this period it was desirable for me to meet members of the extended family who I should know or who should know me. This entailed visits to several people to get acquainted and also for my mother occasionally to invite some people to our family house at James Town to meet me. I think this was a very wise move by my mother because, here was I, about to leave sometime in the near future to spend a minimum of five years abroad. Therefore if she did not do that it would mean that I would really be estranged from my family for a period of seventeen years or more by the time I came back home. As it turned out, I left thinking I would be away for five years only. However, I was away for eight whole years, because after five years I stayed on for another three years. So I think my mother's decision for me to get to know the members of the family and vice versa was a very wise one indeed.

I was now in my twenty-third year, and had to think about some other aspects of my future life. At Achimota, a co-educational institution, I made many friends of both sexes, but had no special girlfriend. Achimota teaches one to regard members of the opposite sex as equal partners. I, therefore, treated my girlfriends like my boyfriends. During the post-secondary course, the two-year course, I made friends with someone whom I had known at school, she was my classmate and we really got to know each other quite well. By the time that I was ready to go abroad, we had become friendly to the extent that we had decided that it would be a good idea if when I came back home after my studies we got married. Before I left, therefore, a gentleman's agreement was struck between us and I left knowing that as far as my love life was concerned, it had been taken care of. I must say that this was my first love and it sustained me throughout my stay in the United Kingdom. A picture of my girlfriend stood on my mantlepiece throughout and it acted as an effective protection from those who might try to park in this "No Parking" lot. For me, it was also a constant reminder of the agreement that we had made. The agreement was, in circumstances which I shall recount later, nullified when I was obliged to take another course!

For security reasons, even after the ban on travel abroad to Europe had been lifted, such travel was always shrouded in secrecy, so that as the time approached for us to leave, which eventually came sometime in early July, we made all preparations, known to ourselves and our immediate family only, and we were warned that when the time came, we would be given very short notice. There was not to be any elaborate send off party which might have the effect of advertising that we were about to travel sure enough, that when the time came we were given only twenty-four hours notice to travel!

One thing which I did whilst waiting, was to travel within the country. My late cousin, Mr. Jonas Coleman, was then teaching at Tarkwa, so I drew up an itinerary and went to Sekondi by road and then took the train to Tarkwa, where I spent a couple of days with him and his family. I had no idea that years later I would spend two-and-a-quarter years there as a medical officer. From Tarkwa, I went by train to Kumasi and spent another two days. At that time, my uncle, Dr. Charles Reindorf, was practising at Kumasi, but I did not stay with him. I stayed with some very good friends of mine; Mr. and Mrs. E. T. Odoteye. Mr. Odoteye was an old-boy of Osu Salem school, who, when I was there, took a very keen interest in me. He had left the school for maybe ten years or more before I entered. He invited me to come and spend a couple of days with them in Kumasi. His wife, Eva Odoteye, was the daughter of Mr. Lokko, whom I believe I have mentioned already. Mr. Lokko lived at Pakro when I was a young boy and he grew coffee and I got to know him and his family quite well. I had an interesting two days' stay in Kumasi. That was my second visit after the 1937 visit to play hockey at Wesley College. From Kumasi, my next stop was Konongo, where my eldest brother, Ebenezer Anfom, was teaching at the Roman Catholic School. I spent a couple of days there and then came down to Accra by train.

It is almost sixty years ago and I find it difficult to believe that at that time, the train service was much better than it is today. The coaches were comfortable, which made travelling by train very pleasant. Almost sixty years later, when we have been independent for over forty years, the state of our railways is in such a sorry mess. It really baffles and saddens me. Clearly, we have to work hard to move forward!

During this same period, my good friend, E. L. Quartey, and I spent a week at the Evans Family House at Mampong Akuapem. We invited Kenneth Whitaker, who was a member of staff and also a friend. Whitaker was a down-to-earth person and very much interested in things African. Even at that time, he started learning the local languages. He was learning Twi and Ga at the same time. The three of us spent a relaxing week at Mampong, at a time when all of us had been working quite hard. Now, it was also at a time fairly close to the time of our departure for the United Kingdon. Nii Quartey, an Engineering student, had also been awarded a scholarship to travel abroad to complete his degree. So we were to travel abroad together. There then occurred an incident which I must recount. We went out one evening on a stroll to town. On our way back home, at about five o'clock in the evening, as we approached the house which was on the outskirts of Mampong, a passing vehicle ran over a cat. When we got to the house, we informed Mr. Allotey, who was the caretaker of the family house. He was quite surprised that we did not bring the dead cat home. He immediately went out and fortunately for him, the cat was still there. It was not run over but was knocked to the side of the road. There were no external injuries so he brought the cat home and announced to us that according to the Ga tradition, if you ate flesh from the head of a cat, then it was sure insurance against dying abroad. He thought that since Nii Quartey and I were about to travel, it was appropriate that he cooked the cat's head for us to taste.

We were, of course, not superstitious but we thought we would try it just to see what it tasted like, for fun. That evening, Mr. Allotey's wife prepared a sumptuous meal, groundnut soup made from the meat of the cat together with the cat's head. So Nii Quartey and I and Kenneth Whitaker also had bits of the flesh from the cat's head. The flesh tasted like chicken! Of course, that was the last time I tasted meat from a cat's head. The interesting thing is that on that trip abroad, both Nii Quartey and I came back safely, thanks to the cat's head! Later on, of course,

Nii Quartey went abroad after he retired and stayed for some years where he died. For this, of course, we do not blame the cat!

During the waiting period, six years after they had left the Gold Coast, Charles Easmon and Eustace Akwei, now doctors, returned home. Both of them became our role models and seeing them going about in their white coats, smart young doctors, really heightened our aspirations to become like them. I did not know Akwei much, but I had known Easmon from my Osu Salem days. I knew his mother and other members of the family also, so I paid occasional visits to him at Korle Bu. The young doctors were living in adjacent bungalows, a bungalow-type popularly called "sweat boxes." It consisted of one bedroom and a sitting-cum dining room and not much other living space. Very uncomfortable and hot like an oven. Easmon briefed me on the medical course abroad and what would be expected of me. I was also able to visit the hospital occasionally. This was also the time when the war was raging and the 37th Military Hospital had a contingent of specialists from the United Kingdom. The most prominent among them was Dr. Ian Fraser, FRCS, a very accomplished surgeon whom, many years later, I met in Manchester at a British Medical Association Meeting. He was then Professor of Surgery in Belfast University and had become one of the top members of the profession in the United Kingdom. He was very interested to know that I came from the Gold Coast and recalled the interesting and happy days he and his colleagues had spent in Accra.

Before I went abroad, one of the things Charlie Easmon gave me was a woollen zipper jacket which he had used himself as a student, and which was very warm very good for the winter, a jacket which I used throughout my medical course. It was only when I became a doctor, when it had become rather worn out, that I threw it away!

As we had been warned previously, when the time came for our departure, we were given only 24 hours' notice. By then, those of us who were to be travelling together were well prepared. During those 24 hours I had to say some hurried good-byes, and I recall saying good-bye to my uncle, Dr. Reindorf and Dr. L. V. Nanka Bruce, who was our neighbour at James Town and our family doctor when we were children, Mr. and Mrs. J. Kitson-Mills, founder of Accra Royal School at Korle Gonno and other aunts, uncles and friends. On the eve of my depature, in the evening, there was a small farewell party. Only close members of the family were there to say good-bye and I recall several members saying prayers for me and wishing me *bon voyage*. About three months before, my mother had had a major operation at Korle Bu and was at that time convalescing. This made the parting more difficult for me but as was usual with her, she gave me every encouragement, saying I should not worry because all would be well. I must say that I thank God because even though I was away from home for eight years, I came back to meet her in good health and for her to enjoy me for eleven more years!

On the eve of our departure, a Government Transport truck came and took our luggage and on the following day another truck came and took all of us. I think there were two trucks because there were nine of us in the group that was to travel. As I recall, there were myself, Henry Bannerman, Matthew Barnor, (Medicine), two engineering students, my good friend, E. L. Quartey, James O'baka-Torto Snr., Frank O'baka-Torto Jnr. (Chemistry), E. K. Twum and Asem, (Agriculture) who were to go to Trinidad, and Atiase of the Education Department (Mathematics). We spent the night in Sekondi. I spent the night with Mr. and Mrs. Francis Awoonor-Williams. Mrs. Awoonor-Williams was my aunt and three of my other colleagues were with me. The day of departure we just looked around Sekondi-Takoradi and in the afternoon, at about 4 o'clock the cars came round and collected all of us and we boarded the ship and then set sail in the evening about 6 o'clock. The name of the boat was SS Copacabana, a Belgian ship, which had come all the way from the Congo. The captain and all the officers were Belgians and most of the crew and servers were Congolese. They all spoke nothing but French so communication was not all that easy. None of us in the group spoke any French though some of us understood isolated words. In any case, we were quite well looked after.

# CHAPTER 7

# WARTIME IN BRITAIN
## The Voyage

The first stage of our voyage ended at Sierra Leone. This took us about four days during which time we noticed that several times a day, a Royal Air Force plane based at Takoradi came and hovered round like an escort plane, I think, to make sure that all was well with us. As our ship was a merchant ship sailing all alone and unarmed, she was highly vulnerable and so needed to have this protection. The day that we missed the airforce flight we suddenly found ourselves sailing into the Bay in Freetown and witnessed a very interesting spectacle. There were many other ships anchored off Freetown, all gathering together to form a convoy which was to travel together for the long trip to Europe. We also noticed that there were three warships that escorted us, one ahead, and one behind and one which wove in and out among the ships inspecting as we went along. Of course, this was wartime and security was very important; so every evening, all the curtains were pulled down as we needed a black-out and then, of course, it was necessary to use the passengers to help in submarine watching. Our duty was only to watch out and if we noticed any suspicious object in the distance, we were to report immediately to the officers so that the matter might be investigated. This watch went on both day and night.

The second important thing was that because of the risky nature of the voyage and the possibility of the ship being torpedoed at any time, we were advised to carry our valuables : passports, any money that we had and other articles in small parcels which we carried around all the time or kept in a place that was readily accessible. Needless to say, we had boat drills every day. These drills came on at odd times and sometimes several times a day or even at night. The alarm would go and we would all assemble ready for the life-boat drill. This happened throughout the voyage. We were just students going abroad for study but most of the passengers were troops going home on leave from various countries in West Africa: civil servants from the Gold Coast in particular, and also miners from the Western Region. In normal times, a passenger ship would take about 12 to 14 days. On this occasion, being wartime, we could not enter Britain through the Bay of Biscay. So for a long time, we did not see land. It appeared that we were just heading westwards in the Atlantic and then going northwards and eventually entering the British Isles by the Irish Sea from the north. The voyage which should have taken a couple of weeks at this time took around 4 to 5 weeks, I believe, and it was quite eventful. At that time, there was the attitude among the white people that they were superior to Africans. Irrespective of the level of education and the social background of the white person, he always thought he was superior, so really there was not much interaction between the whites and ourselves. We amused ourselves, however, by giving nicknames to the various character types that travelled with us. One of our masters at Achimota College, Mr. F. B. Jocelyn, chemistry master, was also going home on leave and he more or less acted as our chaperon. It was very useful to have him because he briefed us on the important do's and don'ts and the sort of things we should expect on arrival.

## Liverpool

So it was that one bright morning, we suddenly found ourselves entering the Irish Sea, in sight of land, and shortly after, we found ourselves in Liverpool, the port of arrival. After the ship docked we quickly disembarked. One interesting thing we noticed was that there were hundreds of shining objects, huge balloon objects, in the sky being held by some unseen devices. These, we later learnt, were balloon barrages full of highly inflammable gas, most likely hydrogen. The idea of having inflammable gas and also keeping the balloons so high was to discourage the German bombers from coming low and having a clear view of important targets like the ports, military installations and other commercial enterprises. These balloon barrages were found all over the strategic areas in the country. We noticed them subsequently when we arrived in London and later on wherever we travelled. Every important city that had something which might be targeted by the German bombers had these balloon barrages for protection. The idea was that if any bomber crashed into any of these, then the inflammable gas would cause some combustion and the aircraft would then be in difficulty because it might just explode.

I must say that we were all a bit disappointed at what we saw: huge buildings but rather dirty-looking, covered all over by soot. Liverpool being an industrial area had much pollution in the air. Our first disappointment was the dirty appearance of the buildings. To our surprise, however, though they looked ugly outside, the interior décor, in most cases was very beautiful and this really helped to redeem the low image we had formed as a first impression. On that first day in Liverpool, we spent part of the time in the cinema house. I remember distinctly the films we saw. There was a Charlie Chaplain film, "The Gold Rush", a very amusing film. The other film was "This is the Army", depicting the life of a new recruit in the army. Someone who came from a higher social class and the initiating process he had to endure. It was more or less like a levelling process every recruit had to go through. The young man who was from the nobility was not accustomed to the harsh life. He had problems, but it was as if he was being chastened through fire. It was to show that however high you may be, when you join the army you really have to come low and go through the same regime like anybody else. Even royalty is not spared.

Our next stop was London. We took the night train from Liverpool Lime Street Station and the train journeyed through the night arriving at Euston Station in London early the next morning. To our surprise, despite the secrecy surrounding our movements, there were some friends to meet us, there were Obuabasa Bannerman, Theodore Dowuona-Hyde and Desmond Buckle. So from there we were taken to the West African Students Union Hostel at Campden Villas; the Hostel otherwise known as WASU. The warden was Dr. Sholanke who had a charming wife. The students' hostel was patronized by West African students passing through London. It also provided club facilities for those resident in London and, over the years, African students from West Africa, and, occasionally from East Africa also, who became leaders of their country, people like Kwame Nkrumah, Azikiwe and others. I recall, for example, that at our first breakfast, we met Mr. Obetsebi-Lamptey who was just about to complete his law studies and Mr. Kankam Buadu, who happily, is still alive. London was not our ultimate destination. We were just there to report to the Colonial Office and to get a briefing. That same day we reported at the Colonial Office to see the Director of Colonial Scholars to get our necessary briefing. Our first allowances were paid to us and then the following day at about 10 o'clock in the morning, we took the Flying Scotsman, an express train, from Kings Cross Station to Edinburgh. The journey took about six hours. To meet us on the platform was Mr. Theodore Clerk, the first Gold Coaster to qualify as an architect. He had just completed his course in Architecture and was doing a post-graduate course for the Diploma in Town Planning. Theodore took us to the Colonial Students' Hostel at 36 Hope Terrace. This was a three-storey building with basement rooms. This was where we were to stay temporarily whilst we looked for lodgings and whilst awaiting the opening of the new academic year of the Medical School.

## Edinburgh

Apart from the residential accommodation at the hostel, there were a small restaurant, dining-room and sporting facilities like a billiards room, a library, and a reading room with newspapers. It was really a place where even non-resident colonial students, that is, students from different countries in the British Empire as it was then, could come for relaxation and even highly-subsidized meals. The warden was a frail-looking old lady, Lady McEwen. She was the widow of a retired Civil Servant who had served in India and who had died a few years previously. Lady McEwen was rather prim and proper but kindly and friendly, with a very warm disposition; she was a gracious personality who made us all comfortable during the short period that we were at the hostel. It was an opportunity to meet students from other parts of the British Empire : from West Africa, Nigerians, Sierra Leonians, Gambians, and, of course, students from the Carribean. There were also some Indian students. It was a colonial students' hostel run by the British Colonial office, a great place for meeting students from different places. And even after we had finally got permanent lodgings we could always go back to use the facilities at 36 Hope Terrace.

Edinburgh University is not a residential university like Cambridge or Oxford. It had two main hostels for students, Cowan House for boys and Mason Hall for ladies. In both Halls accommodation was very limited. Only a small percentage of students got in there. There was always a long waiting list to get in, so most students had to get private lodgings, also known as digs. This is a system whereby the owner of a house who has say 3 bedrooms or more takes in students who are given bed-sitters and the landlady, or whoever, makes sure that they are given breakfast and supper whilst they find their own lunch. If the digs are close to the university and you are able to come home for lunch and are lucky to have a good landlady, you may get full board, that is to say, you have all three meals.

The University had a liaison officer for overseas students whose office assisted them to find accommodation. A retired officer of the Indian Civil Service, Mr. J. de Gaudin, was the officer in our time. He managed to get a place close to the university in a tenement house, not a detached house for me. Student digs are mostly in tenement houses and in Edinburgh the Marchmont area is handy for the University as it is full of tenements and digs suitable for students. The only problem is that some of these have six floors, without lifts. If you are young, it is a very good thing for you, exercising every day up and down these floors. These are old houses built before lifts were invented! Now, I was lucky to get my digs secured for me by Mr. de Gaudin on the sixth floor of No. 18 Warrender Park Terrace. After two weeks I gave notice and left because, it was getting quite cold and the landlady was not too sensitive to my needs for warmth, so I had to quit.

Fortunately, in going round I discovered another digs in the same area at No.1 Roseneath Terrace. By a strange coincidence, the room that I was given was that which was occupied for years by Dr. Eustace Akwei when he was a student at the University. The landlady was therefore quite familiar with the ways of students from the Gold Coast. She was full of praises for Dr. Akwei who, at that time was back home. The landlady remarked that he was a courteous and cultured gentleman. Needless to say this fact really smoothened the path for me, because she looked after me very well. She was prepared to give me full board provided I could come home for lunch. I paid £2 a week for full board, when in other places, some were paying £2 a week without lunch. Alas, I was there for one year only. I had to leave not because I was unhappy with my accommodation and the service I was getting, but because some friends of mine, Gold Coast students, with accommodation problems had found a large house which they wanted to share with other students. The house had five bedrooms with a large sitting room and we were to live together and share the expenses. At the end of the day, it proved cheaper for me, but then it meant more work because I had to do my own cooking. The new accommodation was just round the corner from Roseneath Terrace so from time to time I dropped by to see the landlady, Mrs. Wardie and she was always happy to see me and to give me a good meal.!

One interesting thing about Mrs. Wardie was that she belonged to the Jehovah's Witness Sect and she tried her best to convert me to the Jehovah Witness faith. Consequently, every week she brought me one tract or the other, for example, "Watch Tower." She was highly disappointed that I was quite impervious to her evangelization on behalf of the sect.

The hunt for accommodation was one of the utmost priority, because it was very important to be settled in some lodgings, whether in digs or in a hostel before the academic session started. A few days after procuring our lodgings and during the first week of October, we had to register, that is, Reginald Quarshie, the late Henry Bannerman, Matthew Barnor and I, for classes in a process called matriculation. We went to the office of the Secretary of the University at the Old Quad, in the old part of the University Administration to be enrolled. That was the first time that we came into contact with our future classmates. We were in our early twenties, I was 23 then and the others were slightly older. On the other hand, our British colleagues were just 17-year olds straight from secondary school and, needless to say, with this gap in years we were more mature than they were. We were rather appalled at their childish behaviour. It was during the process of actually filling in the requisite forms and the rather rowdy behaviour which made us look over their shoulders and saw their average age to be 17. In their case, they sat for the examination at an early age and, of course, they were entering straight into university, whereas we had to do the first two yeas of university work back home in the Gold Coast. It was quite interesting the sort of questions they asked us about our home. Some of them were quite surprised that we could speak English as well as we did. I am writing about something which happened almost 60 years ago, during the dying days of the British Empire.

It was clear that many Britons did not know much about what happened in their colonies. Officials of the colonial service went abroad to various places where they enjoyed a master-servant relationship with the indigenous peoples. So although we carried British passports we were British "subjects" and not British "citizens." Hunting for digs could be quite laborious for overseas students, especially Africans. Usually, one looked in the newspapers for advertisements for lodgings. One then telephoned to make an appointment to view the accommodation. However, instances abound where African or West Indian students actually arrived at the scene having made a previous appointment with the landlady or the landlord, who on seeing the person with a black skin, would say, "I'm sorry, the accommodation has already been taken". There weren't many African students in Britain at the time, at least not in Edinburgh, and the few who were there were mostly students of the university. There was a sort of subtle prejudice attributable to ignorance. A number of the population as a result of ignorance were not accustomed to Africans and were not prepared to risk taking in a black person as a lodger. Well, 60 years have passed and I feel quite sure that the position has changed quite a bit, as the world is a smaller place now and people have more knowledge of what is happening in other places.

Our first day at lectures was rather interesting. In the lecture theatre one had to climb up many rows of seats and look down at the professor at the lecture table right down on the ground floor. What surprised me really was the rowdiness of the students, especially the boys. They stamped their feet when the professor said something they disagreed with, and made all sorts of hissing noises when he said something unusual or something which they liked. On the whole, one got the impression that the students were rather disrespectful to the professors, but surprisingly, the latter were quite tolerant. Some of them appeared even to enjoy it. Obviously, they had behaved in the same way when they were students and so were prepared to accommodate whatever was happening.

Lectures were not compulsory as one was not required to attend all the lectures. Attendance at a certain minimum number of lectures was required, of course. Such attendance was monitored in a way, designed to encourage us, hence the random nature of the exercise. Students were expected to have their personal cards with their names on them and then during the course of a lecture, the lecturer would announce that the cards would be taken that day. As one went out a janitor standing at the door would collect the cards, so that one did not know when cards would be collected and if you were unlucky and you did not attend lecture on the day and made a habit of it, you might find yourself falling short of the required number of lectures. In any case, at that stage, the style of teaching was quite different. Of course, since my colleagues and I had had two years of university education at Achimota, we were in a way used to this. It was quite clear that one had to do a lot of reading as the lectures were really just to indicate to the student the sort of things that he was supposed to know and it was up to him to refer to the appropriate text books to amplify his knowledge.

On the first day, the professor would give a list of textbooks which it would be useful to have, or books which one could refer to in the library in order to gain fuller knowledge in the subject. In the first year of the medical school, we had lectures in anatomy and also conducted dissection of cadavers, that is, dead bodies. There were physiology lectures and experiments in the laboratory. In my case, I had to do Organic Chemistry as I did not do that subject at Achimota for my first MB course. There were Botany and Physics and Zoology also for those who hadn't studied these subjects up to the Intermediate level. I must say I liked Organic Chemistry, especially the practical work in the laboratory when we had to do experiments, mixing different chemicals and producing very agreeable scents and smells from various esters and alcohols. I really enjoyed it. Most of our young British classmates found it rather intriguing that as Africans we spoke English so well and some of them wondered which school we attended in England and were quite surprised when they learnt that, that was our first time in Britain and that we had had our general education in the Gold Coast!

## Social Life At The University

The University Union is a huge building and is really a social center for all students. All students of the University were eligible for membership and it provided many facilities like a library, restaurant and café. One could also receive one's mail through that address, a facility which was used especially by overseas students. There were also showers and a drinking bar and billiard room. I must say that membership of the University Union was a must for all overseas students and it was highly desirable even for local students. One of the first things I did was, therefore, to join the Union and as I write now, I hold a Life Membership card of the Union. It was given to me when I finished my course and I was going back home eventually, so that even now when I go to Edinburgh I can walk in as a member and enjoy all the facilities, and I have taken advantage of this on my subsequent visits to Edinburgh. Needless to say, throughout my course in Edinburgh, that was my permanent address to which all my mail was sent.

It was war time, of course, and all letters which I received from home were censored. The situation was rather sensitive. It was very important for security reasons to take this measure. I suppose it was especially applicable to mail coming for students and other people from overseas. The Colonial Students' Hostel which I have referred to already, provided the opportunity to meet students from different parts of the British Empire. I was particularly interested in meeting students from the Caribbean. In those days one referred to these students as West Indians but, as we know, the Caribbean is made up of many islands and countries. For example, there were the Gordons from Trinidad, Davies from the Bahamas, Parnell from Jamaica, Andrews from Bermuda, and so on. It was a good opportunity for West Indian students also to meet students from West Africa. One had the impression that these West Indians exhibited airs of superiority but when they came into contact with students from West Africa they found we were all educated and in some cases better educated than themselves. Then of course, there were students from India. At that time there was just one India. In 1947, after the war, the partition of India into India and Pakistan became a reality. So during my student days, there were just students from India, Malaysia, Singapore Hong Kong, and other far Eastern countries. The interaction with these people helped to broaden one's outlook. I think it was good for them also to know about us and about the conditions in West Africa.

There was so much in the University to occupy one's time. There were social activities, extra-curricula activities and a number of societies and sporting organizations; and I made up my mind right from the beginning that I was going to try to get the maximum that I could from them and from the facilities that the University had to offer. Consequently, apart from the University Union, I joined some other societies; most notably the International Club, which met once a month on a Friday evening and which provided the opportunity for overseas students to meet citizens of Edinburgh, and for them to get to know these students and offer them hospitality in their homes.

It was at the International Club that my mates, Henry Bannerman, Matthew Barnor and I made the acquaintance of the Gladstone family and forged a relationship which was to last a lifetime. The Gladstone family took us under their wing. They invited the three of us to teas in their home; they also invited other students from the Gold Coast who came to Edinburgh later. Thus the Gladstone house in the Morningside district became a home from home. Mr. and Mrs. Gladstone had two daughters who had just graduated from the University and one of them, Wilma, who had done a teaching course and was teaching at the Teachers College in Edinburgh, as a result of this encounter joined the Gold Coast Civil Service and spent some years as an Education Officer. I personally kept up the relationship through correspondence with the Gladstone family. Wilma lived to a ripe old age of 85 and died quite recently. My wife and I and some of my children had enjoyed her hospitality and stayed with her in the Gladstone home. Then there was the Harlley family. Mr. Harlley, was a retired officer from the Indian Civil Service. Before meeting in the International Club, we had met on the hockey field and he had actually spoken to me. It was as if we had known each other for a long time. He himself had been a hockey player before and so was a frequent spectator at the hockey games involving Edinburgh University Teams. Then there were others, Edinburgh citizens, whose acquaintance or friendship made a big difference to us during the war time, isolated as we were from far away home by distance and infrequent communication. It was a club which did a lot to make the overseas students feel at home. I believe it is a tradition which still goes on.

There was a Cosmopolitan Club for students only. It was a small club which met in the house of one of the senior lecturers, Dr. Ludlam, who had seen service in West Africa (Sierra Leone) for some years. A small group of students from different countries met once a month in the evenings in his house and discussed various topics of interest and, generally speaking, just got to know each other better. It was a very useful channel for forging friendships among students from overseas and their Scotish hosts.

Then there was the African Association with membership comprising students from all African Countries, mostly West Africa, that is, Nigerians, Gold Coasters, Sierra Leonians and one or two from The Gambia, which met once a month to discuss issues concerning Africa in general and, as I recall, looking ahead to the time when our countries would become independent from colonial rule and the contributions which we could make.

There was also a vibrant Student Christian Movement in the University. I had been a member of the SCM at Achimota, so it was natural that I would look out for and join the Edinburgh University branch. The secretary for the East of Scotland SCM at that time was the Rev. Peter Fraser. Peter Fraser, like Wilma Gladstone whom I have mentioned already, as a result of his encounter with Gold Coast students became so highly interested that within a year, he had applied to and joined the colonial service or, rather, Achimota College, and had been appointed a member of staff of Achimota, where he taught for a few years. For health reasons, however, he did not stay too long, so by the time I returned home as a doctor, he had already come back home. Rev. Peter Fraser came from Inverness. I did not see him again after he left Edinburgh, but I have had occasion on my visits to Edinburgh in subsequent years to speak to him on the telephone.

My friends, Matthew Barnor and Henry Bannerman, also joined the SCM and we found it very useful because we had regular meetings and retreats. In the early years we had a very important meeting in Bristol. Then there was another meeting at St Andrews University. These were two big retreats which were held during the time, away from Edinburgh University. I had the privilege of becoming President of the SCM during my last year at the University, that is, the 1946/47 academic                                                                 year. I might add that on one occasion, we also went on a retreat in the west of Scotland and were privileged to visit the Iona Community which was under the leadership of Dr. McLoed.

During my first week at the University, I made the acquaintance of Fergus MacPherson, a divinity student, whose father, Rev. Dr. Hector MacPherson, was minister-in-charge of the Church of Scotland's Guthrie Memorial Church, at Easter Road. We became good friends and, seeing that I was interested in joining a congregation, he invited me to the Easter Road Church the following Sunday and I had the privilege of meeting his father, the minister-in-charge. I immediately enrolled as a member at that Church. So throughout my student days at the University I was a member of Easter Road Church, and indeed for a couple of years, I was a Sunday School teacher. I found this a most stimulating experience. At first the young lads and lasses were quite intrigued that a black man was teaching them things from the Bible. I think that encounter with the children made a very big impression on them. I may add that during that time I had the privilege of meeting Dr. Hastings Banda in the house of Rev. Dr. MacPherson.

Dr. Hastings Banda was a member of Easter Road Church when he was a medical student in Edinburgh and knew Dr. MacPherson quite well. He was practising in the Sutherland area, Southshields, I believe, and he had come to Edinburgh on a weekend visit. Dr. MacPherson took the opportunity to invite me to meet him at tea. We had a very interesting conversation. He had known Dr. Oku Ampofo when he was also a student at Edinburgh University, so we had quite a good chat about what the latter was doing. Years later when I was back home, I met him briefly, as he was for a short time in the Gold Coast practising in Kumasi, but he had to leave when the call came from home to come and lead the political movement for independence in Nyasaland, now Malawi. Then again, when he became President of Malawi, on one occasion on a visit to Ghana, he came to Kumasi at the time when I was the Senior Surgical Specialist at Komfo Anokye Hospital and I met him at the Residency at a luncheon given by the Regional Minister. This was during the First Republic.

Rev. Dr. Hector MacPherson had served in East Africa (the Copper Belt, as it was called at that time,) as a missionary and that is how and where he got to know Dr. Banda. His son, Fergus, subsequently went back to East Africa. At that time the East African Federation had broken up and Fergus went to Zambia to work. He spent many years in Zambia University, following which he worked for the Kaunda Foundation for some time before retiring and coming back home to Scotland. At a later stage after I came back to Accra from Kumasi, after service at the University of Science and Technology, I got a letter from him to say that he was planning to pass through Ghana and he would like to see me. So it was a delight for me to arrange accommodation for him and take him around to see a few places whilst in Ghana.

Many years later, again, when I was finally settled in Accra, but retired, Fergus came again to Accra and was my house guest for a few days. I was very happy when he invited me on one of my visits to the United States to stop over for one night in London with my wife. I had the opportunity then to meet his wife. After that we met on one or two other occasions. Those were brief encounters. My friendship with Fergus was special. He was highly interested in the welfare of African students. I did not know this at first, but then later when he told me about the history of his father's service in Africa and his own plans at some future date to go back to Africa to work, I came to realize what motivated him. We jointly set up a small club of students from the Gold Coast and a few Scottish students. The club was called "Afro-Scottish Circle", and during the summer we went on walks and strolls around Edinburgh, for example, to the Pentland Hills, the Braids, and Blackford Hill. It was a very informal sort of club and we functioned mostly in the summer. However, the activities of the Club were curtailed when Fergus left to go to Africa, and with the end of my own medical studies approaching, interest in the club waned. However, the spark which was lit continued to burn and has remained alive with the passing years.

Much happened during my first week at the University. One morning as I sat in the lobby of the University Union looking through my mail, a handsome, athletic-looking young man approached and came and sat by me, greeted me and initiated conversation. "Are you Evans-Anfom?" "Yes," I said. "My name is John Eadie and I'm the secretary of the University Hockey Club. I've been informed that you're a good hockey player who might be willing to join us. I'm here, therefore, to extend a formal invitation to you." I was curious to know where he got his information from, and therefore insisted that he told me. "Well, you have to go and ask your friend Ellis Djoleto." Ellis Djoleto, (later Dr. Djoleto) a Gold Coaster, was a hockey player and was already a member of the University Hockey Team. So I readily agreed. We arranged that I should attend the first practice on Saturday, which I did. Following that I became a member of the regular University team and I played for the next six years, including the year of my Post-Graduate Diploma Course in Tropical Medicine.

One thing which I found strange was that I was supposed to provide and pay for my own kit : jersey, shorts, the hockey stick, gloves and any other thing that was needed for the game. At Achimota, I was used to having everything provided by the College. The Edinburgh University practice had been in existence for a long time and who was I to question it? In any case, during the following week I dutifully went to a sports shop near the University and procured all the things that would be required for playing. I had to do this because I had been actually selected to play. Incidentally, at that time, there were other Gold Coast students playing for the university. There was Dr. Francis Martinson, who qualified in July of that year, 1942 and was about to start a course for the Diploma in Tropical Medicine. Then there was Ellis Djoleto who at that time, was in 4th year in the Medical School. There was Kuta Dankwa, a 2nd year Medical student who was the goal keeper. Kuta Dankwa was a member of the junior staff of Achimota before coming to Edinburgh.

## Some First Impressions In Britain

At this point, I think it would be interesting to recount some of my first impressions on arrival in the UK. I have already referred to my disappointment with the sight of the grubby, sooty-looking buildings in Liverpool. An impression which was to be redeemed by the elegance of the interior décor which indeed went for most public buildings. Then, of course, the disciplined silence of the audience at the cinema house where we killed time whilst waiting to catch the evening train for London. For the first time I could hear distinctly every word of the dialogue which took place. It was an unusual experience! Back home there was a lot of noise and shouting, especially during the action-packed films where there was a lot of fighting, so that one just could not hear what was being said. The next thing was the punctuality of the train service. The train was to leave Lime Street station at 10 o' clock in the evening. We got there, bought our tickets, got on the train, and on the stroke of ten exactly, we felt that the train started moving. The arrival time in London Kings Cross Station the following morning was also exactly at the time scheduled. And this sort of thing we were to experience throughout our stay in the United Kingdom and indeed, in other parts of Europe. The discipline and punctuality, were quite unknown to us and something which was the exception rather than the rule back home.

The next thing which impressed me and my colleagues travelling from London to Edinburgh was our view of the countryside. It was as if human hands had touched every bit of land and in some places they just looked like gardens. For us back home, we had been used to wild bush. Travelling from one place to another you just saw nothing but virgin bush. Then there was the fact that every house or office had a telephone. Communication was easy. Whenever one wanted to make an appointment or meet somebody for the first time they asked for your telephone number, the natural assumption being that you would be on the telephone. What is more, the telephones actually worked!! So that made life a lot easier. It would have been really difficult because of the long distances, if one had to move from one place to another every time to see other people. The mail was also delivered regularly every day. It was delivered to your address whether at home or office and it was delivered more than once a day. In fact in some places three times a day. On the average they were delivered twice a day. Within 24 hours any letter posted in the United Kingdom got to its address. So these were some things which really impressed me and my friends greatly. I began to wonder when we, back in the Gold Coast, would catch up with the stage of advancement we were witnessing.

Another thing which impressed me was the orderly manner of behaviour by people in public. Wherever there was service, whether at the post office or buying tickets to watch a football match or at the supermarket, automatically, everybody fell in line to form a queue. So that there was never any mad rush by everybody to be served at the same time. Any attempt to jump the queue was usually stoutly resisted by those in the queue. In this way service became orderly and was expedited, and everybody was happy. Another thing which impressed me greatly was the general attitude towards children. Children enjoy greater freedom of action and of speech than children back home in the Gold Coast. For example, when I was invited to tea by a family and everybody sat around including all the children old enough to sit around and feed themselves, the children took part freely in the conversation, asking questions and making comments. Well, I found this very odd indeed, and even some questions which I thought were rather impertinent and precocious were very well tolerated and handled diplomatically. On the whole, parents adopted a tolerant attitude towards the children. Back home, of course, as a rule, children were to be seen and not heard. I cannot help feeling that this attitude towards children back home tended to stifle their development as the curiosity of children can really be dampened and their learning process obstructed, the general effect being that the child's development was slowed down, whereas in the UK and generally in Europe, as I discovered later, children were given all the encouragement to express themselves, to ask questions and be answered and by so doing, they sharpened their intellect. The overall result was children growing up and becoming knowledgeable and independent-minded, always asking questions and learning as they grew up.

We arrived in the United Kingdom sometime in September when the summer weather was giving way to autumn. With the passage of time, every day one felt the air becoming more chilly, and by the end of October and in November, it was quite evident that the days were getting shorter. In December I noticed that as winter approached the day became so short that about 8 o'clock in the morning, it was still dark and one went to lectures in the dark. By 3 or 4 o'clock it began to get dark again. We had short days and long nights and, of course, the weather became much colder and one had to wear an overcoat to go outside. Every room had a fire place and they had to put the fire on to take the chill off the air. At that time, of course, coal was the fuel which was commonly used. The alternative was gas or electricity either of which was less messy but costly, coal being the cheapest. The responsibility for keeping the room warm was the landlady's. Of course, if you had a landlady who was not so nice, you could get back from lectures and find that your room was freezing cold, the fire was not on and generally speaking, the landlady would make the fire rather late, and be quite economical with the use of coal. Of course, for new comers, it could be very trying if you did not have a kindly, warm, landlady, but with the passage of time, of course, one acclimatized slowly and was able to tolerate the cold weather.

Twice a week, that is, on Wednesdays and Saturdays, in the afternoon, I played hockey and I found it really helpful. Healthwise, it kept me active and healthy. After each hockey game I had a nice hot shower. Believe it or not, later on I would then top it up with a brisk cold water shower! This I found quite invigorating. Most Saturdays the University had matches against some of the hockey teams in the neighbourhood of Edinburgh. There were matches against the Universities of Glasgow and Aberdeen once a year on a home and away basis. Most of the teams we played against were military or air force teams stationed around Edinburgh and on occasion we played a secondary school. These young school lads were very active and really gave us a run for our money. The first year that I played for the University, there were three other Gold Coasters in the team. There were Francis Martinson, Ellis Djoleto and also Kuta Dankwa who was the goalkeeper. The following year, Kwashie Quartey joined us. Kwashie Quartey was a first class player. He played at the center forward position and became a "goal merchant" for the University. In subsequent years, Akiwumi also joined. By then the seniors, already mentioned, had left the University. Later, my good friend, Abdul Mumuni Atta, a Nigerian brought up at Achimota College, also joined. He also played in the goal. So for some years, Edinburgh University really benefited from the skills of Gold Coast hockey players, mostly former students of Achimota College.

Gold Coast students who were already in Edinburgh before Matthew Barnor, Henry Bannerman Reginald Quarshie and me were Francis Martinson (then Dr. Martinson), Ellis Djoleto, a fourth year medical student, E. M. Brown. and G. K. Brown who were dental students, J. E. Bossman, T. A. Morton, Neequaye Robertson and John Vanderpuije, all medical students. Then T. S. Clerk who was a graduate architect undergoing a course in Town Planning, Susan Ofori-Atta had completed a course in midwifery in a Maternity Hospital in Edinburgh and had decided to switch over to medicine, consequently becoming our classmate. We all belonged to the African Association, and the Colonial Students' Club. Then there was Esi Christian, younger sister of Harold Christian, a law student in London.

By the end of November, I had settled down fairly well and was eagerly awaiting the first snow. We had never seen snow and with the approach of winter we waited with some curiosity for that time around Christmas when snow would fall. In November, I received an invitation from my old friend, Dr. Fred Irvine, former Agricultural Science Master at Achimota College, to come and spend a few days with him and his family during the Christmas holidays. Dr. Irvine was working in Kew Botanical Gardens in Richmond, Surrey. Also in Banstead, Surrey was the Rev. Canon H. M. Grace, former Principal of Achimota College. I did not want to miss spending Christmas in Edinburgh because elaborate arrangements had been made by the African Association and also the Colonial Students' Club for celebrating Christmas. So I had to go down to Surrey before Christmas. In all, I was away from Edinburgh for about a week. I spent four days with the Irvines and the remaining three days in London. At that time the Colonial Students' Hostel in London was in Russel Square. Sometime later, that Hostel was razed to the ground as a result of bombing by the Germans.

My reunion with Dr. Irvine and his family was indeed a very pleasant one. When they were at Achimota, it was their eldest child, Keith, who came down on one or two occasions and spent some time at Achimota. I remembered him, as a small boy, riding his bicycle around the Achimota campus. I met their daughters, Alison and Elspeth. During my stay, Rev. Canon Grace telephoned and invited me to come and spend a day with them in Bandsted, which was nearby. It was a very interesting reunion. You may recall that it was Principal Grace who made it possible for me to switch over from a prospective Art career to the study of medicine and who was largely instrumental in getting me a Gold Coast medical scholarship to come to Edinburgh to study. Naturally, he was very interested in my progress and was happy to learn that I was settling down well and was quite comfortable with my studies. Dr. Irvine, I will have more to say about as in later years he and his wife came to Edinburgh to live for a few years. Their daughter, Elspeth, had became Mrs. Elspeth Luce whose husband was a native of Edinburgh. So she settled in Edinburgh. Alison, the elder daughter, got married earlier elsewhere in the UK and I lost track of her. Keith went to America where he became a leading journalist. I believe he even acquired American citizenship.

On that visit I had the opportunity to look around London and I was appalled by the amount of damage which had been caused by the German bombing. Vast areas were dilapidated and I was really impressed by the fortitude of the Londoners. Of course, the war had been going on for more than three years and, in a way, the Londoners had become accustomed to the bombing. Coming from Edinburgh where there was hardly any bombing and destruction of property, I found it very unnerving indeed.

Back in Edinburgh, I discovered that everything was gearing towards the celebration of the forthcoming Christmas. Shopping was brisk and it was really a joy to go from one shop to another to see the exquisite decorations and the goods on display. People were shopping for Christmas gifts, and one could see whole families, husband, wife with children in tow just looking around and choosing gifts, especially toys for the children. The lighting was out of this world and I may say that this was in a period when the interior décor was very bright, but outside it was all dim. Because of the war, there was a complete blackout, and all the shop windows were blacked out at night. Even the street lights were dimmed. If you were in a car, you had to put on the dim lights as it was an offence to use your headlights. Even when you were on the high road going to another town or city, you had to use dim lights. Another thing which impressed me was the music – piped music – especially the songs which were on the popular list and I recall that during that particular period there were two which were being played almost everywhere and all the time. The first was "White Christmas," sung by Bing Crosby, and the second was "You Are My Sunshine, My Only Sunshine." These two were really the most popular. There were others, of course, like "Jealousy," sung by Leslie Hutchinson, a West

Indian artiste. Indeed, I liked these three pieces so much that I bought the records for my personal use.

Among the festivities lined up for Christmas was the Edinburgh African Association Ball – The Annual Ball scheduled for New Year's Eve. There we were, freshly arrived from the Gold Coast - Matthew Barnor, Henry Bannerman and Reginald Quarshie and I - and not knowing how to dance. However, with the coming Ball in view, we started learning to dance mainly by attending public dance halls, for example, *Palais de Dance* which was within walking distance of our lodgings. We had the opportunity to dance with the local girls, some of them friendly and others snooty. One of the attractions was the smartly uniformed girls who were in the Armed Forces - the WAAF – (Women's Auxiliary Armed Forces) and then the ATS (Auxiliary Territorial Service). These ladies who were serving in the Armed Forces were really very smart in their uniforms. Some of the girls came from other parts of the British Isles. I remember on one occasion, one of the girls came up to me and asked for a dance; an unusual occurrence! I discovered later that she had relatives somewhere in Africa, although it happened to be East Africa (Nairobi) and not West Africa. Indeed, for her the only country and town that she knew were Sierra Leone and Freetown. As I have mentioned before, during the war, Sierra Leone was a staging post for ships going to and from South Africa and the Far East. She was very friendly and when she discovered that I could not dance properly she actually put me through the paces.

On another occasion, I was dancing with one of the white girls, shy but quite pleasant. She was quiet for some time and suddenly started making conversation. She wanted to know whether I was a student at the University. I said, "Yes." "I'm sure you're learning to become a doctor", she said. I replied, "Yes." Then she said, "I want to ask you a question, I hope you'll not be offended." I said, "Well, go on." "Are your teeth your own?" she asked. I just burst out laughing and asked her "But whose do you think they are?" "Well, your teeth are so nice, so regular and white," So I said "Actually, yes they're mine." At that time I was 23 years old and had a complete set of teeth. I discovered later on that it was quite common to find young men and women who had false teeth. They had had dental problems at an early age and they had to sacrifice their natural teeth and wear dentures – artificial teeth! This was not the case with those of us who came from Africa. Later on when I got back home and was practising I discovered that whereas in

Europe; the problem was with the teeth, I suppose because of the "sweet tooth" that they had, eating so much confectionery, sweets, chocolates, back home the problem was usually with the gums!

As Christmas approached and the weather became colder, I began to yearn for snow. I had never seen snow and with each passing day I was hoping that it would snow. Of course, we were all anticipating that we would have a "white Christmas", meaning that snow would have fallen and everything would be covered with snow. On Christmas eve I found myself strolling at the West End of Princes Street. Near the West End was Palmerston Road Church, an Anglican Cathedral. I was walking past the Church when I felt the weather suddenly turn chilly and then hey presto! it felt just like flakes, white flakes, almost like manna from Heaven falling on me. They were not heavy, they were not hailstones, but just featherlight and, as they fell, I saw that everything on which they fell turned white as they accumulated. In no time I found the road itself was covered with the white stuff. Snow at last! I found myself hailing the first fall of snow for that year. Snow on my overcoat, snow on my hat and snow everywhere. Of course, I also discovered that one had to be more careful as the ground became quite slippery and one might easily fall if one did not take care. So I walked briskly but carefully back home and found that the people indoors were not aware at all of what was happening outside. So I broke the news to them and we were all very happy that our dreams of a white Christmas, that song they've been singing all along, had really come true!

Christmas in Scotland was rather a low-key affair, I discovered. Whereas in England, Christmas was a very important occasion, in Scotland, the emphasis was more on the New Year, what the Scots call the *Hogmany,* and the main celebrations were all reserved for the New Year. So 31st of December came, New Year's Eve, and with it the African Association Ball which we were all looking forward to. We had the problem of trying to get partners for the Ball. Fortunately, in the International Club, we had met some lady students at the university and I was fortunate to have one of them to agree to become my date for the New Year's Ball. It was a strictly formal affair held in one of the elegant halls in Edinburgh, a very impressive hall, large enough for our purposes. There was a good band and I believe everybody enjoyed it. Certainly, I enjoyed my first New Year's Eve in Edinburgh, especially as by then my dancing had improved. I discovered that in Scotland there was a superstition surrounding an event called "first footing", that at the stroke of midnight on New Year's Eve, people used to carry coal, a piece of coal to go and greet their neighbour in the belief that the black signified good luck for the coming year. So if instead of a piece of coal you had a black student coming to meet you it was even better.

New Year's Day 1943, was our first in Edinburgh. On that day, our elder colleague, T. S. Clerk, invited Matthew Barnor, Henry Bannerman and myself to a Musical Concert at the Ussher Hall where the Edinburgh Orchestra together with a full choir were staging a performance of Handel's Messiah. It was almost a three-hour concert. As the concert went on, I recognized some of the anthems as anthems which whilst at Osu Salem our headmaster, Mr. E. Max Dodu, had taught us! Anthems like "For Unto Us a Child is Born," "And the Glory of the Lord," "Worthy is the Lamb" and, above all, the "Halleluiah Chorus." These were very familiar pieces, but I had never heard them rendered in such a professional manner. All of us really enjoyed it. The following week I went and bought a score of the music just to look through. Later on, I bought the gramophone records to play at home. I may add that during these festivities of Christmas and the New Year, I had several invitations to tea in various homes. The Gladstones, of course, were one, as well as the Cairnes and the Harlleys whom I have mentioned already. In all, it was a very enjoyable first Christmas and New Year for me in Edinburgh. At these teas I had the opportunity to meet members of the extended families and friends of my friends, thereby widening my own circle of friends.

# CHAPTER 8

# THE PRE-CLINICAL YEARS

The first two years of the five-year medical course are devoted entirely to the study of anatomy and physiology. Anatomy, of course, deals with the form, and structure of the human body; the various parts, constituting the body, how they are related to each other, and as organs with minute cellular structures. Of course, anatomy also involves embryology or the study of the development of the human body from the moment that two single cells come together to join, to fuse and multiply and then grow and develop through various stages until full maturity, or rather the full formation of the body which would lead an independent life. The study of the structure and arrangement of the cells is histology. In addition to anatomy there is physiology which deals with the functions of the various parts of the body and especially how they are inter-related. Of course, all this study is necessary to be familiar with the normal. To recognize disease, it is important to really know what the normal should be. First of all, one should have a knowledge of the normal structure and then the various variations which may take place within normal limits. Also the normal functioning of the body should be known and how to measure these functions to determine whether they are normal or whether there is a departure from the normal. To draw an analogy with any monetary system, it is said that to recognize a counterfeit coin or counterfeit currency note, the first thing one has to do is to study what the normal coin or normal note should be. So students spend long periods studying the normal so that as soon they are presented with the abnormal, they recognize it straight away. So it is with the study of disease.

The study of anatomy, therefore, involved a series of lectures on the various systems of the human body such as the circulatory system, the digestive system, the nervous system and the locomotor system.

Then there is the practical aspect which involved actual dissection of the cadaver, that is, the dead body which is well preserved. Students have to spend weeks and months carefully dissecting structures, the muscles, the nerves, the blood vessels and the various organs - and studying their relationship with one another. The dissection room is a long hall, with dissecting tables - cold marble or terrazzo slabs on which the bodies are laid for the students to work on. Two students on the right upper limb, two on the left, two on the right lower limb, two on the left, two on the abdomen, two on the chest, two on the head and neck and another two on the brain.

On entering the dissection room the first time, I was met with a very strange and unfamiliar odour emanating from the bodies which had been preserved.  It was an odour which I had to get used to quickly because for two years, I had to be visiting the dissecting room almost daily to work.  I may say that my first encounter with these dead bodies really provided much food for thought for me. To think that these were the actual remains of people who had at one time lived lives of varying duration, ranging from teen-agers to middle-aged people, that really we were dealing with, just the frame which was once inhabited by the spirit which had now departed and here we were using the body to learn about disease. The study of embryology which dealt with the development of the cell right up to the formation of the complete human body raised questions about how one could reconcile this with the story of the Creation in the Bible. Then I thought about the verse in the hymn, "O God our help in ages past," the verse which runs: "A thousand ages in Thy sight are like an evening gone. They fly forgotten as a dream dies at the opening day." I thought about this and concluded that seven days referred to in the Bible really must be a very, very long time indeed.  If a thousand ages are represented by just one evening then seven evenings must be very many thousand evenings. I concluded that after all there wasn't any conflict.

For generations, one personality dominated the study of anatomy in the Edinburgh University Medical School. It was that of the legendary E. B. Jamieson. Jamieson was the senior lecturer in charge of practical anatomy and during our time he was already past middle-age. I think he was in his early sixties and he appeared to really inhabit the dissecting room.  He had a small office adjacent to the dissecting room but most of the time he was prowling up and down the room when students were busy, giving tips here and there. I can picture him now, a slim figure, with a skull cap looking like a Jewish Rabbi and his dirtied white coat, a stern look on his face, hardly ever a smile. From time to time, he would move up to a table and ask a few questions of those who invited him to come and do what we called the "viva." Viva is an oral examination on the part being dissected. He would ask the names of various parts and their relationship to each other. The interesting thing about Jimmy (popular name) was that he did not make much conversation. He would just pick up a structure and ask, "What is this?" If you gave the wrong answer he would just walk away without telling you anything and it was up to you to find out what the structure was. Despite his eccentricity, Jamieson was really a very good teacher. It appeared his philosophy was that he was not there to spoon-feed anyone. He was there to guide. It was up to you to do the research and find things out for yourself. If you were right, he would just endorse it. If you were wrong, he would just walk away. Jamieson, of course, is well known in the anatomy world. He had a series of booklets, "Illustrations of Regional Anatomy" - beautifully drawn and coloured by himself which were universally acclaimed as one of the best companions for students in learning regional anatomy. He also had a small very tightly-compressed book which was more or less a summary, "Jamieson's Companion to the Study of Anatomy." It was a book which one could almost put in one's pocket and refer to readily.

Some medical bookshops such as Donald Ferrier sold bony parts for the study of Osteology. You could hire a part to take home to study its various features and to learn the various structures which are attached to the bone. Occasionally, you could hire the skull, but some medical students are known to have lost their lodgings as a result of taking home some of these bony parts, especially the skull. Many landladies are allergic to these bony parts. Therefore it was wise, to smuggle them in and to make sure that whilst you had them in your digs they were not exposed to public view!

During the physiology course we were introduced to the stethoscope and its uses. Many people identify doctors by the stethoscope. To many people, it seems as if there is some mystery about it. There is really nothing mysterious about the stethoscope. It is just an instrument, a hollow tube, which is used to elicit the various sounds that are produced in the human body. For example, when we breathe in or breathe out, the sounds produced are heard through the stethoscope. Similarly, the heart produces sounds when it beats as do the intestines when they are moving, the movement called peristalsis. The stethoscope can detect all these sounds. So during the study of physiology one has to learn to be familiar with the normal sounds. Later on, of course, during the clinical years in the wards one learns about the abnormal sounds produced by disease. I may say that one of the things which pre-clinical students used to envy was to see those in the clinical years walking around wearing white coats with the stethoscopes sticking out of their pockets, and yearn for the day when they would reach that stage and begin to parade a stethoscope, sometimes even round one's neck! But the important thing is that during the study of physiology it is important that all the results, whether it is a blood test or urine test or test of the stools or even test for the function, breathing, the circulation, all these are done in the laboratory. So by the end of the physiology course, the student is expected to be familiar with all the normal sounds, functions and results of these functions of the normal human body.

Of the two subjects anatomy was clearly my favourite subject. I liked physiology also, which I found very interesting, but I preferred anatomy. At the end of the second year, the examinations in Anatomy and Physiology were held. To my horror when the results came I had passed very well in physiology but had been referred in Anatomy, which was really surprising to me because throughout I had not found any difficulty with Anatomy. So I was highly disappointed when I was referred in that subject. It meant that I failed the subject but did not fail badly and because I had done very well in the other subject I was being allowed to re-sit that subject, only. I had to re-sit Anatomy before I could proceed to the next year. Of course, this to some extent ruined my summer holiday. Needless to say, in my re-sit I passed very well!

## Summer Camps And Conferences

The University long vacation was normally of twelve weeks' duration and I spent all my summers when I was a student very actively. During my first summer in 1943, the SCM held a conference in Bristol which I attended together with my mates, Matthew Barnor and Henry Bannerman. Bristol was an important city during the days of the slave trade. It saw much activity, receiving slaves from Africa and in turn shipping them across the Atlantic. During that same summer, there was a weekend Retreat at St. Andrews' University which all three of us attended. Following that the Easter Road Church youth group – a boys group, arranged a summer camp in Turnberry, Ayshire. Turnberry is a very famous place for golf.

The summer camp was primarily for harvesting potatoes as during the war there was a shortage of farm hands, many able-bodied males having been recruited for the War, and the school boys and girls and also university students were in great demand to help with the harvest of potatoes and other crops. During the war travelling around was not encouraged. At every railway station or bus station one saw signs asking, "Is your journey really necessary?" This was because space in the trains and other haulage organs was required for moving arms, supplies, ammunition and troops to different parts of the country. The boys at the camp at Turnberry were a very interesting crowd. Most of them were members of my Sunday School Group at Easter Road Church and we had a lot of fun. The camp lasted for one week but I stayed on in Ayshire. Henry Bannerman and I had met a young lady called Jean Edgar at the Saint Andrews Retreat. She lived in Ayr near Turnberry and when she learnt that I would be coming to the camp she invited Henry Bannerman and myself to come and spend some time with her family after the camp. We, therefore, spent a pleasant weekend with the Edgar family.

As an interesting follow-up, in June 1996, very many years later, I received a letter from the UK addressed to "Dr. E. Evans-Anfom, Somewhere in Ghana." The letter got to me through my mail box at the Ministries, Accra. Now this letter was written by a lady, now in her sixties, who introduced herself as a younger sister of Jean Edgar who, in 1943, had invited Henry Bannerman and myself to Ayr, and she was now living in Inverness. She wrote reminding me of that encounter when she was just a little girl and the impressions she formed about Henry Bannerman and me. I replied immediately to let her know that I was still alive and recounted briefly what I had been doing over the years. Her reply was to say how thrilled she was that the letter got to me at all, and that she was not surprised in view of the contents of my letter that, even without an adequate address, the letter did get to me. That same year, in December, I happened to be in Edinburgh to receive an award from the University of Edinburgh as Edinburgh University Alumnus of the Year. She saw the publication in the paper long before hand and wrote to the University to request an invitation to attend the ceremony. So we were able to renew acquaintance in Edinburgh, and to compare notes, because much water had passed under the bridge during these long years. She was in her sixties. I was then in my late seventies. All the same it was an opportunity for her to meet my wife. We had a very interesting time together before she went back to her home in Inverness.

The following summer in 1944, once again, I went potato harvesting with the boys for a couple of weeks. During that same summer Matthew Barnor's friend, Alec Barbour, invited us to his home in Perthshire. Alec's father was a gentleman farmer obviously very wealthy, highly-educated and a graduate of Edinburgh University. He had a huge estate with many farm hands and a number of small cottages. The Barbours were a very devout, well-knit religious family and the few days we spent there really made a very good impression on Matthew Barnor and myself. The early morning prayers to start the day were followed by a hard-working day. Of course, it was during the holidays and we were supposed to be on holiday. However, it gave us the opportunity to see them in action on their farm and also to admire the cordial relationship between the family and the workers.

The rest of the summer was spent at home in Edinburgh, in preparation for the coming academic year. The Anatomy and Physiology examination which we had just passed was usually considered a very difficult hurdle which one had to overcome before being initiated into the clinical course. So we spent these days in great expectation and anticipation of what was to happen during the coming academic year. That year of course was to be the year during which we would start our clinical training!

# CHAPTER 9

# THE CLINICAL YEARS

At long last October arrived. That was the beginning of the academic year and, whereas during the preceding two years we spent our time working with healthy bodies (physiology) and dead bodies (anatomy), trying to find out as much as we could about the workings of the normal human body, we were now about to start what to us was the reason why we travelled all the way to come to Edinburgh; to learn about disease, how to manage or cure disease. This meant that part of our instruction was to be in a hospital. The main teaching hospital for the University of Edinburgh was the Edinburgh Royal Infirmary just next door. There must have been more than a thousand beds distributed in different departments which one had to go through as one progressed through the clinical years. Altogether we were to spend three years in our clinical study.

For our first clinical year we started lectures in medicine and surgery. These were theoretical lectures. Concurrently, there was clinical instruction on the wards. We had to learn how to examine a patient. The clinical instruction involved how to get information when the patient came with his complaint, how to extract information without actually putting words in the mouth of the patient and how to take a detailed history of what was happening to the patient. The physical examination of the patient would follow, and then a decision would be made whether there would be need for any ancillary tests, for example, testing some of the body fluids or waste material from the body (like the urine and feaces) or whether to have certain parts of the body X'rayed. At that time, the range of diagnostic procedures available to the clinician was limited. Now, of course, there is a wide array of tests which can be done, for example scanning, NMR, Echo sound, ultra sound and all sorts of other procedures.

At this stage we were introduced to the subject of Patholody. Pathology is the study of changes in diseased organs in the body and their appearance. This meant attending postmortem examinations to witness these diseased organs, or just study organs which had been preserved in bottles in the laboratories. Looking at them as they are to the naked eye and then, of course, doing a histological examination under the microscope to see the changes in the component cells of the various organs. It was very interesting because we were able, when studying the management of somebody suffering from, for example, pneumonia to examine the patient on the ward and seeing all the signs and symptoms, the pain in the chest, the cough, the rise in temperature and the other manifestations and at the same time study the appearance of the lungs on X'ray and from the laboratory looking at the preserved lungs as they looked in a patient who had died of pneumonia. The teaching was coordinated in a way that gave the student a better understanding of the disease process. I cite pneumonia as an example but the principle applies to other diseases affecting different organs and the way in which one could relate the pathological process to the clinical condition of the patient. All these we started studying during the third year and we continued to do so not only with medicine and surgery, the two big branches, but with all other branches of medicine.

That same year, we started to study the various drugs that are used in the treatment of diseases - the nature of the drugs, whether they were of herbal or mineral origin, the manner in which they were prepared and the standardization of dosage to be applied. At the same time we studied the action of these drugs on the human body. The study of the action of the drugs on the human body is Pharmacology, whilst Therapeutics dealt with the whole system of management of a particular ailment, what one had to do, the drugs to use either alone or in combination with other drugs and what other measures, if any, were to be applied. The manner in which all these studies were coordinated enabled the student to understand what was happening to the sick patient. Of course, we are talking about the physical manifestations now, but we know from our study of psychiatry and the power of the mind over matter that the causes of some of these symptoms may be entirely of psychological origin. Microbiology and Parasitology are the study of the minute creatures, whether visible or not, by the naked eye, which attack the human body and cause a derangement of function of different parts of the body. For example, different types of micro-organisms attack the body to give rise to pneumonia, typhoid or other diseases. The medical student needs to be familiar with the important ones.

Although the study of the effect of drugs on the human body and their application to disease was to continue throughout the three year clinical course, in the third year, we had to sit for special examinations in pharmacology and microbiology for our third year certificate. Right from the beginning, it became quite clear that medicine - and I use the term medicine in its widest sense to cover all the branches - was a field or rather a subject to be studied more on the ward at the bedside of the patient than from textbooks. The longer the time one spent visiting the wards and seeing patients, talking to them, examining them and looking through their notes, the easier it became to be familiar with the patient's problems and how to help him. If one spent time just poring over textbooks in the library and did not visit the wards often, at the end of the day, it would become very difficult because in the words of Professor Davidson, our professor of Medicine, "Medicine is a subject which you cannot study by heart. So do not make the mistake of waiting till the last moment and spending a couple of weeks burning the midnight oil to commit to memory vast pieces of information. At the end of the day, the real test will be in the consulting room, the ward and the operating room where you will be confronted with the patient who requires immediate help. You may, indeed scrape through the examination with difficulty but when you become a doctor, you may find that you really have a problem because you wasted your time as a student reading in the library rather than practising on the wards".

In the fourth year, new subjects were introduced. One was the important subject of Public Health, now generally known as Community Health, which dealt with the health of the whole community rather than that of a single individual. Community Health is a multi-disciplinary problem and indeed deals with the whole problem of prevention of disease, ensuring good environmental practices, good sanitation, good and wholesome water, good nutrition, efficient waste disposal, how to deal with communicable diseases and preventive measures such as inoculation etc.

Another subject introduced in the fourth year was Forensic Medicine and Medical Jurisprudence, and this really relates to the legal aspects of medical practice and the way in which doctors may be involved in medical ethics, that is, doctors' relations with their patients, improper conduct, malpractice and advertising. Also elementary knowledge of diagnosing foul play in cases of unnatural death. In the same year, we were to do what we call the "Specials." These are really specialties which concern specific areas of the body for example the Ear, Nose and Throat specialty, or diseases of the eye, or infectious diseases, skin diseases and as I already hinted, mental diseases.

In the Edinburgh Medical School, special attention is paid to Dermatology or diseases of the skin. The skin is a very important organ of the body. Indeed, it is the largest organ in the human body and it performs very important protective functions. At the same time various manifestations of internal disorder may appear first on the skin. I was to discover later on that in the tropics knowledge of dermatology is far more important than in the temperate regions. In the tropics one had in addition to the common diseases universally known, numerous unusual infections peculiar to the tropics.

In the fourth year also we were introduced to Obstetrics and Gynaecology, a study of the reproductive process in women and diseases peculiar to women. Paediatrics or the study of diseases of childhood was also introduced at this stage. The child is not a little adult. He is quite a different type of person who has special characteristics, special needs and is affected in very different ways by the environment and other factors which the medical doctor should recognize and be able to cope with.

Obstetrics is fairly straight forward – the whole question of conception and reproduction; and although conception and labour in many cases are straight forward and considered as normal physiological processes there may be deviations from health during the period of pregnancy. There may be serious complications during the period of conception (or the ante-natal period) or during the process of labour. It is, therefore, very important that every medical student should have a modicum of experience of how to deal with these complications.

During the fourth year, all the examinations which need to be done are carried on in the Specials which I have already mentioned, leaving the final year, which is the 5th year, to the two important branches and the third one which is perhaps not on the same level, that is, medicine, surgery, and then obstetrics and gyneacology.

Although there was much interesting reading to do, I really enjoyed the clinical instruction, the daily ward rounds carried out quite regularly with the professor or the chief of the ward and his assistant. During the rounds, there was a discussion of the patients' management, then the clinical instruction which took place on individual basis in a side ward. All told, I enjoyed that part of the training very much indeed, perhaps because I felt it was more relevant to what I would be doing in future. A course requirement was that during the summer vacation, all students in the clinical years should spend six weeks in a hospital other than the Royal Infirmary or a Teaching Hospital; a smaller hospital somewhere. In my case, I chose to go to Dumfries Royal Infirmary. Dumfries is a town about sixty miles south of Edinburgh. I chose Dumfries because the chief surgeon of Dumfries Hospital happened to be the eldest son of Rev. T. L. Beveridge who at the time that I was at Osu Salem was the Scottish Mission Secretary, resident in the Gold Coast. He lived at Kuku Hill, Osu, in a large house which for a long time subsequently was occupied by the Moderator of the Presbyterian Church of Ghana and is now occupied by the Clerk of the General Assembly of the Presbyterian Church. Rev. Beveridge himself lived in Edinburgh with his wife who, incidentally, was a doctor and I recall that during their service in the Gold Coast she worked at the Maternity Clinic which is just across the road from the Osu Ebenezer Presbyterian Chapel. Needless to say, Mr. Beveridge was very kind to the Gold Coast students, especially those who had been to school at Osu. So when the time came for me to fulfil this clinical requirement for my studies, he very readily arranged with his son to take me under his wing. For two summers, therefore, I spent six weeks in Dumfries Royal Infirmary mostly in the Department of Surgery but also in other departments in the Hospital. As it was a smaller hospital, I could see more happening and on occasions I was even allowed to do certain procedures like stitching wounds in the Casualty Department.

## A Trip To Dublin – Republic of Ireland

In midwifery, there was a requirement that every student should conduct by himself or together with a mate a domiciliary delivery of twelve babies before he was allowed to sit for the final examination. In the summer of 1946, therefore, Henry Bannerman, Matthew Barnor and I went over to Dublin for that purpose. Dublin had a famous Maternity Hospital, the Rotunda, the world famous hospital which many students went to not only during the basic training but also during the post-graduate training. There was another hospital, the Coombe Maternity Hospital. The latter was in a slum area where the people were very prolific reproducers and of course Ireland, being a Catholic nation, did not favour family planning. So in no time, all three of us had been able to conduct 12 deliveries apiece.

Before going to Ireland I had managed to organize a hockey team of Gold Coast students studying in the universities all over Britain; so that we were able to tour Ireland after I had finished with my assignment, that is, the necessary requirements for the midwifery course. We had a rather interesting group : Kwarshie Quartey, Akiwumi, George Djabanor, Kwesi Bentsi- Enchill (already in Dublin since he was studying in Trinity College), Adjetey, studying Dentistry at New Castle, Annan from London, doing a degree in Education and Adu-Aryee from Edinburgh (a dental student), George Oddoye, Opoku also from London, and Kobina Aba-Taylor, studying medicine in London. We had quite a good team of highly skilled hockey players. We played three matches against Trinity College, a men's team called Three Rock Rovers, and lastly a team which I believe was the Railway Hockey Team.

One interesting thing about the Republic of Ireland is that it was neutral during World War II, so throughout the War, there was no austerity. At the time we visited, in 1946, the War was over, but in the UK and Northern Ireland for some years after, there was some austerity which was gradually loosened with time. Coming to a place of plenty, we behaved like people who had been starved for ages. We went to town on the food and I remember drinking gallons of fresh milk, a commodity which was then rationed in the UK, the allocation being two pints of milk a week. There were no restrictions on what we could eat or drink or even buy in the shops by way of clothing or footwear. I must say that I found it really strange that a country which was geographically an integral part of the British Isles would for some reason stay neutral and consequently make things difficult for the UK. For example, since there was no blackout in the Irish Republic, air raids by the German Air Force during the night were facilitated by the bright lights. They must have helped the Germans in finding their bearings when they wanted to raid installations on the British mainland. To this day, I have never really come to terms with the strange attitude of the Republic of Ireland which I considered callous and unreasonable.

On the whole, I found the natives of the Irish Republic very friendly. Looking back on their history, having in recent times gained their independence from Britain under the leadership of Eamon de Valera may well be the reason for the attitude of the Irish. The friendliness of the population may be attributed to a sense of fellow feeling with Africans, who at that time were still colonial subjects. We were merely subjects of the King of England. Be that as it may, we were nevertheless at that time fighting on the side of Britain, however distant our relationship. I personally did not think that the Irish who were near blood relations of the British would go to the extent of denying them their support in this crucial period of history when they were embroiled in a life and death struggle against Hitler and all that he represented. Later on that year, I was to return to Dublin in the winter months with the Edinburgh University Hockey Team for a tour of the Irish Republic. It was not as interesting as before, because at that time, the weather was very, very cold. In any case, it was a very brief tour lasting just four days.

## International Students Conference – Switzerland, 1946

A few days after returning to Edinburgh in the summer, I had to go over to Switzerland to attend a conference and retreat in a place called Grindelwald, somewhere in the Swiss Alps. I was President of the Student Christian Movement of Edinburgh University, and went to this international conference in that capacity. The War was over and the ban on travel to the European Continent had been lifted, so we crossed from Dover to Calais and took the train through France to Basel. From there I took the train to a place called Interlaken, which was a junction town from where I changed trains for Grindelwald, which was not too far but was on a higher altitude. The Conference lasted about a week. It provided me the opportunity to meet students from a number of European countries and to make many friends. One particular friendship which I made was with Olle Engstrom, then a student of theology from Stockholm, Sweden. When the Conference ended he extended an invitation to me to visit Sweden the following summer, in 1947. That was the year I was to complete my medical studies. He insisted that before going back home, I should visit Sweden.

After the meeting in Grindelwald, I went to Geneva on my own and spent a few days looking round. I had heard so much about that famous city in Switzerland. As I knew no one there, I stayed at very cheap bed-and-breakfast lodgings. During the day I went around the town visiting interesting places. I was particularly keen to see the building which housed the League of Nations. After Geneva, I took the train to Zurich which was in the German-speaking part in the north. I went there for a week-end. I arrived on a Saturday and found the town very busy, bustling with thousands of people, mostly young people from outside Zurich who had come there to witness an important cycle race the following day, a Sunday. Consequently, it was very difficult to get accommodation. I was obliged to sleep in an army barracks for a couple of nights, sleeping on the floor in the company of a Swiss student friend whom I met. We were both operating on a shoe string budget and as the charge for accommodation was next to nothing it suited us very well.

From Zurich on my return journey, I stopped in Basel. Basel was a name well known to me because of the Basel Mission work in the Gold Coast. My own grand-father had been a catechist and a tutor at the Basel Mission in the Gold Coast, so I was very much interested to see the place where, for me, it all began. On arrival I went straight to the Basel Mission House and introduced myself. When the warden of the House got to know that I had attended a Basel Mission School in the Gold Coast, that my grandfather had worked for the Basel Mission for 36 years, and that two students from the Gold Coast, Philip Richter and Christian Baëta, had studied in Basel and actually stayed in the Basel Mission House when they were students, he insisted that I should stay in the Mission House as their guest. I actually stayed with the warden and his family. This, for me, was God-sent, because my money had practically run out. I did not have to pay for accommodation or meals, except when I went out. In any case, as my stay was short, it did not weigh too much on their budget. I learnt a lot about the Basel Mission and actually met one missionary who after the Basel Missionaries had been interned during the First World War, came back after the war and spent a few years in the Gold Coast. His name was Rapp. He was in his old age but he recalled the happy time that he had in the Gold Coast and knew many of the people whom I also knew - teachers, headmasters and pastors of the Presbyterian Church of the Gold Coast.

Now I have already referred to the subtle prejudices exhibited when an African student went looking for accommodation. This prejudice was also shown in various other ways. For example, in a dance hall a white girl who had declined an invitation to dance with an African student on grounds of being tired would, seconds later, accept to dance with a white student! There were many ways in which this prejudice was shown. However, despite this fact I discovered that irrespective of colour, race or religion, the British people, the Scottish people appreciated and respected merit. For example, if you were doing very well in class and you were at or near the top of the class they respected you. Some may not like it but they respected you. This applied to other fields such as Sports or the Performing Arts. So it was that I found myself, in my third year, unanimously elected by the members of the hockey club as captain of the University Hockey Team, which I captained for two years. Normally, I should have been captain for one year, but the person - the Scots student, who should have taken over from me unfortunately fell ill so I was obliged to do a second term as captain. I was very pleased when my friend and colleague, Kwarshie Quartey, succeeded me as captain of the hockey team. Meanwhile in the 1946-47 academic year, the annual matches between the Scottish and English Universities were resumed and I had the privilege and honour of being captain of this Scottish Universities' Team.

Our first encounter with the English team was in Newcastle in 1946. Most of the team were Edinburgh University Team members. There were just four who came from the other Universities. For this reason, there was much cohesion in the team and we triumphed over the English Universities in that match. I am glad to say that the one who scored the lone goal was Kwarshie Quartey who at that time was playing centre forward for the Scottish Team. The following year, on our return encounter in Birmingham, we were paid back in our own coin when we lost by one goal to the English Universities. By participating in sports, I made friends not only in the hockey world but also in other sports such as soccer and rugby through our regular meetings at the University Sports Pavillion at Craiglochart.

My election to membership of the Spartan Club, the highest honour which the University Sporting Club can bestow and which is reserved for people who excel in the field of sports, I shall always treasure. The logo of the club is a yellow dagger on a green background which formed the crest. Once a year there was the dance or Annual Ball organized by the Spartan Club where members were allowed to invite their partners and other friends. At the Ball one came into contact with the cream of sportsmen of the University and their partners. This was a club which I was very proud to belong to. I may add that from year one, first year, and throughout the years that I played for the University I won my full colours, that is, the University Blue. I was "given" a heavy green scarf and also a badge of the Edinburgh University. As usual, I was given a chit and I had to buy the scarf myself from a shop which sold sports goods. Getting the chit by itself was an honour and the Spartan Scarf was highly coveted by all sportsmen.

Lest I forget, the parents of Alice Parnell, then senior music teacher at Achimota College, lived within a stone's throw of the Craiglochart Sporting Field. Old man Parnell was one of the chief supporters of the University Hockey Team because of the Gold Coast students who played in the team, and, quite often, he came and stood on the touchline to cheer us up. We also kept some of our sporting gear in his house. Occasionally when we were not in a hurry, Mrs. Parnell would give us tea with buns after the game. This went on throughout the time that I was a student. Mr. Parnell died shortly after I had left Edinburgh. When I went back a few years later for the Post-graduate course, Mrs. Parnell had also passed away.

Edinburgh University, as I indicated before, is largely a non-residential university. It has two hostels, one for males and one for females. My first year I spent in digs at Roseneath Terrace. In the second year, I moved to a big house, a three-storey house with five bedrooms. This house was found by my good friend, the late Daniel Odoi, who had arrived in Edinburgh some months before then and was looking for accommodation. He was fortunate to find this big house with excellent accommodation but this meant that he had to find others to share. The names which come to mind are Ben Nii Odoi Annan, a practising lawyer in Accra, E. B. Tagoe, a medical doctor both recently deceased, William Richter, then a veterinary student and the first Gold Coaster to be trained as a veterinary surgeon, Kuta Dankwa, who in later life, was director of the Oman Clinic at Kaneshie, my good friend Abdul Mumuni Atta, a Nigerian educated at Achimota College and Willie Lutterodt (deceased). We also took in an old West Indian, Andrews, who must have been in his 50s at the time. He came to Edinburgh originally to study medicine but could not make it. He therefore hung on and as he received money from home regularly he was not about to do any serious study. We gave him a room at the attic of the house. He was a harmless old man full of stories about the Caribbean and very much interested in what was happening in West Africa at the time and hoping that one day he would have the opportunity to visit what he called his "home".

## The Edinburgh Medical Missionary Hostel – Cowgate

The tenancy for the house expired after two years. I then moved to the Edinburgh Medical Missionary Hostel at the Cowgate. The hostel, as its name implies, belonged to the Edinburgh Medical Mission, a mission dedicated to training or sponsoring the training of Scots boys, mostly, and girls occasionally, who would go to work in hospitals belonging to the mission in the Far East, particularly China and India. Later also in the Middle East and Palestine. At the time that we needed hostel accommodation, the enthusiasm among the Scottish youth to go abroad as missionaries seemed to have waned considerably, so there were rooms available for others. So my friends, Matthew Barnor, Henry Bannerman, and I found accommodation there for the final two years of our medical course.

The set up in the dispensary was quite interesting and we found it extremely useful in our training. First of all, the Cowgate is situated in a slum area called the Grassmarket where poor working class people lived.. This slum was the constituency of the hostel dispensary. The hostel itself had a dispensary attached to it. There was a resident medical officer who was himself, a retired missionary, and was back home to settle. So we had the facilities to attend to patients there. They came complaining of all sorts of ailments and we were able to attend to them. Not only that, but there were domiciliary visits also, so we were called from time to time to see patients in their homes. We became exposed to the appalling living conditions of the people who lived in that area. There was so much congestion, with whole families living in one or two rooms. The tenement houses were poorly lit and sometimes one had to climb as many as four or five flights of stairs. There were no lifts, and most approaches were in semi-darkness.

Going to some of these houses could also be quite risky considering the fact that some fathers were drunkards and you might go and find them in a foul mood and be given a rough reception even though you had been called to see a sick child or some other inmate of the house.

But in spite of all this, we found it very useful for our practice. The two years at the Cowgate Dispensary was very helpful in our clinical training. We supplemented what we were doing officially in the Teaching hospital with our Cowgate practice. Needless to say, our colleagues at the Dispensary were sober, serious-minded people, not students given to drinking or smoking or other indescribable behaviour. They were all very nice boys. One thing I liked about the hostel was that as it was a Christian organization, the day started with prayers just before breakfast. We took turns to conduct the devotion. We also said prayers in the evening. It was a distinct privilege for the three of us to be given accommodation at the Cowgate Dispensary. When I thought of some of our colleagues who would be going as far as China to provide service, I thought of my own mission later on when I finished my studies and the task ahead of me on my return to the Gold Coast and the obligation to go to the rural areas to work.

There is another interesting aspect of our work in the Cowgate. For two years we were called "doctors." Long before we qualified, most inhabitants of that area called us doctors. And why not? At the Dispensary we attended to them in the way that doctors would. We also visited them in their homes and they saw us in our white coats with our stethoscopes so we could not blame them for calling us doctors. In any case, psychologically, it was a booster. It encouraged us to work hard so that when the time came we could pass our examination and become real doctors and, therefore, legitimately be called doctors. Obviously, to have been called a doctor for two years by these people and then failing the final examinations would be a real slap in one's face!!

## Our Professors

I shall mention some of the professors and lecturers who made an impression on me. Apart from being a noble and honorable profession, medicine is also a calling in that it is not merely the accumulation of knowledge or the development of skills that is required, but also the way in which as a doctor one handles patients, or what is called the bedside manner. Some of the professors were excellent teachers but theire attitude towards patients left much to be desired. There were others who were not brilliant academically but who we saw were cut out to be doctors. They had very pleasant, courteous manners towards their patients; a good bedside manner. This sort of manner inspired confidence in patients. In medicine the confidence of the patient, especially patients who have a high psychological overlay in whatever is wrong with them, matters a great deal.

One person I found highly intriguing was Sir Sydney Smith. Sir Sydney was a forensic medicine expert and the Dean of the Medical School at the time. (I have already mentioned him in passing.) He was an international figure who had seen service in Egypt and had been widely consulted and had helped solve many murders in different parts of the world. He was a very interesting lecturer, always full of stories. Whenever he arrived in the lecture room, before he started lecturing, we all started shouting "story, story, story!" and indeed, he always had a story to tell, some long, some short. Sydney Smith was a jolly good fellow. Although he was the Dean he had no airs about him at all. He would talk freely to students, but despite the familiarity, we had great respect for him for his competence in his field and for him as a good person.

Then there was Prof Derrick Dunlop, professor of Medicine and Therapeutics. We found his lectures very interesting. Therapeutics deals specifically with the treatment and management of the patient. Derrick Dunlop, how should I describe him? Tall, dark, handsome and eloquent. He himself used to say, "I was born with good looks and brains, and I married money." His wife was alleged to be heiress to a large fortune, so that money was really no problem for him. Like Sir Sydney Smith, he was also full of stories and the way in which he conducted his clinical teaching and the illustrations he used in the stories he told were such that one always came out of Dunlop's lectures with something to remember. I quite recall when, in connection with the subject of diabetes, we were discussing the signs and symptoms and the manifestations and the fact that the diabetic patient passed urine in large quantities and also frequently. "What do you expect? Here you have this unfortunate person with lots of sugar in the blood. He cannot use it because of the deficiency in insulin. The best thing is to get rid of the sugar in the urine. Of course, he cannot pass lumps of sugar in the urine, can he? He needs to dissolve it first. That is why he is always thirsty and drinks water so that he gets the water he needs which leads to producing lots of urine." This is just an illustration of the way Dunlop taught us. In a way that we always remembered. We used to call him Ivor Novello. Ivor Novello was a popular performing artist on the stage, and a prolific composer of many musical scores and lyrics. Dunlop looked very much like him.

Sir Stanley Davidson, Professor of Medicine, was a very good lecturer. He was not as dramatic as Dunlop but he also delivered good stuff and taught us in a way that we did not easily forget. He was noted for his "Davidson's Notes," notes which he prepared, cyclostyled and then distributed. They were subsequently published as "Davidson's Textbook of Medicine," which became a very popular textbook at the time not only for the Edinburgh School, but for all British Schools and even in schools across the Atlantic.

In surgery, we had Professor Learmonth. Prof. Learmonth combined the chairs of Clinical Surgery and Systematic Surgery. Before then the chair of Clinical Surgery had been occupied by Sir John Fraser. Sir John Fraser was called to become Vice-Chancellor and Principal of Edinburgh University. Sir John did not teach us. He was a world figure in Surgery. A few years after he became Vice-Chancellor, he died a very tragic death by falling down the main stairs of the University Administration Offices.

Prof Learmonth was a very fine brain, an excellent teacher, especially at the bedside, but did not himself have much of bedside manner, I am afraid. He was somebody who was very methodical and one could really remember the things that he taught and the manner in which he taught. For example, it is well known that many medical students, when dealing with signs and symptoms of various diseases, tend, when confronted with the patient to think of the rarest things. For example, a cough may be caused by a wide range of conditions ranging from the simple to the serious. A cough is not really a disease. It is just a symptom. You may cough because there is something stuck in your throat. You may cough because you have inhaled something down the wrong way and it is gone into your lungs and you want to get rid of it. You may cough when you get an infection, e.g. pneumonia or you may cough if you have cancer of the lung. There is a wide spectrum of conditions that may cause a cough, a headache or constipation. When you are confronted with a patient and you want to get to the bottom of his complaint you do what is called a differential diagnosis. In other words, you take the main complaint together with the history, how everything happened. Based on the history alone and the bedside examination, you may be able to arrive at a tentative diagnosis and it is always wise to consider the simplest causes first. You eliminate all the simple causes before you think of the serious. A headache may be just due to malaria or it could be due to tumor of the brain. In between that spectrum there is a wide variation in areas of possibility.

So, in trying to illustrate this axiom, Prof Learmonth would ask, "Now, Patterson," - or whoever it maybe - "if you saw a bird, standing on the telephone line, what bird is it?" Patterson just scratched his head not knowing what to say. He started calling the names of all sorts of wild birds. After sometime, Prof. Learmonth asked him "Would it be a sparrow or a swallow? Which is it more likely to be?" "I think it would be a sparrow." "Yes, it is likely to be a sparrow, as the sparrow is very common and it comes at all seasons. The swallow comes seasonally. When you are confronted with any situation just think of the simplest things and get them out of the way first before you think of the most serious things." In this connection I discovered that many medical students during their course suffer from many diseases only in their imagination. Throughout the course I found that on occasion when I felt a pain somewhere at the back, I thought "oh, this must be my kidneys." Or if I became constipated, for some reason or other, I imagined it to be cancer of the lower bowel. The medical student tends in his mind to suffer from many diseases but, in the end, he realizes the truth in the concept of the power of mind over matter. At the end of the day, he finds that there is nothing wrong with him, at all! On the whole, I think perhaps it is a good thing for the medical student to suffer in this way. It reminds him, when he has a patient, of the variations, the many possibilities as long as he remembers not to jump at the most serious but rare possibility before considering the most common.

Then there was Mr. Thomas Millar, FRCS. A soft-spoken, gentle, mild, surgeon, Millar was the type of doctor whom any patient would want to consult because of his charming bedside manner. He was a first class surgeon, very competent; he got very good results and we all admired him. He was very patient when teaching; very polite to students, polite to his subordinates, the clinical tutors and interns. He was very careful, painstaking and meticulous in his teaching and in operating. He was also a very keen sportsman. He was the type of person who was always on the sports field watching one form of sport or another. I suspect that he himself must have been a sportsman in his student days. Altogether, a very likeable gentleman and a very capable person, and an excellent teacher.

Then there was Ian Aird or rather, Brigadier Aird. Brigadier Aird came back from the War, so we had him for just a few months. Also meticulous and painstaking, I can picture him now walking up and down the lecture hall and almost reciting the important features of any topic that was being discussed. He compiled some very good notes, "A Companion to Surgical Studies." which was later published as a textbook. The quality of the textbook was very high and although it was really meant for post-graduate students, undergraduates also found it very useful. Aird was an excellent researcher and many of the things which he put in his textbooks as fine print, at the time, were more or less looking into the future. They were things on the horizon and which could become realities. For example, the whole question of cardiac by-pass. The cardiac by-pass operation at that time was considered a possibility for humans in future. It was then at the animal experiment stage. Ian Aird was a brilliant surgeon and in no time he went to London, to the Post-graduate School of Medicine as Professor of Surgery in Hammersmith School of Medicine. Unfortunately, he died in a tragic road accident as a relatively young man. A fine brain and indeed a great loss to surgery. His book, "A Companion in Surgical Studies." is still being widely used. Certainly, I found it very useful during my post-graduate specialization in surgery.

Last, but not least, there was Professor Crew, professor of Public Health now called Community Health. Prof Crew also came from the War. He was a very scholarly person, obviously very widely-read, very broad minded, but a bit of a maverick. I remember that during our oral examinations in Public Health, we had to wait, and then be called in, one at a time, to face the examiners. In order to make us feel relaxed, Prof. Crew arranged that coffee would be served by his receptionist in the waiting room. I thought this was very thoughtful of him. Indeed, everything was so informal that by the time I got in to face the examiners I was nicely relaxed without any inhibitions. Prof. Crew, was also the one chosen to give the valedictory address at the graduation ceremony of our class. I can hear him now exhorting us to "go forth into the world to alleviate suffering and help humanity to be more comfortable." That was Prof. Crew, a fine teacher, a fine human being who had a very positive impact on his students.

When I arrived in Edinburgh in the late Summer of 1942, and I contemplated spending five years in training to become a doctor, the period seemed to be very, very long. I wondered how I could really endure those five years. Would I have the stamina? I soon forgot the passage of time and as the end of the course of study drew nearer, I wished that there was more time. There was so much to do and so little time. So all too soon, the five years arrived and in June 1947, we were all geared up to take the final examination. I must say that at first I approached things with a little bit of trepidation. Then I decided at the beginning of June that I was not going to do so much reading, but was going to spend more time on the wards. So for the whole of June, I paid visits to the wards every day, chatting with the patients and having a look at the management recorded in their notes. Fortunately, in some cases, some of my friends who had already qualified, especially my sporting friends working as interns in the Royal Infirmary, gave me access to the notes of the patients. I thought, well, I have been reading a lot. I should now concentrate on practicals.

As I have mentioned already, the two years that I spent at the Edinburgh Medical Mission hostel, the Cowgate, or Livingstone Dispensary, were really very useful years which helped to prepare me for the forthcoming final examination. Indeed, as the time approached I did not burn too much of the midnight oil. I used to go to bed early and tried to wake up early in the morning when my mind was fresh, to read over and do some revision. So when the time came for the final examination, I felt reasonably prepared. The examination consisted of a written examination and a clinical examination in the ward at the bedside of the patient. There were two cases, one short case and one long one on which you spent three hours. Then there was the oral examination which was not on the ward. In the clinical examination you were asked questions also by the bedside, on the notes that you had written and to explain how you arrived at the diagnosis, and, in general, to discuss the management of the patient. The oral examination consisted of theoretical questions to find out how abreast you were with developments in medicine. Indeed, you were not expected just to have read textbooks but also to be abreast with the medical literature. Our main source of information was the British Medical Journal which dealt with current advances in medicine. Of course, there were other journals such as the American Journal of Medicine and the 'Lancet'.

So, the time came for the examination. It was a whole week's examination. There were four Gold Coast students sitting for the examination. There were Matthew Barnor, Henry Bannerman, myself and Susan Ofori-Atta (who became Mrs. de Graft Johnson). After the examination we had to wait for about a week before the results came. We knew the day on which the results would be released, so when that day arrived the reader can imagine how anxious we were. Anxious to see whether our labour for the past five years had yielded positive fruits. At that time my cousin, William Bruce-Lyle, a law student, was visiting from London and he was staying with us. So that day Matthew Barnor and I accompanied by Bruce-Lyle went to Dumfirmline across the Firth of Forth and spent the whole day in Carnergie Park just to while away the time. We did not know at that time where Henry Bannerman was. At about 4 o'clock, we thought it was about time to come back and go to the Medical School to look at the notice board where the results were to be posted, to see what the notice board had in store for us. So we came back and got to the precincts of the University. It was about five o'clock. We walked past the Royal Infirmary towards the Medical School. Suddenly, one of our classmates called Atkins came running towards us, obviously happy, waving his hands and as he caught up with us congratulated Matthew Barnor. "What about you?" He said he was okay. So Barnor asked him, "What about Evans-Anfom?" He said, "Well, Anfom, sorry, I did not see your name." You can imagine how I felt at that point. So having been told this, I did not really have the courage to go to the notice board anymore. Bruce-Lyle and Matthew Barnor, however, continued to the noticeboard whilst I started walking, crestfallen, along the Middle Meadow Walk towards home. We were then living at Accra House, No. 25 Warrender Park Terrace.

A few minutes after we had parted, I heard Matthew Barnor shouting and calling out to me. "Emman, you're okay. You're okay. Your name is there!". "So why did Atkins not see it?" Your name is under the Es – Evans-Anfom - and Atkins was expecting to see it under the As." "What about Henry?" "He too is OK." So we hurried home and started looking for Henry Bannerman to tell him the good news. He was nowhere to be found. Indeed, Henry did not return home till about 11 o'clock at night. Of course, before he got home, he had sneaked by the notice board, and so he already had the good news. He had been in the Caledonian Cinema House from about noon and was watching a picture called "Random Harvest" with Ronald Colman as the lead actor, and he had sat through the picture three times until everything was over! All three of us were very happy indeed. Bruce-Lyle joined us in our celebration. Our tears and toil for the past five years had not been in vain! Thank God!

## The Graduating Trio – MB.ChB.(Edin) July 15 1947

Graduation day was fixed for just a few days afterwards. It was the 15th of July, 1947. I am not sure of the number that graduated that day. I think about 100 of us passed out of a class of 140 or 150. Anyway, the important thing was that all three of us passed. It was a very solemn occasion and it was Prof. Crew who gave the valedictory address. Exhorting and encouraging us, advising us as new doctors, emphasizing the fact especially that now that we had graduated and had been 'capped' as doctors, it was now, really that we were going to begin to learn our trade. Before then, we had been junior apprentices. We would still be apprentices for sometime, and, whilst giving us his congratulations, he asked us to be mindful of the Hipporatic oath which had been administered that day and let that guide us. After the ceremony, our landlady, Mrs. Macpherson of Accra House, took us all out and entertained us at one of the restaurants on Lothium Road. Her daughter, Ann Macpherson, was also there. I think Mrs Macpherson was even more delighted than we were. She was so proud of us and well might she be, because she contributed in no small measure in providing the congenial and conducive atmosphere for our study.

## World Conference of Christian Youth – Oslo, 1947

The following day, all three of us went to the Dean's Office to register for the Diploma in Tropical Medicine in Hygiene course which was to start the following academic year in October. A couple of days later, I left for Oslo, Norway, to attend a big international conference of the World Federation of Christian Youth under the theme, "Jesus Christ is Lord." I went there under the sponsorship of the Christian Council of the Gold Coast. The Christian Council of the Gold Coast had invited a number of the Gold Coast students studying in Britain to attend this conference to represent Ghanaian youth. I recall that Rev. Christian Dovlo who was then a teacher on study leave, studying at New College in Edinburgh, George Djabanor, a student of the Exeter University, Kwabena Nketia, I believe was then at London University, Annie Baëta (later Mrs. Annie Jiagge) was a law student in London, Emily Asihene, (later Mrs. Emily Essah) also on some course for teachers in London. We were the ones whom the Christian Council of the Gold Coast requested to go to the Oslo Conference. It was a week's conference

As a follow up Conference, Rev. Christian Dovlo and I were also to go to another Conference in Lund in Sweden for another week.

I have indicated before that the previous year I had met a Swedish student, Olle Engström, in Switzerland who had invited me to visit Sweden. I had, therefore, written to him, expressing my eagerness to meet his family after the Lund Conference. At that time they were not in Stockholm. They were at a holiday resort in a place called Frille Sas. So I went there to meet his parents, brother and sister. They also had a German student as a guest. He was a very interesting student and we conversed about his experiences during the war. I wanted to see Stockholm, so I left after a few days and went over on my own and spent three days just looking round. I stayed with a friend of Olle's who was an architect and a jolly good and hospitable fellow. After Stockholm, I came back to Gothenburg and sailed back home. The boat docked at Hull. I arrived back in Edinburgh to find out what had happened during my absence and whether there had been a response to my request to the Colonial Office to be allowed to continue to do the Diploma in Tropical Medicine and Hygiene Course. By this time, I had moved to Accra House to occupy the room which was vacated by Reginald Quarshie who had then moved to England.

There was no response from the Colonial Office so I decided to adopt a wait-and-see attitude. The trip to Scandinavia was a very pleasant one. Christian Dovlo and I joined the boat at Newcastle and crossed the North Sea for Norway. It was an overnight voyage. The weather was beautiful. Being summertime, it was a long day and a short night. There were many students from Britain on board and a good number from Canada and the United States, both male and female, all heading for the Conference in Oslo. The Conference itself was a world-wide Conference and a very big one. It is difficult for me, now, looking back, to estimate the numbers but there must have been at least a thousand participants, if not two thousand. It was a great big hall and I recall that the Guest Speaker was Dr. Reinhold Neibur from the United States. Apart from the many plenary sessions, we had group discussions. There was also a lot of time when there were no sessions to enable us to get acquainted with each other. I noticed that the Norwegians were extremely simple, open people, very kind and hospitable. They were very much intrigued by the attire of the delegates from Africa, the Nigerians with their flowing "agbada" and I recall that every delegate from the Gold Coast, except me, had a kente cloth. I had been in Britain for five years whilst the others had just been a year or two, so they were more abreast with what was needed for the occasion. They had brightly coloured kente and other colourful and gorgeous garb. We had numerous invitations to meals in the homes of the Norwegians. I hope they are still as friendly as they used to be and, indeed, I would not mind living in Norway because of the friendliness of the people.

The Conference in Lund which Christian Dovlo and I attended was a much smaller and more intimate affair. There must have been only a couple of hundred people there. One thing which stands out in my mind is a young lady, she must have been about 18 or 19, who kept following us, Christian Dovlo and me, wherever we went. In the end Christian Dovlo came and told me, "Emmanuel, this girl seems to be infatuated with you and you have to be careful about her." So we just laughed over it. On the whole, I got the impression that the Scandinavians hadn't come into much contact with people from Africa and much of the reaction was out of curiosity. When my friend, Olle Engstrom, learnt that I was not about to go back home to the Gold Coast immediately and that I would be doing a post-graduate course and also an internship so that I was likely to be around for another couple of years, he made me promise again that I would come to see their home in Stockholm before going back home to the Gold Coast.

# CHAPTER 10

# POST GRADUATE COURSE AND INTERNSHIP
## Diploma in Tropical Medicine and Hygiene (Edin)

Throughout the five years of the medical course my group, that is, Barnor, Bannerman and I, were paid an allowance of £300 a year to cover everything: university fees, our books, board and lodging, holiday travel, everything. The very first year, we started fighting for an increase. We requested that the £300 should just cover board and lodging expenses only and that the university fees, books and equipment should be paid directly by the Colonial Office. Regrettably, after five years, when we qualified as doctors, there had been no positive response. In any case, I had made my plans for the future, to save some money so that if the need arose I could stay on in Britain for another year without depending on anyone else. By this time, therefore, I had managed to save £300. Now this, of course, meant a lot of sacrifice on my part. I sort of ordered for myself a regime of austerity. In a way it was not too difficult. I did not drink, I did not smoke, I did not do other things which would cost me money and had tried to save every penny so that in the event of the Colonial Office failing to accede to my request to allow me to proceed to the D.T.M. & H. course, I was prepared to foot the bill myself and then find myself a job somewhere as an intern for which I would be paid a salary.

When October came and no reply had been received in spite of reminders, I just went ahead and registered properly and started the course in the second week of October when the academic year started. That same week there was a response from the Colonial Office allowing me to continue, but refusing to let Matthew Barnor and Henry Bannerman continue. The responses we had constituted a typical example of a divide and rule policy. The three of us got different responses. I was permitted to continue. One of the others was asked to come back home immediately. I believe the other one was asked to do an internship before going back home. It was the sort of reaction which made it difficult for us to act in concert. In any case, what it meant was that Matthew Barnor and Henry Bannerman decided that they were going to look for jobs as interns before doing anything else. The refusal of their request meant that no monetary allowance would be forthcoming anymore.

I continued with the D.T.M.&H. course alone. It was a two term course of six months duration. I started in October and completed in March of the following year, that is, 1948. The Edinburgh Tropical Medicine Course was really nothing to write home about. There were other Schools, notably the Liverpool School of Tropical Medicine, which is world famous, and also the London School of Tropical Medicine and Hygiene. These two Schools, especially Liverpool, had the advantage of being port cities where the Elder Dempster Lines' boats went to and from West Africa and the Far East. They, therefore, saw many cases of tropical diseases to enable them to mount a worthwhile clinical course in tropical diseases. In Edinburgh it was only occasionally that a case of tropical disease was seen at the Eastern General Hospital, well patronized by seamen who went to and from Edinburgh. On the other hand, the microbiology, parasitology and entomology courses in Edinburgh were really first class and somehow made up for the deficiencies in clinical teaching. Despite this, it was convenient for me to do the Edinburgh Course as it would enhance my knowledge of microbiology, entomology and parasitology. The clinical portion could wait. In the event, there were a few cases of tropical diseases which I saw during the course. Soon six months passed and having completed my course, I was awarded a Post-graduate Diploma in Tropical Medicine.

At the oral examination in medicine, Prof. Murray Lyon, Professor of Clinical Medicine, congratulated me warmly on my "excellent paper" and I felt really very good. In any case, it was not long after I had passed the finals for the general medical course and therefore it was not surprising that my paper was not bad. The month was March and even though he dropped hints as to whether I might be interested in taking up an internship at the Royal infirmary, I showed no interest. First of all, a Royal Infirmary appointment would mean waiting for July before taking up the appointment and, secondly, losing money because to be appointed an intern in a Teaching Hospital, specifically in the Edinburgh Royal Infirmary, was supposed to be a great honour indeed and you compensated for that by losing money. You were paid £72 per annum at that time, whereas, in other hospitals which were not teaching hospitals, you could earn more than twice that amount. In any case, what I needed was not really a teaching hospital. I needed a smaller hospital where I could have bigger responsibility as an intern. This was what I was looking for and if I got more money in the process, so be it.

As I was still doing post-graduate work whilst, doing the course for the Diploma in Tropical Medicine, I was still considered a student and, therefore, eligible to play hockey for the University. So I had another six months, another season with the University. During that time also I retained my captaincy of the combined Scottish Universities Team and it was then that we went to Birmingham for the return match against the English Universities, which we lost, 1:0 as I have indicated earlier. One interesting thing I remember was a young lad in the team called Dix Perkins, a law student. Quite a promising young player. His mother used to come and watch our matches in Edinburgh. On our way to Birmingham we saw her on the train travelling with her son to watch our match in Birmingham. "Mrs. Perkins, it's good to see you coming to support us," I remarked. "Oh, Dr. Anfom, I've come to see you and Kwarshie Quartey play." "Oh, come on! You've come to see your darling boy play," and we laughed over it. It was a good example of how very much interested some parents were in their children and the lengths they would go to encourage and support them. Years after, whilst visiting Edinburgh, I met Dix Perkins who was then a successful practising lawyer at the West End in Edinburgh.

## Dewsbury General Infirmary

A week before the Diploma examination in Tropical Medicine, I started writing applications to various hospitals, looking for a job, either as a House Physician or a House Surgeon. I wrote about 10 applications, looking through the advertisements in the British Medical Journal, and decided that I would take the first offer that came along. Exactly three days after the examination results came, I got a letter from Dewsbury General Infirmary in Yorkshire, inviting me to come for an interview. I sent a telegram immediately to say that I would be coming. So I went down to Dewsbury, the next day. After the interview I was offered a job as House Physician. Within three days which was then about the first week in April 1948, I was back in Dewsbury to start work as House Physician in the Dewsbury General Infirmary.

Dewsbury is about 8 miles south of Leeds. It is in an industrial area noted for wool. There was also a coal mine nearby. The Infirmary had about 120 beds with all the departments, except midwifery. There was, however, a gynaecology department. It was a small hospital, exactly the sort of thing I needed. There were two other doctors, the Resident Surgical Officer, who was a senior officer and would take care of surgical emergencies, a younger doctor, the House Surgeon and Casualty Officer. The Chiefs or the Specialists all came from the Leeds University Medical School, Professors of Leeds University or Leeds Royal Infirmary. There was Prof. Hartfall, Professor of Medicine and Therapeutics. He was my direct boss. Then there was Prof. Vining, a dear old man, very affable, pediatrician and brother of the then Archbishop Vining of the Anglican Province of West Africa. Then there was Mr. Michael O'Field FRCS, a general surgeon, Mr. Leslie Pyrah; FRCS urologist, Mr. J. M. P. Clark FRCS, orthopedic surgeon, and Mr. Currie, FRCOG, gynaecologist. So for me the arrangement was really perfect. The Resident Surgical Officer was senior enough to be able to help with dire medical emergencies. Even though he was a senior doctor aspiring to the Fellowship of one of the Royal Colleges of Surgeons, he had enough experience in medicine to be able to help out a House Physician in real emergency situations. I had direct access to the consultant in Leeds by telephone. As the distance was only 8 miles, if it was necessary for him to come, he would just rush over. It was a very advantageous arrangement for me. I had the very best that you could get at my beck and call. At the same time, I was in-charge completely and had much independence. There was no one looking over my shoulders. It was a good practice, which gave me good experience for what I would be doing when I came back home to the Gold Coast and was assigned to a District Hospital where I would be on my own.

After six months as House Physician I was re-employed as House Surgeon and Casualty Officer for another six months, and that completed the internship requirements for full registration by the Medical and Dental Council. As it happened, when my time expired after twelve months there was no one to take my place immediately, so I consented to be there for another three months before continuing with whatever plans I had. The time that I spent in Dewsbury Hospital was one of the happiest during my stay in the United Kingdom. The staff and patients were very pleasant and friendly. Some years before my time, they had had an Indian doctor but they had not had any doctor from West Africa or the

West Indies. One of the senior ward sisters in the hospital was a lady called Mrs. Moira MacCutcheon, a lassie from Paiseley, Scotland. Her husband, Dr. MacCutcheon, was a private practitioner in Morley, just a few miles from Dewsbury. Sister Moira MacCutcheon really took me under her wing, taking me round the wards and telling them, "Look, this doctor was trained in Scotland. He was trained in Edinburgh, proper Scottish training!" It was very important for somebody like me, a total stranger, an African, to come to work in a place where I was accepted and respected. It made life a lot easier, which encouraged me to work as hard as I could.

During the time that I was in Dewsbury, my younger colleagues, Kwarshie Quartey and A. A. Akiwumi, still medical students in Edinburgh, came to Dewsbury on one or two occasions to do their attachments. They too found the atmosphere very congenial, and they liked it as much as I did. The Resident Surgical Officer was Dr. Kempsy, who, was aspiring to the Fellowship of Royal College of Surgeons, England. He was a soft-spoken, highly competent doctor, both as a physician and surgeon, with a wry sense of humour and pleasant bedside manner. He was somebody who if he discovered that you were prepared to work hard, taught you an awful lot and allowed you to do things to add to your experience. So I was extremely fortunate to have somebody like Kempsy as my Resident Surgical Officer because I was given the opportunity to do minor surgery initially. By the time I left Dewsbury, I was able to undertake quite a number of surgical procedures - repair hernias, remove appendices, resect bits of intestines and join the healthy ends together, and to undertake other procedures of an emergency nature which I was bound to encounter when I got back home. I may also say that it was during that period that I made up my mind firmly to settle on surgery as a specialty. Before then I had my options open. I could have done medicine instead. Indeed, Professor Hartfall, who was my first boss, thought I would go in to do medicine as a specialty and was somehow disappointed when he discovered that my love was really for surgery, although he respected my stand and wished me well.

By Christmas, 1948, I had already completed the House Physician's job and switched over to House Surgeon. For me it was a very interesting Christmas. The emphasis of the celebration was making the children happy. There was a young lad of about four in the Children's Ward who was suffering from chronic kidney disease with accumulation of water in his belly which filled up from time to time, making it difficult for him to breathe. It was my duty to tap the fluid from time to time to make him comfortable. At that stage, there was nothing much that really could be done for him. He was a sweet little child and he and I became very friendly. At Christmas time when there was a party for the children in the out-patients department, they brought Ronnie and other patients to the hall. They asked me to act as Father Christmas, giving me a suitable disguise and all. After I had distributed the presents and I started talking, I heard a shout from the back of the room. "This ain't Father Christmas, this is Dr. Anfom!" to the amusement of everybody. That Christmas too, I put on a musical concert at the nurses home. They had a very big hall for entertainment and other functions including dances. At that time I had a large collection of records of classical music and all varieties of music. The musical concert, which I discovered many of the nurses liked, was apart from the usual Annual Hospital Ball.

Dewsbury Infirmary was in a working class area and I found from the way they spoke that they thought it was refreshing to have somebody who was kind to them and treated them as human beings, unlike the young white doctors who looked down on them. At that time, I was Casualty Officer and I saw many accident cases. The Orthopedic Surgeon came once a week to run an orthopedic clinic at which I assisted. On one occasion, a certain patient who had not seen the specialist before and who did not know about him came to the hospital at a time when I was attending to another patient somewhere in the hospital and not assisting the specialist. Meanwhile the nursing sister started calling the patients to go in to see the specialist. When this particular patient learnt that it was some other doctor and not Dr. Anfom, he refused to be seen by him. All this had happened in my absence. When I came back to the clinic, Mr. Clark, the specialist, said, "Dr. Anfom, you're a very popular doctor here! There is a patient who swears that he would not be seen by anybody but you." A very amusing situation. When they brought in the patient he brightened up when he saw me. I explained to him then that the doctor was my boss. "It's okay, if Dr. Anfom says so," and we all laughed. There were so many anecdotes I could tell about my life and work in Dewsbury Infirmary which were all positive. I must say that being happy, I learnt a lot which stood me in good stead when I came back home to active practice as a doctor in the Gold Coast Medical Service.

During my stay in Dewsbury, the Gold Coast students who were then studying at Leeds University were D. A. Brown, who had been teaching at Achimota School and was on study leave to do a degree in Mathematics, and the medical students, Claude Enin, Emmanuel Tagboto and de Graft Johnson, who were then in the early stages of their medical course. D. A. Brown came to Dewsbury to visit me frequently and the others too from time to time visited me.

Shortly after my arrival in Dewsbury, Prof, Hartfall, my boss, had a very interesting patient suffering from empyema, a condition which is really a complication of pneumonia, in which infected fluid or pus collects outside the lungs and presses on the lungs and causes breathlessness. At that time, penicillin was not in regular use. It was just beginning to receive wide application. It was my duty, from time to time, to withdraw pus from the chest and to ensure constant drainage so that the lung could expand. I did this for a few weeks and the patient recovered after the pus ceased to form. Whilst she was in hospital, her husband visited regularly, so after her discharge her husband invited me to tea to meet their children, two of them. From then on Gwen Hollings and her husband, Arthur, and their two lovely children, Ruth and Roger, became my friends. Throughout my stay in Dewsbury, they really adopted me as a family friend and I visited them from time to time. Long after I had left Dewsbury and come back home and on a visit to the United Kingdom, my wife and my children were able to drive down to Yorkshire to spend some time with them. At the time of writing both Arthur and Gwen Hollings have died, but their children, Ruth and Roger, are still alive. Ruth got married to an Indian doctor who was at one time posted in a nearby hospital, Staincliffe Hospital. Roger was a very keen football fan. In fact, he became a professional referee.

After leaving Dewsbury, I was able to arrange for Dr. Matilda Clerk, after she had qualified in Edinburgh, to do her internship there, and also for some ladies from the Gold Coast to undergo their nursing training in Dewsbury General Infirmary.

My twelve month period of internship ended on the 31st of March 1948, but as there was no one to replace me I was asked to continue until they had a replacement. Meanwhile, having decided to specialize in surgery, I planned to go to Edinburgh and enrol for a three month revision course from 1st July to work towards the Part I FRCS examination. The examination consisted of advanced anatomy and physiology and pathology. Therefore, before extending my time at Dewsbury I asked permission to go up to Edinburgh to arrange for registration for the Course. I took a few days off to go to see to that arrangement. That short visit to Edinburgh was to become the most important visit in my life, the most important few days for me in Edinburgh, because quite unknown to me, I was really walking towards my destiny, an event which was to change my life completely.

## Meeting with Destiny

During my absence in Dewsbury, I gave my room at Accra House, that is, 25 Warrender Park Terrace, to my friend Abdul Mumuni Atta to stay in until I came back. The day that I arrived in Edinburgh, Abdul met me at the Waverley Railway Station. I did not have much luggage, just hand luggage, because I had some clothes in Edinburgh and there was no need for me to bring much with me. We took the bus and came down at Bucchleuh Place. It was a gorgeous spring day, in the afternoon, and we started walking across the Meadows towards Warrender Park Terrace. All of a sudden Abdul stopped to talk to someone, a lady sitting on a bench and obviouslsy cutting classes and enjoying the beautiful weather outside. As soon as I saw this lady, I felt a bump in my chest. As the song goes "When your heart goes bumpity, bump........." - I cannot quite describe the feeling, you know. I saw this really beautiful lady with a very open face and a certain magnetism about her. A certain warmth and, well, I thought to myself, "Be careful, it may be your heart". Abdul stopped and started chatting with her for a minute or so, then she asked, "Abdul, won't you introduce your friend?" I felt a bit awkward but rather pleased that this beautiful lady noticed me and asked to be introduced, so Abdul said "This is my friend, Dr. Anfom. He is visiting for a few days from a hospital in Yorkshire. Emmanuel, this is Leonora, Miss Leonora Evans, from United States. She is in the first year at the University." We stood around and chatted for a while and started to leave. As we were going she said, "Bye, hope we'll see you again." So as we walked towards the Warrender Park Terrace, Abdul said to me, 'Well, Emman, the lady appears to be quite interested in you." I said, "Well, it's okay. It's because I'm your friend, and since you two are friends, maybe, she's just being polite, you know".

The following morning I went to the offices of the Royal College of Surgeons to make a provisional booking for the Course which I would be attending in the Summer. The strange thing was that, try as I could, I couldn't get this lady off my mind. I kept thinking about her and, going back to Dewsbury in the train, I was thinking about her. I simply couldn't shake her off my mind, and I said to myself; "Well it's a good thing I'll be going back to Edinburgh because she's someone I'd like to meet again and someone I'd like to know better".

When I got back to Dewsbury and informed the Hospital Administrator about my plans to go back to Edinburgh to do this three-month revision course, starting from 1st of July, he readily offered to keep me on until then. It was a mutually agreeable development. They would have somebody whom they knew would be working for three months; whilst I would be acquiring additional experience and also putting a few more pounds in my pocket. I felt really very happy, because the original arrangement was that I could stay on until they got somebody, which could have been a week or two weeks. Now I was being offered an extension of my job for another three months, which I thought was very kind of the Hospital Administrator. I may say that my friends in the hospital - the nursing staff, other support staff and also Dr. Kempsy - were all very pleased that I would be staying on a bit longer. Another advantage of the extension was that Dr. Kempsy, now that I was set on a surgical career, allowed me more opportunity to do some more operations. He would assist me and it was a very useful three months as far as I was concerned.

Now, to go back, some years. Even before I left home, I did say that by a gentleman's agreement with my girlfriend at home, she was to come over to the United Kingdom to spend a year during my last year. I was, therefore, hoping that during my internship in Dewsbury she would be able to come. During that same period I got a letter that at long last she had booked her passage to come over and would be arriving somewhere in May, 1949. She called me from London when she arrived and was staying in one of the Colonial Students' Hostel. I, therefore, went to London to spend a few days to meet her and to welcome her.

Unfortunately, that meeting after more than six years or so was not the happy one that I expected. The reason was that quite, unknown to me, she had registered for a course which was to take three years and possibly four. I must say that I was rather upset by this because I was almost at the end of my stay in the United Kingdom. All that was left for me to do was to take the course for the Part I FRCS and then the examination, and then go back home to the Gold Coast to come back after some years to Edinburgh to complete the Part II FRCS. I could, of course, have stayed on for another year or so to complete the full examination before going back home, but, for my mother's sake, now that I had spent about seven years and was about to spend eight years, that was really enough. I needed to go back home so that I would have some time with my mother before her time came to be called to her eternal rest. On this matter, my mind was made up.

There was no way in which I could fall in line with the plans and arrangement which my girlfriend had made which would have entailed my staying on for another three or possibly four years in the United Kingdom. We couldn't resolve this issue at our first meeting. Anyway, we both agreed that we would think about it. Of course, I made it quite clear that I was not going to change my plans, and if there were any plans to be changed they would be hers! She was not happy about this, so I had to go back to Dewsbury, and at the end of the three months I went to Edinburgh to start the revision course.

I quickly settled down to do the three months' revision course in Edinburgh. The city, of course, was very familiar to me and so I found things pretty smooth sailing. Some of my mates at the medical school were also back to take the same course. I also met doctors who were on study leave from the colonies of the British Empire also taking the course. Now, need I say anything about Leonora? Abdul told me immediately I arrived, "Emmanuel, Leonora has been constantly asking about you wanting to know when you would be coming." So at the earliest opportunity Abdul arranged a meeting. It happened to be at the time when that great negro artist, the singer, Paul Robeson, was visiting Edinburgh, and Leonora was at the forefront of the arrangements by the students from the Caribbean and from African countries to organize a programme for him.

A few days after my arrival there was going to be a programme at MacEwan Hall where Paul Robeson would be singing and, of course, I was invited by Leonora. Abdul and I went and enjoyed the concert thoroughly. Later, there were other engagements for the great man, all organized by the African Association and the Colonial Students Club. Then after that, the following Saturday, there was a Dance at the Colonial Students Hostel, which I attended. Leonora was also there as was my friend Timothy Awuku Asabre, who was a medical student and who knew Leonora. As things turned out, Timothy happened to be the person who would act as an intermediary between Leonora and me, carrying messages to and fro. At the Colonial Students' Dance on Saturday night Leonora was there with Alberta Addo, who was then studying at Atholl Crescent School for Catering and Hospitality Management.

Alberta Addo, who later became Mrs. Alberta Ollenu, was Leonora's friend. Leonora later on recounted how at that particular dance I kept on staring at her, looking at her all the time, and when eventually I plucked the courage to come and ask her for a dance and we started dancing the high life I promptly left her and went and started dancing with Alberta, presumably because I was not satisfied with her steps. Well, I do not need to say much, but by this time, I think the reader must have sensed the development of a friendship between Leonora and myself.

We started seeing each other and going out to the movies and concerts. Of course, our relationship was strictly platonic, but I must say that the imminent falling out with my girlfriend could not have come at a worse period for our relationship because, here I was, initiating a new relationship with somebody who clearly had a great interest in me and I must confess that the feeling was mutual, and it was growing all the time. My love for my girlfriend had, however, not disappeared. I still had some love for her and at one point I asked myself whether it was possible for someone to be in love with two people at the same time! Needless to say, since my girlfriend was unyielding in the stand she had taken and there was no way in which I could change my plans, my relationship with Leonora tended to grow and at one point I just decided that yes, the feeling I had for both must be love, the difference being that Leonora seemed to be more understanding whereas my girlfriend had taken an entrenched position, and I began to wonder whether she valued a carreer more than marriage.

Socially, I spent some time renewing old acquaintances, all the people whom I knew who were still in Edinburgh as I resumed my visits. My plan really was to do the three months' revision course and then spend three months working on my own, reading in the library, visiting the museums of the Royal College of Surgeons and the University, looking at specimens and artefacts. I was particularly interested in advanced Pathology. Of course, advanced Anatomy and Physiology were also subjects which I had to pay close attention to, especially, having regard to my experience in my second year when I was referred in Anatomy. I was determined that this should not happen again! So after finishing the course I spent the next three months, from October to December in 1949, working on my own. Meanwhile I entered for the examination in January 1950. I worked hard to make sure that I got through as the "mortality" rate in that examination was very high. Fortunately for me, I was able to pass the examination at the first attempt.

At that time I was told that the percentage that passed the examination was just about twenty, which meant that out of about a hundred that sat for the examination, just twenty passed. I was very happy with this development because, if I had not passed, it would have meant my staying on and attempting the examination every three months, and there was a limit on the number of times allowed for resitting that particular examination. With my passing the Part I FRCS examination and my plans to go back home, after that, what was left now was to get in touch with the Colonial Office to request a passage home and also to apply for appointment to the Colonial Medical Service, specifically the Gold Coast Medical Service, as a medical officer.

## Search for a Job

Believe it or not, but in spite of the fact that there was a shortage of doctors at home, the Colonial Office started playing what I would call "*hard-to-get*" tactics. First of all, there was no response to my application letter. Then when they wrote they said they would only give me an appointment when I got back home and that the appointment would be as Assistant Medical Officer or Clinical Assistant. I refused the offer outright to go home without a letter of appointment. This was January and as the dilly-dallying continued I stopped all correspondence and booked my passage to go to Sweden to keep my promise to visit my friend, Olle Engstrom, and his family before going back home. I spent two weeks in Sweden at that time.

Before continuing I must recount my experience on the trip to Sweden. This time it was winter and the weather was very cold. I took the boat from Tilbury. The passage across the North Sea was really very boisterous, very stormy. I am not one who easily gets sick, but this time I was sick like a dog. I just stayed in my cabin. I was sick throughout the night. I had never felt so rotten before, trying to be sick with nothing coming out, just retching. It was really a terrible night. We arrived at Gothenburg the following morning. I felt really very ill and so when I got off the boat, I could hardly walk. Fortunately, once I got on land the sickness stopped and I was able to take some coffee with plenty of milk, and lots of fluid to restore my fluid loss and to feel better. I had to take the train from Gothenburg to Stockholm. Once I got on the train I felt better all the way to Stockholm. Olle was there at the time and he was, therefore, able to show me round the sights in Stockholm and drive me round the countryside around Stockholm. Even though it was winter there was not much snow and the weather was not too bad.

When I came back to Edinburgh (this was in the middle of February) there was still no definite communication from the Colonial Office. So I just stayed put. Meanwhile, I continued with my shopping, getting ready to go back home as soon as I had straightened things out with the Colonial Office. I was after a letter of appointment before going, and they were insisting that the letter would only come on my arrival home and that my rank would be that of an Assistant Medical Officer. I felt a little bit indignant because here was I, with the basic medical qualification, a Diploma in Tropical Medicine and Hygiene and then having passed the Part I of the Fellowship of the Royal College of Surgeons. In spite of all this, they were going to appoint me to a rank below that of a medical officer! I sent a curt note to the Colonial Office saying that if I did not get any satisfactory answer, I was going to look for a job and also enroll for another year or two to complete the Fellowship of the Royal College of Surgeons' Examination. Immediately, there was a long telegram to say that I should regard the letter that they wrote as a letter of appointment, and that the rank would be that of a medical officer. They were booking my passage for the 6th of April by the MV Apapa sailing from Liverpool. They were following it with a letter. That really encouraged me. I had to do more serious packing and getting ready to say my good-byes. As promised, a short letter came offering me appointment as a medical officer in the Gold Coast Medical Service effective from the date of my arrival in Takoradi. I immediately I wrote back to say that I wanted the appointment to be dated from the date of my sailing from Liverpool i.e. the 6th of April. I think by this time they were getting tired of me so they wrote back to say that the appointment would take effect from the 6th of April 1950!!

# CHAPTER 11

# GOOD-BYE - UK

On the 5th of April 1950, I took the midnight train from Edinburgh enroute for Liverpool. To my delight and utter surprise Leonora offered to accompany me. This gave us an opportunity to really discuss our future. At that point in time nothing concrete had been said. All we knew was that we were deeply in love. At the same time we realized that Liverpool might be the place where we might have to part. There were so many things to consider before taking any definite decisions. It was quite clear to me that on her part, Leonora was quite prepared, if necessary, to come and make the Gold Coast her home. At that time I was not in a position really to make any promises. In the first place, my mother was very fond of my girlfriend, and I knew she would not really be happy with my marrying an expatriate woman, even though that woman was a Black-American.

On the morning of the 6th April, I joined the MV Apapa, and as Leonora stood on the dock waving as the boat moved along, I wondered whether this was the parting of the ways. Whilst we were in the train she had promised that, whatever happened, she would make a trip to the Gold Coast to see how things were there. So I promised that we would keep in touch by letter. We would just leave the future in the hands of the "Almighty" and see how things would work out. At this time I was deeply conscious of the strained relationship between myself and my girlfriend and it was quite clear to me that given the circumstances and the positions that both of us had taken, there was not going to be any future for us, so I might as well cultivate my relationship with Leonora in the hope that, God-willing, something positive and concrete would come out of it. So on the 6th April 1950, after seven and half years away from home in the United Kingdom, I waved good-bye to Liverpool and to the United Kingdom.

Concerning Leonora, I began to ask myself, "Will this be the last? Will we see each other again? Of course, I knew that in a few years time I would have to come back again to complete the second part of the FRCS Examination and to complete my specialization as a surgeon. I did not know how long this would take. It could be three years or four years by which time, of course, Leonora would have completed her course and where would she be then? So whilst there was the certainty of my coming back, there was not at all the certainty that I would meet her when I came back. Of course, she had indicated that she would visit the Gold Coast before going back home and I hoped that this was not just a mere promise but that she would keep her word.

I need hardly say that for the next twenty-four hours I was preoccupied with thoughts of Leonora. Here was someone who I met just twelve months previously, and yet it seemed as if I had known her all my life. I had no doubt in my mind that something had happened to me during those twelve months. It seemed as if Leonora had brought some sunshine into my life. I was very much attracted to some of the very fine qualities which she had. In spite of all the positive attributes or her positive endowments she had absolutely no airs about her. She was so transparent. The whole manner of her life was one which I found very attractive. Something in her really drew me to her, and it looked to me almost as if we were made for each other. I had no doubt in my mind that her love for me was sincere and no doubt also that I loved her. But then what about my girlfriend? I found myself really agitated about the dilemma in which I was.

Leonora, of course, told me about her background, a very modest background. Her parents had come from the Bahamas to the United States as young people even before they got married and she herself was born in the United States at a time when her parents had naturalized as citizens of the United States. At the age of six she had been adopted by her father's sister, her aunt, Aunt Rachel, who brought her up to New York and since then had been responsible for her upbringing, for her education through elementary school, high school, in New York and had strained every ounce of what she could afford to send her to university in Edinburgh. Leonora herself was very keenly aware of this and was very grateful to Aunt Rachel for giving her this opportunity. So this was the person I was dealing with. I myself come from a similar background, a modest background. But for the various scholarships first to Achimota and then to Edinburgh University, I would not really be in the position in which I was. There would have been no hope of my ever becoming a doctor!

In the face of the evidence available, was I really being fair to my girlfriend? Was the attitude that I was adopting really justified? Was it reasonable? Was it reasonable of me to be allowing myself to be pulled into Leonora's orbit without the proper weaning process based on justifiable factors? For reasons that I have assigned for me really to be switching over, as it were, and also bearing in mind my mother's own attitude towards my girlfriend, would my mother really understand why I was about to change my mind? I had to go over these reasons again to convince myself that they were valid grounds for me to adopt the course of action that I was contemplating. I regarded marriage as a very important issue. Enduring happiness in marriage should be based not only on love but also on trust. So I asked myself, "In view of what was happening, can I really trust my girlfriend as a life long partner? Why would she hide from me plans for her future which she knew were bound to affect our relationship? Secondly, do these plans of hers not really confirm my suspicion, and even my conviction that she was more interested in a career than marriage?" I must confess that the more I thought about this, the more convinced I became that marriage should be based not only on love but also on mutual understanding and trust. Frankly, at that point in time, this was something which I was not really prepared to concede to my girlfriend in view of the action she had taken. Without doubt I was in a great dilemma. I had to pray hard and long about this. In the end I decided that since in the case of Leonora there was not even a gentleman's agreement I would leave everything and expect some sign from the Lord which would really guide me to taking the decision which would be positive for everybody's future.

I may say that in due course, the sign that I was looking for came and I knew then that it was the work of the Lord. Based on that I took the decision, knowing that it was a decision approved by the Lord. Incidentally, when I say, "in due course" I do not mean that the sign came during the course of the voyage back home. It came some time after I had arrived back home.

Having disposed of this particular problem to some extent, I turned my mind to look back on the past eight years or so when I arrived in the United Kingdom as plain Emmanuel Evans Anfom, and now I was going back as "Dr. Emmanuel Evans Anfom!" The transition meant that much water had passed under the bridge. First of all, I arrived in the middle of the war when there was great austerity, and so I had the opportunity of seeing what one might call the fine side of the British people : the way in which they remained united during the war, the way in which they sacrificed practically everything in order to fight for their freedom and, indeed, not only their freedom, but the freedom of the free world.

Looking back now, the war had ended some years previously and there had been a gradual change back to conditions which were not altogether normal but were veering towards the normal. Of course, I had a great opportunity to travel within the United Kingdom and even to parts of Europe, meeting so many people and participating actively in the social and academic life of the University of Edinburgh. In short, my outlook had broadened, my horizon widened, and I was going back home as someone with a mature outlook. I felt quite satisfied with my participation in sports and church work and also in the social life, meeting some splendid people, becoming friends with many families all over the United Kingdom and even on the continent. I had learnt, for example, about the proper use of time. Before I came to the UK I had a different conception of time. In the Gold Coast, we did not seem to value time much, in our traditional setting, especially. There was absolute lack of punctuality, there was laxity, a lazy attitude towards time. I had also learnt that in spite of the ethnic or racial prejudice which manifested itself in subtle ways, on the whole, the British really appreciated merit, be it academic merit or merit in some other fields such as the arts, the theatre, or sports. To me, a very good illustration of this was when I was elected captain of the Edinburgh University Hockey Team. Lastly, of course, I was going back having learnt a profession and, therefore, better armed to serve my people when I got back to the Gold Coast.

## The Voyage Back Home

Indeed, I began to wonder whether all that happened in my transformation was real. Was it a dream or a reality? Everything pointed to the fact that it was real, and that I should really brace myself up for active service back home. I must say that I found the voyage quite pleasant. Some eight years before, it had taken me over one month to travel from Accra to the United kingdom because of the hazards of war. It was a troop ship so conditions on board at that time were really very austere. I would not call them primitive, but they were not really comfortable. Now on the MV Apapa, which was a passenger liner, and with my enhanced status as a medical officer of the Gold Coast Service I was travelling First Class and, therefore, in relative luxury.

I must mention some of my fellow travellers. The first were Mr. and Mrs Ofuatey-Cudjoe. Mr. Ofuatey-Cudjoe was a senior police officer of the Gold Coast Police Service who had been in Hendon Police College in London for a course. He was going back home having gained additional skills and experience. Mrs. Ofuatey-Cudjoe had been with him during the year. I later learnt that she was really one of the pioneers of the Girl Guide Movement in the Gold Coast. They were my constant companions throughout the voyage. Mr. Ofuatey-Cudjoe, who was a public servant with some experience, briefed me extensively on the workings of the public service for which I was very grateful. Then as my companions at table there were four young lady teachers who had undertaken some diploma courses in teaching. There was Elizabeth Vardon (who later became Mrs. Elizabeth Danquah, wife of the great Dr J.B Danquah); Esme Gaisie, (who became Mrs. Esme Siriboe, founder of the Morning Star School at Osu) and Ms Lorraine Daniels, a smashing young lady. The fourth was Ms Agnes Ampah-Baiden (who became Mrs. Nyarko, wife of Prof Nyarko of Cape Coast University). These were young teachers who made very pleasant company. Then there were two technicians from the Railway Location in Sekondi, who had spent a year in proficiency courses of training. Unfortunately, one of them had had some mental problems and just before we got to Sierra Leone he just jumped off the ship one night and committed suicide. He was never seen again. That tragedy marred what would otherwise have been a very pleasant and uneventful voyage back home.

By the time that this tragedy occurred my thoughts were already directed towards home. I began to imagine what was happening at home. I thought about my mother. Fortunately, the last report I had before leaving the U.K was that she was in relatively good health and, of course, the news of my imminent return back home must have put new life into her, and she was waiting eagerly to receive me. Indeed, as I have stated already, I could have stayed on a bit longer to complete my specialization in another year or two, but for my mother. She had not insisted that I should come but I felt that having been away from home for a long time, I must really go back home so that at least I would meet her before anything happened to her.

As it turned out, I was really very happy that she lived for another eleven years after my return. I thought about my brother who had, during the past year, qualified as a pharmacist, a member of the Ghana Pharmaceutical Society, and who I gather had a dispensary somewhere at Asesewa, in the Eastern Region; then my eldest brother, my half-brother, Ebenezer Amah Anfom, who at that time was the headmaster of the Presbyterian Middle School at Abokobi. I thought of all my numerous cousins and also my Auntie Lizzie – Mrs. Elizabeth Chinery - my mother's younger sister, and all my friends, especially those who had been in correspondence with me from time to time and, therefore, had helped to break the monotony of being cut off from home, isolated thousands of miles away for almost eight years!

I also contemplated how I would be fitting into the scheme of things. I am talking about what happened more than fifty years ago. At that time it was a rare privilege to go abroad either to study or on business, and very few people had the opportunity to do so. Those who went abroad and spent some time were referred to as *"been-tos"*, and for whatever reason, were treated with a certain measure of deference; as if they had come from another world! I never really understood this, but it was inevitable that this sort of reception and treatment was awaiting me at home. I imagined what sort of changes in infrastructure and government would have taken place. At that time the move towards independence was at its height. Two years before, in 1948, there had been the famous demonstration at the Christiansborg cross-roads and a shooting incident resulting in the deaths of 3 Ex-Servicemen, increased the whole tempo and raised the temperature of the struggle for independence. So much had happened. So many changes had occurred constitutionally. The Big Six – Danquah, Akuffo Addo, Ofori Atta, Kwame Nkrumah, Obetsebi-Lamptey and Ako Adjei, had been temporarily detained. Kwame Nkrumah was in prison as a result of political action, "positive action" and the political fever at home was quite strong. It was also quite clear that the independence which we had all been yearning for was achievable in our lifetime. Frankly, there had been times when none of us at that time felt that we would ever become independent during our lifetime. Now it looked as if this could happen. This meant extra responsibility, especially on the part of those of us who had the opportunity to go abroad and had had further education and skills which we could use in furthering the development of our country. I saw clearly that there was much that was in store for me and colleagues like me, who possessed the training, education and skills required for nation building.

With regard to working conditions, especially the facilities for working in our hospitals, I did not expect too much. I was familiar to some extent with the facilities that Korlebu had to offer and I must say I felt really pleased that my post-graduate and internship experience had been acquired in a hospital like Dewsbury General Infirmary, a hospital which provided the sort of facilities and also the opportunities for the type of work that I would be called upon to do. So whereas I was prepared for the inadequacies in the facilities and the need to improvise, in some ways I knew that I shouldn't really be disappointed if I did not get the sort of facilities I had been used to in big hospitals in the United Kingdom.

In those days, the majority of doctors and practically all the nursing sisters in our hospitals were expatriates, mostly Europeans. With my new status and new outlook I knew that there would be some friction at the times when with the colonial mentality still prevailing one had to fight for change in attitude by expatriate doctors and nursing sisters. There might even be occasions when one would have to take on the establishment!

Our first port of call was Freetown, Sierra Leone. We were able to go ashore for a few hours as the ship had to disembark passengers and off-load cargo. I must confess that I had a big shock at the sight of Freetown. I found the buildings and the streets so shabby and dirty, with lots of filth around. I must say that I was really very disheartened even in the better parts of town, for example, in the shopping area. Of course, driving through Fourah Bay and parts of the residential area gave me a little bit of comfort as those places looked a lot better. I wondered whether things looked that bad at home also.

**RIGHT**
*William Timothy Evans -*
*My maternal grandfather (1854 -1925)*

**LOWER LEFT**
*My dear mother Mary Emma Anfom*
*(nee Evans)*

**LOWER RIGHT**
*My Daddy - William Quarshie Anfom*

**LEFT**
*Edinburgh Scotland*
*aged 23 years -*
*1st year medical student*
*(October 7, 1942)*

**BELOW**
*Livingstone House*
*Hockey team -*
*Achimota College (1937)*

**UPPER:** Scottish Universities Hockey XI - Edinburgh (1947)

**LOWER:** President - Edinburgh Colonial Student's Club (1947)

*Graduation day (July 15, 1947)*

*Leonora graduation day -
M.A. Edin (1952)*

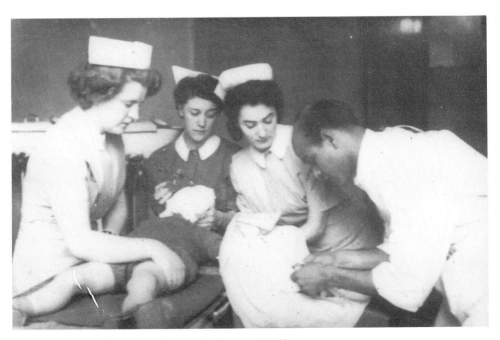

*House Surgeon - Dewsbury General Infirmary (1948)*

*Wedding day (December 13, 1952)*

*Gold Coast
Hockey Team
(1953)*

*The family before
Charlie's arrival -
Tamale (1958)*

**UPPER:** *Congo crisis - Leopoldville*

**LOWER:** *The family - Edinburgh (1964)*

*West African College of Surgeons' delegation with General Gowon Head of State of the Federal Republic of Nigeria*

*On the occasion of my appointment as Vice Chancellor, University of Science & Technology - Osu Salem (1934 & 1932 class)*

# CHAPTER 12

# HOME SWEET HOME

In a few days when we arrived in Takoradi I felt a bit better because Takoradi really looked far better, cleaner and better-kept than Freetown. On the morning of the 18th of April 1950, at last, we docked at Takoradi. Although my voyage to the United Kingdom in wartime actually took more than a month, because of my anxiety to get home quickly, as early as possible, the twelve-day voyage from Liverpool to Takoradi on my the return voyage seemed like eternity! They say a "watched pot never boils." How true! I was so anxious and excited to get home that the voyage seemed endless to me. At long last we were in Takoradi. The Police came to meet Mr. and Mrs. Ofuatey-Codjoe and made formalities for landing easy for them. Mr. Ofuatey-Cudjoe was very helpful to me. He got his men to give me the same facilities and quick passage. At the harbour were my brothers, Joseph and Ebenezer. Before disembarking, I received three letters in my cabin! Two airmail from Edinburgh, from, guess whom? Leonora! The other was an official letter from the Director of Medical Services, welcoming me back home to Ghana and saying that I would be posted in the first instance to Accra.

After all formalities had been concluded I was ushered to a brand new Peugeot 304 car and I was pleasantly surprised to learn that it belonged to my brother, Joe. That was the car which was to take us to Accra. Before leaving Sekondi-Takoradi we called on Mr. and Mrs. Francis Awoonor-Williams. Aunt Nora (Mrs. Awoonor-Williams) was my aunt and the reader may recall that it was at their house that I spent my last day in the Gold Coast when we were about to board the ship at Takoradi enroute for the United Kingdom in 1942. Aunt Nora and Uncle Francis were really very happy to see me. My brother, Joseph, had stopped to tell them of my arrival in Takoradi that day and they were full of praise and congratulations for the fact that first of all, despite the war, I had come back safely home and also that I had managed, in spite of all the odds, to qualify as a medical doctor.

The drive to Accra was rough and bumpy. The roads were not as good as what I had been used to during the past eight years, and it was as if to remind me that now I was back home, home, sweet home! Needless to say, to me it appeared a very long drive indeed. We arrived in Accra around 4 o'clock and I expected to be taken straight to the Family House at Otublohum, James Town. Instead my brother, Joe, who at that time lived at the Osu-La Estates, took me there, and we spent quite a while there; the reason being that he wanted me to rest after the long drive before going home to meet all the people who had gathered there. So we did not get to the Family House till half past six when it was getting dark. You can imagine my amazement to see the huge crowd that had gathered in the house. The yard was full of people, numerous relatives and friends and other people who had gate-crashed to come to see what was going on. Of course, the first thing that I did was to rush and embrace my mother. You can imagine the tearful reception and welcome that she gave me. I felt really so happy that I started shedding tears myself, tears of joy, tears of thanksgiving that the Good Lord had preserved her and that after eight long years I was back home to meet her in good health and to be able to repay some, however small, of the contributions that she'd made to my upbringing and my development; the encouragement that she had given me throughout, especially at the time of uncertainty and suspense before I left for the United Kingdom; at a time when I appeared diffident and rather reluctant to go because of her. She gave me all the encouragement and here we were, God had rewarded her. Her faith that the Lord Himself would be with me and bring me back home one day to meet her had been vindicated!

Well, it was a really happy reunion, meeting all these people : some young ones who were not born at the time that I left, others, who were young and were now teenagers, many who had heard of Uncle Emmanuel somewhere far away in England and looked forward to meeting him one day.

There were speeches galore by my relatives especially. One speech which readily comes to mind was the one which was made by my cousin, Mr. Jonas-Ridley Coleman, who was then headmaster of Bishop's Girls' School, Accra. He reminded me of my antecedentes, of my background, the way in which I had been brought up and the qualities which I had cultivated whilst young. He reminded me that however elevated my status might be, I should never forget my lowly beginnings. I should always remember that without God, there was nothing that I could really have achieved. All that had happened was really to the glory of the Almighty God. He reminded me that medicine was not just another profession, or a trade or a business but that it was a calling. He recalled that when I was young one of my ambitions was to train to become a teacher, a catechist and ultimately a minister of the Gospel. As a doctor, the opportunities that I had to serve as an agent of the Lord would not be too different. I could minister from my consulting room. I could through my relationship with my patients, the sympathy that I would show to my patients and all the qualities which he expected me to exhibit, achieve the same ends as if I were a minister of the gospel. Above all, he reminded me once again that he hoped I had not gone into medicine with the profit motive and to charge high fees as some doctors did, and that I would be modest in whatever fees I charged and always put the interest of the patient before anything else.

Indeed, it was a very good piece of advice and I have always remembered that particular speech on the day of my arrival, and I hoped that future events in my life, which I will recall, would attest to the fact that I have tried throughout to keep to this very valuable advice. Most of the speeches were short and generally congratulated me on my achievement, wished me well in my chosen profession and expressed the hope that I would make notable contributions to the development of the country.

I recall also that when the refreshments were being served, a little boy who was not as shy as one might expect, a six year old boy, wormed his way up to my side and said 'Uncle doctor, Uncle doctor, please when mammy brings me to you do not give me an injection." He said this quite loudly and everybody started laughing. On the whole it was a very merry occasion.

In my reply to the speeches of welcome and advice I tried to be as brief as possible. I thanked all of them for coming and waiting patiently for hours for my arrival. It was an indication of the love they had for me and that I was very happy to be back home. I welcomed especially those who were not around when I left some eight years previously and congratulated the young ones who were now blossoming adolescents and teenagers and wished them well in their studies and various occupations.

I recalled that I left in the middle of the war. It was a period of great uncertainty, a period of danger. Although it was at a time when the fortunes of war had started changing in favour of Britain and her allies, there was still a danger, and I am thankful to God that through His ever present power and His guidance, He had managed to take me safely and to guide me safely and to bring me back home safely. I reminded them that despite all that had happened, and indeed, much had happened in the past eight years, to broaden my outlook in a number of ways, basically I was the same old Emmanuel that they knew before I left. My attitude, my relationship to my God had not changed, I knew the meaning of my name Emmanuel, "God with us". Indeed, God had proved in my life during the past eight years that He had been ever present with me and guided me. I reminded them that I hadn't changed in anyway. I would continue to do things which I thought were right and righteous in His sight, and I knew that for the past eight years He had been preparing me for this great calling to become a doctor and to help to alleviate suffering and to help humanity and mankind with the knowledge and skills that I had acquired whilst I had been away. I expressed the hope that all of them would pray for me to make a success of my chosen profession and that they would all support me in whatever way they could to make the realization of these hopes and aspirations a reality.

I expressed particular pleasure to meet my mother alive and well and to say how very anxious I had been during the past eight years that I might not come to meet her. But God, being so good, He had preserved her to make it possible for me to come to meet her and to thank her publicly for her support and to say that I hoped that God would spare her many more years so that she would be able to see the fruits of her labours. I also thanked all my aunts, cousins and all relations and all my friends who kept corresponding with me whilst I was thousands of miles away when communications were infrequent and rather poor. Their letters were a constant reminder to me that I had a home somewhere where one day I would come back to, and here I was that night fulfilling that hope. After this there was a closing prayer. Just at that point I received a letter delivered from the Medical Department to say that I should report at the Korlebu Hospital the following morning at eight o'clock. I spent that first night in the family house in. The room which I had been accustomed to, especially during my days at Achimota when

I came home on holiday. Everything, really, at that point during the past eight years seemed like a dream. It was as if I had been sleeping all those years and suddenly wakened up to find myself back home!

## Korlebu Hospital

In accordance with instructions in the letter received, the following morning, at eight o'clock, I reported to the medical superintendent at Korlebu Hospital who turned out to be someone who (an expatriate doctor) came to the Gold Coast at a time when I was in primary school, Dr. Hawe. Dr. Albert Hawe was a physician specialist and was at that time acting as medical superintendent. He did not know me personally but he got up from the chair and gave me a hearty hand shake and welcomed me and said how delighted he was to see me because I had arrived at a time when they were really, from the staffing point of view, in a near crisis. Dr. T. A. Morton had resigned and they needed somebody to fill his place very urgently. He apologized profusely for the fact that even though I arrived only the previous night, I would be expected to start work that very day in the afternoon, or latest, the following morning. He informed me that I would be attached to his unit, that is, the medical unit, for a period of about six months. I was rather disappointed with this information because, the reader would recall that I had passed the first part of the examination for the Fellowship of the Royal College of Surgeons of Edinburgh and that I was aspiring to become a surgeon. I therefore, fully expected that I would be posted to the surgical unit. That was my feeling at that time. I was later to change my mind and to revise my opinion about this because I can say without hesitation that the six months that I spent working with Dr Hawe were very profitable to me. It was during those six months that I really learnt the essentials of tropical medicine.

Dr. Hawe had been in the Gold Coast since the mid 1920's, about the time that Korlebu Hospital itself was built, and his experience in tropical medicine was really second to none. Not only that, but he was a very hard-worker, very meticulous in whatever he did, writing down copious notes of the patient, the history, the physical examination - the procedures taught in medical school. Working with Dr. Hawe, there was never a dull moment. If you were a hard-worker then you could work with him, but if you were a lazy person you would dislike him intensely because he was like a slave driver. He did all this to teach you, to impart to you a bit of his vast knowledge and experience and, indeed, I really learnt a lot during those six months of medicine in general and tropical medicine in particular.

Meanwhile, after talking to Dr. Hawe, I reported at the Medical Department to see the Director of Medical Services, I think it was Dr. Shevaton. Dr. Shevaton welcomed me and offered me a chair. "Welcome, Dr Evans-Anfom! I notice you have been playing 'hard to get' about coming back home." "Thank you Sir. I want to say how very happy I am to be back home. Concerning playing hard to get, it is just that I like things to be done properly, and I really saw no need for all the impediments that were being placed in my way, when clearly, there was a great need for doctors at home. Indeed, Dr. Hawe at Korlebu has told me that I might be starting work just this afternoon. So, really, Sir, I saw no reason for those impediments. Having obtained my basic qualification, a post-graduate diploma in tropical medicine and a further qualification in surgery, I thought, really, that'things should have been smooth sailing. In any case, I think we should just put the past behind us. I am glad to be back home and I am ready to start work almost immediately." Dr Shevaton, I think, was struck by my candour and welcomed me again and hoped that I would make important contributions and be an asset to the work of the Medical Department and to the health delivery system in the Gold Coast as a whole.

When I got back to the hospital I was informed by Dr. Hawe that I had been assigned a small bungalow on the campus. That particular building is the building which is currently being used by the Ghana Medical Association as its temporary headquarters. After one month I was allocated one of the small bungalows, a sweat-box, so called, the standard accommodation for doctors on the Korlebu campus and also for other officials in the Ridge area of Accra. They were called sweat-boxes because they were very hot. One needed a fan on practically all the time. I spent the rest of the day getting settled, getting my things removed from the family house to my bungalow. I had no car, of course, so my senior colleague, Dr E.W.Q Bannerman, who lived next door offered me the use of his small car; he had a second car; he also offered me the use of his driver, because at that time I had only a provisional driver's license from the U.K, but no Gold Coast driving license. So until I got my own car this was the car I used.

Now at that point in time the total number of doctors in Korlebu was eleven. Out of the eleven, three were general duty medical officers, Dr E.W.Q Bannerman, Dr. (Mrs.) Coles, wife of a senior expatriate police officer, and myself. The rest were specialists : Dr. Stanley Cooper, the surgeon, Dr. Hawe, the physician specialist, Dr. Bereton, West-Indian radiologist, Dr. Hughes and Dr. Edington, pathologists. Dr. Hughes, I believe, was a micro-biologist. Dr. Goodman and Dr. R. H. O. Bannerman were at the maternity hospital. Dr. Graham, was the anaesthetist. With only three general duty medical officers it meant we had to be on call on a rotation basis. Every three days one person was on call. Being on call meant being available throughout the night, after which you were expected to work during the following day too. The work was really very heavy.

The numbers of patients attending were not as high as they are now but proportionally, and relatively speaking, they were very high for the few doctors that were available. This was years before all the new blocks for the various specialties were built in 1962. The original hospital, I believe, together with the Maternity Hospital had a total of about 350 beds with a very flourishing Out-Patients Department during the day. From the point of view of the facilities and supplies, conditions at that time were then a lot better than now. The wards were kept very clean. Floor patients were not allowed. The hospital grounds were very neatly kept. The dispensary was very well run and well stocked. If a doctor wrote a description for a patient, whether as an out-patient or on the ward, in more than ninety percent of cases, the drug would be available in the dispensary at very moderate cost to the patient. All in all, I would say that doctors derived greater satisfaction working at that time even though our numbers were small. A patient scheduled for a surgical operation was not expected to provide materials for the operation. Everything was supplied by the hospital. The hospital fees were moderate and affordable to most patients. Patients were, however, called upon to pay only what they could afford. No patient was denied treatment because of his or her inability to pay. Certainly, there was no payment up front! In those days doctors, especially specialists, were allowed to charge moderate professional fees in government hospitals. Certain categories of patients for example, children under 5, antenatal, school children, public servants, were exempted from paying private professional fees.

I shall say a bit more about this when I come to discuss my work in the out stations as district medical officer. I must say that on the whole I derived great satisfaction in working at Korlebu at that time. Even though the pay was small the economic conditions were such that one could make ends meet. Loan facilities for buying a car were favourable. You could get a loan quite easily from the government at a small interest rate and it was possible for you to pay back this loan within a short time. There were also loans for buying refrigerators. On the whole the conditions of service, taking into account the possibility of supplementing ones salary with income from a certain measure of private practice, helped to keep doctors at home and to stem the brain drain which has currently become an intractable problem.

My very first car was a Humber Hawk. The agents were Stavely and Co. They had a showroom on Horse Road, now known as Asafoatse Nettey Road, opposite the General Post Office. I just walked into the showroom one afternoon and asked for the price of the car, I was told it cost £680. My annual basic salary was £650. I was given a Government loan at six percent per annum, and as soon as I got the cheque from Government and paid it to Stavely the car was serviced for me and I drove it home! All this happened within a week. At six percent and my yearly salary being almost the same as the price of the car, and the terms of payment being quite generous, I was able to pay for the car within a relatively short time, something which is well nigh impossible at this time.

Because of my interest in surgery and my previous experience in Dewsbury Infirmary in the U.K., whenever I was on duty and accident cases, for example, minor lacerations and other injuries which I could handle were brought in, I just went on and treated the patient. On one occasion the surgical specialist was away at an evening party. They brought in a patient who had multiple injuries to the hand. Some of the fingers were badly lacerated, and a situation which was really quite serious from the point of view of the future function of the hand, so I took it upon my self to deal with this case. After all, I dealt with similar cases at the Dewsbury Infirmary. The following morning when Dr. Cooper, the specialist, was going round the wards he read the notes and was so pleased that he encouraged me whenever possible to do what I could, provided I had the time and other more urgent emergencies, whether medical or not, were not waiting to be seen by me. After that I became good friends with Dr. Cooper and occasionally when I had time went to the theatre to see him work. Dr. Cooper was a fine surgeon, although he did not deal with what I would call very major cases. He was very good at hernia operation and some of these common but important surgical procedures. He allowed me to assist him and to take some of the load from him. This was very good for me because when the time came for me to be transferred to a district hospital I had more or less become accustomed to the ways of doing things in Gold Coast Hospitals. At the end of the six months, I continued working with Dr. Hawe and I was quite happy with the arrangement that I could from time to time visit Dr. Cooper's theatre and handle some straight forward surgical procedures for him.

Certain things bothered me when I first arrived. The first was the intense heat. This happened to everyone who had lived abroad for as many years as I had, almost eight years. The heat was almost unbearable. I recall that every night I slept in my underpants only with all the windows open Sometimes too I had the fan on all night. The other thing was getting used to the new hours of work. Whereas for sometime in the UK, I had been accustomed to starting work at nine o'clock, now I found that my working day started early. Of course, I should have known this, and I had to get used to the hours of work here. I had to be ready by seven and by seven thirty or eight o'clock to start the day's work. Certainly, by nine o'clock most people had already done half a day's work. At the other end was the question of going to bed late at night. I had been accustomed to going to bed at about midnight. Now in order to make sure that I got up early I had to go to bed early. Changing this rhythm was quite a problem for me; so for months it was a problem for me to sleep early and wake up early. This was soon to be rectified. In any case, the irregular manner in which the patients attended hospital and the fact that I was on call throughout the twenty-four hours sometimes soon saw to it that the adjustment was made.

One of the first things my mother did was to take me round to pay courtesy calls on a number of people. The first person was my uncle, Dr. C. E. Reindorf. At that time he was already in his seventies and had retired and settled at Adabraka. Dr Reindorf, it would be recalled, was the one who very kindly offered me the use of his car on the day that I was admitted at Achimota College some fifteen years back, in 1935. He had always been interested in my welfare. Now I had become his professional colleague and he was very happy to see me although I did not heed his advice to specialize in obstetrics and gynaecology and had rather opted for surgery. He wished me well and on my first visit he (at that time I think he was the *Jaasetse* of the Asere Quarter of Accra) promised to get the elders of Asere to donate a piece of land to me at Tesano. The promise which was soon kept made it possible for me to build my first house as far back as 1958/59 at Tesano.

When we were children we were taken to Dr. Reindorf when we were sick and only the Lord knows the number of injections I had received at Dr. Reindorf's clinic. So when I was young I was his patient, but in his declining years when he settled at Tesano, the house just two doors away from mine, I became his doctor. So the roles were reversed!

Our next visit was to Dr L. V. Nanka Bruce, whose practice was just a stone's throw from my family house at Jamestown where I was born. We used to be taken to him also when we were kids and, apart from injections, we dreaded a very bitter and queer-looking mixture that he used to dispense. I gathered afterwards that this mixture was designed to cure a number of diseases. It contained quinine for malaria, iron for anaemia, and a mild purgative to help to dispel worms. The medicine really worked like magic for us. Dr. Nanka Bruce was also very happy to see me. Indeed, on my first leave I did a locum for him. Just one week's locum. Here was I sitting in a chair which was as old as myself and, looking at all the objects in the room, some of which I recognized! It appeared that nothing had changed.

The interesting thing about Dr. Nanka Bruce was that when my mother and I called to see him, he tried to persuade me to come into private practice possibly to come and assist him and maybe take over the practice later on. Of course, when he learnt that I had started a surgical career and that I was half way to specialization as a surgeon he agreed that institutional practice was better. The only thing he told me was, and his words keep ringing in my ears, "Anfom, you're going into the Civil Service. In the Civil Service, remember that you take orders and give orders. So remember that you take orders from those from whom you should take orders, and you give orders to those to whom you should give orders. Just remember this. I don't think that as a medical officer you'll always be giving orders. Be prepared to take orders from your superiors." A good piece of advice, I thought. It was not difficult for an Osu Salem trained-boy to conform. In any case, it was a very useful visit and I learnt a lot from the old man's wealth of experience and wisdom.

I also made sure that my mother took me round to see all the important people of my families, that is, both the Evans and the Anfom families, whom I had to see, and also the senior members of the Presbyterian Church for example, the Moderator and Synod Clerk. I also, personally, went back to my old school, Osu Salem, and it was sort of a feeling of nostalgia to see what was happening at a place where I had had a solid foundation laid for my character and my academic training.

Now there were quite a few things which I found a bit odd and unusual in the hospital. First of all, I was rather sad that a large number of patients came to hospital *in extremis*, or when the illnesses were in an advanced stage. It was almost as if they were coming to hospital to die. When I looked at their histories I could clearly see that had they been brought to hospital early, maybe something could have been done for them. More often than not however, they had been treated by traditional medical practitioners somewhere, and it was when there was really nothing that could be done, that they were sent to hospital, so that in the event of death a qualified doctor could sign the medical certificate of cause of death. The traditional practitioners were not allowed to do this.

The second thing which surprised me was the fact that nurses were allowed to administer intravenous injections. Whilst it is relatively easy and mostly harmless to remove blood from a vein with a syringe and needle, administering any form of medication direct into the blood stream can have disastrous effects. For this reason, elsewhere in Europe for example, only qualified doctors are allowed to administer intravenous injections. This sort of activity is usually delegated to interns, newly qualified doctors in the various hospitals, so that even in small hospitals the Sister or the Matron or the most senior nurse will call a doctor if ever intravenous injection was required for a patient. Very soon I understood why in our circumstances it was necessary that senior nurses be taught how to administer intravenous injections. Some of these people did it very well indeed. Of course, wherever possible a doctor was supposed to supervise this procedure, but it became quite clear to me that, having regard to the number of intravenous injections that had to be administered, without the skill being developed by the nurses, it would have been very difficult, indeed impossible, for the doctors to cope.

Another thing which I came up against was the whole question of the conflict between cultural practices and modern medicine. There was an example of a three-year old twin who had a chronic kidney disease, a condition which was progressive and was obviously threatening the life of the patient. Whilst Dr. Hawe, my boss, and I were busy trying to save the life of the patient, the parents were busy arranging for the patient to be removed from hospital and to undergo some traditional rites which twins were supposed to have performed for them to prevent something fatal happening to them. The interesting thing was that the other twin was a picture of health. There was absolutely nothing wrong with him. He was also a twin who had not had the customary rites performed, and yet nothing had happened to him. The cause of the illness of the other twin was nonetheless being ascribed to the nonperformance of these cultural rites! What illogical logic! I knew the father clearly saw the illogical nature of the situation but, unfortunately, as a result of heavy pressure from relations and friends he was obliged to remove his child from hospital. Needless to say, within a couple of weeks the child died and, at postmortem, just as we thought, he had advanced kidney disease!

Related to this problem, of course, was the frequency with which patients who otherwise were improving were removed from hospital against medical advice and, of course, the regularity with which the measure proved fatal for the patients. Then again, there was the reluctance of relatives to donate blood for their sick relations. In the UK with a very sophisticated and well established, blood transfusion service, I could just write a requisition for almost any amount of blood to be drawn on the blood bank and hey, presto! the blood was supplied with alacrity! Although at Korlebu I felt the disadvantage in the situation, it was when I got to the district hospital, where I had to attend to midwifery cases that required urgent blood, that the impact of the whole thing came forcefully on me.

It may seem a trivial observation to make, but I found whenever I got home and was in my sitting room that it seemed as if something was missing. Eventually, I found out that it was really the absence of a fireplace. For eight years I had been used to a fireplace in the sitting room and a mantelpiece. These seemed to be the focal point in any room for reasons that we all know. In a cold climate a fireplace is needed to keep us warm, whereas in the tropics, of course, one needed to keep cool. Therefore, there was no need for a fireplace. I must say that I really missed the fireplace and a mantelpiece on which I could put photographs and other things. It is an interesting observation which I thought I should make.

To some extent, despite being quite busy in the hospital, I enjoyed a certain amount of social life in Accra. I recall my cousin, Thomas Santrofi Evans, taking me out to a couple of dances at the Roger Club, a club for upper class Africans. It was then very lively and there were organized regular dances, especially on Saturday evenings. The Roger Club building was situated on the ground now occupied by the Headquarters of the Ghana Commercial Bank in Accra. Then of course, I attended a few weddings and other social ceremonies, the most notable being the wedding of my good friend, Dr. T. A. Morton. I felt highly honoured when my friend, Dr. Morton, asked me to be his bestman for his wedding. The lucky bride was a staff nurse in the hospital – Kwadu Prempeh - a very smart young lady, and I was really very happy to perform this service.

One thing which stands out in my memory is that on the day of the wedding, as best man, I had to go to bring the bride to the church. The bride was dressed at a house belonging to Mr. Julius Sarkodie-Addo, who later became Chief Justice of the Republic of Ghana. When I got there the bride was almost ready, but when it came to the point where the ladies had to hand her over to me, they demanded that I pay £2 before they would give the bride to me. I was wearing a new suit and I did not have a penny in my pocket. In any case, I found the request rather strange but Mr. Sarkodie-Addo came to my rescue, not only to inform me that this was custom which had to be adhered to; but he also loaned me the £2, and so an embarrassing situation was averted. The wedding was at Holy Trinity Cathedral and it was very well attended. There was quite a big contingent from Kumasi, the bride being the daughter of Mr. Ernest Prempeh, a well-known lawyer in Kumasi. Now this wedding at which I was the best man turned out to be one of the happiest marriages that I know and one of the most fruitful. I recall that Kwadu on that day promised me that she would have 10 children. Over the years, however, she went on to have 13 children, all well-looked after and well brought-up. All survived and all have done well in life: a very good role model of a marriage for all well-meaning citizens to follow.

At that time the British Council was very active in Accra and was involved in a number of cultural activities - music, the performing arts, exhibitions and sports with particular reference to hockey. Mr. Paul Hill, the cultural affairs officer, was a very keen follower of hockey and with his help my friend Kofi Atiemo and I took the opportunity together with Allotei Konuah, teaching at Accra Academy, to get together with other enthusiasts to form the Gold Coast Hockey Association with me as its first President, Allotei Konuah as Vice-President and Kofi Atiemo as treasurer. I can't recall who was the secretary at the time but there were many enthusiastic hockey players, notably former students of secondary schools like Achimota, Mfantsipim and Adisadel. There were also teams from the Army and the Police. As far as the organization of hockey in this country is concerned, 1950 marked a very important turning point with the formation of the Gold Coast Hockey Association. Within a few months I was transferred out of Accra and Konuah became the President and steered the affairs of the Association from then on.

As the reader might have suspected by now Leonora's photograph occupied a prominent place in my sitting room and, in a way, just as my girlfriend's photograph gave me protection whilst I was abroad, being always on my mantelpiece, Leonora's photograph also started performing the same function. Naturally, my mother was a bit curious about the whole situation. I have already indicated how very fond she was of my girlfriend and, naturally, she wanted to know what was happening. How has it come about that this strange photograph was replacing that of my girlfriend? I had to explain to her as best as I could all that had happened and the reason why I was being forced to go back on a gentleman's agreement which had more or less been sustained for almost eight years. Although she was not quite happy about it because she was not in favour of my marrying an expatriate, I felt that she began to understand my position and told me that the most important thing for her was my happiness. If I thought I was doing the right thing, then so be it. Of course, I told her that I had not made any definite decision. I was waiting for a sign to guide me. The matter had been entrusted to the Lord and I kept praying about it, and at least she could help us in prayer. So it was that, gradually, I sold the idea of the possibility of something happening in the future other than what we had all hoped and were planning for.

Many years before, my mother's elder brother, my uncle, Joe, whom our generation did not know, left home unceremoniously and went abroad. This was in the early 1920s and no one had heard from or about him ever since. It was possible that he might have found his way to the Untied States. My mother wondered whether Leonora could possibly be his daughter, Leonora's maiden name being Evans. So we joked about it and I thought it was a remote possibility; but in any case, if it came to a final decision being made no doubt a thorough search would be made into her background before anything happened.

When word got round that I might after all not be marrying my girlfriend of many, many years standing and that I was planning to marry an expatriate, an American Negro girl, some of my aunties and other senior relatives started making their own plans and trying their hand at match-making. There were several lovely young ladies around and here was I, a highly eligible bachelor, a been-to, newly arrived, from the United Kingdom, and also a member of an honorable profession, a doctor. I was, therefore, not surprised at the many efforts being made by quite a number of people to try to get me involved or interested in their match-making, to make a selection from what was locally available. Needless to say that all that time, my body was here but my mind was very far away. In any case, I was not prepared to start any new relationships at all because a life long partner should be somebody that I had known for sometime, and I was not prepared to start from the beginning of the alphabet! I had really to make a choice between two people, not bring in any third party to complicate matters.

One thing which I found highly amusing was the number of people who came round consulting me about illnesses which they had had for years; chronic conditions. I think at that time there was a general misconception that any newly qualified doctor must have the latest and most effective medicines. To them it seemed the experience of the practitioner did not really matter. Some of them, of course, were patients who had been treated by my own boss, Dr. Hawe, so I was obliged to tell them that "the doctor you've been seeing is the man who is my boss and who is really teaching me all about tropical diseases".

Now at the end of my six months with Dr. Hawe, I found myself very involved and so much interested in tropical medicine and tropical diseases that I was not really fussy about being moved. The only problem was that there was always the possibility of my being transferred to a district hospital and for this reason, it was necessary for me to gain some experience in the surgical department and also the department of obstetrics and gynaecology, that is, the midwifery hospital. In the middle of November, I got a letter from the Medical Department asking me to get myself in readiness to be transferred to Dunkwa-on-Offin in January 1951. The medical officer at Dunkwa, Dr. Dunett, had given notice of resignation and was about to leave at the beginning of the following year.

It was good for me because I had six weeks within which to get myself ready and so I spent sometime with the surgical specialist, Dr. Cooper. Already, I had been unofficially working with him, but now I spent more time both with him and also at the maternity hospital. I hadn't done any post-qualification attachment in any maternity hospital and I had not, for example, performed any caesarian section by myself. I had seen many caesarian sections done and assisted at some, but I had not done any on my own. Since I was going to an out-station, a district hospital, where I would be alone, it was very essential that, at least, I should be conversant with the operation because from time to time I might be called upon to perform such a procedure. Caesarian section is a straightforward operation and for someone like me with the experience I had in surgery, I did not think it would be any problem at all. Nevertheless, it was good for me and also necessary that I did a couple of caesarian sections and other obstetric procedures before going to Dunkwa-On-Offin.

I have said that I was not unduly unhappy about continuing with Dr. Hawe. All the same, I must confess that I had hoped that I would spend a much longer time in a bigger hospital like Korlebu, as I wanted more surgical experience under the supervision of a specialist. All the same, the exigencies of the service demanded that I went to a district hospital. There weren't many doctors in the medical service and it meant that my not going would have meant that an important station like Dunkwa, a very large district, would be without a doctor for sometime.

Since the work at Dunkwa would involve a fair amount of trekking on bad roads, it was necessary to have a much heavier car. I, therefore, managed to do this and bought a secondhand Humber Super Snipe – a much stronger car, and traded it in for my Humber Hawk.

My main problem with my being transferred to Dunkwa was the fact that the facilities there would be inadequate and that was bound to limit what I could do. Already I had been qualified for almost four years and I had acquired reasonable experience in surgery and I felt that the inadequacy of facilities would be a strong limitation on what I could do in my development in the field. I could foresee that because of lack of facilities I would be called upon to improvise a good deal. Although I did not know the extent of this improvisation until I got to Dunkwa. With hindsight, I think it was a good thing for me, because it was a challenging situation. Being called upon to improvise and through the improvisation save a life or minimize suffering was something which must give satisfaction to anybody who might find himself in such a situation.

Dunkwa-on-Offin and its geographical area was one which was not known to me. I was really about to go to a strange country, a situation which posed a great challenge, as I did not know anybody in that area, so I had more or less to assume a missionary spirit. After all, for a long time, we had had missionaries coming from thousands of miles abroad to the Gold Coast for evangelistic work, medical work, and education. So within my own country it shouldn't really be such a problem for me. I really looked forward to going to meet the challenges that Dunkwa had to offer.

I had heard a little bit about the history of Dunkwa. It is in the heart of the timber industry with quite a sizeable expatriate population. There was also some surface mining going on in that area and a measure of commercial activity. The large expatriate population there from as far back as the time of Governor Guggisberg posed some problems because of Dr. Tagoe, the African doctor whose posting to Dunkwa aroused controversy. There was resistance from the expatriate population in the area, backed by some expatriate officials in Accra. It took all the tact, ingenuity and firmness of Governor Guggisberg to insist that Dr. Tagoe should go to Dunkwa, and anybody who felt that he did not want to be attended to by Dr. Tagoe could go elsewhere for his medical treatment. Governor Guggisberg firmly stood his ground, Tagoe went to Dunkwa and, of course, the resistance just fizzled out. From all accounts, at the end of the day, Dr. Tagoe, being a very experienced and competent doctor, was well received by the expatriate population. With this background knowledge, I went to Dunkwa quite confidently because I happened to be the second African to be going to Dunkwa after Dr. Tagoe. Dr. Tagoe's service in Dunkwa was in the 1930s, and here was I going to Dunkwa almost 2 decades later. In any case, I felt very conscious that I had to maintain and, if possible, even improve upon the high standard set by my illustrious predecessor, Dr. Tagoe.

# CHAPTER 13

# DUNKWA-ON-OFFIN

So it came to pass that in the second week of January 1951, I left Accra early one morning for Dunkwa, passing through Nsawam, Swedru, Saltpond, Cape Coast, Takoradi, Agona Junction, and Tarkwa finally arriving at Dunkwa at about 4 o'clock in the afternoon. I made straight for the Government Hospital, and there I met a small staff group awaiting me. Dr. Dunett, the medical officer whom I was going to replace, was at the Rest House, so after the necessary greetings I was taken to the Government Rest House where he welcomed me. He was staying for a couple of days at the Government Rest House prior to his departure from Dunkwa. After we had a drink he accompanied me to the doctors' bungalow which by this time had been got ready for me. We arranged to meet at the hospital the following morning so that he would show me round and hand-over to me officially.

## Surprise – Surprise !!

After Dr. Dunett left, I found a note on the table of the sitting room. It was from Mr. and Mrs. Ofuatey-Cudjoe, who had been my fellow travellers on the MV Apapa on my return voyage home. The note welcomed me to Dunkwa and informed me that Mr. Ofuatey-Cudjoe was the Superintendent-In-Charge of Dunkwa District and his bungalow was just next to mine. I was to notify them of my arrival. Now, that was really very good news for me. When I left Accra in the morning I did not expect that I would meet anybody at Dunkwa whom I knew, and yet providentially, here was I being welcomed by a couple with whom I had struck friendship on board a ship when I was returning home, a couple whom I expected would act as my elder brother and sister. This made

*185*

me feel really very good. Needless to say, even before I finished unpacking I asked the driver to take me to the bungalow which was just next door. I met Mrs. Ofuatey-Cudjoe only as her husband was still at work. They had heard I was coming but they had not got in touch with me because they meant it to be a surprise to meet them there. She made tea and we sat down and had a long chat about our return voyage and, in a nutshell, she made me feel completely at ease. That evening, I had dinner with the Ofuatey-Codjoe's. I felt very much at home and looked forward to a happy stay at Dunkwa under their care.

One of the first questions Mrs. Ofuatey-Cudjoe asked me was, "Dr., have you been hearing from Leonora?" "Yes, I've had a few letters from her and I've written also." "She's a very lovely lady", said Mrs. Ofuatey-Cudjoe. I kept that observation at the back of my mind. The following morning, at exactly half past seven, I met Dr. Dunett at the hospital and he showed me round, introduced me to the chief male nurse, Mr. Quarcoo, and the other nurses. There was Mrs. Hilda Nettey, whom I had known at Achimota College when she was Miss Hilda Vanderpuije. She was now the chief midwife at the hospital. At that time her husband, who was the pharmacist in charge of the Government Dispensary at Sefwi Wiawso, had had an accident causing extensive bodily burns and was a patient in one of the wards. The hospital had about sixty beds, an old-fashioned type colonial district hospital just like Akuse hospital as I knew it when I was a child. There were a variety of cases mostly medical cases and a couple of surgical cases waiting to be operated upon. Fortunately, that day there was no surgical emergency. Although there were mothers coming in to deliver every day, most of the deliveries were normal. Fortunately, the midwives could cope with these quite easily. The handing-over notes were brief. Dr. Dunett was obviously in a hurry to leave, to go on terminal leave.

My first day in the hospital was quiet. This gave me time to unpack and settle down. There was also time for Dr. Dunett to take me round to pay courtesy calls on the District Commissioner, Mr. Mackay, a very pleasant gentleman whom I got on very well with during the time that I was at Dunkwa. We became such great friends that he actually travelled all the way to attend my wedding in Accra. Then we saw the manager of the United African Company. UAC wielded a great influence in the commercial life of the district. We also called on the manager of Barclays Bank.

Later that day, Mr. Ofuatey-Cudjoe took me to call on the Denkyirahene. There were other influential citizens like the Abdo Brothers, Lebanese businessmen, who had been at Dunkwa for a long time and had been in business mostly dealing in arms and ammunition. They also had a motor mechanic workshop. Nassif Nakly and Dagher (Lebanese) were traders. Mr. and Mrs. Plange were old residents at Dunkwa who became my very good friends. I looked upon them as my parents during the time that I was at Dunkwa. Then there was old man Brobbey, also a businessman. When I was at Achimota, one of my classmates was J. W. Brobbey, who I gathered was his nephew, and who was an administrative officer in the Civil Service. I met a few of the important people in timber. Fortunately for me, I inherited Dr. Dunett's cook, Abdulai, a very polite and efficient cook and an ex-service man with a heavy moustache. I was a bachelor at that time who did not fuss much about food. Abdulai cooked what I wanted and it tasted good. That was all that mattered to a bachelor like me.

Although there was electricity, there was no pipe-borne water at Dunkwa. We had to rely on rain water collected in huge tanks in the hospital and also in the bungalows. Whenever I scrubbed for an operation, I used pure methylated spirit afterwards before drying up and putting on gloves. Fortunately, although I was afraid of sepsis, we did not have many instances of operative wounds becoming septic. One of the greatest drawbacks for me in the hospital was the fact that there were no X-rays. This meant that, apart from simple fractures which did not need to be X-rayed, all complicated fractures, after receiving first aid, were referred to Kumasi. At that time, the surgical specialist in Kumasi was Dr. Charles Bowesman. Dr. Charles Bowesman had been in the Colonial medical service and had seen service in the Gambia, I believe, for many years before coming to the Gold Coast. He was an experienced surgeon. In addition to fractures, I had to refer complicated cases to him at the Kumasi Central hospital and he then wrote back to me afterwards when the patient was treated and discharged. Also, occasionally, for cases which I considered interesting, I went to Kumasi myself on a follow-up and was able to witness, even assist, sometimes at the operation. Dr. Bowesman knew that I was aspiring to become a surgeon and that I had passed Part I of the Diploma of Fellowship of the Royal College of Surgeons of Edinburgh. He had great interest in what I was trying to do and, therefore, endeavoured to help me in whatever way he could. Years later, I was to work with him as his assistant in Kumasi for one year.

Thanks to the experience that I got working with Dr. Hawe, I was able to cope with practically all the typically tropical diseases that came to the hospital. So I did not have much problem with that. Also I was able to cope with most of the surgical emergencies. The commonest among them was strangulated inguinal hernia in men, something which I was quite accustomed to and could deal with quite competently. There were a couple of interesting cases which I treated at the hospital which I would like to recall.

The first one was the case of a thirty-year old lady. She was brought into hospital with a grossly distended belly. She was very aneamic-looking and quite breathless. On first sight, I thought that she was in cardiac failure, chronic heart failure. But then on careful examination there were other signs which indicated otherwise. The amount of fluid that had gathered in her belly was such that it was obviously causing the breathlessness due to pressure on the diaphragm. Her anaemia also worsened the breathlessness. Clearly, she required some blood transfusion. She also required to be relieved of some of the abdominal fluid. On withdrawing some of the fluid, I saw that it was highly blood stained, which of course was quite against heart failure. Could it be some cancerous condition? The history did not support this. On close questioning, she revealed that she had missed her period for a couple of months! In any case what needed to be done urgently for her was to give her some blood because, clearly, she was losing some blood somewhere inside her abdomen and she required urgent blood transfusion and also to be relieved of some of this fluid.

When she got a bit better, after being given a pint of blood, I decided that I should take the bull by the horns and have a look and see what was happening. Provided she was not given too much anaesthetic, which would be harmful to her, I could take the risk. So we took her to the theatre, prepared her for operation, and removed about a pint of blood. Because the blood looked so clean, I thought perhaps we should just strain it and give it back to her as it might help her. We could not immediately get one pint of compatible blood, so maybe a bit of her own blood could resuscitate her. So this was what we did. After we had given her, slowly, another pint of blood and she felt a bit better, we were confident to give her the anaesthetic. I opened her up quickly to see what was actually happening. I discovered a tubal pregnancy with a slow leakage of blood from the ruptured tube. The rest was quite straightforward. I removed all the blood available and gave it to her rapidly after I had stopped the bleeding by tying up the bleeding point and from then on she just made a speedy and uneventful recovery. This was a novel case and that experience was to stand me in good stead later on when I encountered similar situations during my active medical practice. In particular I found auto-transfusion a very reliable life saving procedure.

The second case was one which I have already referred to elsewhere. It was a case of a huge muscle absess in a villager. One day whilst I was going on trek to Sefwi Wiawso I was asked to see a patient in one of the villages who had been ill for some weeks. It was quite clear that he had a huge muscle absess of one of his thighs. On my return journey I took him back to Dunkwa and that same evening performed an emergency operation to incise and remove almost half a bucketful of pus. He responded very quickly to this treatment. This was a patient who for weeks had been treated by a traditional practitioner. But for the timely surgical intervention, the patient would surely have died.

The Dunkwa District covers quite a wide area and I had to go on trek once a week. There was a small hospital at Sefwi Wiawso some years before with a medical officer. For some time, however, there had not been any resident medical officer. There was a pharmacist in charge with a couple of nurse/midwives who dealt with straightforward cases and referred difficult ones to the Dunkwa Hospital. One interesting feature of the trek was that, at that time the Yaws Campaign was at its height and, en route to Sefwi Wiawso, I had to stop at almost every village. The children and all those who had yaws would line up by the side of the road and offer their bottoms for intra-muscular injection of Acetylarsan, which is an arsenic preparation. The course of ten weekly injections usually did the trick. Even after a couple of injections the pustules on the skin of the patient began to dry up, and by the time the full course was ended, everything was clear. Later on, we started using penicillin, which was much safer and even more effective. A couple of injections just wiped away the yaws. The skin pustules, which were really very nasty indeed, must have been very uncomfortable for the patients. In my opinion, the success of the Yaws Campaign accounted to some extent for the confidence that the population, especially in the rural areas, had in modern orthodox medicine to the extent that injection to many of the villagers was an indispensable part of patient management. I recall an outpatient who had a course of ten weekly injections. After the last injection, when she came and reported for review she was given tablets only. As she went out, on reaching the door, she turned round and said, "Doctor, Doctor, *ene onwo mi paanie?*" ("Doctor, Doctor, today no injection for me?") It reminded me of my days in Dewsbury when many patients, especially of the working class, were not satisfied with anything that was done, unless an X'ray examination was part of the management. They did not know that the X'ray was just a diagnostic tool. They thought it was also therapeutic!

The work in the hospital itself was very absorbing. On the whole I found it not too difficult to cope with. In the field of midwifery, the midwives were highly experienced, and they dealt with all the straightforward cases. Whenever I was called I knew some sort of surgical intervention was needed, usually a Caesarian Section for obstructed labour, or maybe forceps delivery, or some other condition. I really did not have much problem with the midwifery practice. My predecessors, all expatriates, had run what was called a "sterility clinic." Apart from barren women, they had large numbers of women attending, usually women who had one or two children and wanted more because they had new husbands. Maybe, they had tubal blockage due to some infection or other, and what I discovered was that most of these patients were submitted to a procedure called D&C - Dilatation and Curettage. Opening of the mouth of the womb and curettage was scraping and cleaning the inner lining of the womb in order to have a new lining forming within the womb in the hope that it would provide a more fertile ground for the fertilized ovum. So, D&C had become a very popular procedure with the women, to the extent that, on one occasion a patient came in and when I wanted to know what was wrong she just said, "O!!! doctor I want D&C", much to my astonishment. Of course, the midwife who was assisting me in the consulting room just informed her that "This doctor doesn't work in this way. You just tell doctor what is wrong with you and he will do what he thinks is good for you".

On another occasion, in some other station later, another patient came in and when I asked what was wrong with her she said "Oh!!! I want to buy M&B." M&B of course, stood for "May and Baker," the manufacturers of the sulphonamide drugs, the chemotherapeutic drugs which preceded penicillin. There were drug peddlers and charlatans and crooks who went round the villages selling all sorts of pills and potions. In a few cases, we found pieces of chalk shaped into pellets being sold as M&B tablets!

The nursing and other staff in the hospital were usually very happy when I had to go on trek, not because they wanted to get rid of me from the hospital but because they knew that whenever I came back the boot of my car would be filled with all sorts of produce, cassava, plantain, gari etc - and I would just give it out to the staff to share. After all I was a bachelor and my needs were very modest. They were very happy once a week to get this bonus supply. Needless to say, farm produce was plenty and the price was really very low. I could buy a big bunch of plantains for one shilling!

Shortly after I arrived at Dunkwa, I did a survey among the young men and women around, school teachers, public servants and others, and found that there were quite a few who had been to secondary schools or teacher training colleges and who had played hockey and were quite interested. As soon as I was able to do so I ordered material from Chandirams or Chellarams, in Accra – hockey sticks, pads and hockey balls. Those who could afford to buy the hockey sticks paid in instalments and those who could not afford it I just gave it out to them gratis. We started playing hockey once a week, which really brought some kick into the sporting life of Dunkwa. By the time that I left Dunkwa there was a group of young men and women who had become attached to the game and hockey had become quite popular at Dunkwa.

As there was no Presbyterian Church at Dunkwa at that time, I attended the Methodist Church Services. The priest in the Church at that time was Rev. Wilson, an affable and pleasant old gentleman who became good friends with me. I also had the good fortune to meet the Homiah family who also took me in as a member of the family. They were staunch members of the Methodist Church. I took the opportunity to learn many of the Methodist Hymns and felt quite at home. The worship was very similar to that of the Presbyterian Church, and I used to say, jokingly, that the only difference I found was that the Methodists stood to sing whilst we Presbyterians sat to sing, in church!

## "Educational Visit" by Leonora

In April 1951, I got a letter from Leonora to say that she had booked her passage for early July to come to visit the Gold Coast for a few weeks just to look around, an educational visit as she put it. It was necessary for me to sign certain papers, since she had given my name as her host whilst in the country. As soon as the letter came I took the necessary steps to obtain from the Police and the Immigration Authorities the forms that had to be signed. Needless to say, Mr. Ofuatey-Cudjoe was very helpful in this exercise. So we were able to get the necessary papers for her, and sometime in mid July 1951, she came, disembarking at Takoradi. I sent my car to meet her. Fortunately, my cousin, Thomas Santrofi-Evans, was at that time working with the United African Company (UAC) and also my distant relation, Neequaye Ashison was also working at the Labour Department in Takoradi. I had requested Ashison, to ask for his annual leave, about a month, so that he would be able to chaperon Leonora around when she arrived. So they met Leonora on her arrival, took her through all the formalities and drove her up to Dunkwa accompanied by Neequaye Ashison. Leonora had done all these things at her own expense. She hadn't asked for a penny from me!

Although Leonora hadn't met the Ofuatey-Cudjoes, she knew all about them from my letters. She knew who they were, and on the day of her arrival, we made elaborate preparations to welcome her. Mr. and Mrs. Ofuatey-Cudjoe laid on a very good meal for us in the evening. For sometime the Ofuatey-Cudjoes had admired Leonora from a distance. When they actually met her in person, I could see that she just swept them off their feet, and I was very pleased with the manner in which they treated her, which made her really feel very much at home. Of course, by the time of her arrival at home, I had made many friends in town and later on I took her round to meet some of them.

Leonora had only five weeks to stay in the Gold Coast, and since it was not possible for me to take time off throughout her visit, I made a programme for her to visit Accra to meet my mother and other relatives and friends. Before her arrival I had written to my good friend and senior colleague, Mr. Robert Baffour, who was then the Town Engineer in Accra, and his wife, Akweley Cofie, sister to Kwamla Cofie, (now Nii Kojo Ababio V) my classmate at Achimota College, and they had agreed that whilst Leonora was in Accra, she would be their house guest. At that time they were staying at Korle Gonno in their private house. So whilst Leonora was in Accra, she stayed with them. She tells a story about being taken out by Robert Baffour to meet some of my school friends, mostly old Achimotans, both junior and senior, and the occasion when they called on Mr. A. L. Adu, at a time when J. O. T.

Agyeman and one other person were visiting. According to her, after a while, they started talking about Achimota and completely ignored her. She said well, "You Achimotans think so highly of yourselves." So they countered, "Well, you must think highly of old Achimotans too otherwise you would not want to marry one." After Leonora's stay in Accra, I came down myself to spend a few days to introduce her formally to my mother and all those who mattered and then we came back to Dunkwa. She accompanied me on my treks to Sefwi Wiawso

My elder brother, Joseph, the pharmacist was at that time working with the British Aluminum Company at Awaso. He spent a weekend with us and we were taking him back home on a Sunday afternoon when a couple of miles beyond Ayanfuri our car overturned at a culvert. Luckily there was a shallow stream there and even though the car ended upside down there was no harm done to any of the passengers. The passengers were, my august visitor, Leonora, my elder brother, Joe, my driver, Attoh, and myself.

The trekking that I had to do as district medical officer was quite extensive. Most of the roads were laterite roads. They weren't tarred and, therefore, there was a good deal of reddish dust. Every time I came back from trek I looked as if I had been sprayed with reddish brown powder. My coverage went as far afield as Juabeso, 104 miles from Dunkwa, and near the Ivorian border. I paid a couple of visits to that place during my stay at Dunkwa. There was a dispensary there manned by a pharmacist and a couple of nurses.

Needless to say, as the only District Medical Officer manning the Government Hospital, the only time that I was free really was when I was out of the station visiting Kumasi, Accra or Cape Coast; otherwise I was expected to be on call 24 hours a day. There was one interesting case which I must mention. An old lady approaching 70 was brought in comatose from Ayanfuri village, 10 miles from Dunkwa. She was deeply unconscious and all signs on examination and the history given by relatives pointed to the fact that she had meningitis. She was very ill. Fortunately, at that time there was a good supply of penicillin, so after I confirmed the diagnosis, I did a lumbar puncture and administered large doses of penicillin into the cerebro spinal space. After 24 hours I could see that there was some improvement. However, the relatives felt that nothing could be done. The patient had been there a whole day and she looked the same to them so they wanted to take her away. I could not really resist, but I told them that the treatment she was getting was her only hope of recovery. She would not get better if she was removed from the hospital. So they gave me another 24 hours. At the end of 24 hours, one could see definite signs of improvement, signs of regaining consciousness and coming round. Within a week the patient was completely conscious and she went home with them in a couple of weeks from the time of her admission to the hospital. I was told later that her relatives had prepared everything for her burial. They had a coffin and everything. This incident, I think, in a way reinforced the confidence which the population had in orthodox medical treatment.

It was at Dunkwa that I had my first experience, as an adult, of being really ill. I had jaundice and I became very weak with fever and was obliged to stop work and rest at home for almost six weeks. During that time, the Principal Medical Officer in Cape Coast sent a locum in the person of the late Dr. Neequaye Robertson to come and man the hospital. After six weeks, I was well enough to resume work. Since then I have always felt that, considering the amount of work required of the district medical officers, working round the clock, and the variety of diseases that they were exposed to, it was amazing that they were protected from succumbing to a number of diseases. The Lord in a way protects us and keeps us fit so that we can look after our patients and do the Lord's work!

During the course of Leonora's visit, I had the opportunity to join her in Accra for a weekend which enabled us to go round to meet everybody, or rather, as many people who were important to me as I thought she should meet. But she spent most of the time at Dunkwa. Fortunately, at that time, my late Aunt, Auntie Lizzy (Mrs. Elzabeth Chinery) was visiting so that she was at Dunkwa most of the time that Leonora was there. During the visit, we really had the chance to talk about the future, and what I was particularly interested to know was whether from what she had seen going round, Accra, Akuapem, and then Cape Coast, Sekondi and now Dunkwa, Sefwi Wiawso and what she had seen of the country, this was the place where she would really like to spend the rest of her life. I could see that she had no aversion to making the Gold Coast her permanent home sometime in the future.

All too soon, the time came for her to leave because she had to go back to the University for the new academic year. On that day, I took her in my car to Takoradi. Fortunately, there were some important people whom I knew and who were also travelling. I met on board the late Mr. Justice Quarshie-Idun and two other people; so I was quite happy that she was going back in the company of people that I knew. The following day, I immediately sent a telegram to my bank in Edinburgh asking them to transfer a sum of money, equal to double the return fare that she had paid, to her account. Of course, she did not know this before she left but when she arrived she got a letter from me by air awaiting her asking her to buy an engagement ring which she fancied and then send the bill to me. I immediately got a letter from her by air to say that I had a very unusual way of proposing marriage and she wanted me to know that she had accepted it with all pleasure!

Leonora made such a deep impression on my mother, my family and friends that they wanted to know how soon we were planning to get married. Mrs. Ofuatey-Cudjoe, especially, was keen to know how soon the wedding bells would be ringing! She was disappointed when I said we had to wait another year because Leonora had one more year at the University to finish her degree, but I would assure them that as soon as she graduated she would come straight to Ghana to be married, and there was no question of her going home to the United States before we got married. These were the plans that, God-willing, we hoped would be fulfilled, so they should pray for us. I must say that all these happened really to set my mind at rest because I was afraid that there might be some sort of grudging approval, or hidden resistance somewhere. Not that it would have made any difference to me and my plans for the future because to me all that mattered really was what Leonora also wanted. I thanked God that everything really happened according to His will.

I had said earlier that I was awaiting a sign from the Lord before taking the decision. Clearly, the sign was that Leonora, without any prompting from anybody, on her own volition, had paid a return ticket and come down to the Gold Coast to look round and, of course, to see me again. All these to me were the Lord's way of telling me that here was somebody who cared, and provided she was prepared really to make the Gold Coast her home, she was the one for my future. So I had an unusual feeling of contentment. One very important matter had been settled as far as I was concerned, and I felt quite sure, and Leonora later confirmed this, that for her too a firm decision about marrying me in the future set her mind at rest and made her last year at the University a lot easier for her. That feeling of uncertainty about the future had been removed, knowing that it was in the Gold Coast that she would come to settle for the rest of her life, and satisfied that she had actually seen conditions in the Gold Coast, had actually met my family and friends and, on the whole, she liked what she saw. As a result things moved smoothly for her in her final year.

Although Leonora's real parents were both alive and living in Miami, Florida, it was her Aunt Rachel, who had adopted her from the age of six and brought her up, and had been responsible for her education up to the University, whom she considered her *de facto* mother. The next thing for me to do was to write to Aunt Rachel in New York to inform her of the plans which Leonora and I had and the decision that we had taken about the future, also that she might not see her immediately after her graduation. We had arranged that she would come to the Gold Coast for us to get married and then as soon as possible, both of us would come over to New York to meet her people. In response I got a very nice and warm letter from Aunt Rachel to say that she'd heard so much about me through Leonora in her letters; so much so that she felt as if she already knew me. From the tone of my letter she felt here was somebody who really loved Leonora and was prepared to look after her for the rest of her life; that Leonora's happiness was her primary concern that was the reason why on some occasions she had to do two jobs in order to make it possible for her to provide for Leonora and give her the best education possible. Needless to say, she gave her blessing to our plans and from that moment on I began to look forward to meeting this very precious lady; the opportunity to visit New York after I got married to Leonora.

Official policy regarding cost-recovery for health delivery in our hospitals allowed doctors working in Government health facilities to charge professional fees to certain categories of people. Broadly speaking, there were the categories such as children, lactating mothers, all children of school-going age, students in secondary schools, teacher training colleges, universities and public servants. All these were supposed to have free treatment. Apart from that any other person, privately-employed people and farmers were liable to pay professional fees to the doctor. Of course there was a very wide section of the population who were unemployed and anyone who was prepared to be categorized as a pauper could get free medical care. This meant that at the end of the month the hospital was able to collect a certain amount of money from the professional fees for the doctor, which was available to be shared among the hospital staff. The fees were really meant as professional fees for the doctor but, of course, since the doctor could not work alone without the support of the other members of the hospital staff, what usually happened was that the doctor took a certain percentage - at least that was my practice - of the professional fees, and the rest was shared among the hospital staff, so that every category of staff got something to supplement his monthly salary. This was a sort of incentive for health workers.

Frankly speaking, if doctors were expected to rely on their monthly salaries only, the brain drain would have started a very long time ago. I cannot imagine the average doctor undergoing the stresses and strains and the long hours of work, the responsibilities, the risk to life and health working at what really even at that time amounted to a mere pittance of a salary, without the welcome supplement from the professional fees that were charged. Therefore, despite all the work that one had to do, there was a certain measure of compensation which made one feel that one was not being exploited. At a point in time subsequently the professional fees were abolished and were replaced by what was called "allowance in lieu of private practice" for doctors. In a way, since then, there hasn't really been peace on the health delivery labour front. Doctors, nurses, pharmacists, hospital and all categories of health care delivery staff since the abolition of the private fees have not been satisfied and there has been much instability. The resultant brain drain now continues to assume alarming proportions.

There were other unusual conditions under which the district medical officer had to work. Unlike big hospitals like the Kumasi Central Hospital or Korlebu where food for patients was provided by the hospital, the patients in the district hospital were expected to be given food by their relatives, except in a few cases where the patient had to be given special diet because of the nature of his disease. For this reason the patient's relatives were allowed free access to them in the hospital. Indeed, there were facilities available for cooking by these relatives. This meant that on the hospital compound, there was free flow of human traffic. It was not unusual, for example, to hear a relative shouting across the compound to another relative just as they did in their villages, thus creating a certain amount of nuisance, inevitably. Also, a patient might be given food which he should not really be eating. There had been instances where a patient, who had had a fairly major abdominal operation, within a few days, was being given heavy solid food by his relatives. The nurses and doctors had to observe strict surveillance on the relatives and the type of food they gave to the patient. Because it was useful to have the relatives of the ill-patient around who would alert the nurse on any change in the patient's condition, it was also not unusual to find a patient's relatives sleeping under the bed of the patient. Of course, given all these circumstances, hospital staff had to put up with a certain amount of interference by patients' relations. Interference in the sense of the relatives doing things which they were not supposed to do. The nurses' eyes were, therefore, always on them.

By April 1952, I had completed a two-year tour of duty and was therefore entitled to annual leave. Indeed, I should have taken my leave in 1951 but because of the exigencies of the service, I could not do that. One might, of course, say that my being confined to bed for 6 weeks when I had jaundice was more or less one way of nature forcing me to take some rest. Sometime at the beginning of March, therefore, I received a letter from the Ministry of Health asking me to get myself in readiness to proceed on leave by the middle of April. At that time I had to ponder over the previous 15 months and to take stock of what I had been able to achieve. There was no doubt that from the point of view of work, there had been work galore. There was never a dull moment. There was also no doubt that within that short space of time, I had gained enormous practical experience in all fields of medicine. There was no doubt at all also that I had done a good deal of operative surgery and that I had gained independent experience in the management of surgical cases, especially trauma, and also added to my experience in the field of obstetrics and gynaecology.

I had also managed to build upon the firm foundation of tropical medicine which Dr. Hawe had given me at Korlebu. All told, therefore, I felt more confident in my profession and looked forward after my leave to be posted to a hospital where the surgical facilities would be better to enable me to do more major operations. Quite unknown to me at that time, whilst I was at Dunkwa, a certain young boy in elementary school was drawing inspiration from me, and looking forward to one day becoming a doctor himself and playing the sort of role which I was playing at that time. I was quite gratified to know that many years afterwards, this young boy not only became a doctor but rose rapidly to the very top of his profession, a professor in one of our Medical Schools and the President of the Ghana Medical Associations. So history in a way was repeating itself in the same way that many years before Dr. Charles Easmon had inspired me, so at that material time I was also inspiring at least one young lad. I am happy to note that his aspirations came true for him and that senior members of the profession will continue to inspire and encourage young men and women to become members of our honorable profession.

On the political front, the year 1951, marked a very important turning point in the history of the Gold Coast. When I arrived in 1950 Kwame Nkrumah was in jail as a political prisoner, having been convicted for allegedly agitating and inciting people to violence. A couple of years before, he had formed his Convention People's Party which had grown rapidly into a country-wide Party. It was no surprise, therefore, that the CPP, won the general elections that year under a new Constitution. Nkrumah had to be released from jail to become the Leader of Government Business. For the first time, the Legislature was completely Africanized and the cabinet was all African with the exception of the portfolios of Finance and Defense and Interior. I believe it was a notable year in the history of Ghana. Expatriates in the country had taken note of passing events and were keenly aware of developments and the way in which these political developments would affect their own future in the country.

As an aside, I may note here that the Denkyira Traditional Council under the leadership of the Denkyirahene, who had become my very good friend, petitioned the Medical Department to extend my tour at Dunkwa. They had been very satisfied with my work and they thought transferring me from Dunkwa would rob them of the services of a good doctor. As usual, they received a short and very polite reply from the Medical Department to say that it was good they had been satisfied with Dr. Anfom's work and that it was felt that people in other parts of the country were also entitled to the services of Dr. Anfom in the future. For that reason, and for reasons of equity, the Medical Department could not really accede to the Traditional Council's request.

## First Leave of Absence

Accordingly, sometime during the first week of April 1952, I packed bag and baggage and said farewell to all my friends at Dunkwa and went down to Accra on my leave and to await further instructions. I believe at that time I had approximately two months' leave and, in spite of everything, I really felt tired and needed some rest; rest during which I could really sit down and plan my future and contemplate the different paths along which the future might lead me. I stayed in Accra with my relative and good friend, Mr. Vincent Richter to whom I had been a house-boy during my childhood. I stayed in the out-house and from there I went out and spent short periods at various places, including our family house at Mampong-Akuapem. During that period, I did a ten-day locum for Dr. Oku Ampofo who had a practice at Mampong and dispensaries in various places in the Akuapem area which he visited from time to time.

It was during this ten-day period that my interest in traditional medical practice was aroused. In Dr. Oku Ampofo's absence I had a few traditional practitioners with whom Dr. Ampofo had been on very good terms bringing different kinds of medicinal herbs to show him. I gathered later that Dr. Ampofo had for some time been doing research into these medicinal herbs and their application and had established a very good rapport with the traditional medical practitioners. Dr. Oku Ampofo's interest was sustained and it led eventually to the establishment by Government of the Centre for Scientific Research into Plant Medicine at Mampong. This centre was established when I was Vice-Chancellor at the University of Science and Technology. It was at the tail end of my Vice-Chancellorship of UST and so I was able to help the process along. When the Council was first set up, I became the first Chairman of the Council of the Centre for Scientific Research into Plant Medicine, Mampong-Akuapem.

Just before leaving Dunkwa, I had acquired a brand new Opel Capitan Saloon Car and so I took the opportunity to visit my relatives in Lomé. My aunt, Mercy, my father's elder sister, had married an Olympio from Lomé, and their daughters were all in Lome, so I thought it would be a good idea to visit them. The youngest had married a Cornelius Santos. It was a wedding which I had the privilege of attending in the New Year of 1936, so I looked forward to seeing Lomé again and to a reunion with my cousins and others whom I had known in Lomé. For the trip, I had to drive myself as my driver, Attoh, was having problems with his vision. I was accompanied by my cousins, Willie and Phillip Evans, and our nephew, Kenneth Evans-Lutterot, who at that time was at school at Achimota. It was a very interesting trip. My cousins had never been to Lomé and it was a new experience for them. None of us spoke or understood French. All the same we were able to get by. What I recall is that we had to rush to catch the last ferry at Teflé, which left at 6 o'clock. This was long before the Sogakope bridge was built. After crossing the Volta about half an hour later, we had a very severe rain storm, so for a couple of hours, I had to drive most of the way in very heavy rain. There was no air-conditioner in the car and at times we had to crawl at snail's pace, or stop until we were able to see where we were going. But it was a very interesting journey and we did not arrive in Lomé till 9.30 in the evening. We drove around looking for Ada House which was Mr. Caeser Olympio's house. After several enquiries, we were able to get there. We were then taken to my cousin, Mrs. Josephine Santos.The visit was most unexpected, but she did everything to give us accommodation and to make us happy for a whole week. It was at a time when her husband was away on duty in France. So our holiday in Lomé, in a French-speaking African country, was a very unusual but welcome change for all of us .

   I recall that whilst spending some time at Mampong I went on a day's trip to Kibi where my good friend, Dr. Ellis Fleischer Djoleto and his wife Muriel, were stationed. I arrived at the hospital at a time when Ellis was in the theatre and was actually performing a hernia operation. It was a pleasant surprise for him to see me .As soon as I entered the theatre, he turned round and said, "Emmanuel, come and take over! "I've been very tired and you're on leave resting and not doing anything. Why don't you come and take over?" So we just laughed and I stood and watched him performing the rest of the operation. After he had finished we went home for lunch after which I spent a couple of hours in Kibi. The visit was very instructive for me because I had just finished a tour at my first district hospital. Kibi, I believe, was the second or third district hospital for Ellis Djoleto. We compared notes about our experiences and I came away carrying very useful tips from my senior colleague - tips about how to handle patients and their relatives in a district hospital, especially one's encounter with traditional authorities and other organizations. This was at the time when the doctor's position was an important one in the District. Whenever the District Commissioner was away, the medical officer was required to step in his shoes and act as district commissioner. This did not happen often, but at least on paper, that was supposed to be the arrangement and I got some very interesting stories from Ellis Djoleto about what happened to him, and his experiences at the different stations where he'd been.

# CHAPTER 14

# TARKWA

About half way through my leave, I got a letter from the Medical Department asking me to get myself in readiness to proceed on transfer to Tarkwa in the mining district of the Western Region. As I have indicated earlier, I was hoping that after my first tour I would be working in a bigger hospital. But the Director of Medical Services had explained to me that they were really very short of staff and that there were certain hospitals that they felt needed doctors who had good experience, especially those who had experience in surgery, and would be able to handle most of the surgical cases and other problems and that in Tarkwa, apart from the district hospital there were smaller hospitals - The Tarkwa Mine's Hospital, the Nsuta Manganese Mines' Hospital and the Aboso Mines' Hospital. In a way, therefore, the Tarkwa Hospital would be acting as a first point of reference for certain cases and he thought it would be useful experience for me. So with this explanation, I did not protest, and at the end of April, I packed bag and baggage and proceeded to Tarkwa.

Now what really surprised me was the lack of planning because Dunkwa was quite near Tarkwa and it would have saved a lot of energy and money if the decision to transfer me to Tarkwa had been made earlier, so that some of my heavy luggage could have gone straight from Dunkwa to Tarkwa, but this was not what happened. I felt a bit annoyed about this because it entailed an awful lot of bother carrying things round, a situation which was likely to lead to damage to personal and other property. Be that as it may, when the time came, I was prepared to go to Tarkwa to open an important chapter in my life and also in the service of the Medical Department.

With his failing eye sight, it wasn't advisable to retain my driver, Attoh, so I could not take him to Tarkwa and he fully understood this. I managed to get him a job with one of my friends, not as a driver, but as a security man. Then there was Lantei, my house-boy. As I indicated earlier, Lantei went to Dunkwa with me at an age when he should have been in school. After fifteen months, on my return home, I felt that something should be done. So I left him in Accra and made arrangements for him to attend school. Needless to say, he did not survive long. He spent just a couple of years and then dropped out.

Now, my relative, Mr. James Allotey, or Ataa Allotey, as we called him, was at that time the caretaker of our family house, Evans Family House – at Mampong-Akuapem. Ataa Allotey was a very experienced driver. He had over twenty years' driving experience. At that time he had no job as a driver and no vehicle, and I was quite surprised when he volunteered to go to Tarkwa with me. Of course, I thought, well, he might be rusty and I had to be careful in employing someone who, however long his experience, had not been driving regularly for some years. However, I took a chance and agreed to take him, provided adequate arrangements could be made for the security at Mampong. He left his family and some of his young children in the house.

My half-sister, Juliana Anfom, or Auntie Okailey, as she was popularly known ,was at that time dealing in textiles. As she was not doing particularly well she felt that she could come with me because 1952 was the year that Leonora would be finishing her course in the University and then come to the Gold Coast for us to get married. Apart from everything else it was very important that I had a reliable person to be with me, somebody who would look after the house, cook for me, and, when Leonora arrived she would have somebody dependable, a relation, as a companion. Subsequently, God-willing, she would be able to help with any fruits of the marriage! So together with Ataa Allotey and Auntie Okailey I went to Tarkwa. I did not bother to look for a steward boy for the house. I thought that when I got to Tarkwa, it would be possible to recruit household staff. Indeed, it might be possible even to take over the house help of the doctor that I was going to relieve. Fortunately, this was what happened.

Tarkwa was a bigger town than Dunkwa. The hospital was bigger and better endowed with better facilities. It had no running water, but it had electricity. The laboratory was better equipped and, above all, it had an X'ray machine which meant that I could do a lot more. At

Dunkwa, I had to refer cases that required to be X-ray to Kumasi, but now, with an X-ray machine of my own, I would be able to have many cases X-rayed and dealt with myself. This was something I was looking forward to. I had heard that I was going to take over from Dr. Chelmicki. Dr. Chelmicki was a Pole, who had been in the country for a few years and was resigning to come to Accra and take over the Nima Clinic on the Ring Road.

I had not met Chelmicki personally but I knew of him and was pleasantly surprised to find that he was a very quiet and courteous gentleman. Obviously, someone who was about my age and who had had a good experience in tropical medicine, perhaps not much experience in surgery, but he was an experienced doctor and from his handing-over notes and the manner in which he managed patients whom I saw in the wards and from the records, I knew that the hospital had been in good hands. Clearly, this was a challenge for me to be able to maintain and, if possible, surpass the standard set by Dr. Chelmicki.

Tarkwa, of course, was accessible by road and by rail, and in that respect it was not as isolated as Dunkwa. The facilities that I had in Tarkwa were far superior to those available to me at Dunkwa, so I could really do more. One advantage of Tarkwa too was that I could drive quite easily to Sekondi, Effia-Nkwanta Hospital to see and confer with the surgical specialist there. In any case, all major surgical cases which were not within my competence, I referred to Effia-Nkwanta Hospital. At first the specialist there was a New Zealander, Dr. W. R. Phillips, but within the year, he was replaced by Dr. Charles Easmon whom I have referred to in other parts of this narrative. The arrangement was perfect for me. What happened was that whenever I could afford the time I ran down to Sekondi to assist Dr. Easmon in major operations. In some cases I was actually given the opportunity to do the operation while Dr. Easmon assisted me. In this way, I was able to improve upon my surgical skills. So in Tarkwa, the volume of work was really high in the sense that the smaller hospitals around, fed me with straightforward surgical cases like hernias, hydroceles and hemorrhoids and other abdominal emergencies. I was kept busy there. Anything that was beyond me I sent to Sekondi and I was able to follow-up some of them right through to the end.

For me it was a perfect setting, I had a large measure of independence and at the same time I always had the avenue for referring cases to my senior colleagues and it helped me to acquire additional skills. This was very important for me as in a way, it made up for the fact that I was not working in a major hospital as I had hoped, but at the same time the set up was such that it made up for my not being able to work in a big hospital. In a way, it was even better because if I had worked in a big hospital I would have had fewer cases to operate on.

From the professional point of view, the reader should not forget that I still had before me a major obstacle, that is, the Final or Part II of the examination for the Diploma of Fellowship of the Royal College of Surgeons of Edinburgh. I, therefore, had to work out a system which, within the framework of two or three years, would make it possible for me to be ready to sit for that examination. The way things were, it was not possible for me to do any systematic reading, but as I have indicated before, all I did was that every case which came which was a little bit out of the ordinary, I went back to the textbook and read it over and over again, so that by the end of two years or so after putting the pieces together I had really covered a whole lot of ground with just a few patches to be filled.

As at Dunkwa, I was very fortunate to have a cadre of very experienced and hard-working senior nurses to work with. Mr. Alfred Gizo, the chief nurse, for example, was a very experienced nurse, the type of person who would even hold the fort in the hospital seeing to straightforward cases and calling in the doctor only for difficult cases. I am now thinking of the occasional situation when I had to be out of the station for some days and I had arranged for a locum doctor during my absence. He might well be the doctor from the main Tarkwa Mines, at Abontiakoo, or the one from Aboso or from Nsuta. So with this solid nursing leadership I did not feel so uncomfortable when I was absent from the station. Of the female nurses, there was Jane Hayfron, State Registered Nurse and State Registered Midwife; a very knowledgeable and hardworking nurse with good control of the staff under her. Jane Hayfron, incidentally, was the elder sister of Sally Hayfron who later became Mrs Sally Mugabe, First Lady of Zimbabwe. Then there were other senior midwives whom I could always rely on and there was Mr. Quarcoo, a pharmacist, a very experienced person, and finally a radiographer in charge of the X'Ray Department who was also very good indeed. He produced some excellent pictures and, of course, I had to read the pictures and interpret them. Because of the quality of pictures it made things a lot easier for me and I was able for example to do diagnostic procedures such as investigation of gall bladder function,

X-ray of the chest, barium meal or barium enema and other investigation of the digestive tract, and, of course, fractures, and dislocation of joints. In a nutshell, the fact that the hospital had an x-ray machine really enhanced the quality of work which we were able to do there.

Mercifully, there was hardly any trekking that had to be done. It would almost have been impossible because the volume of work in Tarkwa was a lot heavier that it was at Dunkwa. I had the responsibility for a district which stretched to as far as Enchi. But I recall that during my two and a quarter years' stay in Tarkwa I only visited Enchi on a couple of occasions. Like Sefwi Wiaso, Enchi had a pharmacist or a government dispenser at that time at a health post from where he referred difficult cases to hospital, in particular Tarkwa Government Hospital.

Apart from the fact that Tarkwa was a much larger town than Dunkwa, I also spent a longer time there, two and a quarter years whereas I spent only fifteen months at Dunkwa. From the social life point of view I made quite a wide circle of friends. First there was Mr. E. K. Dadson, the politician and businessman. At the time of my arrival he was the Member of Parliament for that area, but lost his seat to Mr. Ocran, a private pharmacist there, during a later election. There was no sizeable Presbyterian Church. There were a catechist and a primary school there, so I associated myself with them. The catechist was Mr. Mate, later Rev. Mate who shortly before he died was the district priest in-charge of Dodowa Presbyterian Church. The Methodist Minister was Reverend Graham, and the Anglican Father was Fr. Lemaire, a young man at that time who years later became Anglican Archbishop of the Province of West Africa. He was then a young priest at the Abontiakoo Parish. There were visits from Archdeacon Elliot, from Sekondi. We also had visits by the magistrates from Sekondi, Mr. Samuel Azu Crabbe, and later for a short period, Mr. Lanquaye Bannerman, Senior Magistrate. Both subsequently became Chief Justices of Ghana.

On my arrival at Tarkwa and before I settled down, I was taken by Mr. E. K. Dadson to pay a courtesy call on the Omanhene. I believe it was Nana Gyan Kokora at the time. Then I also called on Mr. and Mrs. Mills, a very important couple who had been in Tarkwa for a very long time and, throughout my stay they were very kind to me. There were also Mr. and Mrs. Brookman Amissah. Mr. Brookman-Amissah was a manager of the United African Company (UAC). Mrs. Brookman Amisah was a de Heer and younger sister of Nana Sir Tsibu Darku, Omanhene of Assin Atandasu. Then there was my old friend, Mr. J.

O. T. Agyeman and his wife Felicia. Mr. J. O. T. Agyeman, an old Achimotan, was also a manager at UAC. At that material time, I think, he was still the president of the Old Achimotan Association. He was, incidentally, the father of Nana Konadu Agyeman Rawlings, the immediate past First Lady of Ghana. Then there was Mr. F. O. Squire, who was the manager of the Methodist Book Depot at Tarkwa and Mr. Alfred Hutchful, a businessman and the father of Kweku Hutchful who became very prominent in Christian circles and died tragically just a couple of years ago. Then there were Mr. F. D Laryea who was Assistant Government Agent, Mr. G. L. Markwei, also Assistant Government Agent, and Mr. Lantei Mills, a Junior UAC Manager .

The Senior Officers of the police hierarchy, whom I came to know, became very important and went on in later years to hold the highest posts in the Police Service. When I arrived, the Superintendent of Police was an expatriate, David Lavell. David and his wife, Maryse, were a friendly couple. David was a real gentleman, a very courteous police officer. The late Erasmus T. Madjitey succeeded David Lavell. Madjitey, became the first Ghanaian Commissioner of Police. As a deputy to Mr. Madjitey and Assistant Superintendent of Police was Mr. J. W. K. Harlley. Mr. Harlley, as we know, went on subsequently to become the first Inspector General of Police. Then there was Mr. Ben Fordjour, who also rose rapidly through the ranks, especially in the Special Branch, and was at one time Ambassador to Togo. All these were police officers who were with me at Tarkwa at one time or another during my stay there.

Mr. Alex Quaison-Sackey came to Tarkwa shortly after my own arrival in Tarkwa. Alex was a Labour Officer. The Labour Department was a fairly new Department in Government and the senior people in that Department were relatively young within the Civil Service and mostly university graduates. Alex and I became good friends and there was a time when I felt that he really valued my opinion and advice. This was the time when, with the impending independence for the country, the then Nkrumah Government, that is, the Self-Government government, decided to start training officers for the foreign service. The way was open for brilliant Ghanaian university graduates to offer themselves to be selected for training as foreign service officers. Alex was very much interested in this proposition. At the same time, being quite senior in the Labour Department, he could foresee within a few years rising almost to the very top as Chief Labour Officer. He had the option, therefore, of just remaining in the Labour Department or offering himself for selection for the training for future Foreign Service of Ghana.

I recall that Alex came to see me one evening and we sat through from 9 o'clock for about six hours weighing the options and examining the pros and cons to enable him to take a decision. It was very tempting for him to decide to remain with the Labour Department where his prospects were very bright. He indeed had a problem of choice, choosing between a career in the Labour Department and a foreign service career. On the other hand, though the foreign service was new, it was also clear that the competition was going to be very keen because Government would be looking out for very bright young men and women and getting to the top eventually was bound to be more laborious. I am glad to say that eventually, the long-term view prevailed. Subsequent events really proved Alex right in the decision he took because we know that after a very short period of service he was appointed Ghana's Representative to the United Nations and he had the distinction of being the First African to become President (or Chairman) of the General Assembly of the United Nations. He also held important posts subsequently culminating in his becoming Minister for Foreign Affairs of Ghana.

## Marriage

That summer (1952), Leonora completed her course in Edinburgh and graduated a Master of Arts in July. The plan was that she would come straight to the Gold Coast after graduation and it would be sometime after we got married that both of us would visit the United States. Now, there was quite a lot for her to do before leaving the United Kingdom, involving winding up her affairs. To this end, there were also problems with obtaining a visa as an American citizen who would in due course become a Ghanaian. I must say that the Superintendent of Police at Tarkwa at that time was very useful. He worked very hard with the immigration and visa papers and all that was required. He took over completely and expedited the whole process of Leonora's coming down to the Gold Coast, so that round about mid-October she came by air. I could not go to Accra to meet her but, of course, all arrangements were made. This time she was to stay with Sir Arku Korsah. Mr. Justice Arku Korsah, then a Judge of the Supreme Court. Sir Arku Korsah's daughter, Anne, had been a roommate and a friend of Leonora's in Edinburgh for a couple of years. She was, therefore, like a sister; so the Korsah's were very pleased to have Leonora staying with them because at this time Justice Korsah looked upon Leonora as one of his daughters.

I was, therefore, very happy when he graciously consented to give Leonora away on her wedding day. On the morning of 13th December 1952, Leonora and I got married at the Achimota School Chapel. This was long before the Aggrey Chapel was built. The original school chapel was in the main Administration Building on the top floor. The officiating minister was Rev. Fr. Perry, the School Chaplain, and the pianist for the wedding was the late Robert Kwami, who had been one of our music teachers at Achimota. It was quite a small wedding on a Saturday morning. There were, however, quite a number of important members of society there, apart from my family members and members of the medical profession. Refreshments were at the Achimota School Staff Club.

We spent our first night in our family house in James Town, the Evans Family House where I was born, in quite a noisy part of town. Leonora was quite amused when at 6.30 the following morning, one of the old ladies in the house came and knocked on the door, her excuse for the early disturbance being that she had come to congratulate us! Leonora found this very odd indeed. Well, it was the beginning of a long string of customs and usage that she was going to have to get used to. The following day, we proceeded on our honeymoon. I had taken just one week's leave and we spent a couple of nights in Kumasi. The interesting thing about the drive to Kumasi was that the late Mr. and Mrs. Assimaku-Idun had invited us to stay with them and had organized a party for us on the first evening at about six o'clock. Having started late, we were hurrying, trying to get there in good time before the party. On this occasion we were so deeply engrossed in conversation that when we got to Nsawam, Ado-Agyiri, I instinctively made the left turn towards Swedru. It was not until we had driven for almost an hour that we realized we were supposed to be heading for Kumasi and not Tarkwa. So we had to drive all the way back to Nsawam and then proceed on the Kumasi road. Needless to say, by this time, we had wasted so much time on the road that when we got to the party some guests who had been waiting for a long time had left, thinking that we would not be arriving. Fortunately for us, many of them were people whom I knew, and were eager to see this unique bride from the United

States, so they stayed on even though we got there after 8 o'clock. It was highly embarrassing for the Assimaku-Iduns but then it was understandable for love birds to be absent-minded when in an amorous state!

After Kumasi, we stopped at Bibiani where my good friend, Mr. B. M. Kufuor, a timber magnate, had a bungalow. We spent a couple of days with him at the bungalow at Bibiani. When I was at Dunkwa, one of the friends I made, Mr. B. M. Kufuor, came to Dunkwa to do business from time to time. From Bibiani we drove to Tarkwa. I did not want any pomp and circumstance or any fanfare with the welcome. Therefore, we took pains not to advertise our arrival, except for the members of my household and the senior staff at the hospital. Despite this attempt to keep everything secret, when we arrived at the house, there was a big welcoming party - all my friends whom I have mentioned already, for example, there were Quaison-Sackey, Superintendent Lavell and Mr. F. D. Laryea. Practically, all my close friends at Tarkwa were there to meet us. It was a very joyous occasion. Of course, they had met Leonora before the marriage as she had spent some time at Tarkwa. But there were others who had not met her and for these people we organized a small party a few days after our arrival. Leonora quickly settled in and interested herself in the activities of the Peoples' Educational Association (PEA). Alex Quaison-Sackey was also very much involved and I recall that there were a series of lectures in which Leonora and some of the teachers and senior civil servants participated. That really kept her busy, which was good because as medical officer I was very busy and right from the start, she knew that she wouldn't really see much of me. She, therefore, did her best to keep herself busy with these extra-curricular activities.

Now there was a an interesting development. Barely a month after Leonora's arrival, I got a letter from Mr Bartels, headmaster of Mfantsipim School, saying that he had been informed that Leonora for her masters degree did modern languages and he wondered whether she could come to Cape Coast to help them with teaching French in the lower forms. Of course, this was something that Leonora could do, but it would have meant her spending most of her time in Cape Coast and only coming to Tarkwa on occasional week-ends. The question of my going to Cape Coast for a week-end was completely out. I was so terribly busy that this was something that the Medical Department would not countenance. Regretfully, therefore, I had to write back to Mr. Bartels to explain the situation. Here was someone who was far away from home. I was practically the only friend she could rely on in the country. She had just newly arrived and had not come for employment. Well, she had come for employment – the greatest career of all – marriage. But it was not fair, I thought, to both of us that we should start our marriage living miles apart. I did not think it would augur well for the future. So, much as I would have liked her to help the school, I must respectfully decline. I got a very nice letter from Mr. Bartels to say that he perfectly understood the situation and he wished us well in our marriage.

Leonora was someone who made friends very easily. She, therefore, settled down quite quickly. After a short time, I was quite surprised when she showed me two short plays that she had written, one called "The Letter Writer" and the other "The Consulting Room." "The Letter Writer" was based on her experiences of what she had observed, from the gentlemen who usually sat outside post offices, especially in the Central Post Office in Accra writing letters for illiterate members of the population and the manner in which sometimes the messages were twisted when translated into English. It was indeed a very interesting and gallant effort and extremely humorous. The sort of messages the clients gave and the sort of distortions that sometimes took place in the translation and how it ended. "The Consulting Room" was based on little anecdotes from the consulting room as told my me. The sort of answers patients gave when their histories were being taken. For example, "How long have you had this headache?" Answer: "Well I have had it since my uncle died", thus forcing one to probe further into the history of where, when, and how the death took place and if possible relate it to events natural, or otherwise. "I have had it for a very long time, doctor, round about the time that the kukrudu took place" or "when Nana Asantehene came back from the Seychelles." Leonora had managed to get a collection of interesting situations with questions and answers in "The Consulting Room." "The Letter Writer" was adapted for Radio by the late Efua Sutherland in 1953.

Now, just as I did at Dunkwa, I got together some young graduates of our secondary schools or teacher training colleges, who were teaching in primary schools at Tarkwa, or junior civil servants, especially those who were interested, and encouraged the playing of hockey by buying hockey sticks and giving them out either free or on very favourable terms of payment and getting the game of hockey going at Tarkwa. As fate would have it, my old friend of Achimota days, Kofi Atiemo, who actually taught me how to play hockey, was transferred to Tarkwa at that time and was working at the Department of Community Development. He and I together worked to promote the game. It was there that we discovered Ato Hayford, who was a teacher in one of the schools. Ato Hayford, was an excellent hockey player and it is noteworthy that in 1953, the three of us, Ato, Kofi Atiemo and myself, were selected to play for the Gold Coast Team and from then on and for a decade or more we were regular members of the National Team until my retirement from active hockey in 1962. First of all hockey was threatening my professional work by the amount of time it took and also by the physical risks I was taking. What decided me finally was when I had a knock on my right thumb causing a crack fracture which put me out of action for six long weeks!.

## Arrival Of Our First Child

The following year, 1953, when we were expecting our first baby, Leonora had to go to Accra about three weeks before the expected date of delivery for the terminal stages of ante-natal care. On the morning of 18th October 1953, at about 5.30 I had a telephone call from my uncle, Dr. Charles Reindorf, to announce that my wife had had a bouncing baby boy at the Ridge Hospital, Accra. The doctor who supervised this great event was my good friend, Dr. George. So that morning, I telephoned him at the Ridge Hospital and he gave me a situation report. Mother and baby were fine. At the time, I was so busy that I could not really come down to Accra immediately. So I decided that as soon as Leonora was able to get to the telephone, a call was put through and I spoke to her. She was very happy with the way she had been treated at the hospital, red carpet treatment! I did not come down to Accra until Leonora and the baby were fit to travel.

Meanwhile, the usual out-dooring was performed on the eighth day. Leonora had an interesting account of what happened. On her return to Tarkwa, the Ga-Dangme Community there insisted that we had another out-dooring ceremony, which we did, with some modifications with regard to the ceremony in Accra. Leonora was intrigued and surprised that early in the morning, when it was so cold, a young baby, eight days old and stark naked would be put on the concrete floor for almost half a minute exposed to the elements as a part of the ceremony. According to her, when after our baby, named Nii Okai, was lifted up subsequently he quite irreverently did a little bit of fountain spraying right in the face of the old man who was performing the rites, and it always amused her as she thought it was a legitimate way of Nii Okai registering a protest! That was a custom which she thought was outmoded. So at Tarkwa we took care that this ceremony did not take place outside, but indoors, on the veranda, where Nii Okai had adequate protection. This was really the early stages when Leonora was being indoctrinated into some of our customs and traditions which she found rather bizarre. Even though she did not protest vehemently, she thought it was about time some customs were discarded and we often joked about these things.

As the year 1954 approached, I started thinking about the assignment which I had before me, viz, the completion of my specialist examination for the Post-Graduate Diploma of the Royal College of Surgeons of Edinburgh. Four years was enough time for me to go back to Edinburgh, so I started making arrangements for study leave. I started writing my application letters and also wrote to Edinburgh to register for the examination. Nii Okai was baptised early in the year 1954. Dr. Charles Easmon came over from Sekondi to be god-father to Nii Okai. That same day, my good friend and relative, Soas Jones Quartey (later Professor Jones Quartey) drove up to Tarkwa accompanied by an American Dental Surgeon practising in New York, by name Dr. Robert Lee. They were present at Nii Okai's baptism. The reason Soas brought Dr. Lee to Tarkwa was really for the latter to meet Leonora. Dr. Lee, who was a very staunch Pan-Africanist had been bitten by the bug of coming home to his roots in Africa. He therefore, wanted very much to talk to someone, a black-American living in the country. He was trying to make up his mind whether he should transfer or uproot himself from New York and come back to settle in his ancestral home in the Gold Coast. He therefore, needed to know the views of people who would tell him something which would make sense to him. He had a long chat with Leonora and, I think, you can guess what Leonora told him. As far as she was concerned, she was quite happy in the Gold Coast and if someone felt he wanted to come back to his roots, there should not be anything to stop him. It was for him to come and make the adaptation that would be needed.

My request for study leave was granted during the year 1954 after I had spent two years and a few months at Tarkwa. By this time I had my own earned leave of two months. Ten months were added to make it a one year study-leave for me to go back to Edinburgh to do what I had to do to become a Fellow of the Royal College of Surgeons of Edinburgh.

## Study Leave – Fellow of the Royal College of Surgeons, Endinburgh

In July 1954, together with Leonora and our baby Nii Okai, we set off from Takoradi on the Holland West African Line cargo boat MV "Congostroom" to go to the Untied Kingdom. The cargo boats were not like passenger boats which had precise schedules of departure and arrival. The schedule was very flexible and so a voyage which took a passenger boat twelve days, could easily take another three or four more days because of the uncertainty of cargo delivery when taking cargo from various stops on the way. In any case, I was not in a hurry. I needed much rest after Tarkwa. The voyage by the "Congostroom" took about sixteen days. We made quite a few stops: in Freetown, in Monrovia, Las Palmas and then le Havre in France. On board the ship, we had a certain interesting old Liberian called Blyden Roberts who joined the ship in Freetown. Despite the short acquaintance, just a couple of days, he gave us quite a bit of history of the founding of Liberia. We changed boats in Le Havre. The other boat, I have forgotten the name now, docked at Hull in the United Kingdom from where we went by train to Edinburgh.

We found the trip on the cargo boat quite relaxing. The accommodation was not as luxurious as on a passenger liner, but it was ample and there was just room for twelve passengers. Even then there were just six of us. It was something like home. The food was extremely good and abundant. Fortunately, none of us was seasick. The weather was perfect. So we really enjoyed the trip and arrived in the United

Kingdom nicely refreshed to start a new course. I had then registered at the College of Surgeons to attend a revision course for three months, October, November, and December. My plans were to take another three months, after the course, just studying by myself, going round the wards, putting finishing touches to my preparations for this great examination whose "mortality" rate was very high. Before we arrived in Edinburgh we had instructed an estate agency to look for lodgings for us. Guess where we got? Number 18 Warrender Park Terrace!, the address of my first digs in 1942 as a medical student. That was the digs where the landlady and landlord were very economical with the heating arrangements and I had to run away after two weeks. This time, of course, we had a whole apartment of three bed rooms with a living room and a dining room and kitchen on the first floor. It was a comfortable and spacious apartment which we were later on to share with my friend and classmate, J. K. Oddoye, who was a dentist with the Gold Coast Medical Service also on a post-graduate course in Edinburgh.

Time was of the essence and I was anxious that I should complete what I came to do in record time. So even before the course started in October, I had started visiting the Library of the Royal College of Surgeons, the College Museum and the wards of the Royal Infirmary to see patients. Luckily for me, some of my colleagues or contemporaries at the medical school were now clinical tutors at the Royal Infirmary. They were Hugh Dudley, who was a top student in surgery and J. Clark. So I started visiting the Infirmary and seeing patients. In the second week of October, the course of lectures and clinical instruction started.

With seven years' post-graduation experience, I found the lectures very interesting, I was more attentive in listening to these lectures. One interesting thing which I observed was that some of the lecturers or professors whom I thought were rather dull when I was an undergraduate, I now found extremely interesting. A good example was Sir Walter Mercer who lectured in Orthopedic Surgery. When I was an undergraduate, I found him extremely dull. I now found him very deep and highly informative. I suppose because, now, with the experience that I had I could really understand what he was saying. It might well be that when I was an under-graduate I felt he was talking above my head. I have already said that when I was at home, I found it difficult to do any systematic study. Now, with the revision lectures, everything seemed to be falling in place. Whatever gaps that were in my knowledge were being filled. So by the end of the course, I felt quite confident. All the same, I really needed time on my own to do some more leisurely review of what I had done, not only during the course of lectures but also the sort of practical experience that I had acquired since I qualified seven years previously. I found more time to visit the Royal Infirmary and I must say that I found the help of my friends, Dudley and Clark, extremely encouraging and useful.

At the end of March, I entered for the examination and, fortunately for me, despite the high casualty rate, I was able to pass the final examination at the first attempt. In January of 1955 in order for me to have some peace and quiet for what I had to do, I sent Leonora and Nii Okai to the States. After all, Leonora had not been home for almost seven years and she needed time with her people. So the plan was that after finishing I would join them in April. So in January I saw them off at Southampton and they boarded the "SS America", a very huge luxurious liner, for the States. It was possible for them to telephone from time to time from the States, so we kept in touch. As a precaution, of course, I booked my own passage for the first week of April 1955 and, as things turned out, I was able then to join them as planned.

For me the interesting thing about the examination was waiting for the results. The last bit of the examination was the oral examination and, to my delight, one of the two examiners was Mr. Tommy Millar FRCS, who was a great sports enthusiast and who was aware that I was a hockey blue in the University of Edinburgh and had actually seen me play. The other examiner was Professor Sir Ernest Rock Carling from Liverpool. What I discovered from the oral examination was that the examiners wanted to know how much I knew of course, but even more importantly, they wanted to know how prepared or competent I was to apply what I knew in the performance of my professional duties. Of course, Mr. Tommy Millar at that examination made things easy for me by the questions he asked, about my sporting days in the University. We started with quite an innocuous question, something related to the practice of surgery in the tropics. Once we got on it was as if I was giving them an account of the difficulties encountered in surgery, the types of cases, improvisation. We discussed the principles involved, and I suppose they got all that they wanted from me. In spite of all this, I was a little bit diffident. I thought I had done enough to pass but at the same time the history of the casualty rate of the final FRCS examination really inhibited me from premature rejoicing.

Incidentally, one thing which I noticed in comparing notes with candidates who were on the course with me, especially those who had been my contemporaries and who had been practising in the United Kingdom in hospitals, was the vast difference between the experience which I had acquired, including even the practical skills in operative surgery, compared with theirs. Whilst they had seen a lot done, relatively speaking they had not done much themselves.

Twenty-four hours after completing the oral examination the results were published. The following morning I received a letter in the post announcing the result. I was afraid to open the envelope, to see what had happened. Fortunately, at that time, even though Leonora was away from Edinburgh I had my friend, Kojo Oddoye, and his wife, Margaret who were sharing the flat with us, so after a long while when Margaret saw that I was being hesitant, she just snatched the envelope from me, opened it, and, lo and behold, I had passed! I need hardly describe the feeling that I had. It really meant that all the programme that we had arranged and the time-table were going according to plan and that it would be possible for me to travel in a few days to go and join Leonora and Nii Okai in America!

## CHAPTER 15

# THE UNITED STATES OF AMERICA
### (My First Visit)

Accordingly, during the first week of April, I boarded the French passenger liner "L'île de France", which took five days for the trans-Atlantic crossing. Even though it was just five days, it seemed like eternity, because I was eager to see Leonora and Nii Okai again. Even though Leonora received a telegram announcing the result, I was looking forward to really telling her myself! On board the ship, I met a young doctor, Dr. Clyde Rowe, who had just spent a year in France doing an internship in a French hospital. He worked in the Surgical Department of Harlem Hospital, so I gave him my telephone number and promised that I would look him up when I was in New York.

After about a week's rest, I paid my first visit to Harlem Hospital, where I made the acquaintance of Professor Aubrey Maynard, a very distinguished black professor of surgery of the Columbia University Medical School and Chief of Surgery in Harlem Hospital. He invited me to come on a few occasions for teaching ward rounds with students and residents. After some time, he suggested to me that perhaps I might want to come and join the staff at Harlem Hospital and work as one of his assistants — a situation which would give me teaching experience in the Columbia University Medical School where he was Professor. Of course, attractive as this offer was, I could not really accept it and when I discussed this with Leonora she would have none of it. She had been in the Gold Coast for a little over two years and she had seen the conditions under which I was working and the real need for my services in the Gold Coast. So the answer to Professor Maynard was "No". He had roots in the Bahamas, like Leonora, and therefore he fully understood my position and hoped that anytime I was in New York I would visit them in Harlem Hospital.

I may say that years after when the West African College of Surgeons was established and I was President of the College, I extended an invitation to Professor Maynard to come as our Guest of Honor at one of our Conferences. Unfortunately, it was not possible for him to accept our invitation because of commitments in the United States. Had I accepted Prof. Maynard's invitation and joined the staff of Harlem Hospital, that would have constituted an early brain drain as far as health delivery in Ghana was concerned. Today, it is possible that we have more qualified surgeons outside Ghana than in Ghana itself, a sad reflection on the way things have turned out in our country!

There were certain impressions which I formed on my arrival in the United States. First of all, I was amazed at the size of the taxi that came to take my luggage at the harbour. A very long limousine, as they call it. It had so much room. All the time I was afraid that the huge mahogany box that I brought from Dunkwa would be too big for any taxi. Certainly, it would have been too big for a London taxi. Secondly, I was awed by the sheer size of the vehicular traffic; I got the impression that there were more cars than people, whereas it was the other way round in London, where there were fewer cars. Then, of course, relatively speaking, the buildings were huge and the avenues were very, very wide : very broad avenues allowing five lanes on double carriage-ways. These were the impressions, on my first arrival as we drove to Aunt Rachel's house.

As we got nearer the Bronx, we saw a lot more black faces, more than what I had been used to in the U.K. Of course, it was to be expected that the black population in the United States would be much larger than that in the UK as at that time there wasn't yet an influx of blacks in Britain.

Leonora and I started some sort of a game which lasted throughout our stay, based on the stark resemblance of some of the Afro-Americans to some people we knew at home. Some of them were really dark. Indeed, there was a story about a Gold Coast student who, having newly arrived in New York, saw across the road someone whom he thought was a friend of his from Accra whom he had not seen for some time. He walked across the road to the other side and, without checking, gave the chap a slap on his shoulder and asked him in Ga, "*Kwe, tshiènuu. Meebe oba biè?*" Meaning, "Hey, old chap! When did you come here?" So the fellow just turned round and asked him in a broad American accent, "What you talking, man?" So he immediately realized his mistake and apologized profusely. But he could never get over the resemblance. It was almost as if the fellow and his friend were twins. It showed that for generations since the Slave Trade days there had not been any integration in some black families. There were various shades therefore from jet black to almost lily white. I found it very interesting from the historical point of view.

I do not know what Leonora's friends and family expected to see. They had heard so much about Leonora's husband, Dr. Evans-Anfom, from Africa, and some had even seen pictures of him, but they did not really believe that a person looking like me, a half-caste, was from Africa. When they actually saw me and I opened my mouth and started speaking, they wondered even more whether I was really from Africa and speaking such good English. On my part I found it difficult to make out from their broad American accent what they were saying! On many occasions, I just had to say, "Pardon, pardon" and Leonora, in very bad cases had to act as my interpreter! For the three months that I stayed, I cannot say that I got used to the way some friends and relations of Leonora's spoke, even some who had been to College. Aunt Rachel was very pleased to see me in the flesh. I had only spoken to her over the telephone and I am sure that she was looking forward, as I was, to that day when we met. On the whole, I suspected that her first impression was one of approval. Needless to say, I quickly got used to getting around to adjust myself to some new situations. I thought, well, this is a country where one could get the best and also the worst, a place I would like to visit but certainly not to live in permanently.

There were very few Gold Coasters in the United States at that time. I have already mentioned Dr. Schandorf, who left Ghana in the late twenties to study medicine and had been in America for almost a quarter of a century. He was then a doctor working in a hospital in the Queens, one of the Boroughs in New York. It was very good to establish contact with him. Then there was Mr. Smart Abbey, who was employed at the temporary offices of the Gold Coast in New York. Dr. Owoo, a lecturer at New York University, had been in the United States for a very long time. Leonora and I had the pleasure of meeting him in his house where we had tea.

Our visit was an occasion to meet Dr. Robert Lee, who had visited the Gold Coast the previous year and had actually come to Tarkwa and had discussions with Leonora. We were able to visit him and his wife, Sara, also a dentist in Westbury, where they lived. Dr. Lee at that time had a good dental practice in Brooklyn. He had the opportunity to have further discussions with us for him to confirm the decision he had already taken, namely, to move to the Gold Coast. I learnt from Dr. Lee that when he was in the Gold Coast he was really shocked at the sort of salary I was getting as a public servant. He made comparisons which were not really what one would call genuine comparisons as he was comparing dissimilar things.

He gave us the reasons why he wanted to come back to settle in the Gold Coast. The first reason was that he wanted to provide service. The second reason was that in the Gold Coast, he would be making a worthwhile contribution which would be appreciated. He would feel like he was somebody; that he would be respected, whereas in America, he was just a number among thousands of dental surgeons, and nobody really paid any attention to him or the service be provided. I thought it was a very profound reason.

Following that visit, Dr. Lee, just before independence, moved down to Ghana and has remained in Ghana ever since, acquiring Ghanaian nationality meanwhile. Incidentally, one of the attractions to Ghana was Kwame Nkrumah who had been a college mate of Dr. Lee's at Lincoln University, as was Mr. Robert Freeman whom I met at an Alumni party with Bobby Lee. They were all graduates of Lincoln University. Incidentally, Bobby Freeman had not been to the Gold Coast at the time but he was contemplating a visit before making up his mind to move. I like to think that the discussions he had with me helped him to make up his mind, to bring the Insurance Business to the Gold Coast, to start a company which was eventually taken over by the state, and is now the State Insurance Corporation. Of course, Bobby Freeman did not come with any intention to settle in Ghana like Dr. Lee. However, he made a very valuable contribution to the development of the insurance business in Ghana.

During our three-month visit to the States, Leonora and I had the opportunity to drive to Canada. The Lees very kindly put their second car, a Ford, at our disposal. I had to do the driving all the way to Canada and back. Before then I had to take a driving test. Even though I had the Gold Coast and International Driving Licenses with me, they insisted that I did a test. So I did the test and passed and got my driver's license. This made us more mobile because we were able to borrow other people's cars. We went to Canada through the New York Thruway to Buffalo and the Niagara Falls, then via the Queen Elizabeth

Expressway to Toronto, then to Montreal and on to Quebec. Whilst in Montreal, we were pleasantly surprised to meet a black Canadian doctor, Barry Rapier, who had studied medicine in Edinburgh while I was there. After Quebec we drove back to New York through the New England States. On another occasion, we borrowed a Chrysler car belonging to one of Leonora's cousins and drove to Washington and back. At that time, there was still some subtle racial prejudice and we encountered a bit of this in some cafés and fast food joints.

I must say that one thing which I found rather unnerving throughout was the sort of silly questions which were asked by some black Americans. In Britain, I had been accustomed to being asked those questions by whites. However, they did not sound too well coming from fellow blacks. But then, I remembered that the American educational system and the whole culture was to show the negative side of anything which came from Africa. Clearly, the system did not think anything good could come out of Africa. Therefore, what most of the Americans knew was really what was depicted in films, that is, primitive practices. Now it is interesting to compare the attitude of black Americans at that time to what pertains now. With the independence of Ghana in 1957, and later that of other African countries; and the appearance of statesmen and politicians like Kwame Nkrumah on the world scene and coming to the United Nations, black Americans began to take more interest in black Africa. There was a time when some of the black Americans in some ways became more African than the Africans themselves! They were assuming cultural postures and usage which to them denoted one's *Africanness*. Mercifully, this attitude is changing as more of them have had the opportunity to travel to Africa to see things for themselves. They have become more realistic in their attitude to African culture.

We had planned a three month visit to the States. So when the time came we returned to the UK by air, this time. Well, I must say that judging by the attitude of the members of Leo's family and her friends I was introduced to, umpteen friends of Leo's, school mates who knew her childhood days through college, it was quite clear that she was a very popular person with all these people. I then realized how lucky I was to have such a person as my life long partner.

We traveled to London by BOAC and then went up to Edinburgh by train. Before leaving for the United States, I had ordered a new car, a small Ford Prefect, which was ready when we arrived. After taking delivery of the car we were able to drive around Scotland and down to

Wales and to London and back to Edinburgh. Whilst on the trip we stopped in Gloucester and called on Rev, A. G. Fraser, first principal of Achimota who was, at that time quite old. He was not bedridden then but he had been involved in a minor accident and confined to bed temporarily when we called on him. He was nevertheless very pleased to see us. I have already mentioned that whilst I was a student in Edinburgh, he attended a couple of our Old Achimotan Annual Reunions as our Guest of Honour. As one of the Triumvirate founders of Achimota, he was always proud and happy to see the products of Achimota get on in life and do precisely what Achimota was set up to do, to train people to go out as living water to the thirsty land of the Gold Coast.

# CHAPTER 16

# KUMASI I
## Kumasi Central Hospital

After the visit to the United Kingdom we came back home. I recall that a little over five years previously, I had returned home to join the medical service with an initial basic medical qualification. Now five years later, I was back with an additional Post-Graduate qualification, Fellowship of Royal College of Surgeons of Edinburgh, a much coveted qualification which made me eligible for promotion in due course to the post of Specialist. This time I came back by air and I did not come alone, I came with Leonora and Nii Okai, our two-year old baby. I had no idea where I would be posted on my return. The day after my return, I reported at the Head Office of the Medical Department where there was a letter waiting for me, instructing me to get myself in readiness to proceed to Kumasi Central Hospital on transfer.

The Kumasi Central Hospital had been newly commissioned. It is now, of course, called Komfo Anokye Teaching Hospital, the Regional Hospital for the Ashanti Region and the areas of the country north of Ashanti. It was a brand new hospital and I believe at that time, the finest hospital in West Africa. I must say that I was very happy when I started work there. The construction of the hospital had been in progress for some time but now it was ready and commissioned. Everything was spick and span. The long corridors connecting the different blocks, provided good exercise every day. The total bed population was somewhere between eight hundred and a thousand. This of course comprised all sections of medicine, including the maternity and pediatrics sections. The hospital was very well equipped and it was a pleasure to work in a place where there were five air-conditioned operating theatres. One of these theatres was reserved for septic cases and also for orthopedic cases which required plaster of paris application. The others were all in a row and centrally air-conditioned.

The fact that I was going to work as an assistant to Dr. Charles Bowesman, Senior Specialist in-Charge of the Hospital Surgical Department, also made me happy. I had had dealings with Dr. Bowesman when I was medical officer in Dunkwa, when I used to refer difficult cases to him. Dr. Bowesman was the most senior surgeon in the country. Before coming to Ghana shortly after the War, he had seen service in The Gambia, so it was a great privilege for me to work under him. Apart from his vast clinical experience and surgical skills, he had an excellent bed-side manner and was also a very good teacher and very courteous to all. As my time with him would be used to under-study him for future promotion, he made every effort to give me the facilities for independent work. I cannot remember the total number of surgical beds that were available, but what he did was to allocate one-third of the beds to me. These beds were entirely mine, to admit my own patients and care for them and only consult him in times of difficulty; so that I was able, for many months before I left Kumasi, to work independently. Cases requiring surgical consultation or surgical treatment were referred either to Dr. Bowesman or to me, depending on our consultation days.

Before I left Accra, my uncle, Dr. C. E. Reindorf, had advised that at the earliest opportunity I should call upon Otumfuo Asantehene; so by the end of the first week when I was fairly well settled, I sought audience with Nana Asantehene. Quite unknown to me, my uncle had already sent him a letter about me, and he himself was eager to meet me and was making enquiries as to when I could come to see him.

I must say that Otumfuo was very gracious when my wife and I together with our two-year baby called on him, and he was highly interested to know that I was related to his very good friend, Dr. C. E. Reindorf. I found him an extremely knowledgeable person. By the time we left him, we had learnt quite a bit about both Ashanti and Gold Coast history. I discovered that he was rather concerned about the unhealthy political climate at that time. It would be recalled that at that time the secessionist movement was at its height in Ashanti. The National Liberation Movement had been formed and there was a good deal of political violence. Nana was very much concerned about this and hoped that good sense would prevail and that it would not be long before things settled down and the country gained its independence.

Because of the political violence, we were very busy at the hospital. Because at one point in time the violence was fairly widespread. The antagonism between the Convention Peoples' Party and members of the opposition in Ashanti often ended violently and we had many casualties to deal with. Whilst it was a matter of great regret that such an unwholesome climate should prevail, for us in hospital, it was a very busy period with injuries varying from minor to very major ones.

My good friend, the late Dr. K. Kurankyi Taylor, one of the leading lawyers in the country, was a member of the Opposition and was counsel for the Opposition in many of the court cases that were in progress at that time. He happened to be my patient, and on a number of occasions, I visited him in his house. His wife Dorothy, was a native of Manchester, UK, and I recall that it was in Kurankyi's house that I first met Mr. Geoffrey Bing Q. C. who at that time was appearing with Kurankyi Taylor for the Opposition in the difficult cases that they had. This was 1955. We know that after the death of Kurankyi Taylor, Geoffrey Bing stayed on and he actually became the Attorney General of the Gold Coast during the remaining period of self-government and early independence, becoming a very close adviser to Kwame Nkrumah.

On the education front, quite a lot was happening in Kumasi at that time, especially in higher education. The Kumasi College of Technology was newly established. In 1952 it was mostly housed in prefabricated and temporary buildings. By 1955 there was a good deal of physical development going on when the permanent buildings - the administration block, some of the students halls of residence, and some of the classrooms - were being put up. For me, it was interesting because the Teacher Training Department of Achimota College had been moved to Kumasi, as had the Special Art Course, so quite a number of the staff were known to me. Despite the fact that the College had its own hospital, surgical cases were referred to the Central Hospital to be dealt with by Dr. Bowesman or myself.

There was quite a dynamic Old Achimotan Association also in Kumasi and also very vigorous British Council activities going on. I became a member of the British Council and, as usual, the Council sponsored a number of literary and also sporting activities, including hockey. I joined the British Council Hockey Team and we played matches against the Armed Forces, Training colleges and Secondary schools. Our matches against Wesley College reminded me of my first visit to Kumasi when I was a student at Achimota College to play against Wesley College.

Kumasi was not as highly congested then as it is now. It well deserved the name, "Garden City of West Africa", especially when the vegetation was lush. Social life was also very active and one felt that after work there were plenty of avenues for recreation. My old school friend, Toufeek Majdoub, now Toufeek Bedwei, was resident in Kumasi. He had a textile store in the Kejetia area. I had the opportunity to renew my friendship with the Bedwei family. Through Toufeek, I was introduced to a large number of people in the Lebanese community. Some later became my patients and others my very good friends, and our friendship has persisted even up to the present day! Examples are the Mattouk and Adas families.

On the 16th of January 1956, our second child was born, a beautiful baby girl whom we named Rachel, after Leonora's Aunt Rachel. Far from being jealous of the new arrival, Nii Okai welcomed his little baby sister and we were really quite pleased with this, as it meant that there was peace at home. Sometime in March, barely nine months after we came to Kumasi, I got a letter from the Ministry of Health asking me to hold myself in readiness to go to Sekondi-Takoradi on transfer. The surgical specialist, Dr. Owen, a Canadian, was about to proceed on leave prior to resignation or retirement, I do not remember, but I was to go there to hold the fort after he had left. So a few weeks after that, in April, once again, we moved to Sekondi-Takoradi.

# CHAPTER 17

# SEKONDI - TAKORADI
## (Promotion – Surgical Specialist)

I was not a stranger to the place for on several occasions in the past, Sekondi-Takoradi had been a transit point when leaving the Gold Coast or returning from abroad. This time, of course, I was to go to live in Sekondi and work at Effia-Nkwanta Hospital. The Effia-Nkwanta Hospital itself was a fairly new one, not as new as The Central Hospital in Kumasi and, of course, not as large or well-equipped, but there was a job to be done, so I readily agreed and in April we moved to Sekondi-Takoradi.

When we arrived, Dr. Owen was getting ready to leave and, after a short time most of the work fell on my shoulders, as he made preparations to say his final good-byes to his patients and friends. This meant that after Dr. Owen left, I was solely in charge of the department of surgery of the hospital. The medical superintendent at the time was Dr. Mark Davy-Hayford, an old-timer general practitioner, who had seen service in different parts of the Gold Coast and had very wide experience. This was very good for me because from time to time, I relied on him, for advice, especially on my relationships with people.

At the end of April, after Dr. Owen left, I got a letter, quite a surprise letter, from the Ministry of Health, promoting me to the rank of Surgical Specialist. At once I knew that my former boss, Dr. Charles Bowesman, had been behind this. He must have given a strong recommendation for me to let the Ministry promote me so early after my return from the completion of my specialist course. Of course, this now meant that I was firmly in the saddle, and indeed it was a very great encouragement to me. It was a great boost to me and an incentive for me to work hard and give of my best. My only regret was that at that time, the junior doctors who were working with me, two of them, were both expatriates, Dr. Dalby, from Denmark and Dr. Ferrari, from Switzerland. I thought that it was an odd situation indeed. The country was on the eve of independence. There should, therefore, be expatriates who would be training Ghanaians. But here I was, a Ghanaian Specialist, far senior to these two boys from Denmark and Switzerland respectively and, instead of their teaching me, I was rather teaching them! It was a highly anomalous situation, and I prayed hard that as soon as possible we might get enough young Ghanaian doctors who would be playing the role that these young expatriate doctors were playing!

About the middle of 1956, Dr. Stanley Cooper, Senior Surgical Specialist stationed in Accra, was transferred to the Takoradi Hospital. The Takoradi Hospital incidentally, was once a European Hospital, a hospital for Europeans and senior officials, like the Ridge Hospital in Accra. Dr. Stanley Cooper had just a few months left to go on retirement and I think he was beginning to tire already. Accra was certainly too busy for him so he was transferred to Takoradi. His place was taken by Dr. Charles Easmon, Surgical Specialist.

Takoradi was not a busy hospital and Dr. Stanley Cooper had very little to do. Even what little he had, sometimes he passed on to me when he could not be bothered. I did not really mind because I looked back to the year that I arrived in 1950 and considered what I learnt from him in operative surgery prior to my transfer to Dunkwa. I knew Dr. Stanley Cooper was very fond of me and he told me even at that time he thought that I would go far. I remember distinctly the piece of advice he gave me on one occasion, "Anfom, do not go after money, if you do your work well, the money will come. If you do not do your work well the patients will just run away from you. If you work well, you will not have time to receive money." This was good advice that I kept at the back of my mind throughout my practice as a doctor. So Dr. Stanley Cooper spent the last few months of his service in the Gold Coast in the Takoradi Hospital. I believe he left permanently on retirement shortly after independence in March 1957.

Now, I must record two incidents during my practice in Sekondi. The first one is the day that I was called early in the morning at half past six to see an emergency case in the hospital. It was a dire emergency. The day also happened to be my regular operating day and a number of cases had been listed for operation. The emergency case had to be dealt with almost immediately so I did not go back home at all. I stayed on and did the first operation and from then on, even though some of the regular cases had been cancelled, there was a stream of emergencies, both surgical and gynaecological and obstetrics. Together with my two expatriate doctors as assistants we stayed in the hospital right on to the night. I did not get home till about eleven o'clock. It was quite a memorable day in my practice, standing, operating most of the time with assistance from my junior colleagues. That was an unforgettable day!

In connection with these long periods in hospital, normally when I had to be in theatre for a long time, my wife would usually pack some lunch for me, some coffee or soft drinks together with sandwiches. Normally, I was more thirsty than hungry and more often than not, I did not eat anything but drank whatever there was and gave the sandwiches to the theatre staff, the nurses. I believe, however, that my wife suspected that I had not really been eating the sandwiches myself, so on one occasion, on an operating day, when I got back home very tired she asked me, "Well, daddy, how did you enjoy your sandwiches?" I said, "Oh, they were very nice." "What was the filling?" I had no answer for that, I had no idea what the filling was because I had given the sandwiches away. This time I was really caught pants down. It confirmed what she'd been suspecting all along that I had on most occasions not been eating the sandwiches .So from then on I always inspected the filling. From then on, I always ate at least one sandwich.

My stay in Sekondi-Takoradi coincided with the last few months of the life of Paa Grant of blessed memory. The week after my arrival in Sekondi, Auntie Efua, Paa Grant's wife, came to the hospital to see me. I had met her on a couple of occasions while I was at Dunkwa. She came to Dunkwa because Paa Grant had some properties there. I recall that it was a UAC manager at that time who brought her to see me in the hospital. At the time of my arrival in Sekondi, Paa Grant was not feeling too well. He was mostly in bed, so Auntie Efua invited me to come and see him professionally at home. So throughout my stay, until I was transferred, I paid regular visits to see Paa Grant. It was very interesting talking to the old man. I learnt a lot of history, both ancient and modern: the part that he played and was still playing in the struggle which was now coming to an end. I was very much impressed by the narrative because he told me about his life, how he struggled to make it and the need for hard work, perseverance and resourcefulness. His motto was that "if you want to get on in life then you have to work hard. If you sit down, you would not get anywhere. If you want to get somewhere, get up and get cracking, get walking." So I was able to see the old man fading gradually and I was very sad that a few months after I had been transferred from Sekondi he died at a ripe old age.

Shortly after our arrival in Sekondi, our daughter Rachel was baptized. There was a well-established Presbyterian Church and the District Pastor was the late Reverend Akita. I recall that my good friends, Mr. and Mrs. J. K. Adoteye from Osu were stalwarts in the Church. Mr. Adoteye was a Presbyter and, on occasion I was invited to play the organ for Church Service or to accompany the church choir of which Mr. Adoteye was the choirmaster.

Shortly after our arrival in Sekondi, also, the late Mr. Charles Quaye, who was then headmaster of Fijai Secondary School and whom I had met but did not really know well, came to see me and to discuss the possibility of Leonora coming to teach at Fijai. Of course, Leonora readily agreed. Therefore throughout our stay, she taught at Fijai. She taught English and French to the junior classes and she enjoyed it thoroughly. My other friends in Sekondi at the time were His Worship Mr. Samuel Azu Crabbe then Senior Magistrate. He was the godfather to our daughter, Rachel, at her baptism. Then of course, Mr. Kwartey Quartey, who was the Town Clerk whom I had met on one of my transit passages through Sekondi-Takoradi, and his wife became our good friends. Incidentally, Mr. Kwartey Quartey was the father of Ms Eudora Quartey, who now, I believe, works with an important Commission as a lawyer. Then in the mercantile fields there were some friends, Mr. Lantei-Mills who had been at Tarkwa with us for a brief period, and also Mr. Ayittey, a Manager of UAC. Mr. Ayittey was the father of Ms Sherry Ayittey, the prominent politician and member of the 31st December Women's Movement. Other distinguished personalities resident in Sekondi-Takoradi were Mr. and Mrs. Francis Awonoor-Williams, (Aunt Nora) It was in their house that we spent our last night in 1942 when our group was travelling abroad for studies. Then there was Mr. Abbenssetts, a prominent lawyer and the leader of the Bar in the Western Region. His son, Johnny Abbensetts, also a lawyer in the public service rose to become the Solicitor General of Ghana. Then there was Mr. Gwira, also a prominent lawyer, a private practitioner resident in Sekondi whose son, also a prominent lawyer, became a member of the Council of State in Limann's Government, of the Third Republic.

1956 was a very important year in the history of the country. It was more or less the eve of the approaching independence of the Gold

Coast which was to become Ghana on March 6th, 1957 and there were so many things happening, especially in the first few months of 1957. Unfortunately, I was then, by Independence Day, that is, March 6th, 1957 far too busy to be actively involved in the activities for the celebration because I was packing, ready to move from Sekondi to go on my annual leave in Accra. I must confess that I was fully expecting just to go on leave and then come back to continue at Effia-Nkwanta Hospital. But this was not to happen, so we packed everything and came to Accra. Now, at this time, moving around posed much inconvenience because the children were young, one was not quite four years old and the other was just a year old. We had a well-planned holiday. It was a six-week holiday. We planned to go to all sorts of places including Lomé, to our relations there and, generally speaking for Leonora to see a little more of what she had not seen in Accra and its environs. Unfortunately for me, I was not to have much rest because, mid-way through my leave, I got a letter from the Ministry asking me to get ready to proceed within four days on transfer to Tamale, far away Tamale!

I must say that when I received the letter, I had a little bit of a shock. To interrupt my leave in such an abrupt manner, and to give me very little time, and to move to a place which I considered too far from my home base and really not to allow me to finish my rest was patently unfair. Here was I just half way through my leave and being asked to resume work. I immediately went to see the Director of Medical Services to launch a protest. It wasn't a strong protest, it was rather mild, and my good friend, Dr. Eustace Akwei, who was then the Director of Medical Services asked me why I did not want to go to Tamale. I replied that Tamale was just too far away. "TOO FAR FROM WHERE?" "Too far from Accra, Sir." It was after I had given my answer that I realized how foolish that answer was. Here was I, a public servant who should be prepared to go to any part of the country to work at any time. I felt really bad when the new Director, Dr. Akwei, told me, "We are transferring you now because Tamale is in dire need of not only a doctor but also a surgeon. Right now there is just one doctor there. Someone has left abruptly, an expatriate. The doctor who is left there is a young doctor without much experience and it is really necessary for the service that someone goes there immediately to save the situation". I thought really I could not argue. At that point, I realized the folly of the position I was taking and I apologized profusely, and indeed said that I would go because the young inexperienced doctor was from far away Europe, Denmark, much farther than Accra, my hometown, and he'd come to work in Ghana, so why should I complain? I was a Ghanaian who really had something to offer, experience-wise. So I accepted the posting, and came home and narrated the incident to my wife. I was not at all surprised when she said, "Of course, you have work to do. We have made our plans for the holidays, but if there is need for your services somewhere in Ghana, however far, you just have to go." So with this support from my wife we set out in a few days to go up to Tamale. At that time, Leonora was supervising the construction of our house at Tesano, so I had to go ahead with the children, for her to follow in a few weeks after we had settled down.

# CHAPTER 18

# TAMALE
## (Too far from where?)

Naturally, I did not like the idea of going so far away from home. Another reason was that just recently I had been working in bigger, better hospitals in Kumasi and Effia-Nkwanta, both well-equipped hospitals. From what I had heard about Tamale Hospital, it was really a glorified District hospital!

The Government Transport vehicle carrying our heavy luggage left the day before our departure because it had to break the journey in Kumasi. So on the appointed day, the children, myself, Auntie Okailey, (that's my sister) and the driver, Ataa Allotey, left for Tamale in my Chevrolet car, a newly acquired car, very well appointed and strong, so I was not apprehensive about its performance on the road to Tamale. We left very early so that we could make the journey slowly and, as a consequence, we arrived quite late at Tamale. We arrived at nine o'clock, having left Accra at six o'clock in the morning, and breaking our journey for two hours in Kumasi. We also had a meal with my friend, Toufeek Bedwei.

The bungalow in Tamale was an old, burnt brick bungalow adjacent to the West Hospital. The West Hospital was a small hospital for Europeans and senior African government officials. My bungalow was also next door to the army barracks. Some of my army officer friends were then stationed there. As I expected, the hospital was just a bigger version of a district hospital that I had been used to. I had known Akuse Hospital in my childhood. I had worked at the Dunkwa and Tarkwa hospitals. The pattern of architectural planning was very similar and, frankly, I felt a bit unhappy about this because even the operating theatre was nothing to be proud of. All the same, there was work to be done. The Principal Medical Officer in-Charge of the Northern Region was very happy to see me and so was the young Danish doctor, Jorgensen, who was getting really very tired. Apart from that, he needed supervision. I wish I could say that my working relationship with him was a happy one, but I cannot. He was the type who, though young in age and experience, thought he knew everything. He was, therefore, quite capable of undertaking things which were beyond him. Of course, I had to put my foot down as firmly as possible because we were dealing with human lives! He did not like that very much. Whether he thought because he was a European he could do as he liked, I do not know, but I really had to put him in his place. At the end of the day, even though I cannot say that he liked me he respected my professional competence. Whether he liked it or not, he must have learnt something from me. In any case, there was work to be done and I was very lucky to have the working support of very highly experienced nurses, both male and female, especially the midwives. Among the male nurses there was one who had been given further training in anesthetics by Dr. Bowesman in Kumasi, who was, therefore, a great asset, because I was able to do certain surgical procedures, which required efficient anesthesia.

Before I arrived, there wasn't much major surgery being done, but by the end of my stay, we had managed to build up quite a viable and efficient surgical service in the hospital. The theatre nurses whom I met also, I think, benefitted because whereas in the past they had been used to doing things and just trying to cope with only emergencies, now they were able to assist at important surgical procedures. I was able to help quite a few people with their goiters, removing their goiters and also carrying out different plastic procedures which patients found helpful. For example, elephantiasis of the scrotum, over-grown breasts of different sizes and shapes, and huge umbilical hernias. I must say when I first arrived I was a bit disappointed but increase in the work load and the variety of cases helped to uplift my spirits. When the time came for me to leave I did so with a certain measure of regret.

On the social side, I have already alluded to the fact that there were army officers who were known to me. Major Ankrah and Major Michel, as they were then, were both serving at Tamale at that time, and there were other officers of lesser ranks who later on became quite senior military officers. Then there was Mr. Justice George Djabanor, a High Court Judge at the time, The Honorable Lawrence Abavana whom I knew at Achimota College when he was training as a teacher and who, as a matter of fact, in 1941/42 when I was a temporary, staff member, I had the privilege of teaching mathematics. Abavana was the Northern Regional Minister. Then my own friend and classmate, Dr. Kodjo Oddoye, a dentist, was also there with his wife, Margaret. Then there was Mr. Gilbert Fleischer, who was the Regional Director of Education, and a Dr. and Mrs. Reed. Dr. William Reed was the leader of a USAID team responsible for a series of irrigation projects in different parts of the North. Leonora and I became friendly with the Reed family. Leonora, herself an American citizen, made them feel much at home. They were very happy that they were in Tamale and that the wife of the surgical specialist -in-charge of the hospital was an American. The friendship between the Reed and the Evans-Anfom families has lasted up to this day. Indeed, our youngest son, Charles, for four years, when he was at University in Greensboro, North Carolina, stayed with the Reeds. Dr. Reed himself, had retired from the faculty of the A&T College in North Carolina where my son Charles also studied. To this day, whenever I go to the States with my wife or any of my children, the Reed home in Greensboro, North Carolina, is an obligatory stop, if even for one night!

At the time that I was in Tamale, the medical officer in charge of the Bolgatanga hospital was Hans Schwendler, a German. He was a general duty medical officer but he had been in the country for a long time and had good experience. Whilst in Tamale, I paid a couple of visits to Bolgatanga to see what was happening at the hospital. I recall that on one occasion, at the invitation of the doctor, I performed, a couple of operations at Bolgatanga. When the time came for me to leave Tamale, it was Dr. Schwendler who was posted to Tamale to replace me. Dr. Schwendler was an interesting character. He had good experience. He had no special post-graduate training in surgery, but he had quite a good experience in surgery and could cope with most surgical emergencies; he was someone who could hold his own in medical emergencies. His replacing me in Tamale was supposed to be a temporary measure because after me it was decided that there should always be a trained surgeon in Tamale to keep up the work and the standard that had been set.

Wherever I have been, I have always wanted to play hockey. In Tamale the secondary school at that time provided a useful outlet for me. I used to go to the school to play hockey with the boys. Years later I was quite interested to find that some members of the National Redemption Council Government were old boys of Tamale Secondary

School who were at that time students at the school and remember my coming there to play hockey with them and to coach the school team. Names that come to mind are Felli, Yirimambo, and Sadik. They recall with nostalgia those days, in 1957/58 when they were secondary school students and I was the surgeon in-charge of Tamale Hospital.

The hundred-mile stretch from Tamale to Bolgatanga was the best road in the country at that time. One hundred miles of dead straight road, very well kept. There was not much heavy traffic on it so it lasted for many years. Of course, later on, with the volume of traffic increasing, it started to show signs of overuse and, for some time, it suffered a lot from wear and tear and neglect. I am told that it has once again become one of the first class roads in the country. Regretfully, I was not able to travel much in the North. The distances were long, the roads were not all that good and, of course, there wasn't much time for me to travel around.

With the Reeds, the Oddoyes, and the Michels, (that is Joe Michel and his wife Victoria), George Djabanor and his wife, Janet, and ourselves, we formed a small social group, and on Sunday mornings after church service we went to each other's houses and had mini parties just to enjoy ourselves. This we did in rotation and it was something which we enjoyed greatly. After one year, in April 1958 another letter came for me, this time to come down to Accra to relieve Dr. Charles Easmon, the Surgical Specialist, who had been granted a travelling Fellowship for the USA for six months, and during that time, I was to hold the fort in Accra. As it turned out, after Dr. Easmon's tour of the States, he took his earned leave. So in the end I was in Accra for close to nine months, after which I was posted to Kumasi. All along, it was in accordance with the Ministry's plan that I was to be posted to the Kumasi Central Hospital to take charge of surgery on the retirement of Dr Bowesman. For the next four a and half years I was Surgical Specialist in-charge and for the latter two years of that time I was also part-time medical superintendent of the hospital.

My son, Nii Teiko, was born in Tamale on 12 December 1957. Nii Teiko arrived a few weeks earlier than he should have done, and by so doing disturbed whatever plans my mother had for travelling both as to the time of travelling (sometime near the expected date of delivery) and also the mode of transportation. Mama had sworn that she would never travel by air. Not that she'd ever done so, but the mere thought of being high up in a narrow plane just frightened her. Somehow this fear had to be relegated immediately to the background. As soon as she heard that Nii Teiko had arrived; she jumped on the next plane for Tamale and by so doing, discovered that there was absolutely no mystery about flying! When the occasion presented itself at a latter date, she had no problem at all, flying!

The first time we arrived in Tamale, I found the heat quite overbearing. Mercifully, it did not take long for the rains to start and to cool things down somehow, but one thing which I really remember was that I found myself suddenly having to start drinking beer. Even though water was quite satisfying, on occasion one needed a change. So it was in Tamale that I started drinking beer seriously. There was the alternative local drink, pito, which I tasted once and no more! Many people seemed to like it, but, in my opinion the taste was rather unpleasant, and since then I have neither yearned for nor touched pito! My one regret is that I did not really take the opportunity to learn Hausa during my year's stay in Tamale. Looking back now, I think I could easily have done that. I was quite content with my limited Hausa vocabulary applied to diseases and symptoms - Consulting Room Hausa! I like the sound of Hausa and the fact that it is widely spoken in the sub-region makes it an additional attraction.

Nii Teiko was baptized in Tamale. At that time there were no separate Presbyterian and Methodist Churches there. There was a United Presbyterian Methodist Church but, even then, one could see the problems in store for any idea for a future union of the Protestant churches in Ghana; there were differences regarding many inconsequential matters pertaining to worship. So I was not surprised at all when many years later at the national level, the attempt at church union, having advanced quite far, was surreptitiously sabotaged by people who never had any conviction or faith in the idea. In Tamale, now there are separate Presbyterian churches. Mrs. Mattye Reed, our American friend, was the godmother for Nii Teiko.

It was whilst I was far away in Tamale in 1958, sometime in March, that my eldest brother, Ebenezer Armah Anfom, headmaster of the Presbyterian Middle School at Big Ada, died at Korle Bu at the age of 50. This event upset me greatly because I had looked up to him since my childhood as one of my mentors; someone who encouraged me all my life from my childhood up to the time that he died. It was really a big blow to me. When I consider what has happened to me since his death, the various positions that I have occupied, how I wish he had lived to see what happened to his dear younger brother whom he loved so much.

In April 1958, we had to move down to Accra. I knew that this was to be temporary, and yet we had to pack everything just as we had done on previous occasions. At this point, I want to point out that from the time that I joined the medical service in April 1950, I had served in the following stations, Accra, Dunkwa-on-Offin, Tarkwa, Kumasi, Sekondi-Takoradi and Tamale. Now I was going back to Accra temporarily. I had served in as many stations in as many years! I think it is important to record this at this point. I invite the reader to consider the great inconvenience to myself and my family; having to move from one place to another at short intervals. The result of all this, now that I have retired for many years, is that some of my boxes containing important papers and books still remain unpacked, and I concider this a really great handicap, now that I am writing my memoirs! But it is a clear illustration of the discipline one had to go through and the sacrifices one had to make in those days, all forming part of the history of the development of this country!

## Accra -Temporary Locum

When the time came I moved down to Accra to hold the fort for many months. It was indeed a big jump, from a district hospital, relatively ill-equipped, to the premier hospital in Accra, that is, the Korlebu Hospital. Despite the big jump it was a situation, which was not unfamiliar because I had a few years previously worked at the most modern hospital in Ghana, the Central Hospital in Kumasi, later to be renamed Komfo Anokye Hospital.

It was with a heavy heart that I left Tamale when the time came for me to go to Accra. I recall that a year previously when I was asked to go on transfer to Tamale I staged a mild protest. Now here I was, after one year, I had really come to be fond of the place and of the people, and I had come to really appreciate and realize the enormous amount of work that needed to be done; the need for better health service delivery, not only in Tamale but in the whole area of the Northern Region, which at that time comprised all the three northern regions that we know now - Northern, Upper East and Upper West Regions. I had come to make some good friends and acquaintances. Socially also, I really appreciated the relative quiet in comparison with the hustle and bustle in a place like Accra.

The Korlebu Hospital at that time had not seen any extensions. It was just the old Korlebu buildings as they were built. It was not a teaching hospital. I must say that I really preferred it architecturally and also environmentally; it was a very handsome looking piece of property, with nicely kept lawns and clean looking wards. There wasn't much congestion either. Floor cases were minimal.

I believe the bed strength of the hospital was around three hundred and fifty. In any case it was fewer than four hundred. That was the official bed strength, but if one counted the floor patients, that number quite exceeded 500. Professionally, and from the work point of view it was a welcome situation, because in Tamale even though I was a Surgical Specialist I was really doing general duties. I was seeing all sorts of cases and not concentrating only on surgery. But at Korlebu, I was just heading the Department of Surgery and dealing only with surgical cases referred to me from within the hospital or from medical practitioners outside.

Accra, being the capital also, and very cosmopolitan, the type of patients covered a wide array. They represented a whole cross-section of the population ranging from workers, labourers, right up to high Government officials and members of the Diplomatic Corps. Compared with the present time, I must say that Korlebu was relatively well equipped. Also there was no "cash and carry system" and generally speaking, things went on smoothly. No patient was asked to pay up front before being treated, and any patient who was treated and who could not pay was asked to pay just what he could afford or allowed to go home as a pauper. Of course, things have changed considerably and at this stage, I do not want to go into the pros and cons of the cash and carry system, which has been highly politicized, except to say that, on balance and speaking as a doctor, I think it is detrimental to the welfare of the patient!

The staffing situation was quite good. For example, there was a specialist anaesthetist at post, a very pleasant Indian lady, Mrs. Sharma, who was a very good anaesthetist and who made it possible for the surgeons to do a lot more competently. Consequently, the range of surgical work that I had to do was really wide. I was able to do, within the limits of the equipment available and, of course, of my professional competence, major surgery, which I was not doing at Tamale.

Professionally speaking, therefore the work was satisfying. At that time also in Korlebu, the medical staff strength was beginning to get better and we had young Ghanaian medical officers at Korlebu. I recall Dr. Quarcoopome and Dr. Oduro whose names readily come to mind. I am speaking of the year 1958, and I was quite happy that we were now getting young Ghanaian doctors in the service, and so instead of working with young expatriate doctors, my younger colleagues were Ghanaians. The other thing was that the patients I looked after were scattered as some were at the Ridge Hospital, mainly expatriates, and senior public officials and important personalities. The Ridge Hospital, several miles away from Korlebu, constituted an additional burden, because it meant that one seriously ill patient at the hospital that needed regular attention saw me shuttling to and fro between the two hospitals, thus taking up much time and energy.

Among the important patients whom I had to see whilst I was in Accra, was the Governor General, Lord Listowel. Dr. Silas Dodu, the Physician Specialist who was attending Lord Listowel at the time, called me, in consultation, to see Lord Listowel. It was quite an interesting time for me when I called on him at the Flag Staff House and quite a privilege for me to be called to see the Head of State, and a representative of the Queen. Readers may recall that at that time, Ghana was not a Republic, and the Governor General was the Head State as the Queen's representative in Ghana, and Osagyefo Dr. Kwame Nkrumah was Prime Minister. Fortunately, his condition wasn't anything serious, but it was an opportunity for me to meet Lord Listowel, a very broad-minded and forward-looking gentleman. It was also an opportunity to talk about a number of things, and to exchange views on what he thought about the future of the country.

At the Ridge Hospital, occasionally, one came across a VIP patient who would cause a bit of trouble. I recall that one such patient was on admission with a straightforward condition, but his wife, naturally anxious about him, kept on going after the nurses to "do this, do that. Why did not you do this?" and so on, and generally interfering with the management of the patient. It could be very irritating for the nursing staff and, on occasion, they had to report to me and I had to deal with the situation in the most tactful manner without hurting anyone. Generally speaking, one felt that these patients, troublesome as they might be, really appreciated whatever was done for them to get them back on the road.

Of course, social life in Accra was quite brisk at that time with lots of invitations to parties, and all sorts of functions. On the other hand, I was kept so busy that my wife and I could not attend quite a number of these parties. It was an opportunity, nonetheless, to meet important people in the diplomatic circuit and in the commercial and other fields.

In January of 1958, the Ghana Medical Association came into being as a result of the amalgamation of the Gold Coast Medical Practitioners Union (or Society) and the Ghana Branch of the British Medical Association, which at that time was fairly strong. The fact was that a large number of doctors, both Ghanaian and expatriate at that time, had been trained in the British Medical Schools and most of them were members of the British Medical Association. The formation of the Ghana Medical Association was a very important step as, first of all, it brought all the doctors together under one umbrella. Secondly, it became the organization which would represent the interest of the medical profession, which also included the dental profession, in their dealings with Government. The aim of the association was not only to strive to promote the welfare of the profession, but also to be at the disposal of the Government for consultation on the measures to be taken to improve the health care delivery in the country. As I was away in Tamale at that time I was not really closely involved with the development. However, later in 1958 when I was in Accra, I joined the Association formally, though indeed, I was already a member of the Ghana Branch of the British Medical Association; so automatically, I became a member of the Ghana Medical Association. I was involved in the preparations for formally inaugurating the Association. In that year, I was to play a very important part in the activities of the Association.

## Holiday In Nigeria

Dr Charlie Easmon returned from the United States in December of that year and just about that time, I received a letter from the Ministry requesting me to hold myself in readiness to proceed on leave in mid-January and after that to go to the Kumasi Central Hospital on transfer sometime in March and to take charge of the Department of Surgery. At that time, Dr. Charles Bowesman had retired and I was to go there as a substantive replacement for him. Before going on leave, however, I sought audience with the Director of Medical Services and pointed out to him that in the course of eight years, I had moved around more than half a dozen stations and I hoped that there would be a certain degree of permanency when I assumed duty at Kumasi as my children were now beginning to grow up and starting school and it might become very inconvenient for me to be moving around so often. I obtained the necessary assurance upon which at the end of my leave I assumed duty sometime in March in Kumasi.

During my leave, I decided that it would be interesting to visit Nigeria. My friend, Dr. Abdul Mumuni Atta was then the medical officer-in-charge of the hospital at Zaria, Northern Nigeria. Now that I had a strong and reliable Chevrolet car I could make the journey by road in stages.  So sometime at the end of January 1959, my wife and I set out to go to Zaria. Our first stop was in Lomé, where my cousins lived. My Aunt, Mrs. Mercy Adjoa Olympio, together with her daughters was resident there, so I thought it would be useful just to stop there for a few days to visit them. So in Lomé we stayed with my cousin, Josephine, who was now Mrs. Santos, and whose wedding I attended with my brothers in January 1936.  She now had a growing family, and of course, it was very good to renew acquaintance and to talk about our childhood days. It was very good also not only for her but also for all the other members of the family, including her father, Mr.Caesar Olympio, to meet Leonora. Mr. Caesar Olympio had been a UAC Manager at Ada and sometime in 1928, my brothers and I visited Ada, getting there by launch from Akuse. Mr. Olympio was now getting on in years and was very happy to see me again. Incidentally, Mr. Olympio was the uncle of Sylvanus Olympio, who became President of the Republic of Togo and was unfortunately assassinated in 1963.

From Lomé, we drove to Lagos; this was in 1959. Of course, I had been to Lagos by air on previous occasions since 1952 in alternate years to play in the Gold Coast Hockey Team.  Mr. Ayiku Bossman, a Ghanaian and a manager of Star Brewery, Lagos, with a Nigerian wife, had become my good friends . So my wife and I stayed with them for three days in Lagos, and after that we drove up to Zaria. Unfortunately, we did not leave Lagos early enough to meet the last ferry at Bida, a place in the north, by the Niger. There was a rest house at Bida and we had planned to stop over there overnight before going on to Zaria. When we arrived at Bida we discovered that the rest house was on the other side and there was no suitable accommodation on the near side. Looking at the map, we realized that we could circumvent the river altogether by going all the way up north through a place call Katangora.

So we kept on driving and arrived in Katangora quite late, almost at midnight. Unfortunately, there was no suitable accommodation there too so my wife and I decided that we might as well just press on. So my driver, Allotey, and I, took turns at the wheel, driving an hour each time, and when we got tired, we just stopped to rest for half an hour. We could not really stop for too long because of mosquitoes. We kept on driving and by early morning we arrived at Kaduna, rested a while, and then continued to Zaria. We stayed with Abdul and his wife, Martha, whom we were meeting for the first time. Martha, a Ghanaian girl, was trained as a nurse in the United Kingdom and this was where Abdul met her. She was a very pleasant and gracious lady. Martha made us very comfortable, so we spent a very memorable week in Zaria. During our stay, we visited Kano and I recall that Abdul also took us to meet the Sarduana of Sokoto in Kaduna. Because it was the dry season, many smaller rivers were completely dry and we actually drove across a river bed to go from Zaria to Kano!

We found it very strange indeed that a whole river could dry up completely during some periods of the year. Anyway, it was a most interesting week. It gave us the opportunity to talk about old times, especially our Edinburgh days, and Abdul recalls that afternoon when he introduced Leo to me, when they were both students in the University and I had come up to Edinburgh, for the weekend from Dewsbury in Yorkshire where I was an Intern in Dewsbury General Infirmary. After a week we returned to Lagos via Ilorin. At that time Abdul's younger sister, Sefi, was the headmistress of a school, a Girls' Boarding School, and we spent a night with her, before continuing down to Lagos. We went leisurely, without rushing, and managed to get back to Lagos rather late. It was a very eventful journey, to and from Zaria in the north and we learnt a lot about the geography of the place and the ways of the people. One thing which interested me was how very clean the towns and villages of Northern Nigeria were. Everything was really nice and clean in the north and it was something which really made a deep impression on me.

# CHAPTER 19

# KUMASI II
## Surgical Specialist - Kumasi Central Hospital

After my leave, in March 1959, I assumed duty at the Kumasi Central Hospital, now Komfo Anokye Hospital. As the reader knows I had been in the hospital three years earlier when I worked as Assistant Surgeon to Dr. Bowesman, Surgical Specialist. So nothing was really new to me. The hospital was still very well maintained and I was very happy to be back. Now, of course, I was to be in charge of the Department of Surgery of the hospital. My colleague, the specialist physician was Dr. Rail. Dr. Rail, a Rhodesian, (I am not sure whether he was from the north or from the south) was the Acting Medical Administrator at the time. Of course, being a big hospital, of almost 1000 beds, its departments were well defined. Also there was a specialist gynecologist and obstetrician, Dr. S. C. Bose, in charge of that Department. Dr. Bose was a very hardworking expatriate doctor. He was the obstetrician to Fathia Nkrumah and who took care of her when she delivered her children. Dr. Bowesman had retired and was on terminal leave outside the country. Dr. Bowesman married Martha, an Ashanti nurse, many years previously, and he had always said that when he retired he would settle in Ghana. So he spent almost two years abroad. But it wasn't an idle time because during that time he wrote his book "Surgery and Surgical Pathology in the Tropics", which is a very unusual book, for practising surgeons and also even for medical students. So after nearly two years, Dr. Bowesman came back, I believe in late 1959, and established a clinic on Ellis Avenue, off Bekwai Road, in Kumasi. It was a small clinic, but he had a few lying-in beds and he was able to do a certain amount of surgery at the clinic. More about Dr. Bowesman later.

The Central Hospital itself had become a lot busier than I had known it a few years earlier and I was very happy because at this time, we had a number of young Ghanaian medical officers who had been posted to the hospital. I recall Dr. K. G. Korsah, who went on to become a surgeon and the first trained orthopedic surgeon. He joined the Ghana Medical School Staff and became a professor and is now retired and in private practice. Then there was Akiwuse Akiwumi, who also became a Fellow of the Royal College of Surgeons. He came back home after a short period after specialization and is now, I believe in America. Then there was Dr. John Owusu Ansah, who worked with me for quite a long time. He also went abroad and studied and became a Fellow of the Royal College of Surgeons and is also back in Ghana as a practising surgeon. At one time he was at the Nyaho Clinic as one of the consultants. And then there was Dr. John Bilson, who had trained in America and who also worked closely with me. But after finishing his internship and practising for a while, he left to establish his own clinic, the Allen Clinic, in Kumasi, which over the years, has made a useful contribution to health care delivery in Kumasi. Dr. Bilson, from time to time, made incursions into politics. I have known him as someone who is very much concerned, not only with medicine or health care but also with the general welfare and development of our country.

The young expatriate doctors who were at the time with me were Dr. Guillermo from the Philippines and Dr. Dimitri Photiades, who worked very closely with me. Regarding Dr. Photiades, some of the nurses called him "Dr. Anfom's shadow" because he seemed to be following me wherever I went. Years after Dr. Photiades was appointed a lecturer in Physiology at the University of Science and Technology. I also had some other surgical specialist colleagues who worked with me. First of all, there was Dr. Rovis, an Italian who was very much interested in orthopedic surgery. Unfortunately, his stay was very short. He left quite abruptly. I believe it had something to do with his wife's health! Then there was Dr. Yasnov, one of a team of three from Russia. He was a surgeon. Shereshewski was a pediatrician, and then there was a lady gynaecologist who was really the leader of the team. I cannot recall her name now, but these three Russians were there for just one tour. Then there was Dr. Peer, an Israeli surgeon. Peer was an older surgeon, much older than myself, and quite experienced, who came and joined the team. Of course, they weren't all there at the same time, but at different times.

The interesting thing about Dr. Peer was that, the day he arrived at the hospital, to report, I was very busy in the theatre treating an Israeli patient who happened to be no other than the Professor and Dean of the Faculty of Engineering of the University of Science and Technology. The professor on the previous night during dinner had had something stuck in his throat. Some of the food got stuck in his oesophagus (food pipe) and he was brought the following morning very distressed. I had to take him to the theatre and, under general anesthetic, passed an oesophaguscope to remove all the debris, to clear the passage. When Dr. Peer arrived, they gave him a gown, and mask and he came to the theatre. When I told him that the fellow on the operating table was his countryman he became interested. Dr. Peer's stay was short but I learnt quite a good deal from him.

My closest assistant was Dr. Azam, an Indian and also a Fellow of the Royal College of Surgeons Then there was Dr. Sen Gupta, an elderly Indian anaesthetist, with very good experience. I can say that because of Sen Gupta I was able to do more as a surgeon. I just hastened slowly, knowing that he would do everything possible to keep the patient alive. He and I got on very well and I shall always remember him for the cooperation we had. When I was performing a thyroid operation he used to say that I was working like an artist. Well, I was working leisurely, and precisely because I knew that my patient was safe. I did not have to rush. I was hurrying slowly, but surely. Then there was old man Jabbar. Dr. Jabbar was an experiesnced Indian radiologist. Unfortunately he died in Kumasi and was cremated. That was the first and only cremation that I have ever witnessed, at the Old Tafo cemetery.

In the course of a doctor's working life, there are times when he is faced with very difficult situations or very serious conditions involving close relations or personal friends. Here I recount two such occasions when I was called upon to deal with patients who were my very close friends whom I had known over long periods. The first was the late Edmund Alhassan, who was then an Education Officer stationed at Bekwai. Ali, as I called him, was my schoolmate at Achimota, in the mid 1930's and we played hockey together. So I was shocked when one evening I was called in to see an "emergency" that had been brought from Bekwai. When I got to the hospital and looked at the patient who was deeply comatose, I recognized that it was my friend Ali. He had fallen a week previously and, following a transient concussion, he became conscious and was able to go about his duties; however, a few days later he started getting drowsy and eventually became rapidly comatose. From the history and the physical examination, it was a classic case of what we surgeons know as "middle meningial hemorrhage" which meant that when he fell down, he knocked his head against the floor thus damaging one of the blood vessels within the skull from which blood was leaking very slowly. The increasing pool of blood formed was pressing on the brain and causing damage to the vital centres. Of course, I had to operate immediately to relieve the pressure by removing the blood and stopping the bleeding. However, he had really reached the point of no return. The effect of the damage was irreversible, and within 48 hours he was gone. Needless to say, it gave me many sleepless nights. Here was somebody who was well known to me, a strapping, healthy person, who suddenly encountered this unfortunate fatal accident, thereby curtailing a very bright career! It was very shattering for me for quite a long time.

Years after, sometime in 1962, I believe, I was called urgently to the hospital to see two accident patients. They were both from the Ghana Army. They had been in a helicopter crash, somewhere in the Ashanti Region. Both patients were suffering from burns. One of them had very extensive burns involving more than three-quarters of the body. To my utter surprise, it was Joe Michel, now Brigadier Michel, who 5 years previously, as Major Michel, had served in Tamale when I was there as surgeon. Despite the very severe injury, as soon as I walked into the ward and I started talking, he said, "Hello, Emman, Emmanuel", so I walked to his bed and asked, " How are you?" "Well as you can see, I'm badly hurt, but I feel alright." My heart sank at that time because, I knew straight away that the outlook was really, very gloomy indeed. I had to rally everybody round, to look after him for another three days. However, the odds were so heavily stacked against him having regard to the extent and severity of the burns. I did not sleep much for three days as I had to be running in and out of the hospital whilst at the same time attending to other patients. It was indeed a sad loss to Ghana that this very gallant soldier, one of the most senior and finest Ghanaian Army Officers, should suffer such a tragic end as a result of a plane crash.

Brigadier Michel's companion was an expatriate from the British Army, attached to the Ghana Army. His burns were not extensive but they were deep on both legs. There was word from Accra that he should be transferred to Accra. Of course, I was going to do that anyway. After about a week I heard news from Accra that he had died at the 37

Military Hospital. It turned out that the burns were deeper, much deeper and had destroyed much more tissue than one could really evaluate on first examination.

These were two examples of people whom I had known very well. Both Ali and Joe Michel, were friends, and it was really very disappointing for me as a doctor that they arrived in such serious conditions that all that I could do could not save them. Incidentally, Michel Camp is named after the late Joe Michel, a fine solider and a noble son of the soil.

## A Royal Patient

On a happier note, sometime in 1960, as I sat down to have my supper, one evening at about seven o'clock, the telephone rang. It was my senior colleague and former boss Dr. Charles Bowesman who informed me that he'd been called by Dr. Roberts, personal physician to the Asantehene, to see Otumfuo, Nana Sir Osei Agyeman Prempeh II. He thought Otumfuo should be admitted to hospital. It was a surgical condition which would require major surgery, after a period of preparation, and that he had informed Otumfuo that he needed to be in hospital and he had agreed that the admission, management, and subsequent discharge of Otumfuo from hospital be treated with the utmost secrecy. As a first step, we should arrange to get Otumfuo taken to the hospital at nine o'clock. I should be there to receive him and we could have consultation together, that is, Dr. Bowesman and myself. I called the hospital immediately and spoke to the departmental sister of the Surgical Block and asked her to get the best side-ward ready for a VIP who would be coming into hospital, before nine o'clock. I would be coming to the hospital myself as soon as I had finished my meal. So we got everything ready, and at about a quarter to nine, when the night staff had taken over and the hospital was fairly quiet, the royal patient was brought in and admitted. I was there to receive him and Dr. Bowesman arrived almost simultaneously.

I must say that I was very happy to see Otumfuo, because as soon as he saw me he smiled, the sort of smile of confidence both for him and for me too. As soon as he was made ready and comfortable in bed Dr. Bowesman and I did the evaluation and we agreed that something needed to be done in a few days. Meanwhile, we would do everything to prepare him and make him fit to withstand the operation. Because of the personality involved, Dr. Bowesman advised that perhaps it would be a good idea to invite our colleague, Dr. Charles Easmon, from Accra to come and also have a look at him. So that, together, the three of us could put our heads together to decide on what would be the best line of action. I immediately called Charlie's number in Accra and invited him. He came by the first plane the following day and, after a quick consultation and, considering many things, including the political climate at the time and the need for Otumfuo to have a smooth convalescence, we decided that, even though we could manage in Ghana, perhaps we should recommend that he should go abroad.

I informed Mr. Henry Prempeh, a leading lawyer in Kumasi and spokesman for the family and awaited an early reaction. Meanwhile, Charlie Easmon went back to Accra by the afternoon plane. Early the next morning, Mr. Henry Prempeh came to my house to inform me that when the proposition was put to Otumfuo about going abroad for treatment, he refused point blank. He was not going anywhere. He thought, Dr. Anfom and Dr, Bowesman and Dr. Easmon could handle the matter here in Ghana, so he wasn't going anywhere. Really, I was absolutely flabbergasted. I think what really impressed me was the indication of the confidence that Otumfuo had in us. I went to the hospital to have a chat with him. By this time he was feeling a bit better. As soon as I entered the ward, he said to me, "Dr. Anfom, haven't you been dealing with cases like this. Is it the very first that you people are seeing?" "No, Sir, we deal with patients with this condition regularly." "So why are you advising that I go abroad?" I must say that I felt a bit foolish at this question and I said, "Yes, Nana, we can do it here, I mean if this is your preference." "Of course, it's my preference if you've been handling cases of this nature, I would feel happier, if I did not go anywhere."

I informed Dr. Bowesman and Dr. Easmon in Accra that Otumfuo had expressed supreme confidence in us and so we just had to do our best. To cut a long story short, in a few days we got Nana sufficiently well to withstand the major operation. All this happened in very strict secrecy so much so that at the time of the operation, which was performed at night, apart from the theatre sister, all the attendants in the theatre were doctors. There were three surgeons - Dr. Bowesman, Dr. Charles Easmon and I. We took turns to execute major stages of the operations. Fortunately, we had the very experienced anaesthetist, Dr. Sen Gupta, to administer the anesthetic. He did it so expertly that everything went very smoothly. Within a week, I was able to discharge Otumfuo. After that I visited him daily, for about three weeks. On occasion, I got the Physician Specialist, Dr. Rail, also to go and see him and examine his chest to see if there were any residual effects of the anaesthetic. I am glad to report that everything went on very smoothly. About a month after the operation, the President, Osagyefo Dr. Kwame Nkrumah on a visit to Kumasi called on Otumfuo and as a result of the visit he arranged for him to go abroad for a couple of months' convalescence. Now, I think it was important to tell this story because for us doctors, to have such an important personality display such confidence in us was really highly encouraging!

## Expedition To The Congo

That same year, 1960, in the month of June, I believe, early one morning at about half past five, the telephone rang. It was Dr. E. W. Q. Bannerman, Acting Chief Medical Officer, calling from Accra. His message was that I was to get myself in readiness, within forty-eight hours to lead a team of Ghanaian doctors and nurses to go to Leopoldville, in the Belgium Congo (as it was then) to man one of the hospitals. I had heard vaguely in the news that there had been a crisis in the Congo involving a mutiny in the army and that the Congolese had practically taken over the government from the Belgians. The leader of this rebellion was Lumumba. In any case, things were rather chaotic and there were United Nations troops being sent there and there were troops being sent by the President of Ghana. The greatest need now was for doctors and nurses, because as a result of the mutiny and the chaos, practically all the Belgian doctors had fled across the Congo River to Brazzaville. It was very important, and the President Nkrumah had so decided that Ghana should help by sending a contingent of about twelve doctors and four nursing sisters as soon as possible to the Congo.

I must say that this came at a most inconvenient time for me. I was about to take my annual leave. My wife had gone over to America to visit her people and the plan was that after a few months I would join her so that I would spend part of my leave in America. This new development had, therefore, come to interfere with our plans. In any case, the situation had to be treated with the utmost priority and urgency. That day I immediately telephoned the USA. In addition, I sent a cable to Leonora to tell her about what was happening and that unfortunately my plans for coming to the United States had to be changed and I had to answer the call to go to the Congo. Indeed, since I did not know how long I was going to be there, it would be necessary for her to curtail her visit and to come back home earlier than planned. My mother was staying with us at that time and also my half-sister, Auntie Okailey who was looking after three children. There was nothing else I could do than to obey. The only thing was that at this point in time, there were only two surgeons, Dr. Azam, the Indian surgeon, my assistant at the hospital and myself. When I enquired why they were not sending Dr. Azam instead, Dr. Bannerman indicated that it would have been inexpedient politically to send doctors of other nationalities. We were to be all-Ghanaian doctors and they were expecting me to be the clinical leader of the team. Of course, there would be occasional supervision from Accra, when Dr. Robertson, who was the Principal Medical Officer at the Headquarters, would be visiting us.

Two days later, I left early in the morning for Accra to join other doctors who had assembled at the Ministry of Health. We were to fly that evening to Leopoldville. I recall that apart from me there were the late Dr. K. K. Bentsi-Enchill, the gynecologist/ obstetrician, Dr. A. Akiwumi, now of the Tudu Clinic, the physician specialist. Others were Dr. Yaw Asinfi, Dr. Bondzie-Simpson, the late Dr. Dankyi, the late Dr. Kemavor, Dr. Tagboto, Dr. Mills who was then working at the Central Hospital in Kumasi and now resident in the United Kingdom, Dr. Portuphy Lamptey, who was really a great asset to us. Having studied in Switzerland, he was fluent in French and since we were not given an official interpreter, he was the one who acted as interpreter for us everywhere we went. There were also the late Dr. Susan de Graft Johnson and four nursing sisters whom I recall as Miss Agyepong, Miss Dorcas Arku, Miss Dorothy Hutton-Mills and Miss Lamptey.

That evening, we left by a Russian Ilyushin plane for Leopoldville. We arrived there at night. It must have been round eleven o'clock getting on to midnight. At the airport to meet us was the late Dr. J. N. Robertson, from the Ministry of Health who had already gone ahead. I must confess that the sight of the Leopoldville Airport was an unexpected spectacle for us. It looked just like an airport in any European city. Our own airport terminal in Accra at that time was very small. The Leopoldville Airport was vast with bright lights and it was just like we were in Europe. The drive to Leopoldville was quite a distance; I believe it was about 15 to 20 kilometers, and a double carriageway.

Leopoldville itself gave us the impression of our being in a European city, not being in Africa at all! The Belgian colonial policy was one of settlement of Europeans permanently in Africa; so everything was done with this in view. The African townships had poor housing and there were some shanty towns from which the African workers came and worked in the cities during the day and went back to their townships at night. Our first impression of Leopoldville was one of surprise and amazement and we wondered whether we were really needed there.

On arrival we were taken to a high-class 4 or 5 star hotel, the Memlin Hotel, on one of the famous boulevards in the city. Driving round the city, we saw evidence of the violence that had occurred. Cars that had been overturned and burnt were on the sides of the streets. Buildings had been burnt and gutted, and it was very clear that quite recently, there had been much violence during the army mutiny.

The next morning, we paid a courtesy call on the Minster for Health. It appeared that even though we were sent by Ghana we were really on arrival to come under United Nations control. We were to get our instructions from the local Ministry of Health. We found certain things strange. First of all, we had to wait for the Minister for a long time. When he arrived, we saw that he was quite a young person. He was wearing a black dinner suit, like somebody who had been to a party the previous night, had come home late and therefore come to work without changing! There were very few senior Congolese public officials to attend to us apart from clerical officers and messengers. This was because the Belgian policy was not to train the Congolese to any high educational levels. Between him, the Minister, and the clerical officer, there were no Principal Secretary and Executive Officers. They had all been Belgians, who had deserted! So although political control was in the hands of the Congolese, the politicians had no efficient civil service support.

We had been told that we were to man one hospital in Leopoldville, but we discovered that this was not so. Arrangements were being made for us to be sent out of Leopoldville to the hinterland to work in district hospitals. As it turned out, we sat around for a whole week dong nothing before this posting was done. Meanwhile, we decided that the atmosphere was not really suitable for our ladies, so we got Dr. Robertson, in consultation with Ghanaian Army chiefs in Leopoldville, to arrange to send them back home. This included Dr. Susan de Graft Johnson.

After one week's idleness, we were separated. Six of the contingent were sent to Boma, which was the old capital of the Belgian Congo, to man a hospital there. The remaining six went in twos to hospitals in different parts of the Congo. Those of us who went to Boma were Dr. Kwesi Bentsi-Enchil and Dr. Akiwumi who were specialists, the three medical officers and myself. The hospital was a small one of about eighty beds. The nursing sisters were all Belgian nuns attached to the Roman Catholic Church. They were all in hiding and only came out when there was a surgical emergency. There wasn't much work to do. I was rather irritated because I had come from Kumasi where I was very busy and now I had come here where there was relatively little to do. The interesting thing was that the first emergency surgical case that arrived was a strangulated hernia. I was getting ready to operate. The nursing sisters had been responsible for giving the anesthesia. When they were called, they asked who was going to do the operation! To cut a long story short they were quite surprised to see Africans doing major surgery. Later there were abdominal cases including maternity and gynecological emergencies which we dealt with successfully. The sisters were quite impressed. I think our performance was an eye-opener for the Congolese also because at that time, there was not a single trained Congolese doctor.

The Belgians had made sure that the training got up to what they called the "medical assistant level," something akin to the health superintendent which we have in Ghana. After a few weeks I suggested that Kwesi Enchil, the gynecologist, Akiwumi, the physician specialist and I could go back home, leaving the medical officers to stay on for a little while. They all had enough experience to enable them to cope with the situation. We agitated every day until, mercifully, Brigadier Michel, who was in charge of the Ghana contingent at the time, arranged for the three of us to come back to Ghana after one month, whilst the medical officers stayed on for another two months.

When the time came for us to leave, we just went to Leopoldville Airport and at about ten o'clock at night an Ilyushin plane arrived from Accra. We were the only passengers on the return flight to Accra. We arrived in Accra a couple of hours after midnight. We were not met as no one knew we were coming, so we found our way to our various homes. We reported the following morning at the Ministry and then went back to our stations. Our medical officer colleagues followed two months later. Now, at Leopoldville airport, I bought a lovely wall piece depicting the torso of a Congolese woman. This artefact now hangs on a wall in my living room. There is an amusing story about this work of art. Nii Okai, my eldest son, then aged 7, in writing to his mother said, among other things, that "Daddy is home. He brought a Congolese woman with him!" Leonora used to tell this story with great amusement, but always omitted to say that as soon as she got this letter, she got on the next flight and came back home, with great speed!!

Our medical colleagues whom we left behind in the Congo were assigned in pairs to hospitals in the rural areas, and they were there for another two months before they were sent back home. One thing which I'd like to note here is that since we came back from the Congo, none of us, as far as I know, has received a letter of thanks for going to the Congo at a difficult and dangerous time, thereby taking great risks. A word of thanks would have been in order. It was over forty years ago, and none of us have had any acknowledgement or recognition of what we did. I feel very strongly about this and hope that our Governments will in future take note of this. A simple letter of appreciation would always help to encourage citizens of this country to work harder for their country.

During this period in Kumasi, I was very pleased with the support which my former boss, Dr. Bowesman, gave me. He referred many cases to me, due to the limitations of his small clinic which did not enable him to deal with certain types of cases, and he always recommended me highly to his patients. I believe the height of his confidence was shown when his own mother-in-law, Martha's mother, had an acute abdominal emergency. The old lady was in her seventies when this sudden emergency occurred. Dr. Bowesman sent her to the hospital for admission and emergency operation. Of course, he himself was there to assist at the operation. Unfortunately, it was a most unusual condition and her age and the state of her health did not allow us to do what we could have done for her. She therefore survived just a few days after the limited procedure.

At that time, the National Cultural Centre in Kumasi was in its early stages of establishment, with Dr. Alex Kyerematen as its first Director. Dr. Kyerematen was an anthropologist. I could see that he was someone who had set himself a mission, namely, the revival and preservation of our cultural heritage in Ghana. He set out, almost single handedly, to build the Center, and assembled cultural artefacts and exhibits portraying Ashanti history and exhibits from all over the country to make the Centre really national in character. Now, there were several activities at the Centre also - cultural drumming and dancing, and lectures by various people on aspects of African History, Ashanti history and the history of other Ghanaian cultures. There was a Cultural Centre Choir and occasional interdenominational church services which Leonora and I helped to organize. The Cultural Centre Choir was under the baton of Dr. Ellis Djoleto, Principal Medical Officer of the Ministry of Health in Ashanti, and Leonora was the pianist who accompanied the Choir. In many ways, we did much to support Alex.

In 1960 when Ghana became a Republic and the Central Organization for Sports was established with Ohene Djan as the Director, the idea of the formation of Sporting Clubs was mooted. For a start, every football club was supposed to be in affiliation with other lesser known sports, for example athletics, hockey, tennis, and boxing. The idea was to have these clubs which would have different sporting activities, so that eventually there would be for instance Hearts of Oak Sporting Club, Kotoko Sporting Club, Great Olympics Sporting Club, and so on. For a start, however, as I was very keen to popularize hockey throughout the country, Ohene Djan agreed to my suggestion that every important football match be preceded by a hockey match for half an hour or forty minutes as a way of introducing hockey to the masses. I therefore joined the Kotoko Hockey Club and we played matches against other hockey clubs, for example, the Army, Police or Old Boys' Association Hockey Clubs. The whole idea was to popularize hockey.

It was during one of our matches against the Army that an opponent, inadvertently hit my right thumb with a hockey stick causing a fracture. I, therefore, had to wear the P.O.P. for six weeks. It was whilst I was watching a hockey match on the Army Hockey field with my hand in POP cast, that the Assistant Commissioner of Police, at the time, Mr. Quarm, came all the way to the hockey field to inform me that there had been an accident involving President Nkrumah at Kulungugu. There was a wireless message that I should be flown to the North immediately. Unfortunately, because of my condition, I could not go so they had to arrange for another surgeon to go from Accra.

Needless to say, at that time I felt that the time had come to say good-bye to hockey. It had taken too much of my time. It had been a good exercise for me. For twenty-seven years I had played every season, and now when I was at the height of my professional career it was threatening, to interfere with my work. So after the plaster of Paris cast came off, I said good-bye to playing first class hockey. Of course, my interest continued in the area of the administration of hockey. I became President of the Ghana Hockey Association at a later date.

Socially too, I joined some friends to start the City Dining Club. It was an exclusive club for professionals, businessmen, and lecturers form the University. We met once a month for dinner at which distinguished guests of honour gave after dinner- speeches. It was also in a way an international club because we had Ghanaians, Nigerians, Lebanese, and Indians as members. I recall Mr. Victor Baboo, one of the leading lights of the Club and the Managing Director of the Kumasi Brewery at the time, were members, and then the Ghanaians whom I recall were the late Frank Mensah-Bonsu, William de Bordes of the Social Welfare Department, David Effah, a leading lawyer and Mr. George Hakim, a Lebanese businessman. Most of our dinners were held at the University in one of the Halls of Residence. When the City Hotel was built we started having some of our dinners there.

## Sudden Death of My Mother

At the personal level, my mother, who had been living with us for a couple of years, died whilst I was away at a Conference in the United States of America. I was in Chicago. It was a Conference of the International College of Surgeons to which I had been elected the previous year, in 1960. My mother died on June 12, 1961. I had to rush back immediately. The Conference was over and I had planned to take a short holiday in the United States, but I rushed back immediately to take charge of the funeral arrangements. Needless to say, this was a big shock to me, considering the important role which my mother had played in my life. I was thankful to God that she was spared another eleven years after my return home in 1950 after my studies abroad. Whilst I was in the States, in New York, I stayed with Aunt Rachel, Leonora's "mother", and the news of my mother's death came to me as I was with her. Aunt Rachel had all the time promised that when she retired, she would come and spend some time with us in Ghana. She was to retire in August that year. She came to Ghana in October to stay with us in Kumasi. An important family event, which took place before I left Kumasi, was that our last child, Charlie was born on May 17th 1963.

# CHAPTER 20

# THE GHANA MEDICAL SCHOOL

When the Korlebu Hospital was built in the 1920s, the then Governor of the Gold Coast, Sir Gordon Guggisburg, had planned that it would one day become a Medical Centre for the training of doctors, nurses, pharmacists and other health delivery personnel. Almost four decades after this original vision by Guggisberg the idea was resuscitated. Shortly after the founding of the Ghana Medical Association, the Government of the first Republic set in motion arrangements and plans for the establishment of such a medical school, I am not really competent to discuss in any detail all that went on behind the scenes, as at that time everything was centered in Accra and, even though I was a senior member of the medical profession, my involvement was in an indirect manner as a member of the Medical Association, which from time to time gave its own inputs. Be that as it may, the decision was firmly taken, but there was a good deal of confusion, in the run-up to the establishment of the School and there are certain points which one must make.

First of all, the idea was that the School would be an independent Medical School initially, independent of the University. President Nkrumah went as far as concluding an agreement with the Americans, to help in funding and managing the School. The assistance was to come mainly from the Temple University Medical School in Pennsylvania. A Dean for the School was appointed, Dean Cross. The implementation of the agreement was stillborn as President Nkrumah abrogated the agreement at the eleventh hour. Ghanaian doctors, were called upon to start the Medical School on their own under the leadership of Dr. Charles Easmon, who was at that time the Chief Surgeon at the Korle Bu Hospital.

## At The Department Of Surgical Science
Edinburgh University

I knew that whether under the American Agreement or not, as one of the senior surgeons I was bound to become involved at some future date with the work at the Medical School. Consequently, I sought to go on Study Leave in 1963, shortly after our son Charlie, was born. I thought I needed at least a year abroad, in a research department to familiarize myself with methods of research and also with methods of medical education before offering myself, for a teaching post in the future Medical School.

It was at this point that an important decision taken at that time went contrary to the position of the Ghana Medical Association. That decision was to use Korlebu as a Teaching Hospital. The Medical Association held the view that a new Teaching Hospital should be built somewhere near the University of Ghana, Legon, and that Korlebu should be retained, as it was, but possibly adding about fifty beds. At that time, I believe the bed strength was 350 or 400. By improving certain facilities, it could be used as an additional hospital for clinical teaching. The Association felt that it would be tidier and that the work at the new Teaching Hospital would go on better if it was separate from Korlebu. This view was resisted in Government circles, and consequently rejected. The result was that Korlebu was expanded by the addition of four high rise blocks, namely, Surgical, Medical, Pediatric and Obstetric Blocks. With the passage of time, new buildings have sprung up in an unplanned fashion and Korlebu, now as a Teaching Hospital, has become a huge metropolis. The administration is rather unwieldy and, we could have done better if we had left Korlebu well alone and built a new Teaching Hospital at a separate location.

So it was that in spite of arrangements by Government to send younger colleagues abroad for training, especially in the basic sciences, I made my own arrangement to go back to the Edinburgh University Department of Surgical Sciences. I had seen an advertisement in the British Medical Journal for a Research Fellowship. Unfortunately, I applied rather late, but Professor Micheal Woodruff, Head of the Department, was all the same willing to take me on for a year. As I was due for leave, I asked for an extended leave for one year, which was granted. So in August 1963, I went back to Edinburgh.

Incidentally, I had to pay the passages of my wife and four young children and that of Aunt Rachel, who was staying with us at the time. I went ahead by boat, "Nasia River" of the Black Star Line. The interesting thing for me was that the captain, Captain Tachie-Menson, and all the officers and crew, were Ghanaians. It was a very relaxing trip which made it possible for me to have a much needed rest. Upon my arrival in the United Kingdom, I waited in London, for Leonora and the children to come by air, before we went up to Edinburgh. Aunt Rachel also came by cargo boat, which docked in Glasgow after our arrival, and I went to meet her.

The main research work going on in Prof. Woodruff's Department was on Transplantation of Tissues and Organs. At that time pioneering work was being done on the transplantation of kidneys. The important aspect of the ongoing research was how to prevent the rejection of a donated kidney by the host; to look into the immunological processes going on and how these could be suppressed so that the patient retained on a permanent basis the new kidney that had been donated. I was, therefore, introduced, to work on laboratory animals, small animals, such as mice and rabbits. I must say that I found it a little bit difficult to get used to the smaller animals, especially the mice. During the year, I took part in research work on mice to get to the bottom of the minute cellular changes that took place; the transformations that took place after transplantation. Very important pioneering work was being done and I was privileged to be a member of the team. After one year my request for extension of time was rejected owing to the urgent need for me to join the foundation staff of the new medical school at home.

Another work, which I did independently, was to study the records of 400 consecutive deaths at the Royal Infirmary, Edinburgh, to find out the conditions of the kidneys. It was a very revealing piece of work which I did not complete before leaving, but the indications were that the possible donors from the cadavers for future transplantation would be very few indeed because of the variety of diseases and the ages of the deceased which rendered their kidneys unsuitable. Now this piece of research was important from the point of view of the availability of donors for kidney transplantation. Once a way was found to suppress the immune mechanism, the next stage would be how to store cadaver kidneys for transplantation. Hence the need for healthy donors.

The transplantation of tissues and organs at that time was at the new frontiers of surgery, especially the immunological aspects. Since then, of course, much water has passed under the bridge, and far-reaching advances have been made so that now not only the kidneys but also the heart, lungs and liver can be transplanted. The transplantation of the kidneys has now become a routine operation. One need not wait to have an identical twin or even a close relative, provided the tissue type indicates that the organ might not be easily rejected. It is possible now by administering immunosuppressive drugs, to keep a patient alive for many years. It is also possible now to have a tissue bank, for example, a kidney bank, where the organ is frozen and kept and, when needed, provided there had been previous tissue typing, to give it to a recipient.

Nkrumah's decision to abrogate the agreement with the American's really placed a lot of pressure on Ghanaian doctors. So I was not surprised when Dr. Charles Easmon Dean-designate, came up to Edinburgh, to persuade me, to come back home to help. Easmon at that time, had been appointed Professor of Surgery and first Dean of the Ghana Medical School. I was therefore obliged to leave important research work that I was doing in midstream to come back to Ghana, with no hope of continuing with my research, considering the inadequate facilities at home.

## The Ghana Medical School and Korlebu Teaching Hospital

Before I left home in 1963, students had been taken in the previous year, to study the required subjects for the two-year pre-medical course at Legon. These subjects were Physics, Chemistry and Biology. Later Mathematics was added, as an option. The students were to do this for two years, so that by the time, October 1964, that medical subjects were to start they would have completed the Basic Sciences at Legon and then move to the Medical School premises at Korle Bu.

The pre-clinical subjects to be studied for the two years were Anatomy, Physiology and Biochemistry and these they were to do for two years. This course started for the first batch of students in October 1964 and I got back home the following month, November 1964. At that time of course, clinical teaching had not started, and therefore some of us were to help with the teaching of Anatomy, Physiology and Biochemistry. Dr. J. K. M. Quartey had to take leave from his clinical work in surgery to set up the Department of Anatomy. So for a little more than one year, Dr. Quartery was solely in-charge of the Anatomy Department teaching with the help of other surgeons, Dr. E. A. Badoe, and myself were the ones who helped Dr. Quartey. Dr. F. Engmann, newly arrived medical officer, who had done a first degree in Anatomy in Cambridge, also joined Dr. Quartey. Just about that time, Dr. Harold Phillips who'd been on a course in Canada, came back to take charge of the Department of Physiology, whilst Dr. Andoh from a German Medical School came to head the Biochemistry Department. The point I want to make is that at that time the staff for the pre-clinical subjects was very thin on the ground, so clinicians had to come to the rescue.

In Anatomy, I gave lectures to the first batch of students. In one of my lectures I had to demonstrate the intricate peritoneal folds of the abdomen. Not an easy matter. However, I tried to do my best to get the students to understand this by using handkerchieves and scarves. Unknown to me I had earned the nickname "Omentum." The Great Omentum is the great "policeman of the abdomen", the troubleshooter who wanders in the abdomen, to trouble spots, trying to contain matters, infection and so on. Years later, I learnt from one of the students who had now become a professor in the Medical School that this had been my nickname all along. Well, I feel quite proud to be named after such a great law-enforcer, the Omentum!

In the training of doctors, there is no way that one could teach the clinical subjects such as, surgery medicine, and what have you. without providing service as well. This is an important difference between training students to become doctors and training to become, for example engineers. In the Engineering School, there are lectures and instruction in workshops, not factories; whereas in the medical school, the lectures and actual instruction are in the wards, consulting rooms and operating theatres whilst providing service.

Despite the rush on me to come back home in 1964, when I arrived, there was no official accommodation for me at the Korlebu campus. Fortunately, my house at Tesano was then vacant, so I had to stay there, miles away from the hospital, for nine months. On two occasions when it rained and there were floods, I could not go to the hospital. Besides even though it was critical for me to have a telephone, at that time there was no telephone in my house. When accommodation became available at the Korlebu campus I had to stay in a small two-bedroom bungalow, really meant for nursing-sisters, for a couple of years. Just before the time came for me to leave Korlebu a third bedroom was added to the house. So I enjoyed that luxury just for a couple of months before leaving Korlebu.

Now to come back to the actual work of teaching students. I do not have to emphasize that the students who had chosen to do medicine were the cream of the science students, especially those who had a natural bent for the biological sciences. The teacher was, therefore, dealing with first class students and had, therefore, to be on his toes when teaching them. They were brilliant students! That was one of the reasons why, despite the handicaps, despite the difficulties that we faced as teachers due to inadequate facilities, these students were able to make the grade and to sail through the course. Personally, I found it really stimulating. My interaction with the bright students really made me feel much younger and active.

After teaching the clinical subjects for one year in the following year, that is 1967, something happened which became an important turning point in my life. I had then been acting part time, in addition to my teaching and clinical duties, as the Chief Medical Administrator of the hospital in the absence of the substantive holder, Dr. E. J. Fleischer Djoleto, who was on a long sick leave in the United Kingdom. At that time, the responsibilities of the Chief Medical Administrator extended beyond Korlebu to cover the smaller hospitals - The Ridge Hospital and also all the Polyclinics.

In the absence of a separate teaching hospital, there was bound to be a clash between the Ministry of Health, which owned the hospitals and the Medical School, which was really camping on the premises of Korlebu and using the facilities of the hospital for teaching purposes. The clamour by the hospital administration to have a really high-powered Management Board with some teeth and which would become the sole employer of those who worked in the hospital, was never really properly addressed. Dr. Djoleto had problems with this matter. For example, those doctors who were employed directly by the Medical School and were teaching in the hospital felt that they owed all the allegiance to the Dean of the Medical School. The administrator who assigned clinical duties sometimes felt snubbed when a member of staff of the Medical School just travelled out of the country without his knowledge. There were so many instances where there was bound to be a clash between the Medical School and the Teaching Hospital. I suppose the fact that I was the most senior doctor after Dr. Easmon, the Dean of the Medical

School, was the reason I was asked to act as the Chief Medical Administrator, in the hope that my having one-foot in either camp, as it were, would make it easier for co-existence between the Medical School and the Teaching Hospital. Even at that time, some of the doctors teaching at the Medical School were still Ministry of Health staff who were paid allowances for teaching. I believe this applied to quite a number of us until the School was firmly established.

# CHAPTER 21

# CALL TO OTHER SERVICE

Now the incident I want to refer to is an important one. Early one morning at 5.30 the telephone rang. The voice at the other end was that of Dr. Alex Kyerematen, who was then the Commissioner for Local Government in the regime of the National Liberation Council. There had been a military-cum-police take-over of the Nkrumah Government in February the previous year. Dr. Kyerematen was appointed Chairman of the Council of the University for Science and Technology. I had not seen or spoken to Alex Kyerematen for quite a long time, and indeed, I had not even met him since he became Commissioner. I was really taken aback when he told me, "Evans, we are looking for a new Vice-Chancellor for the University of Science and Technology. I suppose you know that I am the new Chairman of the Council following the death of Mr. Justice Adumuah Bossman, in a tragic motor accident. The University has been without a substantive Vice-Chancellor for almost a year. We are looking for a new person and I just wanted to ask you, because your name has come up in several circles. It is the responsibility of the Council to appoint a new Vice-Chancellor. Of course, the appointment has to be endorsed by the Government."

"The reason I have called you this morning is to ask whether you would be willing to have your name put forward for consideration by the University Council." So I asked, "Well, what about Professor Twum-Barima? He's acting Vice-Chancellor now. Why can he not be confirmed"? Well, he replied, The reason the University Council has decided to bring in an outsider is that there is so much polarization at the University Campus and we want somebody who can come in as a neutral outsider. Somebody who can bring people together. We want somebody with certain personal qualities." "Well, I hope you know that I'm not even a professor." "Dr. Baffour, who was the Vice-Chancellor for six years, was not a professor, either. Besides, we've looked into your background and there has been some search discreetly and we're all informed that even though you aren't a professor but a senior lecturer, you really are professorial material. In any case we're not appointing a professor, we're appointing a Vice-Chancellor and we want somebody who is a respected professional, somebody who is competent in his profession, somebody who the academic staff, would respect. Of the short-listed names that we have received, yours really tops the list and, in my opinion, you're the one that fits the bill best. I know it will be a difficult decision for you to make, but at the same time, I feel that the assignment that we have as a Council is so important that we must come up with the most suitable person for the post.

"Another thing which I feel very strongly about and for which reason I really called you and would, therefore, urge you to think very seriously about accepting, if offered the post, is that it's quite likely that if we don't find a suitable person, locally, the present Government, a military Government, might quite easily bring in an expatriate which, in my view, would be a retrograde step." "Well, thank you very much, Alex, for thinking about me in this way. But you know that I have to weigh matters very carefully. I know you're in a bit of a hurry, but would you please give me twenty-four hours to think about it? Call me tomorrow morning at about this time. As you know, there's at least one person, who is well known to you, that I have to discuss this matter with." "Okay, Evans, let me say hello to Leonora." So I passed the telephone on to Leonora and after they had finished their conversation, Leonora asked me, "What does Alex want, because he was asking me to try to persuade you to give them a positive answer." So I said, "My dear, we'll have a chat about this. It's something most unexpected, and it concerns the Vice-Chancellorship of the University of Science and Technology. Let's have our breakfast and we'll talk about it before I go to work. Meanwhile, we must pray hard." "What exactly did he ask you?" she persisted. "Well, as you know our good friend, Dr. Baffour, left the University of Science and Technology under pressure last year. The Vice-Chancellor's post is vacant and Alex is asking me if I would agree to my name being put forward for consideration by the Council. He's now the Chairman of Council and he's urging me to say 'yes.'"

The new Vice-Chancellor was supposed to assume office by 1ˢᵗ October at the latest. That is, at the beginning of the academic year,

1967/1968. It was then May, so there was some urgency in the matter. I thought about the work that I was doing at the medical school. We were at the pioneering stages of the School. The sort of teaching I was involved in was clinical teaching. As far as the administration of the hospital was concerned, well, that was just an acting appointment, but I was most concerned about the teaching, and also the clinical work. Fortunately, at that time, my first assistant was the late Dr. Arbenser who was also a competent surgeon, and also a fellow of the Royal College of Surgeons, and also Dr. Henry Tackyi, second assistant, a former pupil of mine at Achimota. He also was a Fellow of the Royal College of Surgeons. Both of them were competent surgeons. So there was no problem there.

I thought about many things. I thought that at that point in time, I had been graduated and been in the medical practice for twenty years, seventeen of which had been in Ghana, first with the Ministry of Health and now the Ghana Medical School. I also thought about my love for education and my initial aspiration to become a teacher and the fact that as far back as 1941, for one year, I was on the staff of Achimota College whilst waiting to go abroad. Also that for three years I had been teaching at the medical School. The question I had to answer was, "If I were to be appointed to the post, would I be rendering useful service to Ghana? Would it be just service in another way?"

Clearly, the Vice-Chancellorship would open many vistas for me, even though it would really curtail my progression in the medical profession. The broad field of education was bound to broaden my outlook. It would seem that from the purely educational point of view, I would be educating myself, and looking at it from that viewpoint was also a problem. The question was, "Would I really be serving Ghana well? Was I equipped to serve Ghana as well, if not better, in that position?" These were thoughts that concerned me.

Now, looking back at the fact that on a personal level, my academic advancement, my research work, had been interrupted mid-stream and in a way, frustrated despite the fact that I was abandoning it to come to help to found a new institution, the Medical School, I thought I had done enough, as a foundation member to help to start the School. We had not yet seen the first products of our labours yet even though I had no doubt at all, considering the calibre of students that we had, that in a couple of years, they would all come out as, excellent young men and women doctors to join the ranks of the medical profession.

These thoughts and more crossed my mind. So after breakfast, Leonora and I discussed the matter for about half an hour. We said a word of prayer and she brought out her own thoughts. The sum total of her reaction was that I had done twenty years of good service in medicine. She had been married to me for fifteen years, she'd known me for almost twenty years and she'd been watching me this past year when the burden of administering the Teaching Hospital was added to my work. She had been asking herself, "Well, he has spent so much time in administration and really his attention must be divided in his medical work - teaching students and providing health care service. I know you my husband. There's no question that you can do the work of Vice-Chancellor admirably, I know that. I know you can be firm and also fair in taking decisions, and I feel that what's happening in Kumasi now requires somebody who's a peacemaker, who can bring people together. If you're able to do this, you'd have made a good contribution. You've always liked education, and this will give you the opportunity to pursue and be involved in general education. It's higher education, but you cannot really divorce it from all education, and I think that you'd be able to see the country's problems in a wider perspective and, indeed, your field of vision would become widened at the end of the day, both nationally and internationally. So I feel that at least you should allow your name to go forward for consideration. If it's God's will, you would be appointed. If it's God's will, I know that you'll be doing the right thing."

Much of what Leonora said coincided with my own views. So, in short, we agreed that if the offer was made, I should take it, but first of all, I had to indicate my interest in it. Of course, I could not really tell what the reaction would be in various circles. My colleagues at the Medical School might think I was leaving them in the lurch. On the one hand, they may feel that it did not really matter. Of course, there was bound to be some outcry about a doctor leaving medical work and going to do full-time administration, even if it was educational administration. So before I went to work, that day, we agreed tentatively to continue to pray about it and then take our final decision at lunchtime.

Lunch was late that day. I came home at about two o'clock. But there was not much to add. We merely confirmed our agreement and what answer we would give to Alex when he called the next morning. So after lunch, I went to see my elder brother, Joe, in our family house at Jamestown and told him about it. To my surprise, he said, "Yes, Emmanuel, take it! Take it if it's offered to you!" So with the support and encouragement of my dear wife, Leonora, and my brother, Joe, I made up my mind firmly about the change if it should come.

Early the next morning at exactly five-thirty, the telephone rang, and it was Alex. All he said was, "Evans, good-morning, I hope you're not going to say 'no.'" So I said, " Alex, yes, you're right, I'm not going to say 'no.' It's been a very difficult decision for me to make, but I've discussed it fully with Leonora and I think we both agree that you could put my name forward and, well, leave it to the Lord." So Alex said, "I'm glad, I'm glad, Evans. I hope that if what I'm wishing comes to pass, Leonora will be a worthy partner for you in your administration of the University." "As it is, now that you're prepared to be considered, I'll ask a member of the Council to come and see you tomorrow to have a chat with you. He's Prof. Sey, who's a representative of the academic staff on the Council. He'll be staying at the Continental Hotel, and since you're a very busy man, he'll be in the hotel and anytime tomorrow evening, he'll be waiting for you. You can go and have a chat with him." "Okay. I'am prepared to meet Prof. Sey tomorrow." "But meanwhile, Evans," Alex continued "I should be grateful if you'd obtain brief references from two people who have known you well for a long time and let me have them as soon as possible." So for one of my references, I asked Rev. Max Dodu, father of Prof. Silas Dodu, Prof of Medicine at the Medical School. Rev. Max Dodu had known me since my childhood, since I was in middle school at Osu Salem and had followed my achievements throughout. He was one of the best persons who could vouch for my character, for my ability and personal qualities. The other person was my senior colleague Dr. Eustace Akwei, Director of Medical Services.

When I called on Dr. Eustace Akwei and told him what was about to happen and the need for him to write something on my behalf, he was quite surprised. "You know, Anfom, I was hoping that someday you would succeed me as Director of Medical Services. In fact, they're thinking of a new post, Director General of Medical Services, and I was hoping that on my leaving you would be appointed to that post." "I'm sorry, Sir, but I think, first things first. This one has come first." I said resolutely, "Okay, I'll give you all the support." So my referees wrote references which I sent on to Alex Kyerematen.

The following day in the evening, I went to the Continental Hotel to meet Prof. Sey. I hadn't seen him for sometime ever since I left Kumasi, a few years previously. He was really the one who put me in the picture about the situation on the University campus concerning academic work and general administration. He also briefed me on the personal relationships on the campus, student behaviour, and how some of them hoped that I would be prepared to come to try to help them sort out things on the campus. We exchanged views on a number of things. I asked about plans that they had at the University and the general direction in which the University was going because I did not want to have to come and take on something which would not offer any challenges and about which I could do nothing, and come back frustrated. Prof Sey thought on the whole, all was not lost, that knowing me as he did from the Achimota days - he was a student when I taught for one year at Achimota - that it was in my capability to make a contribution.

A few days after this conversation, I got a letter from the Acting Registrar, Mr. E. A. Barnor, brother of my good friend and colleague, Dr. Matthew Barnor. At that time, there was no substantive Registrar. The short letter invited me to come and meet the members of the Council on a given date. It would really be in the nature of an interview and there might be other candidates. They looked forward to meeting me on the day of the Council meeting.

The day before my meeting with Council, I went to Kumasi, arriving in the afternoon. I checked in at the University Guest House and immediately went to the National Cultural Centre to see Dr. Kyerematen, the Chairman of Council who, spent sometime to fill me in on the happenings on the University campus and to go into greater detail about the reasons he was anxious that they appointed somebody like me as the next Vice- Chancellor. After that and after resting and having my supper, I called on my friend, Prof. Twum-Barima, who was then acting as Vice-Chancellor. Prof. Twum-Barima had been my classmate at Achimota. Indeed, he was the young lad who walked up the Achimota Hill with me to sit for the Cadbury Scholarship examination and it turned out that we were joint holders of the scholarship. He, of course, went into Agriculture and had become one of the leading Agricultural Economists in the country. I was quite warmly received by my old friend and I enquired from him what was really happening on campus. To be frank, he was highly disappointed at what he called a slap in his face, by the Council. Having held the fort as acting Vice-Chancellor for a whole year, he understandably was expecting that he would be appointed substantive Vice-Chancellor. But no! Rather now what he was hearing was that the Council had decided to bring in an outsider and he felt really snubbed. He did not hide his displeasure at all. You could well imagine what an embarrassing moment it was for me, knowing fully well that really he had no control whatsoever over the situation regarding the decision of the Council and the cogent reasons which they had given for the action they were contemplating. Nothing that I could say to console him mattered; he could simply not be pleased. He ended by saying that well, he hoped that I would be appointed and that he wouldd much rather it was me rather than somebody else whom he did not know.

The exact feelings of Professor Twum-Barima on that occasion were really to be tested by subsequent events. In the morning, I called at the Registrar's office at ten o'clock and, after waiting for about half an hour, I was invited to the Council meeting. Looking round, I saw a number of familiar faces. There was Mr. Justice Henry Prempeh, as he then was, an old friend, Mr. Frank Mensah-Bonsu, a private legal practitioner in Kumasi, Mr. Allotei Konuah, representing the Conference of Heads of Assisted Secondary Schools. There was the Chairman himself and also the Seecretary to the National Council for Higher Education and, of course, Prof. Twum Barimah, Acting Vice-Chancellor. There was a white face also, the face of Prof. Sparkes, Professor of Structural Engineering of the Imperial College, London. The membership of the Council included two members representing universities outside Ghana, one representing universities in Africa; at that time, it was Dr. Davidson Nicol who was well known to me, but he was not present at the meeting, and Prof Sparkes represented universities outside the African Continent.

The reception was cordial and the interview very frank. In the main, members wanted to know from me what my plans would be for the future of the university, and what sort of vision I had knowing what I had come to know and also knowing the mission of the University. I did my best to outline my vision and how I intended to tackle the duties of Vice-Chancellor. The line of questioning was friendly until it came to the turn of Professor Sparkes. His first question was, "Well, as a medical doctor, do you think you can cope with the administration of a technological university?" So I said, "Well, Sir John Fraser, a renowned surgeon of international repute was one of the most successful Vice-Chancellors of Edinburgh University when I was a medical student at that University. The University of Edinburgh, is a much bigger University than the University of Science and Technology, Kumasi, and it has a wide range of disciplines, most of the academic disciplines that one can think of." There was a measure of hostility in Prof Sparkes' line of questioning. So his next question was, "But you're not even a Professor, you're just a Senior Lecturer." So I said, "Well, that fact is well known to the Council, I believe." Immediately a member of Council cut in and asked the Chairman, "Was Dr. Baffour, the former Vice-Chancellor a Professor?" To which the Chairman replied, "No." That really ended Prof. Sparkes' questions. I do not know, whether he had some more up his sleeve, but the rest of the meeting went on smoothly. Altogether, I was with the Council for about an hour. The Chairman thanked me for coming and invited me to stay for lunch with the Council. So after the interview I hung around, and I remember calling on Prof Asihene at the College of Art. I had a word with him to while away the time.

After the Council meeting, lunch was served at the Great Hall, in the upper small conference room. All the members of Council were there. I realized also that a number of senior members of staff, particularly the Deans were present. During the course of the luncheon, Dr. Kyerematen introduced me to the gathering and announced that, subject to the approval of the Chancellor, the Council of the University had decided to appoint me Vice-Chancellor in succession to Dr. Robert Baffour. This action surprised me a bit as I did not think that Dr. Kyerematen would make such an announcement prematurely without actually having the endorsement of the Chancellor. Perhaps he was sure of what he was doing. Maybe he had little doubt that the Chancellor would approve Council's appointment, because he qualified the announcement by saying "subject to the approval of the Chancellor". I returned to Accra that same afternoon to await developments. It was a Friday. Of course, I did not say anything to anybody apart from my wife. I recounted what had happened during my encounter with the Council and Dr. Kyerematen's announcement after lunch.

The following Tuesday, I got a message through my cousin, the late Mr. William Evans-Lutterodt, that the Head of State and Chairman of the NLC wished to see me at the Castle the following day. I must explain that the Head of State, according to the Act of the University, was the Chancellor of the University and, of course, in this case the Chairman of the NLC acted together with the Council. So the following day in the afternoon, my cousin, Mr. William Evans-Lutterodt, accompanied me to the Castle to see the Head of State. The Chairman of the NLC at that time was the late Lieutenant General Ankrah. As soon as we entered the office, he burst out, "Emmanuel, what's this I hear about you? Are you out of your mind? What are you going to do at the University? You are one of our top doctors teaching at the Medical School and now they want to take you from the School and send you to the University. What is this all about?" The tone of his remark, really, appeared to suggest that he had the impression that I was being forced or being coerced to go to Kumasi to take up this job. I had to assure him that everything that was happening was with my knowledge and consent, and that I had been properly briefed before the University Council considered my candidature. After that he piped down a bit and said, "Well, well, in that case I guess you will be making a contribution to the country's development in another way. I know you can do it. My concern was that maybe something was happening against your will. If that is the case then there should not be any problem with the NLC approving". So we sat down and chatted about old times.

I had known General Ankrah for very many years. We grew up together in James Town, Accra. Even though he was older than I by a couple of years or so, we had gone through several situations together and, as I recounted earlier, he was in Tamale at the time that I was there and then, of course, he was with the Ghana Armed Forces in the Congo. during the months that we spent in the Congo. So I came back and informed Leonora that it looked as if my appointment by the University Council would be endorsed by the NLC. It is interesting to note that shortly, or sometime after I had actually assumed duty in Kumasi, there were rumours circulating that Anfom had been appointed Vice-Chancellor by Ankrah as they were both Gas, and an ethnic slant was given to the appointment by certain sections of the public. When I heard this rumour I just smiled to myself. "If they only knew Ankrah's own position, that he nearly vetoed the whole process, they wouldn't be saying or thinking along those lines." However, this was Ghana, where people were always ready to ascribe the wrong motives or wrong reasons for actions taken by persons in authority.

**LEFT**
*Vice Chancellor -*
*U.S.T Congregation*
*(1968)*

**BELOW**
*Vice Chancellor,*
*with U.S.T Students'*
*Representative Council*
*(1969/70)*

*A visit to U.S.T by N.R.C chairman Colonel I.K. Acheampong (1972)*

*Send-off party by U.S.T Ladies' Club (December 1973)*

**TOP LEFT**
Commisioner for
Education & Culture -
UNESCO General Conference,
Paris (1978)

**TOP RIGHT**
Hon. D.Sc. -
Salford University
(July 4, 1974)

**LEFT**
The family - At U.S.T VC's lodge

*Chairman of WAEC with Ghana delegation*

*Dr. Evans - Anfom, Chairman of WAEC delivering his address*
*at the 40th Anniversary of WAEC - Accra (March 23 - 27, 1992)*

*Chairman - WAEC with President Alhaji Sir Dawda K. Jawara of the Gambia*

*West African Congress of the Boys Brigade (1990)*

*Wedding day (June 22, 1984)*

*With Elise*

*My 80th Birthday cake*

*The family on my 80th birthday*

*With Dr. William & Mrs. Reed at Greensboro, - North Carolina - U.S.A*

*Preaching the sermon at the*
*Osu Ebenezer Presbyterian Church - Sunday morning service*

# CHAPTER 22

# KUMASI III
## Vice-Chancellor
### University of Science and Technology, Kumasi

After the meeting at the Castle, things moved rather fast because on Friday, I got a letter by hand from Kumasi signed by the Chairman of Council, offering me appointment as Vice-Chancellor of the University of Science and Technology. During the interview in Kumasi, I was asked how soon I would be able to assume duty if I was appointed. I had indicated then that I would be prepared to start work on August, 1st since I had to give at least one month's notice, to leave my current job. So I wrote back immediately accepting the appointment. It was the end of June. I immediately wrote to both the Ministry of Health and the Medical School asking to go on my earned leave during the month of July and also to resign my appointment as a Specialist to the Ministry of Health and also as Senior Lecturer of the Ghana Medical School at the end of my leave.

I decided to assume duty on 1st of August at the University because I felt I needed time to look through files. Also, in view of what had happened during the previous year, there were so many things that I had to look into so that when the academic year started in October, I would be properly briefed. In July, I took the opportunity to go abroad to Edinburgh to attend the 20th Anniversary/Reunion of Graduation of the 1947 Medical Class. It was a four-day Reunion, the first time that we were all gathering together after we left university and it was a very interesting period, meeting friends whom one knew more than twenty years previously, and with whom for at least five years one had rubbed shoulders studying to become doctors. We compared notes on what we had been doing. They had come from all over - England, Scotland, Canada, America, Australia, India, and so on. There were those who had gone to India and China as missionaries and of course, those of us who came from Africa.

The public announcement of my appointment was made whilst I was out of the country. It was rather low key and the reaction which followed and which was rather mixed was delayed until I actually assumed duty on the 1st of August. The main point of those who were not happy with the appointment was not because they thought I was not fit to do the job, but the same reason that the Head of State gave when he sent for me. Why should a doctor be sent from a medical school to do administration? I may say here that the section of the public that complained most were my own patients, who felt that I was really leaving them in the lurch. Then of course, there was the "Ashanti Pioneer", the newspaper which had its own agenda, and which clearly felt that Council should have allowed the Acting Vice-Chancellor to continue, by confirming his appointment instead of bringing in an outsider. One editorial was very vocal and outspoken on this issue. Well, it just fell short of saying that an outsider, especially a doctor, could not do the work of a top administrator! I decided to stay out of the debate. I must say also that the defence of the action came from many quarters. I was happy that some of my medical colleagues really defended the action, you know. Why should people think that once a doctor, it is only treating patients that you are capable of and that certain posts in the country should be no go areas for doctors? Was it being seriously suggested that a doctor could not become the President of a country? In any case, it did not take long for people to forget about this issue.

Once I got settled, it was put on the back burner! I did not allow the controversy to have any effect on me. Sometime before leaving for Kumasi, I thought it desirable, in fact necessary, to call on my good friend and senior colleague and now my immediate predecessor in office, Dr. R. P. Baffour, to have a discussion with him for him to brief me on the conditions on the campus, the nature of the work and the problems and challenges that lay ahead for me.

It was a very useful visit during which we had a very long discussion. He was able to give me his side of the story, to tell me all about his first appointment when the University was a College of Technology and he had been appointed a Principal in the first instance. Then in a couple of years when the College became an independent University he was appointed the first Vice-Chancellor of this new University which was named Kwame Nkrumah University of Science and Technology. After the military take-over in 1966 the military government changed the name to University of Science and Technology. He gave me a full account, of the nature of the change in the scope of work of the College of Technology and its limitations and explained how now that it had become a full University, its functions and responsibilities had become greater and wider in scope. He also explained the financial problems the University faced as well as the limitations these problems placed on its physical development. He observed that he had been fortunate because, as the then President, Osagyefo Dr Kwame Nkrumah was very much interested in the development of the University, he had done everything in his power to provide the requisite financial assistance. Consequently, there had been much physical development during the time despite the fact that there were problems pertaining to the curriculum for the various courses, to staffing and to students.

Dr. Baffour did not fail to mention that certain disgruntled members of staff had encouraged indiscipline and undermined the authority of the administration. He cautioned me to be wary of troublemakers who might want to make things difficult for me and frustrate my efforts. On the whole, the discussion was very frank. He was aware of areas in which perhaps he could have done things in a different way and I found his advice very useful, especially when later I assumed duty. Dr Baffour ended by congratulating me, saying he had known me for a very long time and that frankly, he was very happy that I was the one who was going to succeed him and not any of those other people who were busy angling for the position!

It is interesting that upon receiving the letter of appointment, suddenly the reality started staring me squarely in the face. I began to think about the major leap which I was about to take; I started arguing with myself, or rather, re-evaluating the whole situation. I asked myself whether I had taken the right decision, whether I was doing the right thing, switching from the practice of medicine, even though there was a certain amount of teaching attached to it, and now going on to do what was essentially full-time administration. I started weighing the pros and cons, going over the whole debate in my mind again. Eventually, I reassured myself that indeed, I was doing the right thing! I had, all my life, since my school days, been interested in education. My first ambition was to become a teacher. I actually taught briefly at Achimota College before my training as a doctor and even at this time, I was teaching at the Medical School. In any case, there was the Komfo Anokye Hospital in Kumasi. It was not a teaching hospital then, but I thought that I could always take the opportunity to do a little bit of part-time practice at that hospital, when I became Vice-Chancellor of the University.

I must say that Leonora became very much involved in this second evaluation, this fresh assessment of the entire delicate situation and she was in no doubt whatsoever that I was doing the right thing. I knew that as Vice-Chancellor, I would need the support and encouragement of my life long partner, Leonora. So once again, any doubts which had been lingering in my mind were finally dispelled, and I decided firmly and definitely that indeed, I was doing the right thing. I was persuaded and convinced that this new opportunity would certainly get me involved more in education. It was true that it would be with higher education, but then could one really be involved in higher education without any real involvement in education as a whole? I took the opportunity to study the Act setting up the University of Science and Technology and I noticed that under the Council of the University, the Vice-Chancellor was the academic and administrative head as well as chief disciplinary officer of the University. It was quite clear that the responsibilities of the Vice-Chancellor were very weighty indeed. "Now, surely, I'm in the saddle and am determined to ride high in it", I said.

Happily, my junior colleague at Achimota College, Alex Kwapong, had been appointed Vice-Chancellor of the University of Ghana the previous year, and this was a very encouraging fact to note. Here was somebody, whom I could rely on, to offer opinion and advice whenever I needed one. The knowledge that in the University of Science and Technology, Kumasi, too there were many of the academic staff whom I knew personally and who had known me for a long time was also most reassuring. Some members also had been my patients, when I was the chief surgeon of the Komfo Anokye Hospital a few years earlier. Not only that, I also knew the University before it came into being, physically in 1951. As a medical officer at Dunkwa, when I visited Kumasi, the grounds for the University were then being prepared for the buildings to be put up. I knew when initially they had the temporary structures and also when the permanent buildings were going up. I was fairly familiar with the lay-out of the campus. This was to be my third tour of duty in Kumasi, having been there on two previous occasions, working in the hospital, first in 1955, just for one year, and then in 1959 for four and a half years, leaving in 1963. This was just four years later, in 1967, and I was going back there again. Not to the hospital this time but now to the University as Head. The appointment was to be for seven years, so, for the first time in my working life I could look forward to being in one place for seven years without transfer, when previously, as the reader may remember, I had been hopping from station to station almost every year. So Leonora especially was happy, because this time, three of our children were at school and it was therefore desirable for us to be stationary for a change, and for a reasonably long period.

On the 31st of July 1967, I proceeded to Kumasi. The University sent transport, to convey my luggage. Accommodation wise, there was a vast improvement, because the Vice-Chancellor's residence was very spacious, with four bedrooms, whereas in Accra, for a long time, I was confined to a small two-bedroom bungalow, extended by an additional bedroom a few months prior to my leaving Korlebu. So I was very happy for the change. With four children, we were to be more comfortable.

Leonora could not immediately join me at the University because at that time she was working as the Coordinator of a project with the National Institute of Health. Of course, she travelled with me on the first day and she spent a few days and then had to come back to Accra. We arranged for her to stay at the University Guest House for some time until she was able to leave her work to come and join the family n Kumasi.

Prof. Twum-Barima, the acting Vice-Chancellor, called on me in the evening at home to greet me, and we arranged that the following morning, we would meet at the Vice-Chancellor's Office, so that we could go through the handing–over notes which he had prepared. The following morning at nine o'clock, we met at the Vice-Chancellor's Office and went through the notes after which we made a quick tour of the campus. It was vacation time and so most of the students and some members of staff also were away from the campus. We saw as many people as possible. Later on when the academic year started, I had the opportunity to go round the campus more formally. From then on, I took over the reins of office. A new Registrar had also been appointed who had assumed duty just one month before me. He was Mr. A. S. Y. Andoh, who before his appointment was Secretary to the Institute of African Studies at Legon. Mr. Andoh, had been a contemporary of Leonora, in Scotland. He studied in St. Andrews' University whilst Leonora was in Edinburgh, so they knew each other quite well. I had only met him casually in the University of Ghana, on occasion, but it was good to know that he was somebody who at least knew Leonora and that our relationship was therefore going to be fairly easy to begin with.

I needed time to unpack, so each morning during that week I spent an hour or two in the office and then went back home to do the unpacking. I may say at this stage that a new house had been built just a stone's throw from the Vice-Chancellor's Residence. The house was near completion. They were just doing the landscaping. It was a four-bedroom house and apparently it was meant for the Chancellor of the University, who was the President, as a lodge in which he would stay when he visited the University. Now that we had a military regime, it was decided that perhaps the new Vice-Chancellor should be given the option to live in this new building or in the old Vice-Chancellor's Residence. Taking everything into consideration, I opted for the new building because it was at a much quieter spot. We decided that the old residence should be used as a guesthouse.

In a short circular announcing my assumption of duty as Vice-Chancellor, Prof Twum Barimah referred to me rather uncharitably, I thought, as "a medical officer from the Ministry of Health who had been teaching at the Ghana Medical School." I could well understand his feelings at that time, but I felt that it would have been better if he had stated my proper credentials in the circular. In any case, I think the members of the academic staff especially, sooner or later, had access to my CV and those who did not know me were able to assess properly for themselves the calibre of which I was possessed. This is just by the-way.

One of the first duties I had to perform during the first week was to pay a courtesy call on Otumfo Ashantehene, Nana Sir Agyeman Prempeh, with my wife, Leonora. As the reader may remember, seven years previously, Otumfuo had been my patient and since then we had struck a personal friendship, so Nana knew both myself and Leonora well. Indeed, I recall that when I said good-bye in 1963 after a $4\frac{1}{2}$ year tour of duty at the Komfo Anokye Hospital, Nana did express the hope that one day, I would come back again to Kumasi, and apparently he had not forgotten about this prophetic statement. He welcomed us warmly and hoped that I would have a successful tenure as Vice-Chancellor. He was happy that I would be at post for a whole seven years. Nana, of course, was quite familiar with the challenges and difficulties confronting me and gave me every encouragement. He knew that I would do my best to succeed. He added that if I had any problems which I thought he could help solve, naturally, I could always call on him.  Indeed, during my stay and until his death in 1970, I called on him occasionally, not with any problems, but just to have a chat, and I know that he was very happy to hear first hand from me about what was happening at the University, not only at the UST, but the higher education front, generally.

As it was the long vacation, quite a number of staff members were also away from the campus and so after the first week, I spent most of the time in the office. I thought I should really see to settling my children, making arrangements for them for school. My eldest boy, Nii Okai who had been in school in London for 4 years came back home and was admitted at Achimota School, my alma mater. Rachel, my daughter, had just passed her Common Entrance Examination and she elected to go to Aburi Girls' School where quite a few of her friends in Primary School had also elected to go. Nii Teiko was admitted to the University Primary School and Charles who was then 4 years old went to the University Kindergarten until he was ready to go to the Primary School.

It appeared that Prof. Sparkes, who was rather hostile during my interview with Council, was not quite happy about my appointment and he continued his campaign against the appointment.  In the third week after assuming duty, I got a copy of a letter he had written to Dr. Mojaben Dowuona, Chairman of the Council for Higher Education. It was a rather long letter complaining bitterly about the Council's decision to appoint a doctor to such an important post, and he feared that standards in the University were bound to fall.  He was very anxious about the future of the University. He thought Council had taken the most retrograde step by appointing me, and although there was nothing he could do about this he thought he should warn the Chairman of Council about this. The general import of the letter was that he did not think that the UST under my leadership had much future. Dr. Mojaben Dowuona sent a copy of the letter to me just to warn me about Prof Sparkes, and to say that there might be other people who might be thinking along the same lines. He personally had no doubt at all that I would be up to the job, but he thought that this hint would put me on my guard and make me resolve to do my best to put people who were thinking in that way to shame.

I found Prof. Sparkes' action quite reprehensible. He did not really know me and, of course, Dr. Baffour, my predecessor, had been his good friend and professional colleague, but for him to think that UST, a technological university, could only be administered by an engineer, I thought was most ridiculous. He did not give much credit to persons from other professions. Dr. Mojaben Dowuona thought that since the letter was not copied to me I should just keep it under my hat. Of course, my first reaction was to write a stinker to Prof. Sparkes, but, on second thoughts, I decided just to leave things as they were for him to find out whether I could do the job or not.

About the time that the academic year started in October and all the students were back and all staff who were not on study leave also came back, I was fairly well settled and it had become quite evident to me that the University was really a small township. It is true that it was an academic institution but the municipal aspects of life on the campus were also the responsibility of the Vice-Chancellor who was supposed to preside over all this. In short the Vice-Chancellor was supposed to be all things to all men on the campus: - academic staff, senior staff, support staff, and students. There were different categories of people resident on the campus and all of them were the responsibility of the Vice-Chancellor on whose desk as far as the campus was concerned, the buck stopped. It is only when he could not deal with any matter that he had recourse to the Council. Fortunately for me, as I recall earlier, there were staff members who had been known to me; they included Prof. Whittaker, Prof. Kuffour, Prof. Sey, Prof. Asihene, and others like Mr. Hulede who was in charge of the Printing Press, and several others whom I could always call upon to get their opinion on various matters. So by the time that the new academic year started, I was mentally ready to face the music.

To come back to Prof. Sparkes. At the first Council meeting which took place in October, both he and Dr. Davidson Nicol, who were the outside academic representatives on the Council, were present. I had only been in office for barely three months and there were important matters to be considered. Davidson Nicol. who was not present at the interview, to my extreme embarrassment, spoke very highly of me. He commended me very highly to the members of Council. He had known me for very many years and knew what I was capable of doing. Well, at the end of the meeting, the Chairman of Council, Dr. Kyerematen, congratulated me. He thought I did very well at my first meeting with the Council and even Prof Sparkes came to me. He did not apologize, but he said he hoped that when I was in London on my next visit I would be able to visit the Imperial College and his Department.

As it turned out, a visit to London had already been scheduled for me.  In November-December, there was to be a meeting in Rabat, Morocco, to inaugurate the Association of African Universities, and it had been planned that after that conference I would go to London for about a week to visit the London Office and to make contact with some of the universities which had links with UST. So on my visit to London, I did go to Imperial College, and it was on that visit that Prof Sparkes apologized profusely and said that he had been rather hasty in his assessment of me and that he thought that my performance at the Council meeting and the testimony that he had heard from distinguished academics like Dr. Davidson Nicol and also from the way in which I had spoken about the plans for the future of UST were all highly impressive and so he felt that he should tell me. He wanted first of all to apologize for his manner and to say that he would give me all the support that he was capable of giving just as he had supported my predecessor, Dr. Baffour. Of course, I did not tell him that I had seen his letter. I replied that I sincerely hoped that he meant what he was saying and that the proof of the pudding would be in the eating. As an earnest of his intention, a couple of weeks later, he wrote a long letter of support to me which I acknowledged briefly, with thanks. As it turned out, Prof Sparkes' two-year at Council was about to end, but it was not renewed.  The Chairman of Council for higher Education did not recommend that it be renewed and so someone else was appointed.

I took over the administration of the University at a time when the University was facing many challenges.  First of all, the economy of the country was in dire straits. This meant that there were financial problems ahead since the subvention to all public institutions had to be cut down and the university had to work hard to make do with the reduced subvention that came to it. Secondly, there was the problem of polarization on the campus for which reason the University Council had had to appoint an outsider as Vice-Chancellor. Then with the wind of change blowing across the universities over the world, for example, in America and Europe, the new-found student power had made its way to African universities. As a result, students were agitating for greater participation in university administration and were demonstrating against the university administration or against government policies. This was really a delicate situation which had to be handled tactfully.

My predecessor had been accused of being autocratic. There was, therefore, the need to take steps to democratize the systems within the university campus and, being a liberal myself, to make sure that fair play and justice prevailed. I was to discover later that the main problem that I had to tackle was the strong resistance put up by some people in the university who were really impervious to change, especially change resulting in progress and, however inevitable the change, there were those who would prefer decay to progressive change, to an act of renewal of or revival to move the institution forward.

My first meeting with Convocation was in the third week of October and it took place in the Great Hall. Convocation is the entire membership of the senior members on the campus. At that meeting I outlined the policy that I planned to follow and invited the cooperation of all. I stressed the importance of unity and hard work with every member playing his/her part. Using the analogy of the human body and the different functions that each part had to perform in order to make the whole efficient, I particularly emphasized the fact that I expected loyalty to the institution in our dealings with each other on campus, and a measure of goodwill and a sense of justice and fair play, and that I was prepared to provide the leadership for the period of my tenure as Vice-Chancellor.

A few days later, I also met the Student Representative Council in the Council Chamber and again outlined the policy that I had planned to follow. I congratulated them on their election by their fellow students and mates which implied confidence in their ability to lead. I stressed the importance of leading and not being led by the general body of students. In other words, there should not be a situation of the "tail wagging the dog." I informed them that 25 years earlier, whilst a student at Edinburgh University, I had been in a similar position; I had been a member of the Students' Representative Council, so in a way I had been in the position in which they found themselves then. Therefore, I knew and understood some of the views that they would express, and I was prepared to lend a sympathetic ear to any suggestions or requests, provided they were just. There were rules and regulations and channels of communication which must be followed. The student power prevailing all around the whole world should not be used irresponsibly, as it did not mean that they should not follow the proper procedures and channels of communication. If there was a law or a rule, until it was changed, it had to be obeyed. If there was a need to change it, then the proper procedures should be adopted in getting them changed in a democratic manner. Demonstrations should be used as a last resort, and, if they had to be used at all, then they should be devoid of violence because an attitude of confrontation really did not make for goodwill and the necessary friendly relationship which should exist between senior members and junior members and also the university administration. They ought to remember that I was prepared to be a father to them, in turn I expected them to be good boys and girls. I would stress again that they should provide leadership. They should not allow themselves to be led by the mob. I got the impression that they were happy with this encounter and the frank manner in which I had spoken to them and they promised that they were going to do their best to cooperate and to work for friendly relations between themselves and the administration. I must say that subsequent events on the whole proved them right.

At the first meeting of Council, one important item which was dealt with was the Report of the Commission of Enquiry into the Disturbances in the University. A committee was appointed under my chairmanship to study the Report and the recommendations and advise Council on what steps to take. Needless to say, the Report itself aroused a certain amount of controversy on the campus. It was severely criticized by the supporters of the former Vice-Chancellor, who felt that he had really been a victim of circumstances and that the Commission had been biased in their work and had taken advantage of the fact that the Nkrumah government had been overthrown and there was a military government. Because the former Vice-Chancellor was a great supporter of that regime, he had become a victim himself. Reading through the Report, one could see instances of the bias which was complained of, but there were other parts of the Report which were factual and about which something had to be done. My committee had to work carefully and objectively in order to make fair and just recommendations on the Commission's recommendations to Council. There were aspects of the Report and the recommendations which were not based on an objective assessment of the situation. On the whole I think my committee was fair in the evaluation of the Report and in the recommendations we made to Council. These recommendations were approved, and during the course of the year I had to see that the aspects of the recommendations accepted were implemented and that in the process there was justice and fairplay.

Before the end of October, the Registrar arranged for a Matriculation Ceremony. This was a ceremony at which the new students were formerly admitted to the university. It took place in the Great Hall. Each fresh student had to sign the declaration whereby he/she promised to abide by the rules and regulations of the University and to be of good behaviour. It also provided the opportunity for the Vice-Chancellor to address the students. In my address, I laid particular emphasis on the fact that there were many students out there and many who would like to have the opportunity of the education that they had had, and that they should look upon their admission to the university as a great privilege. During the course of their stay in th University they should learn to take advantage of all the facilities that the University had to offer, both the academic and recreational. It was an opportunity for them as they climbed the ladder to learn the art and system of democratic government and, in general, to prepare themselves for their future life. As beneficiaries of tertiary education and the standard of education that they would have acquired, they would be looked upon as leaders in the community. I impressed upon them to make sure that when the time came for them to leave the University, they would have made some contribution to the progress of the University itself, that they should not expect to get everything from the University and not give anything in return. I ended by wishing them well in their endeavours, hoping that they would find the three or four years that they would be spending in the University a useful period in their lives and reminding them that the foundation that they would be laying then should be strong enough for them to build on after leaving for the world of work.

I drew their attention to the rules and regulations of the Univeristy, both academic and residential, and emphasized that these were not there for nothing. They were there to be observed and obeyed and if they had any problems and they felt that there were things which needed to be changed for the better, there were laid down procedures which they should follow. If they were ignorant of these, the senior members and tutors in the Halls were there to help them, and these tutors were for the time being that they were in the university, in *loco parentis*, that is to say, taking the place of their parents. They should take advantage of the counselling that they would get from the senior members. I reminded them that the University was really a community of scholars primarily, but in our circumstances, there were others apart from the lecturers and students, namely, the administrative and other support staff; in a sense, therefore, it was a small township and we should all learn to live together in harmony and to respect each other. When that was done, they would find that life on the campus would be very rich and rewarding, and they would go out of the University having in a way become better human beings than they were when they entered the University.

My last meeting was with the leadership of TEWU - Teachers and Educational Workers' Union. They were the representatives of the TUC and they were really representing the non-academic staff on the campus. I had a very interesting discussion with them. I reminded them that even though they were not teaching, and they were neither teachers nor students, we knew that without them, the work of the University could not really go on smoothly. They were as important as the academic section of the University and I expected the same hard work, cooperation and loyalty from them as I would from the academics, that I would always have a sympathetic ear for them in any suggestions or requests that they might make, and that provided these were justified and reasonable, they could expect my support. However, if these requests and suggestions were unreasonable, they would not find favour with me. So we were happy with our encounter and I promised the support and cooperation of the administration.

The Registrar, Mr. A. S. Y. Andoh and I were both new, but I must say that the cooperation between us at this time was very strong and it was for our mutual benefit. He had come direct from Administration, from the Institute of African Studies at Legon and I must say that he was much closer to, perhaps more familiar with, that area of administration than I was. He was, therefore, very helpful and I must say that we got on to a very good start. After about a month, Leonora was able to wind up her affairs with the Research Project with the National Institute of Health at Korlebu and to join us at UST. From then on, she was preoccupied with seeing to the furnishing of the new Vice-Chancellor's residence.

The College of Art, under the leadership of the late Prof. Asihene was very helpful with the interior decoration of the Vice-Chancellor's residence. In particular, the heavy curtains in the drawing room were designed and woven at the College. The material was durable and the colours were very fast. Throughout the six years that I occupied the residence, it was not necessary to change them. There were also some beautiful oil paintings chosen by the College to decorate the walls of the drawing room and other strategic places.

The six and a half years that I spent at the University of Science and Technology constitute a very important chapter in my life. It would take a whole book to write in some detail about my experiences there. As this happens to be an account of my whole life story, that period will of necessity be a short chapter.   I can, therefore, only give some highlights of my experiences as Vice-Chancellor.

The late G. M. Pitcher, former librarian of the University and the unofficial University-sponsored chronicler, in his account covering the first 25 years of the University, was highly critical of my regime. He seemed to have found nothing commendable in any measures that I took, in some of the important issues that arose and in my stand on those matters, to the extent that he rounded off his comments on the time that I was about to leave with the wry statement, "Dr. Evans-Anfom, like his two predecessors, spent six years before relinquishing his post, and although he was fortunate not to have a commission of enquiry to sit in judgement on him, his last year in office was clouded by a violent demonstration of the students against some members of the University Senior Staff".

Clearly, Pitcher thought that there were sufficient grounds for a commission of enquiry to probe my administration. He must, therefore, have been highly disappointed that this did not happen. Of course, this did not happen because of my own philosophy of administration, the high standards that I set myself, and the principles on which I acted.  I was pursuing democratic rule in the university; I was pursuing fair play and justice, and some of the measures that I took were to make sure that where I felt that things were not being done in a democratic way I must rectify the situation. It was in this process that I had some resistance, but I fail to see how my actions which were aimed at what one might call "progressive change" and which were fully supported by the Council could possibly lead to a situation where a commission of enquiry would be instituted into my administration. Be that as it may, I am quite satisfied that I tried to discharge my responsibilities as Vice-Chancellor to the best of my ability and I am really not ashamed at my performance as the head of a University. I quite honestly feel that I made a substantial contribution to the progress of the University and I think any reasonable person in evaluating those years would testify to that.

There were matters which the Registrar and I had to see to right away.  The change of government the previous year had prevented certain things from happening. It had been planned that the College of Art would move to Tema, which was considered an industrial area, as it was thought that the emphasis of the work of the College should be on industrial art. This plan was abandoned with the change of government. Also the Faculty of Agriculture was to move to Somanya to form the nucleus of a proposed University of Agriculture. This plan was also abandoned.

Another problem which we had to deal with was the idea that a technological university should confine itself to Applied Science and not be concerned with what might be called the Pure Sciences. Two committees, the Education Review Committee and the Committee on the Delimitation of Functions of University Institutions, had both recommended that the University ceased to offer courses in the Pure Sciences and only restrict itself to the Applied Sciences. Both the Science Faculty and the Academic Board, agreed that it was highly desirable that even in a technological university there should be courses in the pure sciences as this could only enrich the work of the other technological subjects. The then Dean of the Faculty of Science was very active at that time and he had my strongest support, the result being that we saved the situation. The pure sciences courses continued.

The Department of Liberal Studies which operated during the days of the College of Technology had been moved to Cape Coast University to form the nucleus of a Faculty of Social Sciences. So at the time that I assumed office, there was only a small Department of Liberal Studies, not a Faculty. It was not offering any degrees and the lecturers in that department mainly gave service lectures to the other faculties. There were lectures in Law, Sociology, English, and so on. to engineers, architects and pharmacists. We felt that, though a technological university, it was important that there should be a strong Faculty of Social Sciences to offer some balance to the work of the University. Therefore we worked for the establishment of a Faculty and transformed the Department of Liberal Studies into the Faculty of Social Sciences with the following Departments: Languages, Economics and Industrial Management, General and African Studies, Land Economy and Estate Management. I must say that this measure really encouraged the staff, as they were now in a position to prepare students to offer appropriate subjects in the Social Sciences to degree level. Happier now, they worked harder than before, and it was also possible to attract good quality staff to the Faculty, a situation which had been difficult previously.

Another important measure which we took was to discontinue the 6th Form subjects in the two-year 'A Level Course' which was necessary to prepare students to qualify for entry into the University, especially the College of Art and the Faculty of Architecture. Previously, there were not enough 6th Form schools offering Art to A-Level. However, we felt that now that an increasing number of secondary schools were offering 6th Form level courses in Art, the time had come to discontinue these courses in the University in order to make room for students who would be pursuing degree courses. Another important decision which had to be taken was to continue with the Higher National Diploma (HND) courses until such time that the polytechnics were ready to offer those courses. This was meant to be a temporary measure and we felt that even though it was an undergraduate diploma course, the University was really providing useful service in training middle-level manpower at that time. I believe the HND courses are now being run in our Polytechnics, as they are now better equipped to run such courses to the required level.

One of the early tasks which engaged the attention of the Academic Board was the formulation of regulations for post-graduate work – Post-graduate Diplomas, and Masters Degrees - as early as possible so that the localization of post-graduate work and research work might be expedited. The Statutes were promulgated in January 1967, that is, the year that I took office. It was my duty to ensure that their provisions were adhered to, that the committee system worked well and that everything was done in accordance with the rules and regulations. Where the Vice-Chancellor was given discretionary powers these powers were used responsibly. It was my policy that in every case where I had any doubts, I made the necessary consultations. Of course, it was possible that on occasion the wrong decision was made, but I found it very useful to take advantage of the advice and opinion of people whom I thought could be helpful in any given situation. In particular, I made extensive use of a lecturer in law, the late Mr. Gollo. Whenever there was a problem that had legal implications, I did not fail to consult him. This was necessary because not being a lawyer myself, I might take decisions which might have legal repercussions not only for myself but also for the institution.

Before I took over, the University had existing links with a number of overseas universities. These links were either at the topmost level, that is, at the university level, or at departmental level. Now these links were very useful because they helped to enrich the work of the University, particularly at the departmental level. Where a head of department had personal relations with a head of department in another university overseas, it facilitated exchange programmemes of staff and enhanced whatever work had to be done. This system of links helped the university in its staff development programmeme. The link, for example, at departmental level between the Chemistry Department of the University and the Chemistry Department of the University of Salford in the U.K. provided for exchanges of staff. Salford also undertook to receive post-graduate students for training to come back to join the staff at UST. The Universities that we had links with in Planning were the University of Newcastle and the University of British Columbia. There were also links with the University of Toulouse, and Cambridge (Land Economy). Later on I will recount how these links helped to rescue the University in a certain crisis situation.

## Physical Development

Many permanent buildings of the University had been constructed during the two regimes immediately preceding mine. These were periods when money was available and, therefore, the physical expansion of the University could proceed smoothly. Unfortunately for me, the economy was not at all strong during my tenure and, therefore, not much physical development was possible. All the same we were able to finish work on the Unity Hall of Residence. This enabled us to take in more students during the first year of my tenure. Later we were also able to construct the second Tower Block of Africa Hall (the women's hall) in record time. The new Pharmacy Block was also started, but it went on rather slowly, and at the time that I left it was still uncompleted.

The Central Classroom Block was a key project. If it had been constructed in the project time of 18 months, it would have released space in the various Faculties to be utilized for worthwhile purposes, such as being converted into offices for the teaching staff many of whom were obliged to use their sitting rooms and studies at home as academic offices. This particular project, the Central Classroom Block, took a very long time to build; the simple reason being that the Ministry of Finance and the Ministry of Works and Housing at the time rejected the recommendation of the University Tender Board to award the contract to an experienced expatriate firm. Instead, they awarded the contract to a highly inexperienced Ghanaian firm which had not executed any public projects elsewhere in a satisfactory manner. It was no surprise, therefore, that it could not cope with the job. A job which should have taken 18 months took several years and was completed by another contractor well after I had left the University. I may explain that the Central Classroom Block was designed to contain a number of lecture rooms of varying capacity, and a couple of auditoria also of varying sizes and seating capacities. It was also designed to have closed circuit television and other modern teaching technology facilities.

## Constitutional Matters

The governing body and supreme authority of the University is the University Council. The Academic Board which works under the Council has important powers as far as academic matters are concerned. The Act and the Statutes both confer on the Academic Board powers to take final decisions in academic matters, save in a few cases, for example, in the appointment of Professors. Of course, in addition to these powers, the Council may also confer on the Board any other powers. In a university which is largely residential and which has a campus which in reality amounts to a municipality, there are other functions, other concerns of a non-academic nature. After I had assumed office, I soon discovered that the Academic Board was spending a disproportionate amount of time on non-academic matters. Inasmuch as these matters concerned all residents on the campus and not only the academic members, I thought that there was need to amend the Statutes to take care of this anomaly. The Academic Board has the Vice-Chancellor as Chairman with all the Professors and Deans and heads of academic departments and the Librarian as members. The Registrar is Member/Secretary to the Academic Board.

In the second year of my tenure, I set in motion processes for the amendment of certain sections of the Statutes. Firstly, in the appointment of a Pro Vice-Chancellor, the Vice-Chancellor nominated two professors for Council to appoint one as Pro Vice-Chancellor. I thought it was desirable to bring in the members of the Convocation i.e. the whole body of senior members, to be involved in this appointment; so I proposed that the Vice-Chancellor nominated three professors for Convocation to elect two. It would be these two that the Vice-Chancellor would submit to Council for their selection.

I also felt that on the same principle something had to be done to make it possible for the Academic Board to spend more time on academic matters and also allow the other support staff and even students resident on campus to have a say in non-academic matters. To this end, I proposed the setting-up of a Welfare Services Board. The composition of this Board would take into account other residents on the campus, that is, the senior support staff who were not teaching staff, junior staff and also the students.

The Statutes provided for the Vice-Chancellor to be the chief disciplinary officer of the University and for him to be the Chairman of any Disciplinary Board. From my experience and from some of the cases which came before me, I felt that sometimes the Vice-Chancellor, even before the recommendation was made for disciplinary enquiry, tended to get too involved. Some people who committed offences tended to take the Vice-Chancellor's position in a personal way. To avoid this, I felt that it would be better for the Pro Vice-Chancellor to chair the disciplinary bodies and for these bodies to make recommendations to the Vice-Chancellor.

Generally speaking, I felt that disciplinary matters should be taken care of at the Departmental or Hall level, that there should be a certain amount of decentralization, and that it was only matters which were very serious and which might warrant a dismissal, or suspension for long periods that should get to the Vice-Chancellor. I am glad to say that all these proposals had the support of the members of Convocation and that Council had no difficulty at all in approving them, so that it was possible to amend the Statutes to reflect this democratic principle.

During the second half of my tenure I began to feel that an administrative set up which meant all communication to the Vice-Chancellor had to be routed through the Registrar tended to create bottlenecks. Of course, I knew this was the practice in British universities, whereas in American universities there was more division of labour and more high-powered personnel to represent general administration, finance, development and academic matters. So I set the process in motion to try to get the Statutes amended to reflect this. There was much controversy about this and I set up a committee to look into this. The committee brought a report to the Academic Board where there was very fierce resistance by some members. The report had to be sent back to the committee to look at again and give more reasons why this change should come about. The review was still going on when I left the university. Fortunately, my successor who happened to be the Pro Vice-Chancellor was strongly in favour of the change and managed to get the proposal passed with minor amendments and also eventually for Council to accept.

## Financial Matters

The need for more funds to supplement government subvention was very keenly felt by all sections and so in the first two years of my administration we instituted an Expansion Fund for the University. A committee under the chairmanship of Otumfuo Asantehene, Nana Sir Osei Agyeman Prempeh II, was instituted to find ways of achieving this. We had great hopes that there would be an eager and generous public response to this. Unfortunately this was not to be. I had expected, at least in the Kumasi area, to get support from the Lebanese business community and also from a few Ghanaian businessmen of substance. However, the period coincided with the enforcement of the Aliens Compliance Order and I suspect that this really affected the response which we had anticipated because the response from the Lebanese community both in Kumasi and Accra was almost nil, and from the African business community (both commercial and industrial) the response was also very poor. After some time we were obliged to change the name of the fund to "UST Endowment Fund".

We felt that the word "expansion" gave the impression that the university wanted to expand the physical facilities and that "endowment" was probably a better word; a better concept that did not need to involve physical expansion but at the same time menat denoting money that would be used in improving the performance of the activities of the university. Despite this change, the response remained poor. We had aimed at a target of ¢6million but had raised only about ¢200,000 after a few years of operation of the Fund. All the same, we were not deterred. If we were not going to get more money then we should find some way of exercising control over our expenditure and institute other cost-saving measures.

The problem of shortage of funds applied to all three universities and it was clearly an opportunity for the three institutions to begin to cooperate closely. The first target of our exercise was the London Offices of the three universities. At that time each university had an Assistant Registrar together with his staff in charge of that university's activities and concerns in the United Kingdom, Europe and North America. Fortunately, the offices of the universities were situated in the same building at 15 Gordon Square. We decided that rather than having three Assistant Registrars we should have only one with subordinate officers who would be in charge of the schedules for the three universities. Clearly, there was a certain amount of savings on the rents, salaries for two Assistant Registrars, allowances and all fees paid. This we were able to do.

We decided that we were not going to keep any of the existing Assistant Registrars, so we appointed a new person entirely to take charge of the new arrangement. This cooperative effort in dealing with the London University Office provided an opportunity for the universities to cooperate in other matters at home. For example, one of the issues which concerned the various administrations of the three universities was the question of conditions of service for the staff. Since all the three universities were almost wholly funded by government, we were all fishing in the same pool. We, therefore, felt that the conditions of service of staff of all grades should be the same, so we spent some time in making sure that these service conditions were unified, and so that the staff of one university would not start citing better conditions in another university, thereby causing trouble.

At that time, we were very fortunate that the heads of the three universities were persons who had known each other for very many years. There was Prof. Alex Kwapong at Legon, myself at UST, and Prof. Ernest Boateng, Principal of the University College of Cape Coast. Later when the institution at Cape Coast assumed independent status Prof Boateng became the first Vice-Chancellor of the new University of Cape Coast. At that time, Dr. Modjaben Dowuona was the Chairman of the National Council for Higher Education which was the chief advisory body to Government on higher education matters, and in a sense acted as a grants committee after the fashion of the University Grants Committee of the United Kingdom. We had to work very closely with the Chairman, who, incidentally, had been a former teacher at Achimota College. Dr. Modjaben Dowuona was a very experienced educationist whose whole life had been devoted to education. He taught at Achimota College and then became the first African Registrar of the University of Ghana at Legon, and then spent some years at the Ahmadu Bello University in Nigeria before coming back after the change of government in 1966 to become Commissioner for Education.

In 1969, when the National Council for Higher Education was set up, he became its first Chairman. From then on, the working relationship and cooperation among the three universities was very cordial and the Committee of Vice-Chancellors and Principals started in an informal way. We used to meet in rotation at the three universities until such time that it became necessary and highly desirable to establish a permanent office at the University of Ghana, Legon. The Committee of Vice-Chancellors has now become a very important body in higher education matters and is able to advise the Council for Tertiary Education and Government generally on all higher education matters.

I must confess that I found it very strange that at a time when the Vice-Chancellors of the three universities were working under very difficult conditions to cooperate, to maximize the resources of our three institutions, a letter should appear in one of the local newspapers signed by someone who called himself a "concerned citizen." His concern was that he found it rather surprising and very strange indeed that the heads of the three universities were all Akuapems. Of course, he was wrong in this regard. It is true that Profs. Boateng and Kwapong are Akuapems from Aburi and Akropong respectively, but I am not an Akuapem, even though my family had had strong and long-standing relations with Akuapem through the services of my maternal grandfather at the Akropong Seminary and who had also settled at Akuapem Mampong on his retirement. In any case, even if I too had been an Akuapem, I would have found the criticism still strange indeed because we were all Ghanaians working for the good of Ghana. As a matter of interest, all three of us were products of Achimota College. We attended Achimota College and knew ourselves. Indeed, the Chairman of the Council for Higher Education himself, Dr. Modjaben Dowuona, was also a product of Achimota. Besides, all three of us were Presbyterians! I shudder to think what the tone of his letter would have been if this "concerned citizen" had got this additional information!

I am talking about something which happened more than three decades ago. Since then much water has passed under the bridge. There have been lots of changes and the heads of all three universities may have certain things in common, but certainly, they are not all of the same ethnic origin or bound by the same old school tie or by religious denomination. I make this point because of a rather unhealthy tendency, even at that time, to read certain motives into situations which clearly were not taken into account by those who made the appointments. All the three universities are independent universities and the Councils act independently in making their appointments. So I do hope that the "concerned citizens" in future will be concerned about worthwhile matters rather than make mountains out of molehills. The interesting thing is that our concerned citizen did not complain about the incompetence of any of us. What he was concerned about was the fact that however competent we were, whatever good we were doing, we came from the same ethnic group, and that was something which should be condemned!

## Student Affairs

In the area of student affairs, Pitcher, the unofficial-sponsored chronicler of the University of Science and Technology covering the period 1951 to 1976 makes the following statements which I shall quote in full and then comment on: "The regime which took over the administration of the university after the removal of Dr. Baffour took due cognizance of the new student power which was manifesting itself throughout the institutions of higher learning the world over." After giving several examples of the use or misuse of this power, Pitcher concluded, "The students are riding high on the crest of their power and are conscious of the influence they wield in the administration of this university." It is true that the latter half of the 1960s saw the origin and then the growth and spread worldwide of this student power which manifested itself in all forms. I have already mentioned that students started agitating for more participation in the affairs of their universities and that sometimes they went on demonstrations to support this. At other times, the demonstrations were not aimed at the university administration at all but at government policies. The fact that they demonstrated on the campus and sometimes broke loose and went out on the streets, all testified to the fact that they felt that if they acted in this way they might be able to force some concessions out of government or university administration.

Many years ago, when still a student, I was a member of the Students' Representative Council of the Edinburgh University and so I was in a position to appreciate the meaning of some of the things the students wanted to say or to happen. I know that when we are young, we sometimes say things in different ways. There is the tendency for us to see the world in black and white hues only whereas, as we know, there are several shades of colour represented in nature. My philosophy of interacting with the students was quite different because I believe firmly that it isn't everything that the students would ask for that was unreasonable. Indeed, if we are to be true to ourselves, some of the practices in our academic institutions dating back to medieval times were beginning to be meaningless and even archaic, like some of our local cultural practices and traditions!

A liberal mind is always open to new ideas and to change, provided that change is in the positive direction and will lead to progress. Therefore it was my philosophy to spend as much time as possible with the student leadership, especially when the requests or demands that they were making were found to be impracticable and unreasonable, and nothing could really be done about them. On the other hand, where I found there was some reason behind the demands and that changing certain outmoded practices would not really affect progress but constitute a removal of obstacles to progress, I was quite prepared to discuss this with the students and work through the committees of the university, as provided in the Statues, to make changes. Wherever possible I led the move for change and, of course, when change was not necessary I led the move to resist it, but not without having first explained to the students the reasons why certain things could not be done.

The constant demand by the students to be represented on the Academic Board, I found unreasonable and I explained to them that academic matters were not matters of democracy. The teachers were the ones who should make decisions in academic matters. Therefore there was no need for any student to sit on the Academic Board. There were however, provisions at the lower levels (Departmental and Faculty) for the students to make their representations. On the other hand, on non-academic matters, concerning the estate, welfare, health, housing, and other issues, clearly, it was their democratic right to ask to participate. This was the reason behind my advocacy for the establishment of a Welfare Services Board, which, happily Council endorsed. Even then I was highly criticized and as Pitcher put it "I was pursuing democratic ends through undemocratic means." This is where I beg to differ, because a careful reading of provision 15:2c of the University Act shows that in non-academic matters Council can amend the Statutes without reference to the Academic Board. It is only in academic matters that Council is obliged to refer the matter to the Academic Board. Of course, the existing practice had been that it was the Academic Board which made recommendations to Council for amendment of Statutes, and this had gone on for so long that it had been taken as the only way by which the Statutes could be amended. I think the opponents of that move were quite wrong and they can go back and read the Act of the University more carefully. In any case, the point I wish to make here is that I was prepared to spend hours with students and, indeed, I recall that on a certain very controversial issue, I spent almost six hours in my office discussing with, and explaining to, the SRC leaders why a certain thing could not be done, at the end of which they were perfectly satisfied. This is easier where the student leadership is reasonable, that is, where you have really good leaders and they are able to understand the situation and also overcome the next hurdle, which sometimes becomes even more difficult, that is to say, explaining it to the rank and file.

But it must be a leadership which is prepared to lead and not to be wagged by the tail! If you have such leadership then it makes for smoother administration. At this point I recall three presidents of the SRC during my tenure P. V. Obeng, Mohamed Abdulai and Kwame Saarah-Mensah, who were outstanding. There were others also but these three were, in my view, excellent leaders who were prepared to listen. Indeed, even the fact that the Vice-Chancellor or the head of the University was prepared to sit down with them and spend time to explain matters to them, in my view, always meant a lot to students. It showed that you were not an insensitive administrator but somebody who was prepared to listen, argue and debate with them to arrive at an amicable conclusion. This was my style of leadership which Pitcher mistook for weakness. If this was what he thought, the students knew better. They knew what a tough negotiator I could be. By spending six hours in discussion, the Vice-Chancellor could save six months or more of agitation and unpleasantness!

When Pitcher implies that the demand for students to be represented on the Academic Board, was "given short shrift when the Vice-Chancellor brought the matter to the Board" and therefore that I agreed with the students' position, he was quite mistaken. Of course, I could not take a decision by myself and say NO to the students, without bringing the matter to the Academic Board. So the fact that the Academic Board rejected it was no reflection on me whatsoever! Indeed, I feel that it was the mark of somebody who really believed in democracy.

Much fuss was made about the fact that I allowed one of the older staff bungalows to be released to the students to use as their Club House. In any case, the decision was not mine alone. I had to argue for it at the proper quarter and I had the support of the appropriate committee. The argument against the decision was that the students had the Junior Common Rooms in the Halls so why should they have another building?

Indeed, those who argued in this manner quite forgot that a lot of money had been spent in building a whole staff club for the senior staff, despite the fact that all the Halls of residence had Senior Common Rooms, whereas the students had no central place where they could meet. So I found the criticism of this move rather strange. The fact that the students did not manage affairs well at the club house did not detract from the correctness of the decision. To give the students a central place where they could all meet for recreation and other activities was a fair act. If the situation arose again I would do the same thing, knowing that it was perfectly justified!

I think this is an appropriate point to recount the occasions when students demonstrated during my tenure. I remember three occasions. The very first occasion was a demonstration in sympathy with the students at Legon. The previous day, soldiers and police had been sent to Legon to quell a demonstration on the campus. I do not know the reason why the students went on demonstration, but in the course of quelling the demonstration, there had been some violence which the students thought really amounted to Police and Army brutality. Therefore the demonstration at UST and I believe also at Cape Coast, was really supposed to be in sympathy with the students at Legon. It took the form of a boycott of lectures and the students parading around the campus with appropriate placards. This clearly was a demonstration against government (it was a military government at that time) and it was aimed at what the students termed "brutalities." There was no violence on our campus and when the University Council called the student leaders and spoke to them after a day or two they went back, having made their point.

The second occasion was also a sympathy demonstration by only a section of the students, the students of Engineering at a time when the staff of the Engineering Faculty had some problems with the Council. This is something which I shall narrate in some detail later on. But the students were a bit apprehensive about what was going to happen to them as a result of the problems which had arisen with the Engineering staff, and went on a march with placards on the campus, which ended at the precincts of the Administration. They just stood there for a while and made speeches. I was in my office but no attempt was made by any of them to come upstairs to present a petition. They would just hang around for a while and then disperse. This went on for about three days, but I did not intervene in any manner because my dealings with the students was at a different level. When the leaders of the Engineering Students wanted to see me and they asked for an appointment, I saw them in my office and explained matters to them. Clearly, the problem was not with the Vice-Chancellor. It was between the engineering staff and the University Council; the body that appoints staff and lays down the conditions of service of the staff. That was really the issue.

The last occasion, which was a demonstration with a certain measure of violence and really rowdy and unruly behaviour by the students, was something which transpired during my absence. I was then away in Athens attending a function at the Technical University of Athens. On my way back I changed planes in Rome to get on Ghana Airways. On board the flight I saw an article in the previous day's "Daily Graphic" with bold headlines on the front page. I cannot remember the actual words but then it referred to "violent demonstrations by students at UST." This really came to me as a complete surprise. I was away for only one week and, before I left, had not had any complaint from any quarter that something was amiss.

When I came back I got the full report. Apparently, it had started as a result of the alleged assault by the wife of a senior member of staff on a student at the University Hospital and this gave rise to the demonstration. For many days there was tension on the campus and the University Council and even the Regional Commissioner had to intervene. It was altogether a very unpleasant situation and by all accounts, the students' behaviour on that day was really reprehensible. When I called the student leaders on my return, I expressed my displeasure in no uncertain terms. Be that as it may, this happened near the end of my tenure as Vice-Chancellor. It really saddened me a lot because all the time I had had cordial relations with the students and for this unfortunate incident to happen at a time getting to the end of my tenure I found really very sad indeed. As could be expected, Pitcher gave quite a detailed account of this unhappy event in his chronicle. The reader who is interested may refer to pages 43 and 44 of the publication called "The Knot of Wisdom" by George McKenzie Pitcher, Fellow of the Library Association, who was then the University Librarian.

The new students admitted to university are registered at a matriculation ceremony. After registering, the Vice-Chancellor normally addresses them. Each year I took the opportunity to point out to the new entrants how privileged they were to be admitted to the university in view of the fact that the places were limited. For each vacant place, there were three applications from students who were qualified and therefore if one of them was chosen, he should consider himself very lucky. He was chosen because he proved himself to be the best of the three. It was very important to remind them that there were other students who had equal ability and who could be in the university but for the limitations and constraints on the university facilities.

It was also an opportunity to point out to them the opportunities they had for both work and play. At secondary school there was more control on their activities. Now as university students there would be relative freedom. They were more free to organize their time. I stressed the importance of making sure that they took advantage of all these opportunities and facilities at the university. They should make sure that they concentrate on their academic work, but remembering that "all work and no play makes Jack a dull boy," use the recreational, sporting and library facilities and participate in entertainment. The university provided more facilities than the secondary schools from where they had come. I reminded them of the importance of participating in the governance of the university and in electing their leaders.

In the secondary schools, they would have met students from different parts of the country. In the university this would continue and should become the place where they would strengthen the bonds of friendship between themselves and members of other ethnic groups and other religious persuasions. Indeed, the university was a melting pot where they would be practising good governance and nationhood. They should make sure that at the end they did not come out with just a degree or some letters after their names, but also as mature and responsible citizens of Ghana.

Shortly after the matriculation ceremony the newly-elected Student Representative Council would be inaugurated and sworn into office. This was an occasion when the whole student body was expected to be present. It was an occasion for the new president of the Students' Representative Council (SRC) to say something about the policies that his administration intended to pursue. Needless to say on occasion some of these leaders got carried away and made all sorts of promises which could land them in difficulties later.

In addition to the president's speech, the Vice-Chancellor has to address the student body. On this occasion if there were any contemporary issues I would bring them up; if there were certain matters in which the students' cooperation was required, I would appeal to them. If there had been some difficulties, especially during the period when the student power was at its highest, with so many issues cropping up, I took the opportunity to explain to them why certain things which we dearly wished and hoped for could not be done. By that time, I would have gone through the process with the Students' Representatives (the SRC) but it was an occasion for the Vice-Chancellor to personally explain matters to the whole student body. If any student had any problem, this would all be channeled through the new SRC that was being inaugurated.

The third occasion when the Vice-Chancellor addressed students was at the graduation ceremony when the students who had passed their various examinations come to receive degrees, diplomas and certificates; and I took the opportunity on that occasion to remind them of their time in the university and all that they had learnt there. Some years previously, they had come to the university, gone through its walls and some of them had gained top-notch education in the university. Indeed they were better equipped for service to the nation than they were when they were admitted. All this reminded them that their degrees and diplomas and the skills that they had acquired would be meaningless unless they applied this to service to the country, especially in remote and rural areas where this would be most needed. I always reminded them that they were going out as ambassadors of the university, and since the university would be known by its fruits, if they turned out to be bad fruits then they would be giving a bad name to the university.

When I assumed office as Vice-Chancellor I noticed that each Hall of residence had a magazine produced by the students. These were cyclostyled sheets of paper containing all sorts of articles. After a year or two I realized that the standard of contribution was rather low. There was a tendency for contributors to attack personalities and to make libellous and incorrect statements. Despite the overall mediocrity I could occasionally detect journalistic talents from some of the contributors. It was clear to me that, with the needed help and guidance, something better could be done. I suggested to the SRC that perhaps they could combine their efforts and come out with one student magazine that would be edited properly, and which would allow issues on the campus to be discussed in a more objective and responsible way. I am glad to say that my advice was heeded, and with my encouragement and help and that of some of the Hall masters, the students decided to establish a magazine called "The Focus" which, as I expected, helped raise journalistic standards in the various Halls of residence. I do not know whether this magazine is still in production, but it survived for some years and after I left the university, from time to time, I received copies but I have not received a copy for quite a long time now and I sincerely hope that it has not become defunct. If it has, I would urge that it be resuscitated and that the students tackle the task of producing a journal of requisite high standard as soon as possible.

One of the things which really pleased me throughout my tenure as Vice-Chancellor was the fact that the students of the University of Science and Technology took sports very seriously, especially, athletics, football, hockey and tennis, and I went regularly to watch them perform. I was happy especially that for some time, whilst I was there, in athletics the UST were the national university champions and I looked forward to the time when they would become champions of West Africa. As the reader may know, my specialty as a sportsman was hockey, and one of my greatest regrets was that even at that time, a nagging spinal problem prevented me from participating actively; in joining the students on the hockey field, but I paid frequent visits, watched and encouraged them, especially outstanding players like Saarah Mensah and others whose names I cannot recall now. But I must say that I was really very happy that they took sports seriously and that they did well at the national level and even at the sub-regional level.

## Attempted Intra-Student Coup!

In my interaction with students throughout my tenure, one thing which I stressed repeatedly was the fact that they should pay attention to rules and regulations, especially those in whose formulation they themselves had participated. I will recount briefly an incident to illustrate this point. In an article which I wrote for the *"Focus"* some years ago titled *"My Days with students at UST"*, I have given a vivid description of the incident. One night between 10.30 and 11 o'clock, after a particularly busy day I had just retired when the telephone rang. The voice at the other end was that of a student. I could hear a distinct background noise and it was quite clear he was not alone. Knowing that he had disturbed my sleep, he apologized profusely, but informed me that a crisis situation was developing and a few of them thought I should be notified immediately before things got out of hand. Judging by the background noise, I knew that it was most likely quite a serious situation so I asked him what was the matter. He informed me that at a student meeting which was taking place at the Republic Hall from where he was speaking, a decision of "no confidence" in the Students' Representative Council had been taken, so they had dismissed the SRC! The problem now was that the SRC president had refused to hand over the keys of the SRC office which was then in Republic Hall. I told him that they should not do anything rash but that I was going to send the Registrar to come there immediately to take and keep the keys, and also that they should come and see me in the morning. The Registrar was not at home so I spoke to the Finance Officer, who went to the spot and got the keys and I asked him to bring them to my office in the morning. Meanwhile, I told the leader of the attempted "coup", if I may call it so, to come and see me in my office at half past seven in the morning.

The following day, when I got to my office, I saw this chap, who introduced himself as the student who spoke to me the previous night. He was with six other students whom he introduced as his "government." I told him that I was receiving him and his friends just to listen to them, but that did not mean that I recognized them as the new government for the student body. When they got into the office, I asked him whether he was aware of the provisions in the students' constitution for removing the SRC, and he said yes. So I said, "We have to check on this" because I was very strict about these matters, viz, adhering to rules and regulations. I called the Registrar to bring the SRC file. Looking at the SRC constitution, we discovered that a quorum was required and that a notice had to be given for a special meeting to discuss a resolution or a proposal for removing the SRC. The *"no confidence"* motion had to be spelt out. As we read through it was clear that none of these conditions had been fulfilled; so I asked him whether in the circumstances he thought they were acting constitutionally. After they were confronted with the evidence, which showed that clearly they were not familiar with the regulations, they conceded that they had acted unconstitutionally. I, therefore, informed the leader that without these conditions being fulfilled, there was nothing that I could do and that the sitting president and the SRC were the only body that could be recognized by the University. If they wanted to remove the SRC then they should go and fulfill these conditions.

The interesting thing was that this SRC was the carry over from the previous year and they had 10 more days to complete their term before a new SRC was to be installed. In spite of this, the "rebels" thought that the offence that they had committed had something to do with the accounts of the students' club house, which the reader may remember I was instrumental in allocating to the students and warranted their punishment and dismissal! I assured them that if really there had been some embezzlement or some malfeasance, I would see to it that those who committed the offence were dealt with, whether in or out of office! They then went and set in motion the processes for calling a special meeting, giving the due notice and also making sure that they would have a quorum. I sent two officers from the Administration to supervise that meeting. To cut a long story short, they were not able to comply with the provisions of the constitution. The new SRC was elected and the rebels did not have their way, although the rebel leader was elected to represent his Faculty!

When the new SRC was being sworn in, I took the opportunity to express my displeasure at the manner in which a section of the students tried to violate the constitution, and told them that we, in the University were in a civilized society and did not approve of violence for changing governments, and that I expected that in future they would all act in a responsible manner. I also pointed out the fact that one of the reasons it was possible for a group of students to try to behave in this way was the reported apathy among the student body in attending meetings to discuss relevant and important issues. I recount this story to emphasize the position that I always took with students. I believe that many of the students of that time came to appreciate the importance of constitutional rule, the importance of law and order, the importance of obeying regulations and not trying to circumvent or bypass constituted authority, or short-circuit the proper channels to gain their objectives.

## The Engineering Crisis

A matter which was of great concern to me and caused me much unhappiness was what I would call "the Engineering Crisis." In April 1970, all the 24 Ghanaian academic staff of the Faculty of Engineering tended in a notice of resignation to take effect from October, that is, the start of the following academic year. This was in keeping with the requirements of the conditions of service that they had to give six months' notice of intention to resign. This came as a bit of a shock to me but not much of a surprise because several months before, these same members of staff had petitioned the Council for an increase in their salaries. They argued that because they were professionals, they needed to be paid higher salaries than what the other academic staff of equivalent status of the other disciplines in the University were receiving.

Of course, the Council could not accede to this request and decided that in accordance with the unified conditions of service for the three universities in Ghana, there would be no differential in salary to be paid to academic staff in the universities based on their discipline. In other words, the professor of mathematics would have the same pay as the professor of engineering. In fact, all professors, lecturers, and research fellows, irrespective of their discipline would be receiving the same salary attached to their rank. Secondly, in the conditions of service for the university staff, the academic staff were allowed to take on consultancy work to augment their incomes, provided they got permission from the Vice-Chancellor and, of course, in accordance with regulations which were formulated by the university, the most important being that such additional work should not interfere in any way with their academic work.

The notice of resignation came in one letter signed by all the 24 members of staff! I could not accept this. I had to return it for each member of staff to write a separate letter since they were not all appointed *en bloc*. It was necessary to make this legal distinction, and after they fulfilled this request I submitted the matter to the Council. Council of course could not, on the grounds of the notice of resignation, vary its decision, which had been taken as a matter of principle. Therefore I was charged by the Council to appeal to the members of staff involved to rescind their decision in view of the adverse effect which their resignation would have on the academic work of the Engineering Faculty in the subsequent academic year. Therefore for a month or two, I spent much time holding meetings with the leaders of the group, appealing to them in the best manner that I could, explaining to them the Council's decision, and encouraging them to take on consultancy work. The provision existed to make it possible for the academic staff, especially those who were professionals, to augment their income.

I must say that most of what I had to say fell on deaf ears. At one point I was invited to come to the Faculty to discuss the matter with them, which I did, but to no avail. In the end, during the notice period, 10 of the number withdrew their notice of resignation, whilst the other 14 stuck to their guns, so that by the time the new academic year started, these 14 had left the university. This meant that some make-shift arrangement had to be made so that academic work might not suffer during the academic year 1970-71. I have already mentioned that the Engineering students, when this matter came up, went on a demonstration in sympathy with the members of staff. The situation called for some very urgent and serious work to be done and I had to travel extensively within the United Kingdom to visit a number of universities in order to make arrangements for academic staff to be released to Kumasi for varying periods according to the subject that required to be taught.

At the end of the day, I got help from the University of Edinburgh, Herriot Watt University, Salford University and Bradford University. In one case the academic member came for a whole year! In other cases members came for a term or two terms but it was arranged in such a way that no position ever became vacant and that they came in relays to make sure that on no occasion would any subject be without a lecturer.

The arrangements which were made were such that all relevant teaching work was covered during the academic year and there was no complaint at all by the students. I may say that the experience we had then underlined very strongly the importance of the establishment of links between universities, especially between the developing and developed world. It was a good demonstration to us of how very useful these links could be, especially in crisis situations such as we were faced with. Needless to say, during the course of that academic year, the university had to do intensive recruiting for new staff, because we needed at least 14 lecturers to fill the vacancies created by those who had left the university. This meant encouraging the University's own staff who were on study leave from the University to complete their work on time and come back early, as well as advertising for these posts to be filled. To cut a long story short, we had to work very hard during that year.

By the beginning of the next academic year, all vacant posts had been filled. I must say here that one thing which I was happy about was that of the 14 who left the university only two went abroad. The remaining 12 stayed on in Ghana and they were mostly in industry. They stayed on to provide service in Ghana. So it was in the nature of an "internal brain drain." Moreover, after one year, two of this number came back to the university. They reapplied and, of course, we took them back immediately. They had been in industry, acquiring practical experience which I felt would be very useful in their teaching. I looked upon that one year as a form of sabbatical leave for them in industry, and I think they were also quite happy that they were re-engaged by the University to continue with their academic work

Concerning this episode, I must say that I have often wondered why the engineering staff acted on their own. One of the reasons which they advanced in support of the petition was one which could equally be advanced by other professionals in the university, especially the architects, the pharmacists, the industrial artists, and so on. but unfortunately they chose to act on their own. Not that the result would have been different, but I felt that in such an endeavour, it would have looked better if all the professional academics had acted together.

## The Technology Consultancy Centre

Fortunately, out of this crisis situation was born something which was really good and positive for the university. It hastened the establishment of the Technology Consultancy Centre. As we know, the three principal objectives of the university are to teach, to engage in research and to provide service to the community. Of course, teaching is a very straightforward matter. When it comes to research, one needs more funds and facilities - laboratories, equipment and a very good library. The third objective of the university, viz, providing service to the community is one which, especially in developing countries, has always been a problem in the sense that governments provide the money for running the university and expect to see something visible or tangible to show that the university is interested in this third objective. Many had tended to look upon the university as an ivory tower, an inward-looking institution confined to teaching and research only. In the university, we have a pool of talent and expertise in the academic staff, and this is a pool in which government does not often fish. There is a tendency for governments, especially in developing countries, to marginalize (either by default or intentionally) and ignore this source of expertise and then bring in outside "experts" to try to solve problems, problems which indeed could be solved equally well, if not better, by local experts who can be found in the universities.

I have already mentioned that among the conditions of service of the academic staff was a privilege of doing consultancy work and in so doing, provide service. At the time that the engineering crisis came about there had been isolated instances of individual members of staff helping individual small businessmen. Indeed, there was in existence an informal group called "*The Technology Group,*" which was offering advice to small-scale industrialists and helping them to improve on their skills. What happened after the engineering crisis was that the university started thinking seriously about formalizing the whole situation and creating a machinery whereby all the expertise in the university could be mobilized regularly to solve particular problems for industry or government. I became personally very much involved in this, and I was very happy when, on introducing this proposal to the Academic Board after having discussed it with the Deans of the Faculties, the Board accepted this and Council approved the establishment of The Technology Consultancy Centre.

The idea of having a centre was to have a point of contact between the University and the outside world, where requests from industrialists, big or small, would come to the University and the Centre would in turn identify the experts in the University and farm out work to them. The Centre was very useful in projects of an interdisciplinary nature. Associate Prof. Powell, who had been very interested in this whole area of intermediate technology was appointed as the first director of the Centre and, under his leadership, the Centre became an important place in the University. Gradually, it made contacts with small-scale industry, with artisans and craftsmen and technicians in Suame Magazine, Kumasi, and also helped small-scale industrialists by teaching them methods of improving on their skills and production processes. The Centre, over the years, has become very important in the development of the country.

Upon the establishment of the Centre I listed its main functions in an address to members of Convocation (the academic staff) as follows:

1.  *to provide consultancy services to industry, large and small;*
2.  *to assist small-scale enterprises to organize themselves more efficiently and effectively;*
3.  *to assist small-scale business enterprises to improve upon their technology;*
4.  *to introduce new technologies to indigenous craftsmen with the view to increasing their skill and productivity*
5.  *to conduct research and feasibility studies and to support production units by pilot plants and projects.*

The Centre was meant to be the main channel through which requests would come from the general public and outside organizations. Through it also, the research results of the departments and faculties would be made available to outside organizations. It was quite clear that this was a very important development in the University and I know that members of the academic staff especially welcomed the development with great enthusiasm. The hardworking staff members found it an avenue through which they could develop their own skills, conduct research, and last, but not least, supplement their income. Indeed, if I was asked to name one achievement, the most important achievement of mine as Vice-Chancellor I would say it was the establishment of the Technology Consultancy Centre!

It is interesting to note that the Centre established itself very quickly and indeed, whilst still young, became quite famous internationally. Some universities in Africa sent people to come and study the workings of the Centre, the whole philosophy behind its establishment and the manner in which it had been performing.

## The Vice-Chancellor's Travels

Before taking office as Vice-Chancellor, I knew there would be a fair amount of international travelling but, after assuming office, I realized that I had to do more travelling than I thought. Besides, there were occasions and circumstances which made it necessary to undertake some unscheduled travels. The University is a member of international organizations, mostly academic, such as the Association of African Universities, Association of Commonwealth Universities, the Inter-University Council, and the International Association of Universities. These organizations hold conferences annually or bi-annually and the matters which are discussed are so important that whenever necessary it is important that the head of the University himself attends. Usually matters which are discussed relate to university cooperation; in some cases the establishment of formal links either at university level or at departmental level. The discussion of staff and student exchange programmemes and of joint research programmemes also take place. Other travels to be undertaken involve recruitment drives, and usually the destination is London where interviews may be held at the Ghana Universities Office under the chairmanship of the Vice-Chancellor of applicants, both Ghanaian and expatriate, who have applied for specific posts within the University.

As a result of the engineering crisis it was necessary for me within the course of twelve months to make several visits to the United Kingdom. Then of course, there were travels and visits that had to be undertaken, as well as official invitations, either by governments or educational institutions of the inviting country. I recall that in 1968, the three Vice-Chancellors of the universities in Ghana were invited to Germany, for a ten-day visit to German universities. At that time, Dr. F. O. Kwami was a Research Lecturer at the Technical University of Berlin. I was able to have discussions with him and persuade him to come home to join the staff of the University of Science and Technology. I would like to think that as a result of my persuasion, he came the following year. The reader may know that since then Prof. Kwami has made invaluable contributions to the development of the university. He himself rose through the ranks to become Associate Professor, Full Professor, Dean of the Engineering Faculty and eventually Vice-Chancellor of the University. He is still exerting great influence in the field of technical education in the country.

I recall also that in 1968, I was invited by the African-American Institute in the United States with a grant by the Carnegie Corporation to undertake a travelling tour of several universities in the United States. I was able to visit the University of Miami, Florida (and incidentally took the opportunity to meet my biological mother-in-law for the first time) the University of Houston, Texas, Tuskegee Institute in Alabama, Caltech in Los Angeles, the University of California at Los Angeles, Stanford University, the University of Illinois, Northwestern University in Chicago and Northeastern University in Boston, Harvard University, Columbia`University and St. Paul's College, Minneapolis, a predominantly women's college. I was also able to visit a number of junior colleges which provide two-year college work which could later on be topped up with another two years for a full degree. The graduate of junior college could also go into the world of work. Incidentally, during that visit in 1968, I had to break the tour for two weeks to go to Australia where the Association of Commonwealth Universities was holding its biennial Congress in Sydney. There were visits to Melbourne and also Canberra. Unfortunately, because of my commitments in the United States I could not go on to New Zealand for a mini-congress so I had to come back via Hawaii, where I spent the weekend in Honolulu, a weekend which I would prefer to forget, because I had a heavy cold and spent most of the time in bed in my hotel!

The Inter-University Council in Britain is a very important organization which facilitates and sponsors cooperation among universities. It helps out with the recruitment of staff, and makes recommendations about capacity building. In 1972, there was an important conferences in Hong Kong after which there were post-congress visits to Singapore and Malaysia. The Inter-University Council also arranged conferences in different cities, in Malta and also in Sussex, UK. In 1973, the Association of Commonwealth Universities Congress was held in Edinburgh, my alma mater. I was happy to go back to my second home. I recall that some of my contemporaries and some of the staff in the University arranged an informal meeting for me to talk to them about higher education and other matters in Ghana and West Africa generally.

## Honorary Awards

During my tenure, the university awarded honorary degrees to several distinguished Ghanaians. At my first congregation in 1968 the honorary degree of Doctor of Science was awarded to Otumfuo Nana Sir Osei Agyeman Prempeh. It was through the generosity of Otumfuo that the University was given such a vast area of land on which to develop. Conferring the honorary degree on Otumfuo in 1968 was an act which was long overdue. At that same ceremony Dr. Robert Gardier who was then the Executive Secretary of the Economic Commission for Africa, a very distinguished international public servant and son of this soil, was also awarded an honorary degree of Doctor of Science. A very popular award was also made to Mr. E. A Barnor, the Deputy Registrar who had been with the University Administration right from the beginning, rendering meritorious service. He was awarded an MA Degree. Then Dr. Alex Kyeremanten on his retirement from the Chairmanship of the University Council in 1972 was awarded an honorary Doctor of Letters Degree. The following year, two distinguished Ghanaians, Mr. Justice Nii Amaa Ollennu, an eminent jurist and former Speaker of Parliament, and Mr. E.L. Quartey, a distinguished engineer and Chief Executive of the Volta River Authority were awarded Doctor of Science Degrees.

## Changing of the Guard at Council

After nearly five years, Dr Alex Kyerematen relinquished the chairmanship of the Council of the University. He was replaced in early January by Dr. Daniel Chapman Nyaho, a distinguished educationist, former headmaster of Achimota School and retired international diplomat. The Busia government which appointed him was overthrown by the military government of the National Redemption Council on 13 January 1972. Dr. Chapman Nyaho's tenure as Chairman was rather short-lived. He attended two meetings of the Council, one of the Council itself and the other of its Development Committee. On the eve of the 1972 Congregation, just a few days before, the new military government summarily terminated his appointed as Chairman and appointed the Catholic Bishop of Kumasi, Bishop Akwasi Sarpong, as Chairman of the University Council.

The shabby, capricious and cavalier manner in which Dr. Chapman Nyaho was removed by the military government caused Dr. Modjaben Dowuona, the Chairman of the National Council for Higher Education at the time, much embarrassment and pain, because it was on his recommendation that government appointed Dr. Chapman Nyaho. I know that it took a great deal of persuasion for that distinguished Ghanaian, Dr. Chapman Nyaho, to accept to serve as Chairman of the University Council. I need hardly point out that the manner in which some distinguished citizens have been treated over the years since independence by successive governments has resulted in some leaving the country and others feeling unwilling to give useful service or advice when needed. Fortunately for the University, Bishop Sarpong who succeeded Dr. Chapman Nyaho, was himself an experienced educationist who rendered very useful service to the University.

One major issue for the universities had been the question of funding, specifically the funding for students. The National Liberation Council Government before handing over to the Busia government had appointed a committee, with Dr. Modjaben Dowuona as chairman, to consider a proposal for loans to students. Hitherto, all students had been on "scholarship." They were entitled to ¢500 (five hundred cedis) a year out of which ¢400 (four hundred cedis) was given to the University for their board and lodging and ¢100 (one hundred cedis) was given directly to the student for his other expenses. There were three student representatives on the Modjaben Dowuona committee, one student from each of the three universities. The Committee Report recommended the abolition of the scholarship scheme and putting in place a Loans Scheme with a system of recovery. There was no proposal for interest on the loan. There was to be a one time payment of ¢50 (fifty Cedis) for servicing the loan. The recovery was to start six months after the graduate had secured employment and was to be spread over a period of twelve to fifteen years. I must say that the terms of recovery were very generous. The idea was to set up a revolving fund.

The students understood the reason for establishing the fund but they resisted it fiercely, even though their representatives also signed the report. There was student agitation and resistance against the whole idea of the students' loan which dragged on for some time. At the start of the academic year 1971/72, the Busia government introduced the students' loan scheme. This made the government highly unpopular with the students. To curry favour with the students, one of the first things which the NRC government led by Colonel Kutu Acheampong did was to abolish the students' loan scheme. By so doing he got initial support from the students. This support was to be short-lived, as I shall narrate later on.

## The Vice-Chancellor's Wife

I cannot end this narrative on the UST without mentioning the exemplary role which was played by the Vice-Chancellor's wife. That morning when Alex Kyerematen called me on the telephone and asked whether I would be prepared to have my name put forward for consideration for the Vice-Chancellorship and he had been trying to persuade me to respond affirmatively, he said in passing, "Leonora will help you." This statement was made rather casually but, of course, Alex knew Leonora well from previous years, and he knew what sort of support Leonora, as the Vice-Chancellor's wife, would give me. I must say that during nearly seven years of my vice-chancellorship, I came to value and appreciate the importance of having a wife such as Leonora as my support.

Throughout those years, she was the rallying point for university ladies, not only wives, but lady workers also. They looked upon her as their natural leader, they looked upon her as a mother and through her leadership they were able to establish a children's library on the campus and also engage in many other humanitarian activities. Also she played the role of a counsellor for many of them. I am happy to say that in two cases, Leonora and I were involved in the private married lives of two members of the academic staff. Fortunately, we were able to help to resolve one. The other had been long standing and rather intractable and proved insoluble. There were many examples that I knew of when some of the girl students came to see Leonora at home with their problems. Altogether, she played a really positive role and had a beneficial influence on the social life on the campus. Indirectly of course, she earned much goodwill for me personally as the Vice-Chancellor. Indeed, I feel that she succeeded better as a Vice-Chancellor's wife than I did as a Vice-Chancellor!

In our second year, 1968, after she had accompanied me on a trip to Winneba where I had been invited as guest speaker on a Speech and Prize Giving Day of the Advanced Teacher Training College, on our return she had an acute heart attack which really disabled her for some time. This made it necessary for her to go abroad to Edinburgh for a major cardiac operation subsequently she went back annually for check-up. Despite this physical handicap, she was able to do all that she did to support the Vice-Chancellor.

Apart from Charlie, our youngest son, who was four when we assumed duty in Kumasi, and therefore went to the kindergarten and later to the University Primary School, the older three children were all in boarding school. The two boys were at Achimota and the girl at Aburi. I was, therefore, able to spend much time with Charlie; the time which I did not have when I was working in hospitals all over the country and was on call round the clock! Charlie was lucky. As Vice-Chancellor I was very busy, of course, and had quite a fair amount of travelling to do, but then whilst in Ghana, I saw more of him at home.

## Kicked Upstairs

Sometime during the first quarter of the year 1973, the Chairman of the Council of Higher Education, Dr. Modjaben Dowuona, on a visit to Kumasi informed me of his impending retirement on 31st July that year, adding that there was a search going on for his successor. He wondered whether I would be prepared to curtail my contract with the University by one year to enable me to leave the University in July of that year and assume the chairmanship of the Council for Higher Education. I had already decided that after my seven years with the University I was not going to seek a renewal of the appointment for any further period and that I would go back to Accra, preferably to private practice with an arrangement for teaching at the Medical School. Dr. Modjaben Dowuona was quite persuasive. He was anxious, or rather the government was anxious, that whoever succeeded him would be somebody of stature who would be respected by the universities preferably a former Vice-Chancellor. It appeared that my colleagues, Prof. Kwapong at Legon and Prof. Boateng at Cape Coast had much longer periods of their contracts still to run and it was thought that I would be the one who would make the least sacrifice by leaving early.

I did not give an answer immediately because I had to think about many things. Definitely in staging a re-entry into professional practice, I would have to return to Accra to spend some time and it may well be that if I were to be appointed the Chairman of the Council for Higher Education for a short period, and, therefore, to be resident in Accra, the transition period would help me to make some more solid arrangements. In the end I agreed to a compromise; that I was prepared to leave after six-and-a-half years, which meant that I would end my contract with the university on 31st December 1973. As Dr. Modjaben had made up his mind to leave at the end of June by all means it meant that someone would have to be appointed to act in the interim; perhaps one of the members of the Council On his return to Accra, I telephoned to say that I would be prepared if appointed to take over from him but only after 31st December and provided I would be permitted to do part time clinical work in one of the hospitals.

My wife, had no objection whatsoever to the appointment. She was quite prepared, although with mixed feelings, to leave the University six months earlier than the scheduled contract date. From then on, I began to look back on the six years at the University so far and wondered whether they had been worthwhile years, from my point of view, and also from the point of view of the University. Had I made any contribution at all to the University's development? Had I also gained anything from the University?

I had arrived at a time when there was supposed to be polarization on the campus, when allegedly there wasn't the desired unity among staff, when there wasn't that peace which would make for forward movement and development. I had decided that the best way to handle such a situation was to adopt a posture of positive neutrality. As a doctor, such a thing was not difficult for me. After all our profession does not allow us to discriminate in matters concerning the management and treatment of our patients. I would remove the appendix of a pauper in the same way that I would that of a prince. The management would be the same. The profession had taught me to treat everybody equally, at least as far as professional skills are concerned. I had worked for some years previously at Komfo Anokye Hospital as Chief Surgeon and I had adopted the same attitude, so really it was not difficult for me. Judging from what I perceived from the campus, apart from the unfortunate incident at the university hospital concerning the wife of a member of the teaching staff and a student, which led to a student demonstration with a certain amount of violence resulting in tension on the campus, I thought on the whole relationships on the campus were quite good.

My evaluation of the six and a half years' tenure, had to take into account, in broad terms, what contributions I had made to the university on the one hand and on the other what I had gained personally from my service as Vice-Chancellor. Generally speaking, in accordance with my mission, I felt that the most important thing was the effort I had put into democratizing the systems within the university. In this area, I think, I had made quite useful contributions. Also, I had endeavoured to continue the far-sighted programmeme of staff development which my predecessor had initiated. I continued to send post-graduate students and members of staff abroad on post-graduate work or study leave for higher qualifications. I had increased and strengthened the bonds existing between UST and other universities both within and outside Africa. Certainly the cooperation with our two sister universities in Ghana had been strengthened during this period. I had endeavoured to bring the university closer to the people : that is to say to bring town and gown together and through the activities of the Technology Consultancy Centre, underscored the importance of one of the principal functions of the university, viz : SERVICE. All this had taken place during six years.

On the whole, I thought, as my successor Prof Bamfo Kwakye subsequently remarked that "I laid bare the enormous potential of the University for rendering effective service in the development of Ghana".

On my part, there was no doubt at all that the six years helped to widen my horizon, to broaden my field of vision and to increase my knowledge of so many things. The many welcome addresses that I had to give at conferences on the campus organized by the various faculties/ professional organizations meant learning more about disciplines other than my own. Also the invitation to be guest speaker, at speech and prize-giving days of secondary schools and training colleges all over the country meant that I had to learn a lot in order to be able to deliver. Without doubt I was now able to see both national and international problems in better perspective through the opportunities that I had had: opportunities which I would never have had if I had just remained a teacher at the Medical School practising my profession.

Before coming to the University, as a doctor, I knew much about the human body: its structure and its functions. After six and-a-half years as Vice-Chancellor, I found myself becoming quite an expert on human behaviour, the workings of the human mind and, not only the individual mind but also the group mind. For example, I was able to predict at a meeting say of the Academic Board or of a committee, the attitudes or positions which various individuals were likely to take on a given issue and what they were likely to say. I found myself being correct in my predictions in quite a large percentage of cases. Certainly, the truism in "unhappy lies the head that wears the crown" became more real to me. One thing which bothered me was the anonymous letters that I received concerning persons in the University. I could see that some of these letters came from within the University itself, but others also came from outside the University complaining about various officials of the University, in the administration or in the academic section of the University. At first I found it rather strange and I was not quite sure how to handle the situation. It gave me the opportunity to consider carefully what had been written, and to evaluate it and, quite frankly, I found that in most cases, whilst not ignoring completely any information which I got, the best place for these letters was the waste paper basket! Interestingly, in some cases I found that there were complaints about decisions which I had taken myself, as Vice-Chancellor, and yet the complaint was against the Registrar!

One issue which cropped up regularly, especially at the beginning of every academic year, was the question of admission to the University. Parents or guardians usually did not understand why their wards having fulfilled the minimum requirements for entry into the University were not admitted. Some of them understood the situation of constraints on accommodation and other facilities on the campus which prevented the University from admitting everyone just because they fulfilled the minimum entry requirements. However, they refused to accept that it was necessary to draw the line somewhere and for selection to be based on academic merit.

It was a regrettable fact that the growth of the University was stifled to a large extent by the paucity of facilities - accommodation, classroom, workshop, and laboratory facilities. The fact that at that time there was emphasis on residential accommodation made it even more difficult. With the passage of time, students have come to accept to share rooms. Where originally a student room was meant for one person now it is being used by up to four persons, leading to a good deal of congestion on the campus. The increase in numbers is not matched by an increase in facilities. I am glad that at this point in time, the policy of non-residential accommodation has come to stay, since students, parents and guardians now understand that to increase access to higher education, it will be quite impracticable to provide comfortable accommodation and all the facilities to satisfy the increasing number of aspirants to university education.

By this time also I had become quite an expert in counselling students in their choice of careers, something which I found quite an asset, which would become useful in future.

Dr. Modjaben Dowuona retired in July 1973 and Mr. K. B. Ayensu, a former clerk of the National Assembly and member of the Council for Higher Education, was appointed to act as Chairman until a substantive Chairman was appointed to take over. Shortly after Dr. Modjaben Dowuona's retirement, I received a letter of appointment from the government. My appointment was to take effect from 1st January 1974. Now in order for the University Council to have a long enough period to search for my successor, I sent in my letter of resignation. After a thorough search, Associate Professor E. Bamfo Kwakye, who was then my Pro Vice-Chancellor, was appointed Vice-Chancellor to succeed me. When I assumed office in 1967, Prof. Bamfo Kwakye was on study leave. He was among those mentioned in the Manyo-Plange Report on the Affairs of the University as having benefited from favour shown by my predecessor, Dr. Baffour. It had been alleged that he benefited from rapid promotion because his wife was a relative of Dr. Baffour. When Prof. Bamfo Kwakye came back from study leave, I was soon to discover that he was a highly competent professional and a very good hardworking teacher, who exhibited qualities of good leadership. So it did not take him long to rise through the ranks as Head of his department and to become Dean of the faculty of Engineering and eventually Pro Vice-Chancellor. I found in him a very good worker, extremely loyal to the University, and, therefore, I had no difficulty at all in supporting the recommendation for his appointment as Vice-Chancellor.

# CHAPTER 23

# FINAL RETURN TO ACCRA
## Chairman Of The National Council For Higher Education

Despite the fact that I was to leave the University after a few months and therefore my administration during that period might be described, as a "lame duck administration," I just continued as if nothing had happened, as if I was not leaving. I pressed on with the policies that we were pursuing. Happily, the Pro Vice-Chancellor, who became Vice-Chancellor-designate, was someone who strongly supported these policies.

In December, I realized that I was quite tired. Therefore before making any move, I wrote to request that the date of my assumption of duty as Chairman of the Council for Higher Education be changed to 1st March 1974, to enable me to take part of my accumulated leave, during which period I hoped to get the necessary rest. Also since that move from Kumasi to Accra was to be the last move I would have to make in my chain of transfers for more than twenty years, I thought I needed this period to pack and transfer my belongings to Accra. Fortunately, the application was approved and therefore I was able to continue to stay on in the University. Fortunately, the new Vice-Chancellor, after taking over from me on 1st of January, agreed that I could stay on in the Vice-Chancellor's Lodge during my leave. Leonora and Charlie could stay on a bit longer for Charlie to take the Common Entrance Examination sometime in March before we made the final move to Accra. I left Kumasi in the last week of February 1974 to come to Accra to get ready to take up my appointment on 1st March. Leonora and Charlie joined me later and Charlie spent the last term of the academic year at the Ridge Church School.

The Council for Higher Education is the body which advises Government on all higher education matters. In particular, it performs functions akin to the University Grants Committee of the United Kingdom in advising on the allocation of funds to the three existing universities. It is quite a high-powered body with the three Vice-Chancellors together with three other representatives of the universities, representatives of government, for example, Ministries of Finance and Economic Planning and Education and also some prominent Ghanaians who had knowledge of education. It was quite a formidable body. Apart from the Chairman, who was full-time, all the other members were part-time.

The Council was directly under the office of the head of government. The Decree establishing the Council made provision for this. Somehow, it was felt that higher education had peculiar problems which required special action. So the Council was placed under the purview of the head of government allegedly also to avoid the possibility of politics influencing matters of higher education.

The Chairman of the National Redemption Council, Colonel I. K. Acheampong, held many positions in relation to the Universities : he was Chancellor of both the University of Ghana, Legon, and the University of Science and Technology, Kumasi, Commissioner responsible for Higher Education, Head of Government and, finally, Head of State.

When I assumed duty on the 1st of March 1974, all the universities had been closed down. I did indicate earlier on that the cordiality which existed between the students and the Acheampong Government was rather short-lived. For some time the students had complained about what they called "military and police brutalities" being inflicted on civilians. The straw that broke the camel's back on this occasion was when a university student was alleged to have been brutally assaulted at Ho by the military. Immediately, there were demonstrations against the government on all three university campuses. These demonstrations were highly disliked by the government and, on the same day, the universities were closed down without any consultation with the Council for Higher Education or the university authorities. The reader may recall that when Col. Acheampong abolished the students loan scheme, he did so without consulting the universities or the National Council for Higher Education. On this occasion too, the order to close the universities came directly from him. In addition to instructions that the universities be closed down, it was also decided by Government that before they were reopened the loan scheme should to be introduced.

It was a matter of great concern for not only the Universities but also the Council and I recall that the two Vice-Chancellors and myself had a couple of sessions with the Chairman of the NRC, trying to prevail upon him not to make the introduction of the loan scheme a condition for re-opening the universities. He had abolished the scheme without consultation, and was going to reintroduce it, again without consultation, and we felt it would not do the image of the Government any good. Although we agreed that the loan scheme was necessary, it was important that it be carefully thought through over time and therefore we advised him to drop that particular requirement.

It took us some time, but in the end reason prevailed, and it was agreed that at some future date the matter of the loans would be reintroduced. We were happy about this because the whole idea of the loans scheme was to make it possible to have a revolving fund which would facilitate the funding of students and make it possible for a larger number of students to access higher education.

Now, in advising Government on the funding of the universities, the Council held annual preliminary budget hearings with the universities before submitting the budgets of the universities to the Ministry of Finance. This was very helpful because, traditionally, the universities had to fight hard for their proposals to be accepted by the Ministry. The recommendations which came from the Council after these budget hearings made it easier for the Ministry to accept whatever proposals the Council put before them.

During my tenure as Chairman, the Council had to advise Government on three matters where new institutions were to be established. The first one was the proposal for the establishment of a university in the north. This proposal was first embodied in a memorandum prepared by the Honourable Mumuni Bawumia, when he was Regional Minister of the Northern Region in 1963 and had been submitted to the President of the Republic, Osagyefo Dr. Kwame Nkrumah. No action was taken on it. When the National Redemption Council took over (and it is well known that it was a government which was very sympathetic to the Nkrumahists çause) the request was revived, and the Office of the Chairman of the NRC sent the proposal to the Council for Higher Education, which then appointed a three-man committee to examine it. They visited the North and had discussions with all the relevant stakeholders, and, in the end, Council advised that it was better to start in a modest way. There already existed research stations at Nyankpala and Pong-Tamale and we thought that the University of Ghana, Legon and UST, in Kumasi could be involved in strengthening the research work there and gradually raising the standard, attaching some teaching functions and starting something like a Workers' College which could be under their supervision. With time it would become a university college and eventually an independent university after the manner of Legon and Kumasi. We thought it would be most unwise under the circumstances for a new institution to start from scratch.

Nothing much came out of this, but we now know that as a result of the recommendation of the University's Rationalization Committee which was appointed by the Government of the PNDC in 1988, a university of the North was started as an independent university. Since then, as was to be expected, they have been experiencing extremely painful growing pains.

The second proposal was for the establishment of a medical school at the University of Science and Technology. Again, a committee was appointed. Its recommendations to Council which were passed on to Government were that it was rather premature to start a medical school then, and that time was needed to plan for its establishment as there were many implications. The university itself felt that it would initially start with the first degree in human biology to be topped up by clinical training for doctors. Other graduates would specialize in subjects like biochemistry, microbiology or chemical pathology. We also felt that it was necessary for the medical school in Accra to find its feet properly before some resources were diverted to the second medical school. This advice was allegedly understood by Government but all the same the medical school was started in 1975 and, as a result of the premature start, there have been difficulties. When the time came for clinical teaching, the Komfo Anokye Hospital which had been designated a teaching hospital was not properly organized for clinical teaching and it became necessary for the first batch of students to complete their clinical training at the medical school in Accra!

The last proposal concerned the establishment of the Department of Agricultural Science in Cape Coast. Here there was not much controversy. There were people who felt that the two faculties of agriculture in the existing universities were enough and that the graduates of these universities could go and top it up with one year's diploma in education; but, in the end, the views of the advocates for the Department to train students in Agricultural Science prevailed.

In the strategic development plan for the work of the Council (with plans for development of higher education) which was prepared during my first year as Chairman, one of the important recommendations made was that the polytechnics should come under the orbit of higher education since they were already in the tertiary sector. Unfortunately, both the human and material resources of the polytechnics did not make it possible for their work to be of the requisite academic standard and so the polytechnics were placed under the Ministry of Education. We had to be careful when we were making this recommendation because we did not want to be seen as empire builders, wanting to have more institutions of higher learning. The polytechnics are now under the administrative purview of the National Council for Tertiary Education, as it is known now - tertiary rather than higher education.

As Chairman of the Council for Higher Education, it was arranged that once a month, I had audience with the Commissioner for Higher Education, that is, the Chairman of the NRC, to brief him on the situation of the higher education sector and also of the universities. The Chairman was at liberty to call me at any time if he wanted information urgently on this. So it came as a great surprise to me when one evening when visiting Kumasi I went to the Independence Hall where two of my children were resident, and heard on the six o'clock News that certain officials of the public service had been dismissed by the NRC; they were the Chief Justice, the Governor of the Bank of Ghana, the Commissioner for Income Tax and two senior professors of the Medical School. It was quite unconstitutional for a professor of the university to be dismissed by Government. This prerogative was that of the Council of the University.

As I was coming back to Accra the following day, I called the Secretary to the NRC to make an appointment for me to meet with the Chairman immediately on my arrival, which he did. By the time I met the Chairman, he was shocked that within 24 hours all the doctors at Korlebu, and not only the staff of the Medical School but all the doctors in Accra had downed their tools. The reason behind this was that the Chairman had been mistakenly informed that the two professors involved were antagonistic to Government policies. As a result this hasty action had been taken, so the Chairman was not expecting the reaction that followed. He had been given the impression also that these two professors were very strict and rather unpopular with their colleagues and their students so he was quite surprised at the turn of events.

There was an interesting background to this whole matter. Initially, Col. Acheampong with his "Operation Feed Yourself" and self-reliance programmeme was quite popular but by the time this incident happened, which was somewhere at the beginning of 1977, he was becoming increasingly unpopular, primarily as a result of his UNIGOV campaign. The whole idea of the UNIGOV was to have a national government in which the military and the police would also be represented. Of course, this had been resisted by the professional groups, students and the TUC. The whole idea of UNIGOV was derided by the well-informed sections of the public.

As a result of my confrontation with the Head of State on the dismissal of the professors, relations between myself and Acheampong became rather cool. I thought that even though I was not yet 60 years, I was well past 55 and could therefore retire at any age. I duly gave notice of my intention to retire with effect from 1st October and to leave after I had taken my earned leave. On the 1st of October that year, I handed over to Mr. Casely Mate who was much older than I and had retired from the work of UNESCO. He was also a member of the Council. After taking my earned leave, I left the service in mid-December in 1977 and that was the end of my paid pensionable public service.

Before leaving Kumasi to come down to Accra, I had started making arrangements to purchase a house which would be where my family and I would live after my retirement. Fortunately, there were a number of available houses and bungalows belonging to the UAC and my friend, the late Henry Gbedemah, who was one of the managers of UAC put me in touch with the Properties Manager who took me round to see a couple of houses which had been earmarked for sale. I made arrangements to purchase one and indicted the amount that I was prepared to pay. Just before I came down to Accra, I got a letter from the UAC through the Properties Manager that they had decided not to sell any more of the houses until further notice. So when I came down to Accra, I started making a fresh search for a house to buy. I went to see Mr. Richards, the Chairman of UAC who gave me the reasons why they had taken this decision. He hoped that when the ban was lifted I would be able to get one of the houses if by that time I had not succeeded in getting another house. A few months after Mr. Richards left, I went to see the new Chairman, the late Mr. David Andoh and discussed the matter with him. I pointed out to him that I had spent a lot of time corresponding with them and was practically promised the house, only to be let down later. Shortly afterwards, I got a letter conveying to me their change of mind. So through the good offices of Mr. David Andoh, the UAC lifted the ban and I was able to purchase the property in which I now live: Leonora Lodge, Gamel Nasser Avenue (formerly Fifth Avenue).

When I bought the house, there were sitting tenants so I could not occupy it immediately, which was okay for me. The transfer was done in 1975 and being in a Government house, at that time, the need was not pressing. When I finally decided to retire. I had to give notice to the tenants and fortunately for me, I did not have much difficulty with their leaving. After renovation and redecoration, (the whole interior decoration and painting was done by my sons, together with their friends) everything was ready. My children and I decided to name the house after their mother, Leonora, and call it "Leonora Lodge." Now Mammy, had been visiting the house, practically every day to see the extent of progress but when this decision was taken and we had prepared the signboards, it was necessary to find some way of preventing her from getting there until the signboards were put up. So for 24 hours they found ways to divert her attention and when she was finally taken to the house and she saw the signboard, LEONORA LODGE, she shed tears of joy!

My terminal leave expired in the middle of December 1977 and I should have moved immediately, but as Leonora Lodge was not quite ready, the new Chairman of Council, Mr. Casely Mate, kindly agreed for me to stay on for a couple of weeks in the official residence. During the first week of January 1978 we moved into Leonora Lodge. By that time, I did not have much money, having spent all that I had in buying the house, I did not really have money to furnish it, so the furniture was very scanty! Leonora and I had to sleep on a mattress in our master bedroom for a month or so. The children had their own beds. For a few months, the conditions were Spartan, but gradually we were able to start furnishing the house to our taste. After all, this was the first time that we were staying in a house which really belonged to us! Since I joined the public service in 1950 I had stayed in Government houses all over the country, and now, for the first time in 28 years, we had our own house. So we took our time to choose the furniture we wanted.

Meanwhile, I was also looking out for accommodation where I could establish a private clinic, and it occurred to me that my old friend Dr. George, was working alone in Salem Hospital, Labadi Road. Dr. George, at that time, was in his 70s and was running the place single-handedly. We got together and worked out some arrangements whereby I would join him and eventually take over the place. There was a lot that had to be done to the place to make it attractive.

## Commissioner for Education and Culture

Now whilst the negotiations were going on, some colleagues of Col. Acheampong, members of the Supreme Military Council staged a palace coup, and he was removed from office. He was succeeded by General Fred Akuffo, who was then the Chief of Defence Staff. I had no idea, at that time, that this event would have any effect on me, but a week after. Col. Acheampong had been removed, the Army Commander, the Late Major General Odartey-Wellington sent a very important personality to come and have some discussions with me. The Akuffo Government had dropped the UNIGOV idea and had decided that there would be preparations for about one year after which they would hand over the government to a civilian administration under a multi-party constitution. As an earnest of their intention, they were going to remove all the military commissioners and replace them with civilians, and they thought that these civilians should be people who would be respected by the public and who had shown no political inclinations. This would show the public that they really meant business about handing over to a civilian government within a year. When I went to see General Odartey-Wellington he told me that he had been asked to find out from me if I would be willing to help out as Commissioner for Education or Commissioner for Health. I chose Education: I had just come out of the Education administration and I was more comfortable with that, although I could easily handle the Ministry of Health too. For a couple of weeks, nothing happened and just as I was beginning to think that "these people are not serious," I was invited to the Castle to meet General Akuffo himself. The following day I got a letter appointing me as Commissioner for Education and together with my new commissioner-colleagues, we were sworn-in shortly thereafter.

In the face of economic austerity, and a changing political dispensation, it was clear that there was nothing much that I could do within that year. I just regarded it as a holding operation to see that nothing deteriorated in the Ministry and to lay a foundation for any future development. It was in the era of import licences, and my first duty was to rectify the anomalies in the import duty allocation in the Ministry.

My relations with my military colleagues in government were not all that easy. I had been in Education Administration for well over 10 years and, naturally, I had a better understanding of issues. I had been accustomed to working out issues and trying to find solutions in collaboration with others. I found that their military training tended to make them impatient, requiring instant solutions to problems. For example, the whole question of funding of feeding in our educational institutions was a problem and, unfortunately, they were always quite suspicious of and ready to assign blame to headmasters or bursars. Now, it *is* true that there was a certain amount of corruption, of malfeasance, in our educational institutions in the area of procurement of food and other things, but it is also true that there were genuine difficulties, especially when funds which should come from Government did not arrive on time and the school authorities had to make other arrangements for this. There were several other issues on which I felt that the military did not always understand what I was trying to say. In any case, it was to be for only one year.

I spent some time visiting schools and other educational institutions, and one thing which stood out quite clearly was that in the allocation of development funds, in attempting to satisfy everybody, nobody was really satisfied. What I saw was a whole array of unfinished building projects, especially in our secondary schools, all over. In that area, I felt there had not been proper planning and prioritization.

## The June 4ᵗʰ Uprising

On one of my inspections of educational institutions, I found myself in Tamale on June 4ᵗʰ 1979. I was then staying at one of the guest houses of the Residency and, according to my programmeme, I was to leave for Bimbilla that morning to inspect the Bimbilla Training College and other educational institutions in that area. As I was getting ready for breakfast, my orderly, who was a military man, came to tell me that the Akuffo Government had been overthrown by the other ranks in the army and that there had been constant broadcasts. This was shortly before the 7.00 news. Before then I heard martial music on the air as we in Ghana had become accustomed to whenever there was a violent overthrow of Government. At 7.00 the voice of Flt. Lt. Rawlings came on the air, shouting in a very shrill voice and saying that the "boys" were very angry and they should not be resisted by anybody and also saying, to the "boys" that they should not seek justice through unjustifiable means. It was very clear that he was a very angry person because he was shouting at the top of his voice.

Now before leaving Accra I knew that Flt Lt. Rawlings was in custody while on trial. He had appeared once before a court martial because of his attempt to overthrow the Government. Knowing he was behind bars I was really quite surprised to hear his voice. Apparently, that morning, a group of soldiers had gone to wherever he was being kept, freed him, and taken him to the Broadcasting House to make the announcement. It was clearly prudent for us to leave the Residency immediately because we did not know what was happening. I went to the Regional Office to await developments. From there I was taken to the Tamale Secondary School to stay in the Guest House. Whilst in the offices of the Regional Administrative Officer, Major General Odartey-Wellington came on the air at about half past ten or eleven to say that everything was under control and that the coup had been foiled! This made me a bit easier in my mind although I was still not too happy. I noticed that my orderly, very wisely, had changed into civilian clothes. The headmaster of the Seceondary School at that time was Alhaji Gbadamoshi. We both kept our ears glued to the radio. In no time Flt Lt. Rawlings came back on the air again to start giving instructions and we knew then that the coup had succeeded. It was announced that all military Commissioners of State should report to the nearest Police Station or Army Barracks.

There was just a handful of military commissioners. Most of them had been replaced by civilians. So we just kept listening to the radio and, later on, it was announced that civilian commissioners also should report to the nearest Army Barracks or Police Station, and that members of the SMC should all go and report at the Army Barracks Headquarters in Accra. The mutineers knew that they were meeting at the Police Headquarters and threatened to bomb the building at a certain time if had they not left the place by then. Now my house, Leonora Lodge, is just across the Ring Road from the Police Headquarters and I became very worried indeed because if any bomb missed its target my house could easily be hit. In any case, I just kept my composure. As I was wondering what to do, the high court judge at Tamale, Mr. Justice Taylor, who had heard that I was in Tamale came to the School and advised me strongly against reporting at any police station or army barracks, because according to him the "boys" were very unruly and disorderly and no one could really tell what they would do. So I heeded his advice. The following morning, he himself came to the secondary school and took me to report at the police station.

I was received by the police and they gave me a bench behind the counter where I sat. The Regional Administrative Officer also came to join me, so the two of us were prisoners for the time being. Now, I must say that the police were extremely courteous and treated us with great respect. They allowed food to be brought to us and then in the evening they allowed us to sleep on mattresses. Mine was brought from the secondary school and so we were quite comfortable. The cells were nearby and were filled with people who had been arrested and detained. They were just bunched together like animals, and were shouting but there was nothing that could be done. The following morning we just kept on listening to the radio with the police who were also waiting for instructions as to what to do with us. It was announced at about 5 o'clock that evening that all civilian commissioners were to be released. So I went out of the police station but did not spend the night at the secondary school; instead I slept at the house of the Regional Accountant of the Education Service.

The following day, I was booked to travel on Ghana Airways back to Accra. Unfortunately, something happened and I missed the Ghana Airways flight, but when I got to the airport I found that there was a military plane on the tarmac and there were several officers who were waiting to be taken to Accra by that flight. At the airport, I met Chief Abayifa Karbo, the Paramount Chief of Lawra, who had been the Commissioner for Health in the Acheampong Regime. He was also to join us to Accra. I presumed he was going to report at Gondar Barracks which was the Headquarters of the Army. Among the other officers was the late Colonel Felli. I noticed that all the other officers had their heads shaven, but Felli's head was not shaven. Eventually, when we got on the flight, which went to Sunyani first to pick up some more officers, I sat with Colonel Felli and we started conversing and I remarked that he had the opportunity to go to Burkina Faso. He told me that he did not think it was necessary because he had not done anything wrong, and as far as he was concerned he was only going to report as instructed.

Now the fact that he had not been shaved, gave me the impression that they were giving him special treatment. So you can imagine my horror and surprise when later on I heard that he was among the 8 senior army officers who had been executed!

When we arrived at the airforce station in Accra, a bus came along and took us all to the Flagstaff House, where there were many other senior officers waiting, some sitting on benches in the hall. I thought that Chief Abayifa Karbo and myself, having been released, could go home, but unfortunately for us, the Captain in Charge at Flagstaff House said he had not been given any instructions about us. So we told him that it had been announced on the radio and we were civilian commissioners so why should we be kept any longer? As we waited, the senior army officers were taken in batches to various destinations. The Chief and I soon found that they had all gone and that the two of us were practically stranded. After some time the Captain, I think his name was Captain Davies, came to tell us that they still did not have any instructions about us. I told him that he was not likely to get any because, really, we should have been freed. He said in that case he was going to take it upon himself to let us go home, and he offered us transport. When I got home, I found that my wife was not there. She had gone to a friend of hers and my driver took me there, and this was where we spent the night.

The following morning, I went to the Gondar Barracks to report and was taken to the headquarters. At that time, Flt. Lt. Rawlings was having a meeting with his colleagues, but when he was told that I had arrived, he asked that I should wait. In about fifteen minutes he came out and apologized profusely for keeping me waiting. The first thing he said was, "Dr., I have heard so much about you." I did not say anything, but wondered where he would have heard about me. When I got back home I remembered that his wife was Nana Konadu Agyeman who had been a student at UST when I was Vice-Chancellor. Apart from that, Konadu's father, the late J. O. T. Agyeman had been a senior colleague at Achimota School. Flt. Lt. Rawlings asked me to go home and wait for instructions. This was Friday, and nothing happened over the weekend. On Monday, we heard over the radio that I had been reappointed Commissioner for Education and, in addition, I was also to be the Commissioner for Health. Needless to say, on the first day when Commissioners were asked to report, it was added that we had all been dismissed. So it was necessary for an announcement to be made that some of us had been reappointed. Under those circumstances there was nothing I could do but to accept the appointment. In those heady days of the "revolution", it was a small price to pay.

Practically, all the civilian commissioners were reappointed. The following morning, I went to a meeting at the Castle which was chaired by Lt. Gen. Joshua Hamidu. Joshua Hamidu at the time of the coup was the Chief of Defence Staff and he was the one who, on that day, in an effort to prevent further bloodshed exhorted the loyalist forces on the radio to surrender. He was therefore, spared the fate that befell some others and he was asked to be Chairman of the Council of Commissioners. From then on he chaired all the meetings of the Council. A few days after we assumed duty, we heard of the execution of Mr. Acheampong and General Utuka. Now, Acheampong by the time that he was overthrown had become a full General of the Army but was subsequently demoted and he became just plain Mr. Acheampong. I must say that in spite of the prevailing atmosphere, the excitement in the air and the general anxiety, people were really shocked at the executions, although there were sections of the public, the students in particular, who kept on urging the soldiers on to "let the blood flow!" About a week after there were six further executions: General Akuffo, General Afrifa, Air Vice Marshall Boakye, General Kotei, Rear Admiral Amedume and, surprisingly, Colonel Felli!

All of the civilian commissioners were really disturbed. We did not know what was going to happen. It looked as if law and order had broken down, and we were not ready to continue to be part of a government that behaved in that way. We, therefore, protested vehemently and threatened to resign *en bloc*. Now, when the message got to the Chairman of the Armed Forces Revolutionary Council, (AFRC) which had been set up under the chairmanship of Flt. Lt. Rawlings, they invited us to a meeting at the Air Force Base one evening. We were all present at the meeting. All the AFRC members were also present. It fell upon me to be the spokesman for the civilian Commissioners to register our protest. I expressed our displeasure at what was happening and let them know that we were all Ghanaians, we were all patriots and we did not think that killing people corrected mistakes. I tried in a most diplomatic and courteous, but firm language to convey our feelings and to let them know that if there were any more killings, all of us would just down tools and resign. That would really take some wind out of the revolution because, politically, it would be very negative for them. There was much discussion after this. We came away feeling that the message had got home, and to cut a long story short, after that there were no more public executions. If anything happened in private I would not know, but there were no public executions.

The junta had wanted to tell us that the "boys" were so angry that they really could not be controlled, but we had to point out to them that having taken on that leadership mantle, they had started something and it was for them to put a stop to it. If they were saying that they could not control the "boys", it really meant that they agreed with our position, so they had to display leadership at that time and use whatever method they had to control the situation. After this, we were all prepared to go on with our work - Flt. Lt. Rawlings had promised that the Presidential and Parliamentary elections which had been scheduled would go on. True to their word, this happened and the PNP(Peoples' National Party) led by Dr. Hilla Limman won the elections. In the last week of September that year, the AFRC handed over the reins of office to a new civilian government headed by Dr. Hilla Limman with his Vice-President as Prof de Graft Johnson who had been Director of the Building and Roads Research Institute of the CSIR for many years.

# CHAPTER 24

# THE THIRD REPUBLIC
## Member of the Counil of State

A few days after the handing over, I got a letter from the Office of the President informing me that the President had decided to appoint me a member of the Council of State, and that in accordance with the Constitution, he had submitted my name to Parliament for vetting and approval. A day or two after, I got an invitation from the Speaker's office and together with my other colleagues who had been nominated, we were interrogated in turn by a Parliamentary Committee in the Speaker's office. Now I thought that was the end of it, but I was informed by the Speaker that having been a Commissioner of State, it was necessary for me to be cleared by the Sowah Assets Commission before Parliament could approve the President's nomination.

I got the necessary forms from the office of the Assets Commission. It was a long, almost endless questionnaire and I was supposed to submit seven copies! I very nearly declined the nomination but I also did not want it to appear that I had something to hide. So I started filling the forms. I then began to wonder what was the rationale in asking members of the Council of State, an honourable body with no avenue for making money or for corruption, to be cleared. So I consulted Mr. Swaniker, a barrister-at-law at Osu. After reading through the Constitution he told me that the Constitution did not require any member of the Council of State to clear himself anywhere before being considered by Parliament. What Parliament was asking for was unconstitutional. I told him that in any case I had decided to fill and hand in the forms. He advised against that, and said it was no longer a personal matter but one of principle and that he had prepared a legal opinion on the issue. After reading the legal opinion, I felt that others in the same position like Major General Nathan Afari should see it. I sent this finally to the Attorney-General who agreed

*341*

with it and advised Parliament accordingly. The requirement that I should be cleared by the Assets Commission was lifted and Major General Aferi and I were duly endorsed by Parliament. So we became members of the Council of State.

The Council of State at that time was under the chairmanship of Mr. William Ofori-Atta, popularly known as Paa Willie. Paa Willie, took the duties of the Council of State very seriously. He was very jealous of the authority of the Council. He understood and made it quite clear to us that we were not an appendage of the President's Office, and that we were there just to advise the President and his Ministers and any other organ of government that needed advice and we were not to consider ourselves as part of the President's outfit. Therefore we were to operate independently. Throughout the brief tenure of that Council, we acted very independently, especially in the matter of approving certain appointments to public office. On this I am glad to say we had very good cooperation from the President's Office. There was one occasion, however, when there was a near confrontation with the President's Office. We received a certain letter which got us all up in arms and I distinctly remember the meeting which discussed this letter. The Chairman of the Council, Paa Willie, sensing the mood of the members asked Bishop Akwasi Sarpong who was a member of the Council to pray. After a very powerful prayer by Bishop Sarpong, the temperature came down considerably; and what could have been a stormy meeting, producing a decision which would not really further cordial relations with the President, was avoided. Everything went on smoothly and I believe that we really acted in accordance with the interest of the country.

The Speaker of Parliament, Mr. Justice Griffiths Randolph, was very much impressed by the work of the Council of State. In fact the Council was very helpful to Parliament in matters of legislation because we regularly examined legislation which was about to be considered by Parliament, and made our views known, especially where there were controversial areas which were likely to disturb or be a problem to members of Parliament. They thought it was helpful for us to give our views on the matter. The Speaker thought that in this area, the Council of State under the chairmanship of Mr. William Ofori-Atta was really very helpful to Parliament.

Before the tenure of members of the Council was terminated abruptly, the Council produced two reports – one on "Discipline and Productivity" and the other on "The Economic Situation", with comments and recommendations. The Council spent a long time considering these Reports and it had actually been arranged that the chairman of the Council would present those two reports to the President during the first week of January 1982. Unfortunately, on 31$^{st}$ December 1981 the military once again overthrew the constitutionally elected government and took over the reins of government. All the same we decided that the report would be submitted to the new body in power. When the first announcement of the take-over was made, Parliament was dissolved and Ministers were dismissed, but there was no mention of the Council of State. This made it possible for us to meet legally on the 2$^{nd}$ of January 1982 and it was at this meeting that it was decided that copies of these two important Reports should be submitted to the new military government which had assumed the name "Provisional National Defence Council". On that same day there was a radio announcement that the Council of State had also been dissolved, but by that time copies of the report had already been sent to the office of the Chairman of the Provisional National Defence Council. It may well be that at that time, they were preoccupied with revolutionary matters and that these two reports were never studied by the new government. So, once again, the orderly democratic development of the governance of Ghana was rudely and violently interrupted by the military!

# CHAPTER 25

# RETIREMENT

The narrative so far has focused on my education and training and on what I may call my professional career in the public service. I shall now come to more personal matters, extra-curricular activities in which I had been involved. My moving from Kumasi to Accra was, in a sense, coming home finally to settle. During the previous twenty-four years I had served in Accra for short periods, but most of my work in the public service was in other parts of the country. Indeed, I think it is correct to say that I served in all the regions in the country with the exception the Volta Region. At that time the Northern Region was one large region, but was subsequently was carved into three regions: Northern, and Upper East and Upper West.

Having been away from home for so long it was important for me to pick up the threads and once more reestablish contact with members of the extended family, with the church, and other social and professional organizations in which I had been involved. For example, it was important for me to re-activate my membership of the Osu Ebenezer Presbyterian Church of which I had been a member since 1934. Leonora also reinstated her membership of Saint Barnabas Anglican Church on the Labadi Road, Osu, Amanfon.

Shortly after our arrival, the Resident Chaplain at the Accra Ridge Church, Rev. Fr. Justice Akrofi, came to see her and to request her to help the choir as one of the organists. At Saint Barnabas she joined the choir and assisted the choirmaster, my late cousin William Augustus Evans Lutterodt. Leonora joined as one of the organists. I became quite involved in the affairs of the Osu Ebenezer congregation. I was particularly interested in the social activities of the Church, and in welfare matters, especially health. Years later I become a Presbyter. This is a matter I shall refer to later on.

## Hon. D.Sc (Salford University)

Sometime in December of 1973, shortly before leaving UST I got a letter from the Vice Chancellor of Salford University in the United Kingdom, Dr. Cilfford Whitworth, to say that the University had decided to confer an Honorary Doctor of Science Degree on me for my outstanding services in medicine and education. The award would be made at a Congregation Ceremony in July 1974. In March of 1974 I received a letter from Professor Phillips of that University, who was to present me for the award, asking for more detailed particulars of my Curriculum Vitae. The University Administration also asked for measurements for one academic gown and cap. In July 1974 Leonora and I went to Salford and on the 4th of July at a Congregation Ceremony I had the honour of the conferment on me of a Honorary Doctorate Degree in Science by Salford University. The other recipient was Doctor Urguhart, an outstanding Librarian and a man of great distinction. I was given the privilege of replying to the citation on behalf of the two of us. I must say that this singular event gave me great encouragement to know that whatever I had been doing had been recognized by a university abroad.

The University of Salford and the University of Science and Technology (Kumasi) had established strong links between their departments of Chemistry whilst I was Vice-chancellor of U.S.T. and I had the privilege to visit that University a couple of times. Dr. Whitworth also visited Kumasi once. I may note here in passing that he was on a visit to Kumasi at the time of the funeral of the late Asantehene Otumfuo Nana Osei Agyeman-Prempeh II. He had the unusual experience of attending the Funeral Service with me and also the subsequent interment at Bantama. He found this most interesting. Dr. Witworth was a person who was highly interested in higher education and, particularly, in the service that the products of higher education, especially in developing countries could make to the advancement of their own countries.

## Chairman, Ghana Hockey Association

On the recreational front, I was pleased to note that hockey had been vigorously revived under the enthusiastic leadership of the Late K. N. Owusu and others. I was happy that shortly after my arrival in Accra I was invited to become the Chairman of the Ghana Hockey Association. That same year 1974 in November the African Championships were coming on in Cairo so we had to work hard to raise a good team. I was thrilled with the enthusiasm among the clubs in Accra. The Ghana Armed Forces had some outstanding players like Major Sam and Otchere and Aboagye. There were stalwarts like Saarah Mensah who were rock-like in defense. The coach at that time was Ashalley Okine the son of Attoh Okine, my former housemaster at Achimota College. Colonel Simpe-Asante was then the special Assistant to the Commissioner for Sports, Colonel Acheampong himself.

Seeing that the hockey team was doing well, Colonel Acheampong gave us every encouragement to go to Cairo. There were only five teams in the championship: host nation, Egypt, Kenya, Uganda, Nigeria and Ghana. I am happy to say that, despite formidable opposition, especially from the Kenyans, Ghana won the championship. The Ambassador in Egypt at that time was the Late Major General C.C. Bruce, himself an enthusiastic hockey player. I stayed with him whilst other members of the contingent stayed in a hotel. Madam Fathia Nkrumah was then in Cairo. She not only came to watch and cheer the Ghana team in all our matches but also one day gave the team a very good lunch. I could sense at that time that she longed to come back to Ghana. I am happy to say that the following year in 1975 the Acheampong Government invited her to come back to Ghana. I also recall that one evening during our visit to Cairo, Kofi Annan, currently Secretary General of the United Nations, called on Ambassador Bruce. Mr. Annan had a short stint in Ghana at that time working on tourism before going back to the United Nations. I did not know Mr. Annan himself but I knew his father very well as he had been a Regional Minister for Ashanti in the Busia Government at the time that I was Vice-Chancellor at the University of Science and Technology, Kumasi.

Having won the championship, Ghana qualified for the World Cup, which was coming on the following year in Kuala Lumpur, Malaysia. I found that we had excellent material to really put together a formidable team. What was required was good coaching. On my return to Ghana, therefore, and on a subsequent visit to the United Kingdom, I got in touch with the Headquarters of the Hockey Federation in Paris and asked if they could recommend an international coach for a short period of say, two months, to come to Ghana. Prior to my leaving for the U.K, I had discussed this with the Special Assistant to the Commissioner for Sports, who was very enthusiastic about it and encouraged me. Luckily, I was given the name of a first class German Coach, together with his particulars and telephone number. I called him and he agreed to come for a couple of months to train our national hockey team. I cannot recall the terms under which he agreed to come, but I thought that they were quite reasonable. Unfortunately, on my return when I reported to the Commissioner for Sports, I was told that there was no money. So the Ghana team went to Kuala Lumpur, not having had the extra coaching which would have brought them up to a high standard. I did not go to Kuala Lumpur with them, but was not surprised that, despite a good performance, Ghana did not come anywhere in the listings. Indeed, I think Ghana ended right at the bottom.

During that year 1974 Charlie, our youngest boy, was admitted to Achimota School where Nii Teiko was in Lower Sixth. Nii Okai was at the University of Science and Technology, studying architecture. Rachel was at Aburi Girls Secondary School. Most of the time Leonora and I were left on our own. In the past, Leonora, in order to relieve boredom, would teach in one of the Secondary Schools. In Sekondi she had taught at Fijai Secondary School. In Kumasi whilst I was working at the hospital she had taught at St. Louis Secondary School. In Accra whilst I was at the Medical School she had taught at Accra Girls Secondary School. Now, of course, she could not work for reasons of health. She continued with her regular yearly medical check-up in Edinburgh and remained well provided she took her medication and necessary precautions. Indeed, in 1978 after her check-up in Edinburgh she went to the United States of America on holiday with the two older boys.

## The Painful Loss of Leonora

Having been given a clean bill of health, she was both looking and feeling very well. In February 1980 she actually attended a Congregation Ceremony in Kumasi at the University, when Nii Okia received his post-graduate Diploma in Architecture. Following that we went to Abidjan to fulfil a long-standing promise which we had made to our nephew. Nii Armah Coleman, then manager of the State Transport Corporation in the Ivory Coast. Shortly after our return from Abidjan she started complaining of breathlessness. I knew straight away what was happening and decided that it was important for her to go back to Edinburgh urgently. Prof. J. Pobee was then her doctor, and he immediately referred her to Edinburgh. She was immediately admitted to hospital and, after a short period of preparation, had a second operation. She responded quite well but, unfortunately, two weeks after the operation complications set in and on the 3rd of May 1980, the Lord took away my precious gift, Leonora.

I must record my eternal gratitude to Kojo and Margaret Oddoye. Margaret, then mostly resident in Ghana, came all the way to Edinburgh at her own expense to look after us as we were staying with them. She really looked after Leonora before she went to hospital. The strong support of Maggie and Kojo at a time when I was really shattered helped to dampen my grief. At that time also Dr.Collison, presently specialist gynecologist and Senior Lecturer at the Korlebu Teaching Hospital, was on attachment in Edinburgh. He was very helpful to me in the arrangements I had to make. Our daughter Rachel came all the way to Edinburgh before the operation on her mother. She had interrupted her studies, preparing for her final year Law Examination. She was there right through and she left after the operation, after her mother appeared to be convalescing smoothly. Indeed, she was still in London on her way back home when her mother died.

I had the almost impossible task of how to break the shattering news to Rachel whilst she was still at a London Airport Hotel. I had to call my cousin, the late Mr Teye-Dornor, to go and break the sad news gently to her. I had called her once to tell her the news myself but I could not bring myself to do it! A really harrowing experience for me. All I could say at that time was, "The Lord gave and the Lord has taken away. Blessed be his name." I looked back over a period of thirty-one years, almost to the exact date and Day in 1949. It was in Edinburgh that I first met Leonora, and now, thirty-one years on we had come back to our original meeting place to say good-bye!

Rachel left for home almost immediately and was the carrier of the sorrowful news. I stayed on in Edinburgh for one week to make all the necessary arrangements for conveying Leonora home for burial.

Meanwhile, the late Mrs. Hannah Armar who was then in London went all the way to Edinburgh to help Kojo and Margaret Oddoye in what there was to be done before Leonora's body would be brought back home. When I arrived home, I found out that my brother, Joe, my children, and close members of the family had started discussions and made a draft programmeme for the funeral. Lest I forget, whilst waiting in the departure lounge at London Heathrow Airport I got the most unexpected news from a Ghanaian doctor who had just arrived from Ghana that my good friend Dr.George, proprietor of Salem hospital, with whom I had been negotiating for a possible partnership, had died at the same week-end that Leonora died. This piece of news of course compounded my confused state of mind and completely knocked me off balance. Throughout the preparations for the funeral celebrations, I was completely dazed; and I shall be eternally grateful to my good friend and brother, Harry Sawyerr, then a Minister in the Limann government, for the prominent role which he played during Leonora's funeral. Of course, it was not surprising, because I knew the love and affection that Harry and his wife, Esther, had for Leonora.

At the wake-keeping on the night of 23rd May 1980, I was really overwhelmed by the number of people that filed past. I must have shaken the hands of countless numbers of people. It was a constant stream of people filing past, from about 7pm to midnight. It seemed as if half of the population of the campus of the U.S.T. were there. The next day, despite a shower, large crowds came to the funeral service at Saint Barnabas, and the subsequent burial at the Osu Cemetery. The late Dr. K. A. Gardiner remarked to an American friend of ours that the funeral resembled a Royal funeral. What really pleased me about the funeral was that most of the people who came did so because of Leonora and not because of me. To me this will be an undying testimony to the esteem in which Lenora was held. She had won the hearts of so many people by her unique personality and her charm, all the desirable virtues one would look for in a good person and a human being. I am glad that Leonora's mother visited Ghana in Leonora's lifetime. Leonora's younger sister, Adele, never did so, despite many promises in her letters, but on this occasion she just had to come to the funeral. She confessed to me she was really flabbergasted at the size of the funeral. She indeed regretted that she was not able to visit whilst Lenora was alive.

To say that the children adored their mother would be a gross understatement. They almost worshipped her. She in turn showed much love and affection for them. The children's grief was intense. I was very fortunate they were there, so we could share the grief and so lighten it. Leonora's very good friend, Gloria Nikoi, in her attempt to console me, remarked, "Doc. Just see what a beautiful legacy Lenora left. Four wonderful children." Indeed, I am grateful to Lenora that she left me something to constantly remind me of the love we had for each other.

Despite the most unhappy events which interrupted her schedule, Rachel was able to go through her final examination and to be called to the Bar about a couple of months after her mother's funeral. I must say that I was anxious for her all along and constantly prayed that the harrowing experience wouldn't affect her examination results.

For my part, I do not recall for how many months I went about completely dazed. Everything seemed like a dream to me. To think that Lenora and I had been married for twenty-eight years, had been together, moved together, and had gone out together everywhere that was practicable! Eventually, when I came out of the daze into the world of reality, a frightening sense of loneliness descended on me. How, how could I face the future all alone? The children at this time were all grown-up and would be leaving home, and what would happen to me? Dr. George's death made things worse for me, and of course, shattered all hopes of my ever inheriting the Salem Hospital. There was so much to be done to rehabilitate the Hospital, and, without Leonora there wasn't much really that I could do.

I was getting on in years. Being sixty-one at the time of Leonora's death, I was past the retiring age for public servants. In a properly organized society I would be retiring on a good pension. I was in no proper frame of mind to plan for anything and decided to leave things and let things just go as they were. I really needed time to think. I needed a holiday. A couple of months after the funeral, Rachel and I went over to the United States to see Leonora's family and we spent sometime in London on our way back. Having been called to the Bar recently, Rachel had to start looking for a job. She could not really afford to stay away for too long. Fortunately, I was a member of the Council of State so I had something to occupy my time. I had also been elected a Presbyter of my church, Osu Ebenezer Presby Church, and that, of course, entailed some responsibilities. My membership of some committees of the Ghana

Academy of Arts and Sciences also provided an outlet to keep me busy.

Although at sixty-one I was past the retiring age, it was possible to arrange for some part-time teaching at the Medical School. In any case, I dismissed the idea because I did not want any arrangement where I would just give lectures without actually doing some clinical work, including operating, and this I had to rule out entirely because for some thirty years I had been taking hypertensive drugs to control my hypertension. I had to keep well. Former patients of mine consulted me for medical advice. I succumbed to the pressures and had to convert one of my outside garages into a small consulting room. I saw patients for medical examination and medical advice. In a way it was more or less like charity because patients who came to see me were not well to do and could not afford to pay high fees. In any case, I was not interested in making money. I was quite content to live on my modest investments. All my children had passed out of school so I did not have to pay any school fees.

In the end my good friend, Dr. Awuku-Asabre, prevailed on me to come and assist in his clinic, St. Patrick's, at Tema. The clinic had a small operating theatre and one room with two beds like a recovery ward for minor surgery on cases like hernias, hydroceles, lumps and bumps and a fair amount of cosmetic surgery. I agreed to this and went to Tema once a week in order to see patients and to operate. The medical officer in charge of the Ghaip Hospital arranged to have the patients needing surgery to come to see me at Saint Patrick's. I did this for a few years just to keep my hand in. Also, of course, it was good for me to see patients for my good friend, Dr. Awuku-Asabre, and to offer a second opinion. Even though I was not doing any major surgery I think my small consultancy was useful in the sense that I used to refer patients who needed major surgery, including gynecological cases, to the Korle-Bu Teaching Hospital. I was acting more or less like a "sorting officer," just examining patients and sending them to the right place. This service was really much appreciated. The patients were quite satisfied that I was sending them to the right people who could deal efficiently with their complaints.

At this time I also arranged with the Edinburgh Medical Mission to send drugs to the Osu Ebenezer Congregation. What they did was to collect unused drugs from patients, and from some of the pharmaceutical firms and send them over to us in a drum. The drugs were used for patients in the congregation. In all two drums were sent in successive years. Whilst we found this quite useful we noticed that some of the drugs were expired by the time they arrived. It entailed a good deal of work which Miss Angelina Adjei, a nurse and a presbyter at the church, sorted out at the Customs Department. We were able to salvage useful drugs, some of which were very expensive. I think at the end of the day the service we provided was much appreciated as patients had prescriptions from various doctors on which they would have spent lots of money. However, they were able to get these drugs free from the supply that was sent from Edinburgh! We could not continue this because the manner in which the drugs were collected was very laborious and it took a long time to fill one drum. Besides, when the drugs arrived there was a lot of red tape to take delivery so we had to give it up. But whilst it lasted we felt it was providing some help which was good for the patients.

In 1982, when Charlie finished the 'A' levels and was ready to enter the University, all three Universities in Ghana had been closed down for an indefinite period. Although the policy that Leonora and I followed in the matter of the education of our children was that they were to complete tertiary education in Ghana and only go abroad for Post-graduate studies, Charlie's had to be treated as a special case. I was not prepared to let him mark time and kick his heels in Ghana. I therefore went over to the United States to make arrangements for him to be admitted to one of the American Universities. The fact that Charlie's mother was an American citizen and, indeed Charlie held an American passport, made it a lot easier. Fortunately, our friends, Dr. and Mrs. Reed, who the reader may recall were with the USAID Agricultural team in Tamale in the year that I spent in Tamale, were back home. Even though Dr. Reed had retired from the faculty of A&T, University in Greensboro, North Carolina, he still had some influence and he was able after Charlie had fulfilled all the requirements to enter a University in the United States to assist him to gain admission at A&T to study Business Administration. Therefore on my way home on reaching London I sent for Charlie who met me there, and then continued to the United States. He was able to enter the University for his course immediately, being more than qualified for admission! He graduated with first class honours in 1986. Incidentally, shortly before her death, Charlie's mother heard in hospital that he had been elected Senior Prefect at Achimota School. This made her very happy indeed.

## Second Marriage

Now I began to look back on the time Lenora and I had been together and gone everywhere together, and together honoured the invitations to various parties and so on. I was not really accustomed to going out alone. I really began to wonder how long this would last. I began to suffer from moods of depression and I imposed upon myself the regime of not accepting invitations to go anywhere. Clearly, for sometime I was not myself at all. Occasionally, I would dream of Leonora, and I remember on one occasion her telling me not to make myself unhappy. I should continue with my life, which meant I could have another partner, a thought which from time to time crossed my mind and which I promptly dismissed. I could not imagine having a partner who could adequately fill the shoes of Leonora. On the other hand, I felt that my standing in society would be better enriched if I did not remain single for the rest of my life. And so with the passage of time the idea of getting a partner became more of a reality. When I finally accepted the possibility it dawned on me then that it was desirable to have somebody who would be approved by Leonora. Somebody who was known to the children. Somebody they would accept.

In the end I decided on Miss Elise Henkel, younger sister of Mrs Susan Alhassan whose husband, the reader may recall, was my patient when he died. Elise had been a friend to Leonora, a younger sister. I knew that Leonora was very fond of her. Indeed, both of us were very fond of her. The children also liked her, so it was not difficult for them to endorse my choice.

Whilst all this was happening, Rachel was also having problems with her choice of partner. I must say I felt rather anxious for her. After her mother died she did everything to make sure I did not go off my mind. I was very pleased when in 1983 whilst on a visit to the United Kingdom, she informed me about her friendship with Dr Henry Baddoo, son of my professional colleague, Dr. Michael Baddoo, and the possibility of their coming together. I knew the Baddoo family well. Michael and Barbara Baddoo brought up their children to be humble. They were a Christian family. The children were all bright without being arrogant. Although I knew Henry when he was a boy on the Korle-Bu Hospital campus I had not seen him since he became a doctor. I had no difficulty at all in giving my blessing to his relationship with Rachel. Knowing the background of the parents, I knew also that Rachel and Henry belonged to the Scripture Union and I felt that Rachel couldn't go wrong if she chose Henry to be her future partner.

Henry was at the time working in a hospital in Northern Ireland and Rachel was a State Attorney in Ghana. Rachel had gone abroad for a short holiday when they decided to get married finally. The date for the wedding was fixed for 30th June 1984. I arranged for Elise and me to get married in London. We tried hard to fix the date a week before Rachel's wedding so that she would have a mother. So on the 22nd June 1984, Elise and I got married in London. My son Nii Teiko was the best man at our wedding. Rachel's wedding followed on the 30th of June 1984 also in London. Elise's maid of honour was Mrs Cecilia Campbell, Elise's long-standing friend and sister of H.E.President Kufour! Henry's younger brother, Jimmy, was his best man whilst Rachel's maid of honour was Dr. Florence Apaloo, a bosom friend and school mate at Aburi Girls Secondary School.

I was very happy that all Rachel's brothers were able to attend her wedding. Nii Okai came all the way from Nigeria. Charlie was at University in the United States but also managed to come. Everything was complete for Rachel's wedding and this made her very happy. My friends tell me that after my wedding I brightened up. For four long years I was pining! The wedding or the marriage more or less came to my rescue. This marriage has survived almost nineteen years! I shudder to think what would have happened to me if I had remained single. I can most certainly say I wouldn't have survived as long as I have. The constant thought of Leonora would really have conspired to bump me off!

Elise is an Akora like myself; and the granddaughter of Heinrich Ludwig Henkel, one time German Commandant at Kete-Krachi in the German Togoland. Her father, Wilhelm Henkel, was an outstanding educationist who has done more than any one else for the development of Basic Education in Northern Ghana. Elise herself lived and worked in Paris for a number of years and holds honors Bachelors' degree in French. She was at one time a tutor at the Ghana Institute of Languages and at the time of our wedding a freelance interpreter and translator.

We were both keenly aware that we were not a young couple starting life, and that the aim of the marriage was one of companionship rather than the desire to raise a family. We were a more mature couple. We both realised we had to accommodate each other's strengths and weaknesses and that, provided we did that, everything would go on well. To my surprise, I adjusted to this new situation more readily than some of my friends and relations who gradually came to accept that I had taken the right decision to get married again.

## Chairman, National Education Commission

In the year 1984, that is, the year that I remarried, a high-ranking functionary of the P.N.D.C. Government came to see me. He had been sent to discuss the whole question of education in Ghana with me. The idea was to set up a committee to review the entire education system, and I could sense that there were some extremely radical views on the direction in which this exercise should move. I myself had been much concerned over the years that there had been several reports by committees set up by succeeding governments. It seemed that every government that came into power set up a committee to review the education system. When you read these reports carefully you find that there are certain recommendations that keep on recurring. My personal view was that if some of these important recommendations were implemented, there would be no need to upset the apple cart. I made it quite well known that I thought the thing to do was to get hold of these previous Education reports and then search for those important recommendations that had been made over the years and implement them!

I thought I was saying this to escape from the request that was being made but I discovered that the request was persistent. The messenger came to see me several times. I finally agreed to the request that perhaps I could head a committee, which could look at all previous Education Committee Reports and advice Government on important recommendations which needed to be implemented. With this in view the National Education Commission was set up with me as Chairman. It was a small body with about fifteen members from different backgrounds. This Commission was inaugurated by the Chairman of the P.N D.C. himself. I had thought the idea was to have a once and for all assignment, and that we were not going to be a standing Commission. To my surprise, however, during the launching of the Commission the inaugural address implied that we were to be a Standing Commission and to produce reports from time to time for Government.

Our very first Report of course was to look at previous reports. We had a lot of problems with this because, to our surprise, some of these reports were either unavailable or available only as library copies. In the end, we were reduced to just studying the recommendations in these reports. In one or two cases, we did not have the advantage of studying the reports themselves in order to have an idea of the reasons behind some recommendations, although with the important recommendations, these were self-evident. Repeated emphasis was made on technical and vocational training, on agriculture and women's education. We did not need anybody to give us any reasons why they were important. We managed to produce a Report which highlighted the important recommendations which we thought should be acted on with urgency.

Before we ended the first assignment we got an urgent request from Government to study the whole question of funding feeding in educational Institutions. In our Report we attempted to break down the ingredients or those items under the umbrella term "fees." We identified ingredients which did not constitute education and which we thought should not be a fair charge on the Government – for example, feeding and residential accommodation. We did our best to separate academic facilities, i.e. tuition, from board and lodging.

After this exercise, we looked at the structure of the education ladder. Our first report in this series was on Basic Education and we produced a short Report in which we spelt out what we thought should constitute Basic Education, which the Constitution mandates should be free when funded by the State. The idea is that funding of Post-Basic Education is not a constitutional obligation immediately. Funding by the State should therefore be gradual. As the requirements of the lower levels are satisfied, Post-Basic Education also will be taken on board gradually up to the tertiary level. In my view, our Basic Education Report written in simple language covers much ground. After that Reports on Secondary Education, Teacher Education and Moral Education were produced.

I resigned the chairmanship of the Education commission after 4 years in 1988. There were two reasons for my resignation. Firstly, I felt that the status of the Commission had not been properly defined, and that it should really have been a Commission to advise Government and not be treated as a Committee of the Ministry of Education. Secondly, the fact that at that time the National Council for higher Education and the Ghana Education Service Council had both been abolished and their powers assumed by the Secretary for Education I found utterly wrong.

Funding for the Commission was inadequate for which reason we were not able to travel to different Regions to collate views on some of the matters under consideration. I was really tired of the marginalization of the Commission, and thought I was really wasting my time. However, the Commission continued and I know that subsequently they did work on moral education and Technical education.

In 1992 with the return to Constitutional rule the Commission was abolished. This was done because throughout the four years that I was Chairman we applied pressure on Government to reinstitute the Ghana Education Service Council and the National Council for Higher Education. Fortunately, the Constitution of 1992 made provision for these two bodies. Whilst we were considering the whole Basic Education question the Secretary of Education announced the PNDC government's decision to introduce the new educational Reforms with the 6-3-3-4 structure as the framework for formal education as proposed in 1987. In my opinion there is nothing wrong with the reforms proposed. The problem really was with implementation. The Education Commission earlier on advised that there should be a period of planning and public education and putting together of resources. The problems which arose after the introduction of the new reforms in 1987 were quite unnecessary and could have been avoided. There were not enough trained teachers and the facilities were inadequate. Besides, the foundation, that is, the six years primary school preceding the three years junior secondary school had not been properly dealt with. The foundation had not been strengthened in quality. The Reforms sought to reduce the number of years of Pre-University Education and at the same time improve the quality of education, the assumption being that the foundation would be strong enough to carry the superstructure, which would be built on it.

Initially, there were complaints about entrants to the J.S.S. programmeme from Primary School not being able to write their names! The problem with English and Mathematics had not been properly dealt with at the Primary Level. Things came to a head in 1994 with the first graduates of the Senior Secondary School programmeme. The first S. S. S. examination results were disastrous. This was a wake up call that all was not well. Something had to be done. The result has been review exercises culminating in the recent appointment of the President's Committee to review the Education System and whose report was recently submitted.

I shall now deal briefly with a number of organisations and bodies in which I have been involved through the years but it is not my intention to recount in detail the history of these organisations but rather the part which I played in them. I shall start with the Ghana Medical Association.

## President, Ghana Medical Association

The birth of the Ghana Medical Association, in 1958, that is the year immediately following the declaration of Ghana's independence, by the coming together of the erstwhile Gold Coast Medical Practitioners Union and the Gold Coast Branch of the British Medical Association, was a historic landmark in health delivery in this country. Some readers may recall that at that time it was only British or Commonwealth qualifications which were recognized for professional practice in this country. For example, Dr. Adjei-Schandorf who was trained in the United States had to obtain a Canadian qualification in Halifax, Nova Scotia, before returning home. That made him eligible to practice in Ghana.

At the time of the formation of the Ghana Medical Association the majority of practising doctors in the country were expatriates, mostly British, but there were also Indians and Pakistanis who had Commonwealth qualifications. However, quite a sizeable number of doctors, especially the British, opted out of the new Ghana Civil Service. They were soon replaced by doctors from other countries, notably Germany, Italy and Eastern European countries including Russia, after legislation was introduced to give recognition to the qualifications of doctors from these other countries. At the same time a number of Ghanaian doctors trained abroad were also returning home.

Membership of the Ghana Medical Association was not compulsory, and it was possible for a doctor, whether Ghanaian or not, provided he was registered by the Medical and Dental Board, to practise in the country. Later on, things changed and a decree was passed which made it mandatory for all doctors to be members of the Ghana Medical Association before they were registered by the Medical and Dental Board and thereafter became eligible to practise in Ghana. Needless to say, the majority of doctors worked in the public service, mostly Government Hospitals and health facilities. One big change which the formation of the Ghana Medical Association brought about was that for the first time, all doctors came together as one body which was to be recognised by Government and which was to speak on behalf of all doctors and dentists. It was, therefore, important that the new body be quickly recognised by Government. For some inexplicable reason, it appears that this recognition was not immediately forthcoming. One would have thought that Government would welcome the idea of having to deal with only one body in matters concerning the welfare of doctors. Meanwhile, there were battles to be fought as the majority of the doctors and dentists were in the Public Service, as I have already indicated.

The primary concern of the Association was with the conditions of service and salaries of doctors and dentists in the public service. I have already said elsewhere that at that time private practice, or the charging of professional fees by doctors in government hospitals was allowed, provided this was under controlled conditions. Needless to say, this made it possible for doctors to augment their salaries and also share whatever proceeds came from professional fees with other health personnel, particularly those in the district hospitals who assisted them.

The Nkrumah government which was socialist inclined saw this as a violation of socialist principles. Therefore one of the first things it sought to do was to abolish this system of private practice in private hospitals. In order to weaken the Medical Association front, it was first abolished for medical officers whilst specialists were allowed to continue. This was a mere ruse, however, because in a couple of years the privilege was withdrawn from the specialists also. Now it is fair to say that following this action the payment of allowances was introduced: allowances styled "Allowance in lieu of Private Practice". These, however, were grossly inadequate and it was not possible for the doctor to give anything to other health personnel, who did not enjoy any allowances. Needless to say, there were protests from doctors and dentists and grumblings from the health workers. From that time, there has never been peace in connection with the salaries, remuneration and conditions of service for the health personnel.

The prevailing climate of dissatisfaction may well be at the root of the brain drain, which started in a small way and has now assumed alarming proportions. As long as doctors were trained abroad and therefore needed to spend long periods away from home and could be attracted by the bright lights and other conditions in European countries, it was understandable why some refused to return home to serve. When the Ghana Medical School was started it was hoped that there would be an increase in the number of doctors in the country. After all the majority of doctors would be trained locally and would, therefore, not have had any exposure to the conditions and opportunities which their colleagues who trained abroad would have. It is really unfortunate that the majority of doctors trained at the Ghana Medical School since 1969 now live and work abroad! Something must be very wrong indeed!

It would be entirely wrong to say that the Association was formed mainly to fight for conditions of service for doctors and dentists. It also provided the opportunity for the organisation of annual meetings to discuss matters pertaining to the health delivery system in the country and to share these concerns with government and other sections of the Ghanaian society. These meetings also provide the opportunity for members to prepare and read scientific papers concerning their practice, and to compare notes in connection with unusual cases that they have seen.

Earlier on also the Association pressurised the government to establish a Medical and Dental Council to replace the Medical and Dental Board, which existed at that time, with the Director of Medical Services, as the Chairman. It was felt that the Council should be a body independent of Government. It should, therefore, not be chaired by the Director of Medical Services, so that government influence would be reduced. The Association fought for this and eventually a decree was promulgated to establish the Ghana Medical and Dental Council in 1975.

During the discussions prior to the establishment of the Ghana Medical School, especially the siting of the School, it was the considered view of the Association that a new Teaching Hospital should be built in Legon at the site where the Noguchi Memorial Institute now stands. There should be modest improvements to Korlebu Hospital to retain it also as a Teaching Hospital. This view did not find favour with the Nkrumah Government and instead extensions were made to Korlebu Hospital to turn it into an unwieldy cluster of buildings, and, as a Teaching Hospital, an administrator's nightmare, with so many problems seemingly insoluble!

Last but not least, there was the fight for compulsory membership of the Medical Association to strengthen it with numbers and also for members contribution to be a source of income. Concerning the peculiar problems of private general medical practitioners, there was a proposal by the Nkrumah government that every private medical practitioner was to devote six hours a week to give free service in public hospitals and clinics. The Association had to take it up with Government and to point out the difficulties and implications of its implementation. In the end the matter died a natural death.

The Association was an umbrella for all medical and dental practitioners and its Constitution made provision for groupings within the Association, that is to say, it was possible for special groups for example, Specialists to form their own groups, within the framework of the Association. Initially, the general practitioners felt that they should also have an Association because of the peculiar problems with their practice. There was, therefore, the danger of division within the ranks of the profession, and this had to be handled in a rather delicate manner. There was justification in the general practitioners' feeling that they had peculiar problems. It cannot be denied also that every medical or dental practitioner in the public service is a potential general practitioner, because if you were a specialist in the public facility the time would come when you would retire and practise privately. It was in the interest of the profession generally that the problems of general practice and general practitioners be attended to. In the end, this matter was settled amicably and the imminent split was averted. I am happy to say that when the final decision was taken, I had just assumed the Presidency of the Association. The spadework for agreement had already been done, it was just left to me to give the final push. The general practitioners agreed to form a "Society" and not an "Association." Currently, the Society of General Practitioners is a major pillar of the Association.

At this point, I may say that when I was appointed Vice-Chancellor in 1967, I was then the Vice-President of the Association. I was very happy therefore that, despite the fact that I appeared to be deserting the ranks of the profession, at the following Conference of the Association, I, as Vice-President, was elected President. As I write now, the Association is well over forty years and although over the years I have played a diminishing role in it, I have nevertheless watched with admiration the manner in which our younger colleagues have kept the flag flying, I think it is true to say that the Association under the leadership of successive active Presidents and members of the Council has really become an important force in the life of Ghana. In 1970 I was made a life member of the Association in the company of very eminent senior colleagues. In 1998 I received an additional honour of "Fellow of the Ghana Medical Association"

## President - The West African College of Surgeons

I was privileged and honoured to be President of this College from 1969 to 1971. The idea of establishing a College of Surgeons in West Africa originated during a discussion between Dr. Charles Bowesman, and Dr. Victor Ngu. Dr. Bowesman I have already mentioned earlier in this narrative. He had then retired as a surgical specialist and I had succeeded him in 1959 as specialist in charge of Komfo Anokye Hospital, Kumasi. On the return voyage from leave on board of one of the Elder Dempster Lines boats he met Dr. Ngu, a Cameroonian, and a senior lecturer, (Surgery) at the University of Ibadan Medical School. They thought about the idea of establishing a College, but thought the first step would be to form an Association which would over the years develop into a College. It was in early 1960. Victor Ngu came to Kumasi shortly after arriving back home in Ibadan. I joined in the discussion with Dr. Bowesman.

Victor, being the dynamic and active person that he was, on his return to Ibadan soon set about organising an Inaugural Conference to take place in Ibadan in the latter part of the year 1960. Dr Charles Easmon who was the Surgical Specialist at Korlebu, Accra and I were privileged to attend this Inaugural Conference. It was not a large gathering, but the important thing was that Victor had managed to get in touch with surgeons from different parts of West Africa - Nigeria, Benin, Togo, Ivory Coast, Sierra Leone and Senegal. It was a fairly representative body of surgeons in West Africa. The proposal for the establishment of an Association was endorsed heartily by all the colleagues there gathered. Victor had prepared a draft constitution which was looked at and, as I recall, adopted immediately with amendments, and the Association was privileged to have as its first President Sir Samuel Manuwa, a very distinguished Nigerian, an eminent surgeon and scholar, a physician, and a man of very great distinction. He was the first President of the Association of Surgeons of West Africa. The following year as I recall, our sister Association was also formed: "The Association of Physicians of West Africa." Sir Samuel Manuwa, being a distinguished physician with the highest qualification in internal medicine, was also its first President.

It was arranged that after the Ibadan meeting, there would be annual meetings in different parts of West Africa, especially those parts which were represented at that inaugural meeting, and it was decided that the

Association would just provide the platform for members to prepare and read scientific papers at the annual meetings. Foremost in our minds also was the formulation or outlining of a programmeme of training for younger colleagues within the sub-region. This was at a time when these colleagues were trained in different parts of Europe and America. There was the British tradition, the French tradition, the American tradition, Eastern European tradition, and so on. It was decided that eventually, there should be established a College which would have a programmeme of training and also a system of examination and certification to enable our younger colleagues to qualify to become specialists. I am happy to report that this idea was embraced with great enthusiasm. Since that first inaugural meeting in Ibadan, the Association has grown from strength to strength.

In 1969 I was privileged to be elected President of the Association. This was at the time when plans were ripe for the establishment of the College. There was a programmeme that had to be endorsed by the Association, but before then it was necessary to take a formal decision to convert the Association into a College; so that the machinery could be put in place to establish a system of training to cater for the different faculties representing the different disciplines of surgery. I recall quite vividly the 1971 meeting in Dakar as this meeting coincided with my last year as President. It was at this Dakar meeting that the proposal was discussed. We all expected that the decision would be automatically endorsed to convert the Association into a College. However, we did not take into account the resistance from a certain French Professor of Surgery in the University of Dakar Medical School, who vehemently opposed the whole idea of the College. He thought it was enough to remain as an Association, arguing that the systems of specialist training differed so much between Britain and France that it would be very difficult to mix them. At that time one got the impression that our francophone colleagues were very much under the thumb of the French, and so it required a great deal of persuasion to get them on board and to agree with us that the decision must be taken. The objective that we had was not impossible to achieve; so after a long, sometimes very heated, discussion the decision was taken and from that time on the Association become a College.

Things were put in place for subsequent meetings of the new College to establish the structures and programmemes of training. Over the past three decades, much has happened and the College is now well established and is part of the West African Post-Graduate Medical College system. The idea of bringing together of different systems of training into the programmeme has materialized and there is now a qualification of Fellowship of the West African College of Surgeons (F.W.A.C.S.). I must say it has followed fairly closely the lines of organisation of the British Colleges. With time of course, we have established reciprocity with a number of sister Colleges in different parts of the world. The College is now firmly established and is one of the recognised professional colleges for the training of surgeons in the world. The chapters of the College in the constituent participating countries are all very active and the training programmeme is very vigorous and well patronised.

## Chairman, Ghana Medical and Dental Council

The Ghana Medical and Dental Council was established by N.R.C. Decree 91 in 1975 to replace the erstwhile Medical and Dental Board which was under the control of the Ministry of Health with the Director of Medical Services as Chairman. It was felt that the nature of the functions of the Council required that it should be an independent body. In 1979, I was elected Chairman of the Council by my colleagues at the first meeting of the newly elected Council. It is interesting to note that I succeeded the late Prof. Charles Easmon who almost simultaneously changed places with me as Chairman of the Board of the Centre for Scientific Research into Plant Medicine at Akuapem-Mampong.

I think it would be true to say in a nutshell that the function of the Council is really to protect the interest of the public. The Ghana Medical Association, of course, was formed primarily as a body to see to the welfare of doctors and dentists and by so doing enable members of the profession to discharge their professional functions more effectively and efficiently for the public.

The Medical and Dental Council, however, has as its primary function the protection of the interest of the public. It discharges this function in several ways. First of all, it is the body responsible for the registration of all medical doctors and dentists before they are allowed to practise their profession. Before registration, the Council has to satisfy itself that the qualification of the doctor is from a recognised medical school. The W.H.O. has a register of medical schools throughout the world which are recognised by the World Organisation and this is a source of great help to the Ghana Council. The Council is also required to monitor the actual professional performance of doctors and dentists in hospitals, whether public or private.

Finally, it has disciplinary powers over doctors and dentists in cases of malpractice or professional misconduct. Reports made to the Council are investigated by the Council and appropriate sanctions applied according to the nature of the offence. These sanctions range from a mere reprimand, through suspension from practice for a stated period, to outright removal of the name of the practitioner from the Register, which means that the practitioner can no more engage in professional practice. No practitioner may be registered who is not a member of the Ghana Medical Association. This is an important requirement.

As an example of the way in which the Council operates also, any hospital to be used as a Teaching Hospital would have to be inspected by the Council to make sure that the facilities of the hospital, for example, well qualified teachers, the facilities for professional work and also for teaching are of a certain minimum standard. This was done for the Korle-Bu Teaching Hospital before it was accredited by the Medical and Dental Board before the Council came into being. When the School of Medical Sciences was established in Kumasi it became necessary for Komfo-Anokye Hospital which had been designated as a Teaching Hospital to undergo a rigorous inspection by the Council, but because the facilities at the Hospital were at the material time considered inadequate, the Council withheld its approval for the hospital to be used as a Teaching Hospital. The first batch of doctors produced by the School of Medical Sciences of the University of Science and Technology, therefore, had to undergo their years of clinical training at the Korlebu Teaching hospital in Accra. This was during the period of my predecessor, Prof. Easmon. When I took over as Chairman, the Komfo-Anokye hospital had still not attained the required standard. On our first inspection, therefore, we were unable to give the necessary approval. The Council had to apply pressure on the Ministry of Health to improve facilities urgently in order to satisfy the basic requirements for a Teaching Hospital. When the time came and the facilities at Komfo Anokye satisfied the minimum requirements, the Council was able to give its approval and thereafter, clinical teaching started at that hospital.

With regard to discipline, for the Council to act, it is necessary that a complaint should be made to it formally. At this point I would like to draw a distinction between a medical officer or dentist being dismissed by the employing authority, whether government or not, and being banned from practising. It is only the Council that has the power to enforce the latter. Therefore, if a medical officer in the Ministry of Health, for example, commits and offence which amounts to professional misconduct or malpractice the Ministry may dismiss the officer without prejudice to what the Council may do. The Council then upon receipt of a complaint from the Ministry will proceed to institute a disciplinary enquiry and thereafter act and apply appropriate sanctions. The Disciplinary Committee of the Council has an assessor from the Attorney General's department on it and the accused has the right to engage counsel.

Although many cases are reported to the Council, it is sad to say that when an official disciplinary enquiry is instituted, often it has been difficult to get the complainants to attend as witnesses and to give evidence, so that unfortunately, some doctors and dentists who have committed certain offences may escape sanctions. In criminal cases where the practitioner has been convicted by a court, the Council automatically removes the practitioner's name from the Register.

There have been instances where the law enforcement agents, for example, the police, have been uncooperative in enforcing decisions by the Council. As an example, when I was Chairman there was a notable case where a practitioner in Kumasi was found guilty of gross negligence of duty and malpractice and a long period of suspension was imposed. The duty of the law enforcement agency was to see to it that the practitioner culprit did not at any time during the period of suspension practise his profession. On this occasion, the officer in charge was alleged to have stated that it was rather odd that when there was a shortage of doctors in the country, the Council should prevent some qualified doctors from practising. A very ironical situation indeed. Obviously, such an officer did not understand the whole idea of making sure that those who would commit offences against the public interest should be sanctioned. To him it was better to have someone who has been trained as a doctor to work, however incompetent and dangerous he might be, whether or not through his action people die!

## Chairman Centre for Scientific Research into Plant Medicine

The Centre for Scientific Research into Plant Medicine was established by N.R.C. Decree 344 in 1973. The establishment of the centre is a very good example of collaboration among scientists in Ghana. The reader may recall that on my first leave after a tour of duty in Dunkwa, I spent sometime as a locum at Dr. Oku Ampofo's clinic and came into contact with the work which was being done by Dr. Oku Ampofo in the field of herbal medicine. He collected medicinal plants and herbs from traditional healers and established good rapport with them. Now whilst Dr. Oku Ampofo was continuing with this work, the Faculty of Pharmacy in Kumasi under the leadership of Prof. A. N. Tackie was conducting research into the active principles in certain medicinal plants. At the same time Profs. F. Torto and J. Quartey at Legon were also doing chemical analysis on some of the active principles in the herbs. Eventually, these three groups came together and submitted a memorandum recommending the establishment of a Centre where not only scientific research into the herbs might be carried out but also clinical tests to ascertain the validity of the claims made by the traditional practitioners. Dr.Oku Ampofo was appointed the first Director of the Centre. When I moved to Accra in 1974, in my capacity as Chairman for the National Council for Higher Education I also became Chairman of the Centre's Interim Board for a number of years.

For the benefit of the reader, I would like to quote in full the functions of the Centre as outlined in the decree establishing it:

1.  To conduct and promote scientific research relating to the improvement of plant medicine.
2.  To ensure the purity of drugs extracted from plants.
3.  To cooperate and liaise with the Ghana Psychic and Traditional Healers Association, research institutions and commercial organizations in any part of the world in matters of plant medicine.
4.  To undertake or collaborate in the collation, publication and the dissemination of the results of research and other useful technical information.
5.  To establish where necessary, botanical gardens for medicinal plants.

6.      To perform such other functions as the government may assign to it from time to time."

The Centre was further charged

(a)     "To encourage the use of medicinally proven preparations as effective substitutes for conventional drugs.
(b)     To advise government on the presentation and restriction of the exportation of certain medicinal plants.
(c)     To advise the government from time to time on the desirability or otherwise of importing certain medicinal plants or their preparations into the country."

Since the establishment of the Centre, its activities have been concentrated on the following areas:

(1)     Data collection
(2)     Documentation
(3)     Upgrading the preparation of traditional medicinal substances
(4)     Clinical trials
(5)     Establishment of a herbarium and the cultivation of an arboretum.

There are two traditional herbalists permanently attached to the Centre, but others also come to the Centre from all over the country to give information. Needless to say, among these are a few quacks who will just come and give any information at all knowing that they will be paid some money, and also knowing that the information they give is false. However, over the years, much has been done and a systematic documentation of whatever information is received has been made. There is a botanical artist who makes drawings of the plant parts, whether they are leaves, fruits, roots or barks. The leaves are dried and preserved in albuim form. Here is also an experimental garden near the Centre where specimens of these medicinal plants are planted and labelled. The silviculturist attached to the centre goes round the country collecting medicinal plants for research work. Clinical studies done on patients to test the validity of the therapeutic claims using the preparations on them are based on two factors :

(1)     First, the diseases that traditional practitioners claim they can treat more successfully than modern practitioners and

(2)     Secondly, the diseases commonly present at the Centre.

Using this yardstick certain diseases have been selected. These include asthma, diabetes, hypertension, peptic ulcer and skin disease, sickle cell disease, arthritic conditions with the omnibus designation "rheumatism," malaria, guinea worm and haemorrhoids.

Having done a fair amount of investigation into the background into traditional medicines and traditional practice, I would like at this stage to draw a distinction between the herbs or plant parts that are used as medicines and the system of medical practice by which the practitioners decide on which herbs to use and which conditions to apply them to. With the first there should be no problem at all. The Centre was set up so that what had been done in the past in a non-scientific manner might be put on a proper scientific footing. For example, it is important to find out for a given plant part what the active principle is, and whether it is alone or in combination with others, which work together.

It is also important to establish a dosage which may be applied in given conditions for example, for children, adults, or patients with other medical conditions. It is generally known that our traditional herbalists have the handicap of not really knowing the standard dosage which should be applied. The measurement is faulty, and even the method of preparation which indirectly affects the quantum of the active principle in a given herb may vary from preparation to preparation Also it is necessary that the form of presentation may be more precise and more hygienic. We are all familiar with some of the concoctions which are peddled in trotros or at our markets; substances with plant and animal parts which are dried up, dirty, gathering fungus and other material and, altogether an unsavoury sight. On the presentation of these drugs, much leaves to be desired.

Above all, it is important that the practitioner should really know the condition that he is dealing with, and it is in this area that there is a vast distinction between the traditional practitioner and a practitioner scientifically trained in orthodox medicine. Indeed, some of the traditional practitioners do other jobs and practise part-time only. They may be carpenters, masons, or other artisans. Besides, they have not had any systematic training, apart from apprenticeship in a tradition that has been passed on from generation to generation. It is true to say that most traditional practitioners are completely illiterate and, if we are going to make any headway in the development of traditional medicine, it is important that all our traditional practitioners should have a minimum of education for them to understand scientific principles and the nature of the disease process.

The results of research are necessarily slow because the process has to be thorough. Anything which is hurried is usually not done satisfactorily. It is only when adequate research has been conducted and a particular drug of plant origin has been tried and tested and found to be effective in treating disease that the next stage, that is, the production and manufacture of the drug in commercial quantities can be done. The point I wish to make is that the Centre at Mampong is a Research Centre and it can only go as far as the production stage, that is, to the point where the Centre comes out with a drug that has been tried and found useful and can now be produced in large quantities. It is only at this stage that an entrepreneur can take over and produce the drug in commercial quantities. It may be a drug manufacturing firm or other institution. What should be pointed out here is that since we are dealing with medicines of plant origin we have to take into account the nature of the plant. Is it a small shrub which grows in weeks and which can be harvested and used immediately, or is it the leaf, root, bark or fruit of a huge tree which may take years to fruit to enable the fruits to be used? At the end of the day whether a particular herbal drug can be produced in large quantities depends on the plant part that has to be used.

The next thing to consider is the question of land. If you are going to cultivate large areas of a particular medicinal plant you have to go through the process of acquiring the land, in the appropriate part of the country, for example, the savannah area or the forest area. All these things must be taken into account. I can see that at some future date some of the medicines which will come out of the research Centre at Mampong may lend themselves to this kind of consideration.

There may then be large scale cultivation of medicinal plants to feed the pharmaceutical factories to produce drugs locally. At that time when everything has been scientifically tested and documentation done, the drug can find its way into the pharmacopoeia. The modern orthodox practitioner would use it and prescribe it and will do so with confidence knowing that this drug has been tried and tested.

As far as the traditional practitioner is concerned, we should make sure that he has a certain measure of education and that he has a system of medical practice which is up to date. After all, the modern scientifically trained practitioner goes through a system of training, which is recognised world-wide. On the other hand, the traditional practitioners have no recognised system of training, which is universal. In Ghana, one might even say that there are as many systems as there are practitioners! It is common knowledge that the traditional practitioner learns his trade mainly through apprenticeship, by oral tradition handed over from the master. Nothing is written down and, indeed, the master may not teach him everything, for fear of competition. The master may die with certain secrets. Is it any wonder then that traditional medical practice has remained stagnant because of the handicap of education and because of professional jealousy and envy among the practitioners and their colleagues? The problem is not competition between the traditional and the modern but professional jealousy among the traditional healers themselves!

# CHAPTER 26

## CHURCH MATTERS
### Chairman of the Inter-Church and Ecumenical Relations Committee of the Presbyterian Church of Ghana

In 1983, I became Chairman of the Inter Church and Ecumenical Relations Committee of the Presbyterian Church. Rev. S.K. Aboa was the secretary. Rev. Aboa in a sense could be described as the "Foreign Minister" of the Church, as he handled relations with other churches, notably partner churches of the Presbyterian Church of Ghana, especially in Europe. The main partner of the Church was the EMS, the organization representing the churches in South West Germany. There is a Basel Mission also and churches in Scotland, and in the Netherlands. The Interchurch Committee is really a sub-committee of the Synod Committee and considers matters pertaining to relations with other churches, including churches in Ghana. It, therefore, considers matters of partnership and the work of fraternal workers, whether Ghanaians in Europe or European workers in Ghana.

During my tenure there was occasion to send fraternal workers, mostly ministers of the Presbyterian Church, to different places in Europe, especially Germany, to cater for the needs of Ghanaians mainly, but generally, African students in those places. An important responsibility pertains to the London Chaplaincy. The London Chaplaincy was established in 1961 during the moderatorship of Rt. Rev. E.M. Odjidja who, on a visit to Britain, realized that it was desirable to have a Ghanaian minister to administer to the spiritual needs of the students in London primarily and in Britain generally. The Rev. F. W. K. Akuffo was appointed first chaplain and he assumed duty in 1961 for a period of five years. He was followed by Rev. E. Mate Kojo also for a period of five years. By this time, the EP Church in Ghana was also interested and became partners in the enterprise. So, in 1972 a Minister of the EP Church, Rev. Wurapa, was appointed.

During my tenure, I had the privilege of attending a Consultation with the partner churches held in Atlanta, USA. The Consultation is an annual affair held alternatively in Ghana and at a place outside the country. It is really a meeting which considers the needs of the Church for the forthcoming year and also reviews the work of the Church in a way, after the study of a situation report. The partnership of the church with outside churches has been a tremendous help, and materially, there have been enormous inputs, especially into the medical and educational institutions of the Church. I also had the opportunity to attend a consultation in Bad Boll, which is a small village near Stuttgart, headquarters of the EMS. It was a small body of representatives of partner churches of the EMS from all over the world. Subsequently, we were able to attend a Synod of the churches in Pfalz in South West Germany.

The most important event during my chairmanship was a meeting I attended in Cambridge in 1985 to review the work of the London Chaplaincy. This was shortly after the Rev. Anthony Beeko assumed duty as the chaplain in London. Rev. S. K. Asamoah of the EP Church accompanied me and Rev. Beeko was also at that meeting. The Chaplaincy had been in existence for a little over twenty years, and the time had come to take stock of what it had done and to decide whether it was necessary or desirable to continue. After a brief discussion, it was the unanimous agreement of the meeting, which was held under the chairmanship of a representative of the United Reformed Church in Britain, that the work really had grown. With the increasing number of Ghanaians in Britain over the years the responsibilities of the Chaplain had become more pressing and wider in scope. Indeed, over the years, the Chaplain had been available not only to students but non-students as well, and indeed to residents from other African countries! Before that time, there had been some difficulty with Rev. Anthony Beeko's immediate predecessor as there had been some reluctance on his part to leave when the time came. It became necessary to emphasize the point that the tenure of the chaplain should be five years. No more.

Rev. S. K. Aboa was succeeded as Inter-Church Secretary by Rev. Isaac Fokuo for a number of years and by the time I left, Rev. Dr. David Kpobi was the new secretary. My tenure as Chairman ended in 1998.

## President of the Ghana Boys' Brigade Council

After several years as one of the National Vice Patrons of the Ghana Boys' Brigade, I was elected President of the Boys Brigade Council at the Council meeting in Takoradi in 1987 in succession to Mr. G. K. de Graft-Johnson, an eminent engineer and former Managing Director of the Black Star Line. There had been eminent predecessors in office. There were Mr. Creedy, a missionary with the Methodist Church and a former Principal of Komenda Teacher Training College, and Mr. Justice Nii Amaa Ollennu, an eminent jurist and a former Speaker of Parliament. The Boys' Brigade was introduced into Ghana at about the time of the First World War and for many years it flourished in Basel Mission and Methodist schools. However, by the time of the Second World War, its activities had been diminished somewhat and the Brigade had become almost defunct. It was in the 1950's that it was revived, the principal participating churches being the Methodist and Presbyterian Churches and, to some extent, the Anglican Church.

The Object of the Boys Brigade is "the advancement of Christ's kingdom among boys and the promotion of habits of obedience, reverence, discipline, self-respect and all that tends towards a true Christian manliness." It is therefore a section of the youth movement in the church and, considering the ages of the boys involved, one could rightly term the Brigade as the nursery of the church, where the young boys would be trained in such a way that they would become future leaders of the church. The Ghana Boys Brigade is part of a worldwide youth movement called the World Conference together with analogous youth organizations from different parts of the world, principally the British Commonwealth but also a number of European countries. The headquarters is in Britain. It is unlike the Girls' Brigade, which is really a branch of the British Girls' Brigade.

One of the main problems of the brigade is funding. Surprisingly, some leaders of the participating churches, especially pastors in charge of congregations, do not seem to appreciate the value of the Boys Brigade. Where the pastor in charge of a congregation is broadminded and forward looking, the congregation gives all the support to the work of the brigade. However, as the Brigade solicits funds from outside the church some pastors look upon it as a rival organization in sourcing for funds. One has to work hard to educate pastors in charge of congregations to support the Boys Brigade. One difficulty I found was in getting dedicated leaders to lead the groups within the brigade. Where good leaders are available the companies flourish and parents are willing to let their children join the brigade. Another problem is the fact that some of the children do not take the Brigade seriously. They are only attracted by the uniform. Once they join, they are difficult to deal with, because apart from the teaching of the scriptures, there is the physical side; physical fitness exercises and also learning other skills, especially, self-preservation skills and first-aid skills, which make it possible for the brigader to help others in difficulty. The Boys Brigade to some extent could be regarded as a Christian counterpart of the Boys' Scout Movement.

The organizational structure of the Brigade provides for regional branches under the General Council, which meets once a year. Of course, there is an Executive Committee chaired by the President and comprising the various Vice-Presidents, Secretary and regional representatives. The Executive meet more often and implements decisions under policy laid down by the Councils. During my tenure there was an important World Conference meeting in Singapore, which I was privileged to attend. There I met brigade leaders and presidents from all over the world. I was accompanied by my wife on that occasion. An interesting aspect of the meeting was that my wife's profession came in handy. As a professional interpreter (French-English), she interpreted during some of the sessions. As a member of the World Conference Executives also, I attended a meeting in Belfast in 1988.

The Secretary / National Organizer of the Brigade had a lot of work to do, running around the country, and helping the various companies with their work. It was quite clear that there was the need to have two people; a full-time secretary and a full-time organizer in order to make the work more efficient. I advocated this very strongly. Unfortunately, by the time that I relinquished the presidency of the Brigade Council, the participating churches had not implemented this recommendation. Shortly after my departure, however, the decision was taken and a full time secretary was appointed in addition to the national organizer. In recent years, I notice that the work of the Brigade has been flourishing all over the country and I suspect that one of the reasons for this is the implementation of this decision to separate the secretary' work from that of the national organizer.

Before leaving the presidency, a revision of the existing Constitution, which had not been done for very many years, was completed and it made it possible for certain gray areas of the Constitution to be clarified. No doubt this has also, to some extent, helped the smooth running of the Brigade. Altogether, the Boys' and Girls' Brigades are important youth organizations which should be well nurtured by the church as, in my opinion, by doing so the church would guarantee smooth progress of its work in the future, knowing that the young people will grow into responsible men and women who will provide the needed christian leadership in the church. During the Council Meeting of the Brigade at Tema in 1998 I was honored as a "Distinguished Friend of the Brigade".

## Chairman, the Akrofi-Christaller Memorial Center For Mission Research and Applied Theology

The Akrofi-Christaller Memorial Center For Mission Research and Applied Theology was established at Akropong-Akuapem by the Presbyterian Church in 1986. It was established as a Private Company Limited by Guarantee. This means that it has a certain measure of autonomy from the Church itself, and could not be regarded as a mere department of the church in the same sense as the Ramseyer Institute at Abetifi or the Women's' Center at Abokobi.

Christaller and Akrofi, after whom the Center has been named, were important members of the Basel Mission and the Presbyterian Church of Ghana respectively. Christaller was the person who was largely responsible for the translation of the Bible into Akuapem Twi, a translation which is regarded to be one of the finest into any language, by any standard. Akrofi later on did much work on the Twi language itself, specially Twi grammar. He was the author of "Twi kasa, Mmra.

The main object of the Center is as quoted at the back of the Center News, which is published quarterly "the Center is dedicated to the study and documentation of the life, theology and history of the church in Ghana and in Africa as a whole in relation to the African setting in world Christianity. The Center seeks also to equip pastors and other christian workers for more effective mission in the African context." The Church appointed Rev. Dr. Kwame Bediako, then resident chaplain of the Ridge Church in Accra, as the Founding Director of the Center. This appointment was a very important one because the Rev. Bediako himself had for some time dreamt that one day the church would establish such an institution, which would make it possible for the aims as declared above to be realized. Although a Presbyterian initiative, the Center is ecumenical in outlook as is reflected in the composition of the fifteen-member Board of Trustees, which includes nine Presbyterians, four Methodists, one Anglican, and one Baptist!

At the first meeting of the Board of Directors, my colleagues elected me Chairman of the Board with the Rev. S. K. Aboa as Vice-Chairman. The Center was formally launched at the British Council in 1987. It was a very grand occasion and the main stakeholders were well represented : the Presbyterian Church by the Acting Moderator, the Methodist Church by the then President of the Conference, the Swiss Embassy, emphasizing the Swiss connection, represented by His Excellency the Ambassador of Switzerland to Ghana, and the British connection, that is, through the Scottish Mission, represented by the Acting British High Commissioner. There was also a descendant, (I believe it was a great grand-daughter) of Christaller who was visiting from Switzerland. Then there was a representative of the Akrofi family. All made important speeches to launch the Center. At a subsequent date, there was an inauguration at Akropong also.

From the onset, the Presbyterian Church of Ghana helped the Center to get on its feet by donating the old house where Akrofi lived and also the old Basel Mission House, the big building which once housed the Basel Mission Seminary. The Church also gave support by offering to pay the staff of the Center and adding a small grant towards the running expenses of the Center.

The Board of Directors had a lot of planning to do. The question of how to raise additional funds to make it possible for renovations and restoration of the old buildings occupied much of the time of the Board. Also in planning the programmemes for the Center we had to take into account the additional buildings that would be required to sustain the programmemes, which had been envisaged under the dynamic directorship of Rev. Dr. Kwame Bediako. To support this, funds have had to be raised both internally and from outside the country. I must say that there has been much enthusiasm in support from outside, especially by organizations such as Bread for the World, other organizations in the Netherlands, EMS in Germany and other well-meaning bodies in Britain and the United States. Individuals and some organizations within the country have also made modest but important contributions and even at this time they continue to send donations to support the work of the Center. The physical development of the Center has been done in stages.

First of all there was the question of renovating the Akrofi House and also restoring and renovating the old Basel Mission House itself, so that the original architecture was preserved while, structurally, the building was made stronger. For example, important wooden pillars were changed into concrete pillars and old decaying wood was replaced. From the beginning, the Board decided that everything should be done to preserve the architecture and even the appearance of the building so that anyone who knew what the building looked like, visiting it now, would not really notice any difference, despite the fact that it has been restored and made stronger, structurally! Other developments involved the building of a hostel and also a cafeteria. This makes it possible for the Center to receive visitors and also students for varying periods from time to time.

The Centre's programmemes have been varied. There is a programmeme of orientation for newly ordained pastors of the Presbyterian Church of Ghana, prior to assuming duty at their various stations. Ther are also programmes for the continuing education of pastors and church agents through the organization of seminars and retreats. Generally speaking, members of the church, for example, the elders of the church, who wish to use the Center's facilities are entitled to do so. I may say that it is not only the Presbyterian Church but also other churches, especially the Protestant Churches, that have taken advantage of the Center's facilities.

In the academic area, the Center was given accreditation a few years ago by the National Accreditation Board as a post-graduate institution to run the M.Phil (Master in Theology) in African Christianity in conjunction with the University of Natal, Pietermaritzburg, South Africa. Currently, there are three pastors of the Presbyterian Church of Ghana on secondment to the Center who were appointed research fellows and have obtained the M.Phil degree and are working towards the Doctorate Degree under the programme with Natal. The programme requires that part of the tuition be done at the Center and another part in South Africa. The Center is open to students from other churches and other countries, especially in Africa. But in recent times, there have been students from the United States and Europe.

Among the publications of the Centre is the important journal, "Journal of African Christian Thought," which is issued twice a year. Also providing the requisite leadership, Rev. Dr. Bediako and his wife,

Gillian, publish findings of their research and encourage researchers who come to the Centre also to publish. The programmes for the retrieval of archival material from the churches, schools, hospitals and families for documentation has not gone on as well as has been expected. The Centre, therefore, needs to concentrate its efforts in this important area in the years to come to prevent such material from disappearing completely, with the dying out of important members of the churches and families concerned.

The Center has indeed established itself as an institution of excellence, not only within Ghana but internationally, and I feel that the Director and the staff have to be warmly congratulated. It is a great asset to the Presbyterian Church of Ghana and is bound to play an important role in the set up of the new Presbyterian University which is being planned to start in October 2003. I relinquished the Chairmanship of the Center in 2002 after over 16 years' service. I am indeed grateful to the Presbyterian Church for giving me the opportunity to serve on the Board, and to my colleagues for electing me chairman of the Board and for the support they gave me.

# CHAPTER 27

# EDUCATIONAL MATTERS
## President of the Ghana Academy of Arts and Sciences

In the year 1970 whilst I was still at the Kumasi University, I received a request from the Honorary Secretary of the Ghana Academy of Arts and Sciences to send him my Curriculum Vitae, which I did. For months, nothing happened but sometime during the year 1971 I received a letter from the Honorary Secretary informing me that I had been elected a Fellow of the Ghana Academy of Arts and Sciences. To this day, I have no idea of who nominated me for the Fellowship of the Academy! Being a Fellow of the Academy is a very great honor and I must say that I felt highly encouraged in whatever I was doing.

Before moving to Accra in 1974 obviously, because of the distance and my busy schedule, I was not very active, but when I got to Accra, I put all my energy into the activities of the Academy by attending meetings regularly and doing whatever there was to be done. The Academy, of course, is a group of distinguished Ghanaian intellectuals who are presumed to have made important contributions in the various fields in the arts and sciences. The Academy itself aims at promoting the advancement of the arts and sciences in Ghana. When it was founded originally by the first President of the Republic, Osagyefo Dr. Kwame Nkrumah, in 1958 it had additional responsibilities of overseeing a number of research institutes. Years later, this function was removed from the Academy's responsibilities and given to the Council for Scientific and Industrial Research, which then took over the Research Institutes.

The Academy, therefore, became just a body of academicians, and it was called the 'Ghana Academy of Learning'. But the name was very quickly changed to the "Ghana Academy of Arts and Sciences," with no direct responsibility for research institutes. However, it carried on its activities through lectures and symposia and through awarding prizes for outstanding research work of scientists and other intellectuals. These were the gold award and then the silver award was for promising young scientists. In addition the Academy gives awards for undergraduate essays.

Over the years, annually in November, for a whole week, the Academy observes its Anniversary. The celebrations start with the Presidential Address on the first day; then for three days there are symposia to which distinguished academics in various fields are invited to take part as panelists, with audience participation. On the last day, which is the fifth day, there is the Anniversary Address, delivered by one of the distinguished Fellows or occasionally a distinguished outsider. For the whole week, there is a theme chosen from a wide variety of topics, both scientific or non-scientific. It may be in Medicine, it may be in General Science, it may be in Politics or Economics or Government. There is a wide spectrum of themes which have been dealt with over the years and, looking through the list, one could see that the Academy has really done well in dealing with issues which are both topical and relevant to the country's development.

In February of each year, a distinguished Fellow or, occasionally, a distinguished citizen of Ghana who is not a Fellow, is invited to deliver the J. B. Danquah Memorial Lectures, which is a three-day lecture on a theme of the lecturer's choice. These lectures are to honour the memory of Dr. J. B. Danquah, a distinguished Ghanaian who was a Fellow of the Academy. Every new Fellow is expected to deliver an inaugural lecture within a stated period of being elected to the Fellowship. The proceedings of all these lectures - the Anniversary Lectures, the J. B. Danquah Lectures, and the inaugural lectures - are published by the Academy.

Over the years I have found my interaction with the distinguished Fellows, men and women of high intellect, very stimulating, and, of course, highly beneficial to me. I have had the privilege of serving on a number of committees of the Academy, notably the Education Committee and the Committee which plans the programmes for the year and for the Anniversary celebrations, and I have been privileged to be Chairman of these two committees. In 1985, I was elected the Vice-President of the Science Section of the Academy and, a couple of years after, that is in 1986, at the last meeting in December, I was elected President of the Academy. I served two terms of two years' duration, ending my presidency and handing over in 1990. My predecessor in office was the Right Rev. Professor K.A. Dickson, formerly of the Department of the

Study of Religions and the Institute of African Studies at the University of Ghana. In 1990 I handed over the baton to the late Rev. Professor Emeritus Christian Baëta.

The problems of the Academy over the years have been many. First of all, there has been one of identity, that is to say, that of the public really recognizing and getting to know what the Academy is. It has been said that for a long time a large section of the population, when the Academy was mentioned, just thought first of Accra Academy! It may well be that the confusion in the public mind stems from the fact that the public relations of the Academy have not been sufficiently effective. The Academy has not been aggressive enough in projecting itself. Now I do not know whether one can put the blame altogether at the door of the Academy. One would have thought that the enlightened Ghanaian public would support and patronize the lectures, which are arranged and given on the Academy's platform throughout the year, especially during the Anniversary Celebrations and the J.B. Danquah Lectures. Unfortunately, patronage at these lectures has been poor over the years and it is sad to note that public officials who should be interested in the topics, and who should come especially to participate in discussions during the symposia have been conspicuously absent. Even when special invitations and letters are written to ministers, members of Parliament and others, the response has been very poor. The exception has been, of course, when the topic happens to be a hot political one!

Secondly, the Academy has been wholly funded by the Government by subvention over the years in addition to the dues paid by Fellows. Normally, Fellows who are elected to the Academy are the intellectual type not normally associated with wealth, and cannot therefore by themselves contribute in any large measure to adequate funding of the Academy. On the other hand, sponsorship by outside organizations, probably because of the lack of understanding of what the Academy stands for, or what it does, has not been forthcoming.

The response to the Endowment Fund of the Academy has been rather disappointing. Another problem of the Academy is that ever since the split was made between CSIR and the Academy proper, the Academy has been a tenant of the CSIR. Its offices have always been in the "womb" of the CSIR Secretariat. Clearly, there is a great need for the Academy to have its own building. Indeed, many years ago plans were made for a separate building, but these plans have remained on the drawing board because there have not been funds provided by

Government for the purpose. A visit to other countries, especially the European countries, shows that the academies there have a visible physical existence. I recall during my presidency that the then Honorary Secretary, Professor Reginald Amonoo and I visited Bulgaria, and we were really impressed by the imposing building of the Academy of Bulgaria. There, academicians are treated with great respect by the state and by the Bulgarian society in general.

In 1984, I had the honour of delivering the seventeenth series of the J.B. Danquah Memorial Lectures. I chose for the theme of my lectures "Traditional Medicine in Ghana: Practice, Problems and Prospects". I also delivered annual Presidential Addresses during my tenure as President. On three occasions also I had the honour of being the Anniversary Lecturer.

The J.B. Danquah Lectures delivered by Professor Adu Boahen in the year 1988 during my presidency were very highly patronized. Professor Boahen had chosen for his theme, 'The Ghanaian Sphinx,' which is a historical account of years of unconstitutional rule in Ghana, the years of military rule especially, and the reader will recall that the year 1988 was during the regime of the Provisional National Defense Council when the culture of silence reigned supreme. On this occasion Professor Adu Boahen had the distinction of breaking the culture of silence in no uncertain terms. Needless to say, the British Council Hall, which was the usual venue of these Academy Lectures was filled to capacity, for all three lectures to the extent that loud speakers had to be installed on the verandahs outside the hall for the crowds that came to listen to Professor Boahen.

After the second lecture, as President, I received a request from Government through an emissary, for the Government to be given the chance to react to statements made by Professor Boahen during the second lecture. This unusual request was contrary to existing convention and practice. No questions or discussions are allowed after these lectures. I had to consult hurriedly with members of the Academy Council who were available. In the end, out of deference to the government and the way in which they felt strongly about the lecture, we agreed that a representative of the government would be allowed to say a few words after the last lecture on condition that the audience would be told that it was Government that had made that request. The government representative reluctantly accepted this condition. So it came to pass that after the last lecture by Professor Boahen, I mounted the rostrum and announced that at the request of Government, the Council of the Academy had agreed to allow a representative of the government to say a few words, in rebuttal of certain statements made by Professor Boahen in the second lecture, on condition that this representative was not going to give another lecture, and that the presentation would not exceed twenty minutes. In the end, the representative of the government came up and had his say which, unfortunately, was not well received. The audience was quite hostile and it seemed to me that the result was really counter-productive.

Professor Boahen's lecture emboldened the media to be more outspoken and, of course, for the Academy, it tended to strain relations with the government, since the platform was the Academy's even though the views expressed by lecturers are not necessarily the views of the Academy. Views are supposed to be independent views of the lecturers, whether during the Anniversary Celebrations or J.B. Danquah Lectures or any other lecture.

Happily, the Academy's relations with Government at this time are very cordial and it is important, therefore, to take advantage of this situation. There is no doubt that the Academy is a great national asset. The Academy is an intellectual pool in which Government or the State could fish to its advantage. It constitutes a think-tank which could be called upon by Government to help out in many areas of national endeavour, areas pertaining to national development. One of the most important needs of the Academy now is a building befitting its status. In a few years, the Academy will be fifty. It would, therefore, be appropriate for Government to take steps to ensure that before that time, the dream of the Academy to have its own Academy building is fulfilled. I think it would be entirely proper for Government to donate a suitable building to the Academy. Such a move will really be a great encouragement to the Fellows of the Academy to work as hard as they can, to do what they have to do to help in the forward movement of their country.

## Founding of the African Academy of Sciences

In the summer of the year 1985, in my capacity as Vice-President of the Academy (Sciences), I attended a Conference at Trieste, at the International Institute of Theoretical Physics, which was headed by the great Pakistani scientist, the late Professor Abdus Salam. Other members of the delegation were Professor Allotey and Professor Laing, Fellows of the Academy, the late Dr. Kwamena Butler, Director General of the Council for Scientific and Industrial Research, and Mr. Trebi Ollennu, who at that time was working with the Ministry of Finance and Economic Planning. Prof. Adjei Bekoe, a Fellow of the Third World Academy was also there in his capacity as a Fellow of that Academy. At that meeting there were scientists from all over the Third World and there was quite a sizeable number of African scientists also. The African scientists present met and held detailed discussions about the desirability of establishing an African Academy of Sciences. A decision was finally taken to establish such an Academy.

As a follow-up, the following year, in 1986, a Conference was held in Nairobi, first to endorse the Constitution which had been drawn up, and also to inaugurate the new African Academy of Sciences, under the distinguished presidency of Professor Thomas Odienbo, an eminent Kenyan entomologist and Head of the International Center for Insect Physiology, Nairobi. It was decided that all who attended the meeting in Trieste the previous year would become foundation Fellows of the new Academy. Since then the African Academy has grown from strength to strength and it has published on a regular basis the Journal of the Academy which is distributed regularly among the Fellows.

The year 1990 was my last year as the President of the Ghana Academy. I was privileged to attend a meeting of the Third World Academy in Caracas in Venezuela in the company of Professors Allotey and D. A. Akyeampong. Professor Allotey and Professor Akyeampong have since been elected Fellows of the Third World Academy. Other distinguished Ghanaian scientists who were members of the Third World Academy are Professor Adjei Berkoe whom I have mentioned already and also Professor Edward Ayensu.

## Chairman of the West African Examinations Council

Sometime in early March 1991 Mrs. Sylvia Boye, Head of the Ghana National Office of the West African Examinations Council called to see me in my Consulting Room and asked for my Curriculum Vitae. I asked what it was for and she replied that the Ghana National Committee which was about to meet at that time, would be considering a candidate to be recommended to Government for appointment as Chairman of the West African Examinations Council. In accordance with the Convention signed in Monrovia in 1985, the chairmanship of the Council was to be held on a rotatory basis among the five participating countries, namely, Nigeria, Ghana, Sierra Leone, The Gambia, and Liberia. The tenure for Chairman was to be three years, and non-eligible for reappointment. It was Ghana's turn to provide a candidate. The procedure was that the Government of the country involved would recommend a name to the West African Examinations Council at the annual meeting for consideration and formal election. Theoretically, the Council could reject a nominee of the government in which case, another name had to be submitted.

Fortunately, at that time I had a curriculum vitae updated to the beginning of the year 1991 so I was able to get a copy for Mrs. Boye. I started to think about the Council of which I had been a member for nearly seven years when, in my capacity as Vice-Chancellor of the University of Science and Technology, I was a Ghana Government nominee on the Council. Within a week of Mrs. Boye's coming to see me, I received a letter signed by the Acting Director-General of the Ghana Education Service, who was the ex-officio leader of the Ghana delegation on the Council informing me that the government of Ghana had nominated me for election by the Council as Chairman. After that, things moved quite fast. The Council meeting itself was to be held in Banjul within a week. During the course of that week, the Registrar of the Council, Mr. Ezesobor, came to see me and gave me literature and documents about the Council to study. It appeared to me then that my election as the Chairman of the Council was a foregone conclusion. At the same time, the Registrar gave me a return ticket to Banjul for the meeting of the Council. He was to see that I was present in Banjul during the meeting. Accordingly, a day or two before the meeting of the Council, I travelled to Banjul.

On the day of the Council meeting, I stayed in my hotel room, and at the appropriate time, I was invited to the meeting to be informed by the Chairman of the Council, Dr. Lenrie Peters of The Gambia, that the Council had unanimously elected me Chairman of the Council to succeed him. I thanked the Council most warmly for the confidence they had shown in me by electing me Chairman. I have taken the liberty of attaching, as an appendix, a copy of my acceptance speech at that meeting. For the ensuing three years, I was to be very busy, deeply involved in the affairs of the West African Examinations Council which I found very stimulating, enjoyable, and educative. It enabled me to travel extensively within the sub-region in the member countries, with the exception of Liberia, which was by then embroiled in Civil War.

The West African Examinations Council was established in 1952 to take over the conduct of examinations of the Cambridge School Leaving Certificate. Prior to that, these examinations in the four British colonies in West Africa were conducted directly from Cambridge. Over the years, there have been several developments and in addition to its international function, the Council has conducted national examinations, that is, examinations for the individual member countries. It has also continued to conduct examinations on behalf of examining bodies like the City and Guilds and other such bodies in Britain and elsewhere. For some years, following developments in education, the Cambridge School Certificate Examination gave way to the West African School Certificate, that is the 'O' level and the 'A' level and, during the past decade or so, with the reforms in education taking place in the sub-region, the 'O' and 'A' level examinations have gradually given way to an International West African Secondary School Certificate. This has taken place in stages, in all the countries. By the time that the Council celebrated its fiftieth anniversary, which was the year 2002, all the participating countries had adopted one internationally recognized West African Secondary School Certificate.

Liberia, which is the other English speaking country in West Africa, later on, joined the Council as a participating country. The ordinance establishing the Council insisted that the standard of the Certificate issued by the Council should not be lower than  that of equivalent examinations which the Council was already replacing, and one can safely say that this principle has been maintained throughout the years, so that the West African Secondary School Certificate is now recognized as being of an acceptable international standard.

Of the various inter-territorial organizations existing during the colonial period, organizations such as the West African Court of Appeal, the West African Currency Board, the West African Airways, the West African Cocoa Research Institute, it is only the West African Examinations Council which managed to survive the stresses and strains occasioned by the independence of the participating countries. I think it is to the credit of these countries that they realized the importance of the work of the Council and of education in general. It cannot be denied that the Council has played a very important role in making sure that high standards are kept in education throughout the sub-region.

In 1985 a new Convention established the Council very firmly as an independent body during the annual Council meeting in Monrovia, so that whilst the individual governments may have a certain measure of control over their national offices of the Council, no single country has control over the Council itself, which has its headquarters in Accra. I think this measure of independence has made it possible for the Council to act with minimal political interference from any of the member countries. I must say that Nigeria being the largest member, and with its multifarious examinations, has from time to time felt that perhaps it could go it alone. I think in the long run, good sense has prevailed with the realization that it is far better to have an internationally recognized certificate than a national one. There is no gainsaying the fact that a national certificate would not have the same weight and standing as an international certificate. The composition of the Council makes it possible for the member countries to nominate individuals of high distinction, who have a wide experience in education, and therefore the work of the Council and the decisions of the Council which are taken are of good quality, decisions which member countries have respected.

Apart from the Council itself, there are international committees of Council such as the Administrative and Finance Committee, the Awards Committee, the Tenders Committee, the Appointments Committee and so on. Each country has a National Committee with its sub-committees, which in a way mirror the committees at the international level. In addition to that, there are hundreds of subject committees and the whole structure and function of the Council is such that there is extensive participation because all the universities are involved as are experienced teachers, in setting examination questions and marking examination papers. All in all, one would say that the structure of the Council itself has really helped it to survive. The main function of the Council is to make sure that there is proper evaluation and assessment of the teaching and training in the various member countries and the Council has, therefore, acted as a guide in the formulation of the examination and the teaching syllabuses for the various member countries.

My three-year tenure as chairman coincided with the reforms which were taking place in education in the various member countries, in particular the adoption of the 6-3-3-4 structure of education, the introduction of the Junior Secondary School concept and also the taking into account of continuous assessment, that is school based continuous assessment when evaluating the performance of the candidate at the end of the day. Currently, the continuous assessment takes 30% whilst the Council's own examination assessment takes 70%. There have been problems with the continuous assessments and it will take time for all these problems to be satisfactorily solved. These problems are inevitable in view of the varying standards of teaching and resource endowment of the various schools and also even the experience of the teachers in making the continuous assessment. The Council's expertise has been very important in advising and helping the education authorities in the member countries.

The activities of the Council over the years have been bedeviled by examination malpractices in various forms, ranging from leakage of examination papers to cheating by bringing in foreign material into the examination room, impersonation, collusion, copying during the examination period and so on. Over time, these malpractices have become more sophisticated in spite of the severe sanctions which are prescribed for various offences. Sometimes it would appear to the public that the sanctions applied are too harsh; for example cancelling the entire examination results of a whole school as a result of the discovery of a leakage at a particular examination center, or, indeed cancelling the examination results for all as a result of leakage at the printers or elsewhere.

Although the Council is the principal focus whenever something happens, it is true to say that these malpractices and leakages may occur at any stage of the examination process from the setting of the examination questions, which has to be done by human beings and printing of the questions, to conveying the question papers through various distances. In some rural areas, there may be intimidation of invigilators by outsiders including sometimes parents or guardians or even school authorities, and this has not helped to sanitize the whole process. So whilst it may be difficult to eradicate these malpractices completely, it should be possible to minimize them to the lowest level. Needless to say, the bigger the country, the higher the incidence of malpractices, so that one is not surprised to find that Nigeria is the leader, followed by Ghana, Sierra Leone, the Gambia and Liberia as far as the incidence of malpractices and application of sophisticated methods are involved.

My visits to the various member countries and to the various offices and examination centers gave me a good insight into the problems of education in the sub-region and I was also very impressed with the important role which women were playing in educational administration in the sub-region. During my tenure, two of the national offices were headed by women: Mrs. Sylvia Boye in Ghana and Mrs. Grace Morris in Liberia. Ghana has the distinction of producing the first woman Registrar of the Council, in the person of Mrs. Sylvia Boye, who crowned a very long and distinguished service with the Council by becoming the first woman Registrar, a post she very richly deserved and which I supported very strongly. It is interesting to note that she was succeeded as Head of the Ghana National Office by another woman, Mrs. Lydia Kpodo, who had also had a long and distinguished service at the Council. Both women brought credit to Ghana for the part they played at the Council.

My predecessor, Dr. Lenrie Peters, during his tenure, was very instrumental in the establishment of a security printing press in Lagos, a press which was named Megavons. Megavons, I believe, is an acronym using the names of the important rivers in West Africa - the Niger, the Volta, the Manor River and others.

The idea of establishing the Council's own security printing press was for the Council to gain a firm control over the security of the examination papers. It was a very important decision which was implemented during the tenure of my predecessor. Unfortunately, shortly after I took over, it had become apparent that we had to be very vigilant lest the whole idea was undermined by the company being hijacked and the Council thereby unwittingly losing at the end of the day. Consequently, I spent much of my time using diplomatic and legal means in making sure that this did not happen. I must mention the help which Professor Basil Lokko, of Ghana, who at the time of my appointment was Acting Director General of the Education Service in Ghana and therefore the leader of the Ghana delegation at the Council, gave together with other important Nigerians with good business experience in making sure that Megavons remained firmly in the ownership of the Council.

My wife accompanied me to some of these visits to different parts of Nigeria, to places like Benin, Oyo and Jos and Kaduna. We were really exposed to aspects of Nigerian culture. I recall with a certain degree of nostalgia our visit to Benin. The Oba of Benin really received us in grand style as very important visitors to his court. It was at Benin that I was able to establish contact with the family of Mr. Ineh, whom the reader may recall, came to Achimota College when I was doing post-secondary work to teach brass work to the students. Mr. Ineh, of course, had died a long time before, but I was very happy to meet his eldest son who was carrying on the family business of brass work. He was highly intrigued to know that I had known his father whilst he served and taught at Achimota College.

Twice every year, the International Final Awards Committee of the Council met to consider the chief examiners' reports on the various examinations and also to take decisions on the awards to be made, with particular reference to whether there were examination malpractices or not and apply the appropriate sanctions. One important issue which kept cropping up in the examination results was the low performance, throughout the sub-region, in English and Mathematics, and it was quite clear that these two very important subjects needed to be focused on by the various member countries.

I have been talking about visits to the various countries, I had the honour of meeting Sir Jahwara, President of the Gambia (an old Achimotan), and General Momo, who was then President of Sierra Leone. In Nigeria I met the Vice-President. It was during a military regime and I cannot recall his name now, but he was a Vice-Admiral of the Navy.

My three-year tenure as chairman of the Council was a very happy period, and intellectually stimulating for me. All the members of the Council were men of great intellect and I found discussions on the Council very stimulating. I became chairman when I was 72 and relinquished the chairmanship at 75! So you can imagine how mentally rejuvenating it was for me! I handed over to Professor Kamara, of Sierra Leone, a veterinary surgeon. I am happy to say that even after leaving office, the Council Secretariat in Accra have treated me with very great respect and extended courtesies to me. When I travel out of the country, the protocol section of the Council gives me the same treatment as they did when I was Chairman. I have not travelled for some time now, but I daresay that they will continue to render those services whenever I need them, especially when in 1998, four years after I had left the Council, my predecessor Dr. Lenrie Peters and I were accorded the honour of being made "Distinguished Friends of the Council" at the Annual Council Meeting at Abuja.

I have already referred to the survival spirit of the Council and the fact that it was very wise of the leaders of the participating countries to leave well alone the Council and continue to support it to flourish. The effort has been sustained, but as education has expanded and grown over the years, it is important that this support should be strengthened and adequate resources made available to the Council so that it can perform its work of advancing the cause of education in the sub-region more effectively and more efficiently. With the establishment of ECOWAS, such interterritorial international cooperation has become even more important, and what better area to cooperate in than education to make sure that educational standards are kept uniform and the equivalences are properly maintained so that the ECOWAS provision of free movement of goods and services within the sub-region may be facilitated.

## Edinburgh University - Alumnus of the year 1996

In the year 1990, the University of Edinburgh, in collaboration with the Royal Bank of Scotland, instituted an award titled "the Edinburgh University Alumnus of the Year." The award is to be made to an old student of the University who has made outstanding contributions in the arts and sciences or business or in the development of his community. Nominations are invited from the thousands of graduates of the University worldwide through the medium of the University Bulletin, which is widely distributed.

In 1995, my friend Dr. Timothy Awuku-Asabre of Tema, a graduate of Edinburgh University, asked if he could send in my particulars nominating me for the award. I obliged by giving him a copy of my curriculum vitae, which he duly forwarded to Edinburgh. Unfortunately, the nomination was sent in quite late, and by the time that the committee responsible for making the selection received it, it was already late.. However, they wrote back to Dr. Awuku Asabre to say that, even though the nomination could not be considered that year, they were going to hold it over to the following year, so there was no need for him to renew it. Nothing happened for some time, but about the middle of the year 1996, I received a letter from the Alumni Office of the University of Edinburgh informing me that I had been selected as the Edinburgh University Alumnus of the Year 1996 and that the Award would be presented in Edinburgh in December of that year. Consequently, my wife and I travelled to Edinburgh during the first week of December of that year and, at a Graduation Ceremony in the afternoon of December 7th, 1996 I was presented with the award. There is no cash attached to the award but there is a citation and also a certificate together with a replica of the shield. The shield itself is kept in the office of the Principal of the University.

I must say that I was very pleasantly surprised that having left the University almost half a century before, the University was able, on the basis of what I had been able to achieve after leaving the University to confer that great honour on me, an honour which I shall cherish throughout my life. Standing on the mantelpiece in my office now is a replica of the award. It was during wintertime and therefore I was not inclined to stay in Edinburgh for a long time; my wife and I planned just a fortnight's visit.

After the award ceremony in the afternoon, the Principal gave a dinner in my honour. It was a small dinner to which some deans of the various faculties of the University were invited and I was also permitted to invite a number of friends not only to the ceremony in the afternoon but also to the dinner. I wish to record here how very pleased I was that some of my Scottish friends from my student days were able to attend those two ceremonies, especially Rev. Colin Forrester Paton and his wife, Jean, whom I had known since 1942 when Collin was a Travelling Secretary for the Student Christian Movement for the East of Scotland. Subsequently, he came to Ghana and worked with the Presbyterian Church for over two decades. I believe his last assignment was as Resident Chaplain of the Ridge Church in Accra. Then there was Wilma Gladstone. Wilma also I had known as a student, and indeed, the Gladstone family from the very first year of my university days became friends of mine. Wilma also came to the Gold Coast and joined the Education Service as Education Officer for a number of years but had to leave on grounds of ill health and go back to work in Scotland. At the time that we met for the award ceremony, Wilma was in her middle eighties, but still going strong. In the intervening years, I had kept the links with the Gladstone family, and my wife and family have on occasion been their guests when we visited Edinburgh. Then there was my good friend, John Gray, and his wife, Elizabeth. John, by then was a very distinguished lawyer and had been playing an active part in local politics as a liberal. John as a student was president of the Students Representative Council when I was a member of the Council. Although we do not belong to the same profession, we have been friends since our student days and my wife and family have often been their guests when we visited Edinburgh subsequently. On this occasion after we finished with the award ceremony and all that it entailed, we were very pleased to accept their invitation to stay with them in Edinburgh before we left to come back home.

At the ceremonies also were Aaron Madjetey and his wife Muriel. Aaron was a practising accountant at that time. He is the son of Mr. Erasmus Madjitey, the very first Ghanaian Commissioner of Police. His wife, Muriel, is the daughter of my good friends, Kodjo and Margaret Oddoye, whom I have already mentioned in this narrative. At that time Rev. Dr. Sam Prempeh, now Moderator of the General Assembly of the Presbyterian Church of Ghana, was Assistant Chaplain at the University of Edinburgh. He also attended the ceremonies. Last but not least, were Rev. Dr. Kwame Bediako and his wife, Gillian. Dr. Bediako is the Director of the Akrofi Christaller Center at Akropong, the Center whose Board I happened to be Chairman. Rev. Bediako and his wife were spending a short time in Edinburgh in connection with their work at Akropong.

There were some of my contemporaries at the Medical School who were also around, Philip Myerscough, a retired gynecologist, and then Arthur Kitchin and John Loudon, both retired. Kitchin was Leonora's physician at the time that she died, John Loudon was a sportsman. He and I used to rub shoulders on the sports field at Craig Lochart playing in Edinburgh. Incidentally, John and Arthur and another contemporary, Luton, have been responsible for arranging the reunion of the 1947 Medical Graduation Class at various times. I recall attending the 20-year reunion in 1967. Subsequently, there have been reunions in 1977. Unfortunately, it was not possible for either myself or Dr. Matthew Barnor to attend the reunion lined up for 1997, the Golden Jubilee Reunion.

For some months after the award in Edinburgh, I received letters from longstanding friends of mine, who were students in my time in Edinburgh and who remembered me. Others who just read an account of the award in the Alumni Magazine or the University Bulletin also wrote to congratulate me. I must say that this was really a source of great comfort and satisfaction to me. Among the letters was a request from the Editor of the Edinburgh University Journal asking me to write an article on any subject of my choice to be published in the Journal. He indicated that there were so many people who would be interested in what I had been doing during the 50 years or so since I left the University. I obliged by sending in an article entitled "Too Far From Where," an article which gave the highlights of what I had been doing since I left the

University and in an indirect way emphasizing the need for service anywhere in the country, especially by people who had been trained with the tax payers' money and without which they would not have become who they were! I just left it like that. The title, *Too Far From Where?* it may well be that the reader may hear more about this title in this book.

# CHAPTER 28

# MISCELLANEOUS EVENTS
## The Bahamas Independence Celebrations - 1973

In this chapter I intend to list just a few events which have occurred during my life in a random fashion, the very first being the Independence Celebrations of the Bahamas. My interest in the Bahamas stems from the fact that Leonora had roots in the Bahamas. Her parents, as indicated earlier, were young when they migrated to the United States from the Bahamas and became United States citizens. Leonora herself was born in the United States. At the time that I was referring to, Leonora had only been to the Bahamas once. On this occasion, however, she had a letter from some friends in the Bahamas inviting us to attend the Independence Celebrations of Bahamas in 1973. Fortunately, that year, I was entitled as Vice-Chancellor to a paid overseas trip for myself, my wife and another adult, to London and back. So I took advantage of this and paid the difference for a round trip to Nassau in the Bahamas and back through London, for Leonora, myself and our daughter Rachel, who was 17and a student at Aburi Girls School.

The Bahamas is an island in the Caribbean, and the capital is Nassau. Despite its small size, it is a prosperous country. Its main sources of revenue are tourism and banking. There were a number of international banks located there. Incidentally, some of the readers may recall that when King Edward VIII abdicated the British throne, he was later appointed Governor of the Bahamas for some years before he finally settled in France. This fact, I believe made the Bahamas well known among the Caribbean islands. The ceremonies in the Bahamas were very well planned and we enjoyed ourselves thoroughly. At that time, Mr. David Lavell, who was the Superintendent of Police at Tarkwa at the time that Leonora came for our wedding and who was with us at Tarkwa for a few months, had served in the Bahamas for some years

and had retired there. When he heard about our coming, he insisted that
we should stay with him. His wife, Maryse, was there also and in order
to ease the congestion in accommodation, Leonora and I stayed with
the Lavells, whilst our daughter, Rachel, stayed with Leonora's family,
the Davies. Incidentally, Leonora's maternal grandmother was still alive.
She was 102 years old and we were able to pay her a visit. One thing I
remember is that though she was bedridden, her mind was very clear,
her eyes were very sharp and it was possible to carry on intelligent and
intelligible conversation with her.

We took advantage of our presence in the locality of the Caribbean
to visit Jamaica for a few days. As a medical student in Edinburgh I had
known many Jamaicans who were then at the University. The most
outstanding student among them was Michael Beauburon who by then
had become Professor of Psychiatry and was teaching at the University
of the West Indies, which has its headquarters in Kingston, Jamaica.
We were able to meet Michael and his family and others less well known
to me.

My impression of Jamaica was very positive. I felt quite at home
because the vegetation reminded me very much of Ghana. In certain
areas, some of the cultural practices were obviously practices which
have been imported from West Africa, specifically Ghana, or the Gold
Coast, as it was then.

I came back from the Caribbean with the impression that despite
the long years of separation from their roots, there were pockets of
cultural practices in the Caribbean which had still not changed whatsoever
and remained untouched by the interaction with western and Indian
civilization.

## Holiday On Board a Black Star Line Ship
## Down the West Coast

Throughout the time that I was at the University in Kumasi, the most
relaxing and peaceful holiday that I can remember was during the ten
day trip which the whole family, Leonora, our four children and my
niece, Stella, took down the West Coast to Douala in the Cameroon
and back. At that time, the Black Star Line boats were cargo boats
and most of them had passenger accommodation for about twelve people.
The accommodation was not as luxurious as in a passenger liner, but it
was quite comfortable. The trip that we took was in 1970 and the Black

Star Line boat was the Benya River. This particular boat had a presidential suite and we were very fortunate because Leonora and I were given the honor of living in the presidential suite, which as you can imagine, was very well appointed and very comfortable.

The cost per day per person for the trip was ¢3. This included the transportation to and from the terminus and three square meals a day! The meals were of very high quality as the number of people to be catered for was small. As a matter of fact, I do not recall that even all the passenger accommodation was taken up. So the passengers were just 10 including my family of seven. All in all, I spent ¢21 a day for 10 days. I shudder to think what it would cost now! Unfortunately, the Black Star Line has folded up and long before then, that facility for travelling up and down the West Coast had been stopped. I still consider that trip as the most relaxing and quiet period that I have ever experienced. It was very good for me because I really needed rest. There was no telephone, no problems reported to me day in day out. I came back nicely refreshed. The children were really thrilled and to this day, they remember that trip with a certain amount of nostalgia.

## A Trip to the Middle East

This trip did not involve the family. In1966, I had the privilege of visiting the Middle East. My good friend, the late Sleiman Nashief, and his family had been my patients in Kumasi and thereafter very good friends. For years, he had extoled the virtues of his home country Lebanon, what a magnificent place it was, what a happy country, how very prosperous, with very nice people and almost like a Garden of Eden and invited me to visit it one day. I had the opportunity in 1966 to do just that. He had informed me that by paying just a few cedis extra, one could convert a return ticket to London into a ticket which could take one through Lebanon, Rome, London and back to Accra. On this occasion, when I had my annual leave, I decided that since I had planned to go to London on an important visit, I would take advantage of this offer since Nashief was to be in Lebanon at that time and he had offered to be my host. To make it worthwhile, I had planned that I would be in Lebanon for two weeks in order for me to have the opportunity of travelling around the country and meeting some of my Lebanese friends who had been my patients, some who had left Ghana and had gone back home for good, some who were there on prolonged visits. It was an opportunity for me to meet them on their home ground, as it were. I did this trip in the company of Nashief and spent two weeks in Lebanon en route to London.

Nashief's home was somewhere in the southern part of Lebanon, not in Beyrouth. Lebanon is a small country. You can take your car and drive round the whole country in one day. A programme was arranged for me to visit places and people. I must say that I was very much impressed with Lebanon. It had not been touched by war or violence and I found the people to be very friendly. Everywhere one looked around, there were lots of fruits. There was everything in abundance and I recall that on one occasion, Nashief arranged for me to spend the weekend with some friends of mine, Victor Thome and his wife. The first evening of my visit, they arranged a dinner party at a Casino at a place called Jeunie. We did not go there to gamble. There were so many facilities - restaurants, floorshows, variety shows and what have you. This small dinner party was in my honour, but I had eaten so many fruits that day that by evening time, I was so bloated up that I could not touch the food. Here was I with this sumptuous spread before me and I could not touch it. An unforgettable experience! This was an example of the wonderful hospitality of the Lebanese, which I enjoyed during that two-week visit. I must have put on a few pounds by the end of that visit.

The interesting thing is that everywhere we went, I heard Nashief saying "Hakim, Hakim." At first, I did not ask him anything, but I thought the name Hakim must be quite common in Lebanon, because back in Kumasi, I had friends, George and Georgette Hakim, whom I had known for some time. They were family friends. Indeed, during that time they were also visiting Lebanon and I was able to call on them. After a few days I thought: "this Hakim business is too much!' So I asked Nashief, "How many Hakims do you have in Lebanon?" and he explained to me that that word "Hakim" in Arabic means "Doctor." So, indeed, he has been introducing me all the time as Hakim. I found it very interesting indeed and quite amusing!

During the two weeks, I was able to pay a couple of days' visit to Jerusalem. Unfortunately, I could only visit that part of Jerusalem that was in Jordan. I could not visit the part occupied by Israel for obvious reasons. And on this occasion, I took the opportunity to visit some of the holy places, some of the places that I read about in the Bible - Bethany, Jericho, Bethlehem, the garden of Gethsemane, the last route which Our Lord had taken carrying the Cross, even what was considered to be the birth place of Our Lord. It was an educative visit for me, having heard of these names in the Bible, to be able now to actually see them in person.

I left Lebanon with a very good impression of the country. It was peaceful. Everything seemed to be going on well. It was really an important commercial center in the Middle East. Subsequently, I was able to visit, in transit, just on one occasion when I was on my way to Athens; I had to stop overnight in Lebanon and then after the 1974 visit to Cairo with the hockey team we made a brief stop at the airport.

With this picture in my mind, you can imagine my great horror when the hostilities started in the Middle East; the amount of damage, and destruction of all aspects of life in that beautiful country that has taken place since my visit! Happily, at the time of writing this, things are returning to normal. It is my hope that it will not take long for that beautiful country to be restored to the condition in which I saw it in 1966. My prayer is that all the roots of the conflict, be they economic, religious or whatever, may be amicably got rid of so that Lebanon may once more regain its position of a leading commercial centre in the Middle East!

## Sports Writers Award – Past Heroes

In 1979, I was pleasantly surprised when the President of the Ghana Sports Writers Association came to see me to inform me that I had been nominated for an award as a past hero in the field of hockey. I believe the award was started the previous year and, rightfully, the first award in hockey had gone to my great friend, Kofi Atiemo. On this occasion it was my turn to be given the award of past hero in hockey. I felt very proud indeed and I thought to myself that all was not lost yet because there was a creeping tendency, I thought, in Ghana, for people who had made important contribution in various fields, not only in sports, after some time to be completely forgotten. It was almost as if they were being discarded into the dustbin of history. As someone has actually put it, "These people are cast away like the surgeons' soiled gloves". As a surgeon, I know that after the operation, my gloves are very bloody, of no more use, I have finished an operation, I just remove the gloves as they are dirty, contaminated, and just throw them away. So, I was very happy that, having retired from hockey as a player a long time ago and having been in the administration of hockey, I should be accorded this honour at this time!

Early in 1980, at a ceremony at the Star Hotel, among other personalities of the year in the various fields, I was given this recognition in the form of a certificate signed by the President of the Sports Writers Association and a cheque for the handsome sum of ¢200! This is almost a quarter of a century ago and ¢200 at that time had real value!

# CHAPTER 29

# THE JOURNEY SO FAR
## The State of My Health

I entered Achimota College in January 1935 shortly after my fifteenth birthday. Before then I had enjoyed extremely good health and for the next 27 years, I played strenuous hockey every season without fail, retiring finally from first class hockey in 1962. In the interim, especially when I was a medical student at the University of Edinburgh, my weight fluctuated around 11.5 stones. However, in 1962 following a bout of flu whilst I was working at Komfo Anokye Hospital, on routine medical examination, it was discovered that I had a raised blood pressure. Even after I had shaken off the flu, the high blood pressure persisted even though I had no symptoms.

The following year 1963, I had to go to Edinburgh on study leave prior to coming back in 1964 to join the newly established Medical School. During my year in Edinburgh, I had a thorough investigation of the hypertension and, even though I had no symptoms, the pressure was quite high and it was thought advisable that I should start taking anti-hypertensive drugs prophylactically. Since then I have been on anti-hypertensive drugs, which have kept the pressure under control.

My first serious health problem which I had was low back pain. I trace this back to a fall which I had on my return from the United States, when my mother died and I had to rush back. Coming down the stairs of the plane, I fell in a sitting position on the tarmac. The ensuing pains soon disappeared in response to painkillers. There were no radiological changes seen on examination, but, from time to time, and for many years there was a recurrent low back pain which made it impossible for me to take part in the active sports. I have said elsewhere that one of my greatest regrets was that I could not take part actively in playing hockey with the students when I was Vice-Chancellor of the University of Science and Technology.

In the year 1980, I started having very severe pains and I had to go to Edinburgh for full investigation. Osteo-arthritic changes had started taking place with what looked like a burnt-out slipped inter-vertebral disc. After that, I went to Edinburgh on a regular basis for evaluation. In 1985, the question of operative intervention came up. At that time investigative procedures, especially, diagnostic procedures were not as sophisticated as they are now, and the results of operation were not predictable. It was decided that I should continue with conservative measures. On one occasion, I had a spinal manipulation by a qualified doctor specialized in that procedure. This gave me a certain measure of relief.

I continued on the conservative regime prescribed at the Western General Hospital in Edinburgh. This went on for many years and, of course, I had to take an occasional painkiller. However, in 1995, I started having pains which were quite excruciating and debilitating and it was quite clear that something radical had to be done. I started having neurological symptoms in my lower limbs, especially the left one. My doctor, Dr. Ben Kuma (Korlebu) and I discussed the desirability of having an operation for relief. I was just contemplating going back to Edinburgh or to the United States when fortunately, we had a visit from Dr. Edward Kunz, a General medical practitioner in Geneva who was well known by my wife, Elise. Dr. Kunz was born in Ghana of a Ghanaian mother and a Swiss father, who worked in Ghana for a number of years, but Edward was taken to Switzerland at a young age and brought up there. He qualified as a medical doctor and had a good practice. He was especially interested in helping Ghanaians who needed medical attention in Geneva. After discussing my back problem with him, he offered to arrange for me to see a neurological surgeon in Geneva. Shortly after he went back, he made the necessary arrangement and I was able to go to Geneva in the summer of 1995. My wife accompanied me to Geneva and stayed with me throughout my treatment.

All arrangements were made for me to be seen by a leading neurological surgeon. After the necessary investigations, including a C.T.S. scan, I had an operation, a multiple laminectomy to release the pressure on the spinal nerves, which were causing the trouble. After the operation, I had relief for a good many years. I would like to record my gratitude to the surgeon, a young Egyptian-Swiss, Dr. Aymen Ramadan, a delightful professional whom I have a very high regard for, for the good work he did on my back. I am also very thankful to the Wilson family. Ambassador Wilson served in Geneva in the Foreign Service for some time and some of his children were living in Geneva at that time. After the operation, I spent some time convalescing in the home of his daughter, Sylvia, and her husband, and they indeed made me very comfortable.

One thing, which I am very grateful for is that the cost of treatment which would have been very expensive was reduced, through the good offices of Dr. Kunz, to a level which I could afford. This operation was done almost eight years ago. After some years of relief, therefore, I started to have pains occasionally. Because of the chronicity also, I noticed there was a residual weakness in my left leg. Everything was going on smoothly until about the middle of the year 2001, when travelling to Tamale on some official assignment, I was involved in an accident at Nkawkaw. Although we had a very sturdy cross-country vehicle, something happened to the tyre rod and the vehicle went tumbling down a slope into a valley and miraculously coming to an abrupt halt. The jolt that I felt on that occasion, weeks after, started to manifest itself in severe pains. This necessitated many months of physiotherapy, and although my condition is stable at present it is difficult for me to move round. I have problems in balancing and I have to move round with a walking stick.

A few months ago I met a lady who had been a nursing sister who had worked with me at the Komfo Anokye Hospital some forty three years ago, and who knew me as a young active person who used to walk briskly along the long corridors of the Komfo Anokye Hospital, and even run up the stairs. Seeing me walking with the support of a stick was quite an unusual spectacle for her. She herself had put on some weight, grown much older, unable to move as briskly a she did in the good-old-days. We just thanked the Lord that we had been preserved up to that time and could look back on the past with a measure of thankfulness.

There have been times when I have refused to accept what is happening to me, but then I remind myself that I am past 83 and approaching 84, and should be thankful to the Lord that I can still move around occasionally, although not with the same agility. I cannot do the things which I want to do because of this restriction of my mobility. On the other side of the coin, I must admit that this enforced immobility for some time now has helped me to focus on the assignment of writing my autobiography, which inevitably covers a period of many years.

## The Osu Ebenezer Presbyterian Church

My involvement in the affairs of the Osu Ebenezer Presbyterian Church ever since my retirement from public service and also subsequent involvement to some extent in political affairs has been a great source of satisfaction to me. I was raised at Osu, my character formation started seriously at Osu, and therefore Osu is the place which I regard as my home.

There have been many things that one has had to do in the Church, both at the material and spiritual levels. As a presbyter for almost 20 years, eight of which were as senior presbyter, I have been more involved in the social action of the Church than the spiritual. I believe in setting example by action rather than words, therefore I like to interest myself in welfare matters, for example, in health matters and also matters pertaining to education. I have been chairman of the Board of Trustees of the Ebenezer Scholarship Fund for almost twenty years, a Board, which was dissolved recently to be replaced by a Scholarships Committee.

The history of this Board is quite interesting. The whole idea was mooted by Mr. Harry Sawyerr. It was at a special ceremony in the Church when he was chairman for the occasion and mooted the idea of a fund to help in the education of promising children of members of the congregation. This idea was immediately endorsed by the then Session and a Board of Trustees set up. I was the first chairman with Mr. Harry Sawyer himself as the Honorary Secretary-Treasurer together with three other members. It was a small Board and for very many years, Mr. Sawyer paid all the administrative costs of running the scheme. The church since then has given assistance to a number of boys and girls of the congregation to secondary schools. The main source of funds is the second collection of the second Sunday of each month. The money is invested in Treasury Bills. There has also been donations from well-wishers. Starting with a modest assistance of ¢3,000 per scholarship twenty years ago, it has now gone up to half a million cedis per scholarship with bursaries of ¢200,000 per head. The congregation has supported it, not to the extent one would have wished, but at least to a level which has made it possible for the fund to be kept alive for twenty years. It is hoped that the new committee replacing the Board of Trustees will also be helped by the Congregation with the tools to do the job required.

During this time also, much money went into the building of the Ebenezer Presbyterian Church Hall. The important point I wish to make here is that most of the money for building the Hall was raised by members of the Congregation themselves. The Church Hall has become a great asset to the Ebenezer Congregation, a very popular place for conferences of all types organized by professional bodies, Christian organizations, and so on. Altogether, the Church Hall is helping the Ebenezer Congregation to discharge an important social function for the society.

I have also been chairman of the Choir board for a good many years. There have been problems in the choir from time to time and I have been proud to be associated with the Board. For some years I have been chairman of the Awards Committee. Awards of the Gold Medal to members of the Church for meritorious and long service to the Church. Certificates are awarded to promising younger people of the Church. Then for the past two terms I have been privileged to be chairman of the small committee that has vetted nominees for the position of presbyter. It is a very delicate exercise, but things on the whole have gone on well. The presbyter sacrifices much time and energy in his/her work. More people should be willing to make this sacrifice.

In the year 1992, the Ebenezer Chapel celebrated its 90 years of existence. As we know, prior to the building of the Chapel, the services were held at Amanfon. The church itself was in existence before the Chapel was built. At that time, 1992, I was then senior presbyter and I recall writing a brief message in a commemorative brochure prepared for that occasion, expressing the hope that some of us might live to see the Centenary Celebrations of the Church. At that time 10 years seemed very far off. But time indeed flew very quickly and before we knew it, the year 2002 was upon us. The Centenary Anniversary was celebrated in grand style. A year or two before the celebrations, much renovation work was done to the Chapel and its precincts. The interior décor and even work done in the precinct of the Chapel have given it a new look which is admired by visitors, especially those who had known the chapel for some time.

Fine feathers, however, do not necessarily make fine birds, and the fact that the chapel has put on a new look does not necessarily guarantee that everything else would be all right. The Church, for example, at the time of my writing is embroiled in court cases related to financial matters, and one only hopes that all these matters will be resolved amicably. It would seem that some of us christians overlook the fact that matters pertaining to the church should be dealt with in a christian spirit. When the mundane and materialistic spirit submerges the spiritual, then, however good looking the Church may seem outwardly, it cannot in all sincerity say that it is fulfilling its christian mission. The christian mission carries a message of love and fellow feeling, of cooperation, a spirit of reconciliation and forgiveness, and a spirit, which promotes that Christian fellowship which is embodied in the motto of the Presbyterian Church : "That all may be one." How can there be oneness, or the unity, which the crest of the Church symbolizes with the message that it carries, if church matters are conducted in a mundane and materialistic manner?

As the membership of the Church has grown over the years, it has become necessary for Osu Ebenezer to hold two services on Sunday mornings, one at 7 o'clock and the other at 9.30. In my view, the numbers certainly warrant this arrangement. On the other hand, I would like to urge strongly that there should be a certain amount of caution in this. I say so because the first service is conducted in English, whereas the 9.30 service is conducted in Ga. If it were just because of members, then there would be absolutely no reason why both services cannot be conducted in Ga so that all members of the church, both literate and illiterate in English, will have the choice to attend either service. As it is now, there is a creeping tendency for the 7 o'clock service to assume an elitist garb, a service quite different from the second service, so that if care is not taken, at the end of the day, Ebenezer will become two churches instead of two services in a united church! I believe strongly that this matter should be carefully considered.

We know that the Basel Mission philosophy is that evangelization is best done in the mother tongue of the population and not in a foreign language. It is for this reason that the Presbyterian Church should guard this tradition jealously. After all, it was its precursor Church, the Basel Mission, that was responsible for the translation of the Bible into Twi and Ga first, and subsequently into other Ghanaian languages, in the belief that the message would be accessible to all who can understand and who can read the indigenous language.

At this present time, owing to changes in the educational system, we know that Ghanaian languages are not given the importance that they should be given in the curriculum. One of the reasons is the lack of competent teachers and, of course, competent indigenous Ghanaian teachers are an endangered species, a species that is dying out at a time when we have a new generation of young people who cannot speak or write their own language. What is even more serious, they are not even competent in English also! The Church should really take on the responsibility of promoting the indigenous Ghanaian languages, as this cannot be guaranteed in our educational institutions. As a church, we may find ourselves unwittingly contributing to the dying out of our Ghanaian languages, in our case at Osu, the Ga language. So whilst the Ga Dangme Council is busy talking about promoting the Ga language, the Church unwittingly is acting in such a way that stifles the progress and development of the language and, who knows, there may come a time when the Ga language may die out altogether. I have made these views quite strongly elsewhere and my only hope is that they will be taken seriously.

If we must have an English language service, then the Church must put in place an arrangement to make sure that the Ga language is properly taught to our youngsters. Maybe, we should go back to the days when there were Sunday Schools in the Church to make sure that our illiterate fathers and mothers are taught to read and write the Ga language. In this case, they will include our youngsters, our boys and girls who, are gradually losing the advantage of preserving a treasured aspect of our culture, the Ga language.

## Mentors Who Are No More

At my age, I cannot be as active in church matters as I would like to, but I am happy to say that quite an increasing number of our congregation and even some outside the congregation from time to time come to me for counselling on a wide variety of matters. On a personal level, I myself for some time now have missed the wise counsel of some of the senior citizens in our society whom I have looked up to. First of all are my teachers, Dr. Miguel Ribero, and then Dr. Mojaben Dowuona.

At this point, I must make good an omission regarding Dr. Mojaben Dowuona when I discussed my Achimota days. He was indeed the first Achimotan scholar to come back from Oxford to teach at Achimota, his alma mater, in 1935. He taught Latin, English, Ga and a variety of other subjects. Dowuona is a well-known Osu name, indeed of the Osu Royal Family. Mojaben was a product of the famous Osu Salem which was my alma mater too, and, needless to say, we became quite good friends.

It is not necessary for me to say much here, but one unforgettable incident which I must recall is that on the day of Dr. Mojaben Dowuona's wedding to Miss Catherine Konuah, I was the one who pressed the bridegroom's wedding suit. Unfortunately, there was a slight accident, as I burnt one of the lapels of the suit. It was not a bad burn. Fortunately, it was an ash-gray colour, so I enlisted the help of the washman in Anumle village who, very skillfully applied some ash and treated it in such a way that it became invisible. This secret was only between myself and the washman. The bridegroom got to know about it only after the wedding. This was a great feat and it was the skill of the washman which saved me from great embarrassment. I have mentioned Dr. Mojaben Dowuona earlier and the roles he played as First African Registrar of Legon and then Chairman of the Council for Higher Education, whom I succeeded. Then there was Dr. Daniel Chapman Nyaho, about whom I have said much already.

All these three gentlemen lived to ripe old ages and I had the benefit of their counsel as long as they lived. Then there was Mr. Justice Nii Amaa Ollennu, my role model right from my childhood days, also a product of Osu Salem and a self-made man. He became an outstanding lawyer and an eminent jurist and the Speaker of Parliament during the Second Republic. Last but not least was Rev. Prof. Christian Baëta, whom the reader may recall succeeded me as President at the Ghana Academy of Arts and Sciences. I have really missed the wise counsel of these individuals to whom from time to time I went depending on the problem that I had, and who really helped me, and instilled a measure of wisdom into me.

I must also mention my very good friend Mr. S.M. Codjoe, my senior at Ahimota, who played a very important role in my mundane affairs, preparing legal documents for me. Apart from being my lawyer, he was one of my best friends. Alas, he was cut down in his prime after a short illness. As fate would have it, his son, Raymond, has followed in his father's footsteps and is now a well-established lawyer. He happens to be my lawyer too and is performing admirably the functions which his father performed before him.

1997 was a year of tragedy for me. There was a series of bereavements. Several people close to me were called to their eternal rest. First of all, there was Susan Alhassan, my sister-in-law, who was very close to me, whom we lost in January of that year. Then followed my very dear friend and classmate, Prof. Ernest Amano Boateng, a month or two after Susan. He died after a short illness and was buried at Aburi, his hometown. Then my nephew, Willie Evans, formerly of the Black Stars, died, in Lome quite suddenly. Willie had been in Lome for some years coaching several football teams. At one time, he even coached the Togolese national team. Willie's death was followed a few weeks later by that of his son, Sammy, also quite suddenly. As we were at his funeral, my cousin Mrs. Ayo Tagoe, nee Ribeiro, was also called. To crown it all, in July of that same year within the space of eight days, I lost my half sister, Juliana Okailey-Anfom, or auntie Okailey, as she was popularly known, and who, when we started having a family, was with us at Tarkwa and looked after our first three children. She had been bedridden for a number of years and died at the age of 84. Within 8 days, I lost my only surviving brother, Joseph, one month after his 80th birthday. He had been ill for a little over a year, and his death was not unexpected, but all the same coming so close to that of auntie Okailey really put great strain on me. So, 1997 is a year which I would rather like to forget because of the tragedies which occurred that year.

## My 80th Birthday

I did say earlier on that shortly after my second wedding, many of my friends remarked that I had brightened up, and that I looked better and felt happier. I just want to say that this wedding took place in 1984 and as I write now, Elise and I are just round about celebrating the 19th anniversary of our wedding. Considering all that has happened during these years, the reader can imagine the sort of support that I received from Elise. She has given me loyal support, and if I may say so, she has made sure that I did not deviate from the path of health, that is, not doing anything that may affect my health. Surprisingly, over the years I seem to forget that with the passage of time, there are things that one could not do anymore, or as well as before, and in a way, it was like refusing to grow old. Elise has given me good protection from outside influences which might affect my health and through her companionship, I have managed to survive all these years. Originally, I did say that I wondered whether if I had not remarried I would be able to survive so long!

Following the unhappy year 1997 and also 1998, the following year 1999 was the year during which I celebrated my eightieth birthday. Elise and my children organized a fitting celebration. I am happy that all my four children were able to attend the celebrations. Nii Okai and Charlie came down from the United States and we even had a surprise visit from one of Leonora's nieces and her husband. There was a Thanksgiving Service in the Osu Ebenezer Chapel followed by a reception at the Ebenezer Church Hall.

I am really thankful to all my friends who came to celebrate with me on that occasion. The pastors who officiated at the service, Rev. Victor Oko Abe who had just assumed duty as a District Minister of the Church, Rev. Peter Kojo, who preached the sermon - a very stimulating address - Bishop Justice Akrofi, Anglican Bishop of Accra, a good friend of the family who gave the blessing, Rev. Mate-Kojo, former District Minister of Osu and a retired Synod Clerk of the Presbyterian Church and, of course, Bishop Banahene Thompson, retired Anglican Bishop of Accra, who gave the benediction. The church choir was in attendance.

Although the actual birthday as the reader may recall, is October 7th, the celebration took place on October 10th, which happened to be a Sunday. It was an afternoon event. The toast was proposed by my good friend Professor Alex Kwapong, Chairman of the Council of State, with supporting speeches by my professional colleagues Profs. J.M. Quartey and Silas Dodu, and Mr. Kwame Saarah Mensah, the last SRC President during my Vice-Chancellorship of UST.

There is an interesting piece of information which I would like to give to the reader. On the day of my birthday, we had a great surprise from the KLM Airways. As the family was gathered upstairs praying, we were informed that there was a delegation from KLM Airways waiting to see me. We came downstairs, and to my utter surprise, four workers from KLM had brought a birthday cake and a birthday card with them to wish me a very happy birthday.

I must give a background to this. KLM as an airline was born on 7th October 1919, the very day that I was born. So KLM and I had the same birthday! This fact became known to them through my filling in a questionnaire, which occasionally they put on their flights, and I gave this information in passing, not even knowing that it would get anywhere! This was many years ago. Later, the KLM office in Accra got in touch with me, and the first sign that they showed was to send me a christmas card and on one occasion, a birthday card and a birthday cake! To my utter surprise, the visitors had a huge KLM business class ticket for two which I could use to any destination in the world serviced by KLM at any time that I wished.

It was an opportunity for me and my wife to use this ticket any time we were ready to do so. I must say that I was really overwhelmed by this most unexpected and surprising gesture from KLM. First of all, we had to decide where to go and when to go. In the end I decided that we should go to Japan because, even though in my working days I had travelled extensively to all important countries, I had never been to Japan.

## Visit to Japan

So it was that we decided that in the spring of the year 2000, Elise and I would take advantage of this ticket and go to Japan for a week. When spring came, we went to Tokyo and spent a week there. It is interesting to note that the Ghana Ambassador to Japan at that time was Torbgui Kporku III. This is his stool name, but he happened to be a former engineering student of the University of Science and Technology when I was Vice-Chancellor and he informed me that I signed his degree certificate. Need I say anymore? He really gave us red carpet treatment and even though our visit was short, he did everything to make us happy. In addition to Tokyo we visited Yokohama.

I was able to persuade KLM to write the ticket in such a way that we could come back home via the United States so we could visit Nii Okai and Charlie. We returned by the Pacific Route to Atlanta, then spent 5 weeks in the United States before coming back home. The interesting thing is that the flight from Tokyo to the United States arrived in Atlanta at about the same time we left Tokyo! This is because we had to cross the date line somewhere. Elise has always been intrigued by the fact that having been served lunch and having slept for a while, when the stewardess came again to wake her up, she told her that they were serving breakfast. She wondered what had happened to dinner!

An autobiography can never completely cover all the events of one's life, naturally. There has to be a cut off point. I had hoped that, that cut off point would be my eightieth birthday or shortly thereafter. But when writing this autobiography, I realized that the events of December 2000 were far too important in the history of Ghana for me to leave them out. After exciting elections, there was a peaceful change from one constitutionally-elected government to another government, a government of a different party. It was really something that had not happened before in Ghana and I thought I should mention it. At least, I thought that stopping after my eightieth birthday would rob my story of certain important developments which, as a result of these events of December 2000, would be found interesting.

I am not saying this because I belong to any political party. Indeed, I have never belonged to any political party since the advent of party politics. I have always had friends from all parties and as I indicated once before, it is not difficult for a doctor to do this. I have had patients from all parties and, for me, issues matter far more than party, and actions, and the behaviour of people more than their party. All the same, I have been curious to watch developments, to watch what sort of changes would take place after the changeover. I would like to say at this point that at the run up to the introduction of the 1992 Constitution, attempts were made by some people to draw me into party politics, which I stoutly resisted. To this day I do not hold any party card. I prefer to remain independent, to have an independent opinion about issues and be able to comment objectively on any issue without any party or ideological coloration.

As I write now, I am within sight of my 84th birthday, just a few months away. Whether I will reach it or not is in the hands of the Lord, but nothing would please me more than to be able to launch this book, around my 84th birthday or shortly thereafter. Meanwhile, I will continue to play the role of an *Abusuapanyin*, an elder in the Anfom, Evans and allied families and also to put the benefit of my experience in matters medical, educational, and so forth at the disposal of whoever may want to avail themselves of it.

I am happy that for some time now, I have been patron of a number of youth organizations, especially in the church; the many groups within my church, and also choirs of other churches. From time to time also I have one student or another coming to pick my brain on a number of issues and I have always tried to be accommodating. Alas, I am no more in a position to respond or to accept invitations to chair functions or give lectures because of restrictions on my physical mobility. For this reason, I have stayed home most of the time.

I had a very laudable programme of weekly visits to the aged and the infirm in our church. This is something I used to do some years ago, but which I cannot do anymore, and this really saddens me. Those that I am able to reach on the telephone, I call from time to time. The other side of the coin is that, as a result of this restriction of mobility, I have been able to go down memory lane, looking back, recalling some of the important events of my life from the beginning, and which have been the substance of this narrative.

I shall make a political comment at this stage. I believe strongly that when a political party makes campaign promises and is given the mandate by the people, there is a time frame attached to these promises. It is only fair, therefore, that the Party is judged by its achievements at the end of the period for which it is given the mandate. In our circumstances, it is four years, and I do believe that we should all be patient and see what happens at the end of the four years. There are certain things which can be changed over night and others which take time to mature as it were, and to show results at a later date. So, I personally would advise that we should all be patient and see what happens at the end of it all. After four years, hopefully, all of us will still be in possession of our thumbs and if we feel that the progress warrants a continuation, so be it. If we feel that it warrants a change then of course, our thumbs are still there!

In the next chapter, I shall try to look back and comment on a number of issues. So far, I have really concentrated on the narrative with a minimum of comment, although I think after such a long experience of four score years I am entitled to express my views on some of these issues. I shall try to be as objective as possible and, hopefully, some of the views I express may be found useful!

# CHAPTER 30

# RETROSPECT

My story covers a period of four score years and more, from the colonial period, of the days of Governor Guggisberg, through Governor Arden-Clarke, to the independence of Ghana, a self-governing country for three years, and a Republic from 1960 up to the present time. It saddens me to think that after over 40 years of independence, Ghana has not really made the progress that some countries elsewhere in the world, especially the Asian Tigers (Malaysia and Singapore) that were at about the same level of development as ourselves, have made. Without doubt, the most important reason has been the frequent intrusion by the military into the governance of our country. In each case, it appears that rather than propel us forward the intrusion has set us back for some time.

It is said that life begins at forty; but even at the age of forty, Ghana did not get that new dawn of day which should have projected her forward. The question is; "Apart from military intervention, what else is there that has hindered our development?" For someone who has seen life in the colonial days and then during the post independence period, it is rather baffling for me, because Ghana is endowed with rich human and material resources. Yet, we are now where we should not be. We should be far ahead by now! For many senior citizens like me, among whom there is a section which I would call "The brains that refused to drain" and who have worked hard for this country before and since independence, the situation is most disappointing, to say the least.

## Healthcare

It would require a whole book for me to try to analyse the factors which, in my opinion, have cumulatively contributed in the stifling of the development of our dear country, Ghana. For now, I shall list in a random fashion some issues which require urgent attention. I will start with the health sector and refer briefly to the funding of health care, particularly the cost to the patient. During the whole period of my active medical practice, even in the colonial days, there was no occasion that I recall when any patient was refused treatment because he could not pay. In most cases, cost recovery was not made upfront.

Unfortunately, the "cash and carry" system introduced later has resulted in a great hardship for a number of patients. No doubt many patients have died who should not have died. Some patients refuse to go to hospital because they cannot afford to pay upfront. To give just one example. Prior to "cash and carry" if a patient was to have a hernia operation, everything was provided by the hospital. It was after the operation that if there were fees to be paid he was asked to pay! If he could not afford to pay, he was designated "a pauper" and discharged. With "cash and carry," for a simple hernia operation, the patient is given a long shopping list of items to buy, including cotton wool, needles, syringes, medicinal ampoules, and also the cost of treatment. This has resulted in many patients not being able to afford the operation and, therefore, not being treated! Naturally, some of these patients must have succumbed to the ailment. So the "cash and carry" system from the word go brought much hardship, and it is good that at this time it is about to be replaced by a Health Insurance Scheme. A Health Insurance Scheme needs to be carefully thought out because our society is not as well organized as the European society where many things fall in place. But at least, it should be possible to start somewhere. Where there is no properly organized community, we should revert to the pre "cash and carry" system. Even in the colonial days, all patients were treated and, if they could not afford to pay, so be it! They were discharged as paupers to make room for others who needed the hospital beds. So, in the matter of health care, this is the only comment that I want to make. The sooner the cash and carry system goes out of the system, the better!

## Education

In the field of education, there has been much talk about funding. Without doubt, with the increasing numbers of people wanting education and also the constitutional provision that all children should be entitled to free basic education, it is understandable that funding would become an important issue. As the population increases, even if the cost per person did not rise, the total cost to the taxpayer would go up. However, in an economic situation where there is persistent inflation and other militating factors to be considered, it is quite clear that funding would be quite a problem. In my view, the debate now going on is not paying due attention to the priorities given by the Constitution. The priority in the funding of education should be basic education, which should be free. Therefore, in my opinion, any student who has reached the tertiary level and states that the priority in education funding should be tertiary education is really being selfish and unfair. I believe that the focus of any government on education funding should be on basic education. Currently, we have defined basic education to be nine years of schooling. The Constitution, therefore, demands that every child should be given that basic education free; not only free, but it should also be compulsory, which means that all facilities should be provided by the State. The demand for a shift of focus to tertiary education, in my view, is totally wrong, and contrary to the Constitutional requirements.

For many years the percentage of 6 year olds who should be in school but who are not, hovered between 25% and 35%. I gather that it is now about 20%, which is a good thing, as it is coming down. However, I feel that the responsibility of the State is to make sure that these 6 year olds are in school, wherever they may be in Ghana, whether in the urban or the rural area. I am not implying for one moment that secondary and tertiary education are not important. Of course, they are. But to get to secondary or tertiary education, you must first have basic education. Assuming that most of the money is used at the top, it would mean that the numbers who are able to gain access to, or even start formal education, will dwindle and there would be complete social injustice done to increasing numbers of young people in the population. In recent times, attention has been drawn to pre-school education, which is a good thing. The only thing to remember is that by adding another two years to basic education, the net is being cast wider and, therefore, it becomes even more important that resources in education should be focused at the base of the pyramid rather that at the apex!

Of course, tertiary education should be accessible to all who qualify; but it must be remembered that someone has to pay for it. Naturally, with increasing numbers, the State cannot afford to pay for all. It is important therefore that the State sets up a machinery which would make it possible for students entering tertiary education, however poor their economic status, to access loans to pay for their tertiary education. After all, people are prepared to take loans to build houses, buy cars and so on, and yet when it comes to taking a loan to get the most important commodity of all, viz, tertiary education, which may include professional training education and which raises ones market value, then there is a whole lot of noise being made which, in my view, is quite unreasonable. When you consider the fact that a number among these beneficiaries would be some of these people, who after raising their market value would sell their skills at the open market and leave the country to go and help in building other people's countries, it makes it all the more unreasonable that demands and pressures should be put on Government by these people. The university student can articulate and argue his case. However, I have never seen a 5 or a 6 year old, who is denied access to basic education, talking on television to argue his case! These are the silent majority, and it seems to me that the State should make sure that the constitutional provision for these people at that level are be satisfied as a priority, so that every child of school going age should be given the opportunity, irrespective of sex, religious or other background, to gain access to basic education.

Another important reason why the State should focus on sound and good quality basic education is that it is in the interest of good governance that as many citizens as possible should have a minimum of education and literacy. If the quality is of a sufficiently high standard, they would then be able to reason and to think things out for themselves and not allow other people to think for them. All this helps to further good governance. More people would be able to consider issues which are raised, analyse them and make meaningful choices, including choosing suitable representatives to the assemblies and to Parliament.

## Sports

In my view, it is a good thing that Sports has been brought under the Ministry of Education. For too long, we have thought of sports in physical terms only. I believe that the time has come when we should take a holistic view of what sports really entail. There is a saying, " a sound mind in a sound body", a saying which encapsulates the linkage between sports and education. Some people argue that sports are far too important to be put under education and should have a ministry of its own. I beg to differ. It is possible to have an organizational structure in the Ministry of Education which demonstrates the linkage between the mind and the body, and therefore the logic of having them under one umbrella ministry. It is a good thing right from childhood for the individual to cultivate a habit of physical fitness. Many of us know what benefits we have derived from the physical training and the games or sports that we played while in school. When we refer to sports therefore, we should not think only of the physical aspects, but also of the mental and other aspects. Indeed, I feel that we should look at the whole question of sports under the concept of sportsmanship. If we concentrate on the physical only, we lose many of the benefits which sports has to offer.

Apart from the mere physical exercises and motions that the individual goes through during various sporting activities, for organized sports there are rules and regulations governing them, and it is important that all those who engage in these organized sports should know and be familiar with these rules and regulations. Not only that. But we should also know that during sporting activities, especially competitive sports, there is always somebody, a referee or an empire, who is expected to see that the rules and regulations are adhered to by the contesting parties. It is important, as a form of mental discipline that we play according to the rules of the game. Secondly, one should realize that the referee's decision is final and therefore accept it. After all, the referee is a human being, and may occasionally make a mistake. But we must all admit that good referees usually are very objective and impartial, and one small slip which may lead to a wrong decision should be understood and not held against him, and lead to all sorts of conflict situations. So it is important that both participants and the fans and supporters should know the rules and not fault the referee, even when he takes correct decisions, merely because the decision happens to be against what they wished for.

Sportsmanship entails discipline. It also means the acceptance of decisions that are taken by constituted authority. It also means fairplay, in the sense that one does not take undue advantage of a temporary mishap of an opponent. In sum, the aim of good sportsmanship is to play the game well, according to the rules, and to appreciate that sometimes you lose, and sometimes you win. When you win, you do so magnanimously. When you lose, you do so gracefully. And if all sportsmen and all those who participate in or support sports obey these simple principles, all should be well. Such an attitude can be transferred to all aspects of our lives. The Bible says, "teach the child the way he should go and when he grows he will not depart from it." For this reason it is important for sports to be put under education, so that right from the beginning, whilst in school our boys and girls will begin to appreciate and understand the whole concept of sportsmanship, and also to know that it is good for them to keep healthy bodies and by so doing ensure healthy minds as well.

In Ghana, one of our greatest problems in sports is our overemphasis on football. Football, we all know, is the most popular sport throughout the world and it is understandable that many people should follow it. But it is important to realize also that there are other sports. Some of the most ardent football fans play other sports like tennis, hockey, cricket, athletics, boxing, cycling, and so on. There are other forms of sports which need attention and support. In Ghana, we pour too much of our resources into football and in the process deny the other sports the assistance which would help them to develop. Ironically, some of these sports in recent times have brought more honour to Ghana than football.

What is happening to football in Ghana now is that we are living in our past glory when in Africa, Ghana football was of the highest standard. Not long ago, the Starlets won the World Cup on two occasions and were runners up on two other occasions! However, for some years now there has been a rapid decline at all levels and utter confusion in the whole question of administration and organization of football. The retrogression is really amazing and truly, something drastic needs to be done. However, I sincerely hope that, that something would not be pouring even more resources into football, thereby starving the other sports even more!

For some time now, Ghana has been passing through a period of economic hardship and I often wonder whether there is any correlation at all between success in football and the solution of our economic problems. For example, if Ghana were to win the World Cup today, would our economic problems disappear immediately, if at all? I cannot see any logical link between the two. I therefore fail to understand the amount of time, energy and resources being poured into football as if success in football would wipe away our economic woes, pronto!

The new organization in the Ministry of Education makes it possible and easier for sports to be taken more seriously in our educational institutions. Sports need to be regarded as an important part of the education of the individual. After all it is said, "All work and no play makes Jack a dull boy" and we do not want to make boys and girls dull. Therefore, we must make a provision in all our educational institutions right from the basic level, for the promotion of sports. It would be an investment which would yield great dividends in the future. Our nation would be healthier and the educational level of society would be much higher than it is now.

I am a great believer in the capabilities of women, intellectually and in other fields as well. For more than half a century now, women have shown that, given the opportunity, they can do as well as men and sometimes even better in practically all fields. I feel that the emphasis on women education should be stressed. In certain areas there are cultural reasons why the girl child is left at home and only the boys are sent to school. This attitude should clearly be a thing of the past. Girls should be given equal opportunity with boys in education, then there will not be any clamour for affirmative action which in a way tends to suggest that women attain important positions in our society because they are women. Hitherto, it has not been so. Therefore, let us leave it as it is and let women compete with men on equal footing. By all means, give the girl child an equal opportunity to start her education and the Ghanaian girl child will do wonders.

It is my view that if we are able to achieve this objective, it will go a long way to help us in solving many of the societal problems which confront us at this time.

## In pursuit of excellence

The formal education structure is in the form of a pyramid, with basic education at the base and the university at its apex. Sometimes, I get the impression that some people think that everybody who finishes SSS and who gets the minimum grade for entry into tertiary education, especially the university, is entitled as of right, to go to the university. I think it is a wrong attitude to adopt. Clearly, it is unrealistic to hope that everyone who starts in class I will end up at the university. As one climbs the educational ladder, a selection process goes on at different stages - the primary, the secondary and the tertiary. The important point to make is that every child, with the exception of those who are mentally disadvantaged, is endowed with some talent or talents which can find room within the pyramid. The duty of the educational authorities is to endeavour to unearth the talent of every child, and as he or she climbs the ladder to help him or her to develop those talents. Some are academically inclined, whilst others are more useful with their hands. The important issue is that no one should feel, as he climbs the ladder and fails to access the next stage, that he or she is a drop out. There should be options open for everything including the world of work!

At the end of basic education, every child should have discovered where his talents lie. The State should make sure that the quality of basic education is such that every child reaches a standard which will make it possible for him to build upon that foundation, whether in further education or in the world of work. In other words, if the child does not qualify for further academic work, it should be possible for him to be trained for something else. Those who follow in the academic stream must know that there are standards to be kept and that as one climbs the ladder these standards will be used in a selection process.

Ghana, with its rich endowment in human and material resources should strive to build a society of excellence. We ought to be a meritocracy rather than a mediocracy. In a mediocracy anything goes. Excellence is often overlooked whilst mediocre performance is rewarded. It is our own Aggrey of Africa, who, almost a century ago, enunciated the principle that "only the best is good enough for Africa." I think what we should do in Ghana, especially after 45 years of independence, is to always have this aim before us and strive for excellence in all that we do. After all, Ghana has been able to produce world class individuals. The first public servant in the world today is Mr. Kofi Annan, a Ghanaian. We have had world champions in boxing such as Azumah Nelson. In the academic field, we have Prof. Alex Kwapong, who rose to the post of Vice-Rector at the United Nations University. The Ghanaian child, given the opportunity and encouragement, can rise to the highest level in his chosen field. In filling positions of importance in society, whether public or private, we should always look for excellence and avoid the mistake, we have sometimes made in the past, of putting square pegs in round holes, and by so doing, hampering the progress of our country.

## Recognition Of Achievement

I think it is a logical follow up to what I have been saying that the State should reward individuals for outstanding achievement. It is important to do so during people's lifetime, rather than wait and at their funeral pay glowing tributes to the things that they were able to achieve to help the country develop and move forward. All that senior citizens need, especially those who are pensioners and have been on retirement for a good many years and cannot make ends meet, is for the State to take steps to ameliorate their hardships through reasonable pensions and some attractive social privileges. There are thousands of senior citizens whose contributions, however lowly their posts might have been whilst on active service, have nonetheless made very important. Some of these people have moved around the country and served in various positions under difficult circumstances. One must really appreciate and applaud the sacrifices that have been made by our senior citizens in the past. I do not mind saying that the attitude and the sacrifices by these people in those days are not being copied by the present generation, who like their comfort and prefer the urban life to life in the rural areas, where their services are more sorely needed.

## Record Keeping

Related to the issue of senior citizens is the whole question of record keeping in our country. It would appear that the frequent changes in government over the period of our independence have led to the disappearance of important documents, thereby breaking historical continuity. I was quite surprised when some time ago, a public relations officer of the Sports Ministry came to see me to tell him something about the development of hockey in this country. I was even more surprised to learn that there was hardly any record, or documentary evidence of the beginnings of hockey before the Central Organization of Sports was set up. Indeed, I thought that with the establishment of that body, under Ohene Djan, in 1960, everything would be done properly. I say this because before then, sports other than football was organized on a voluntary basis with the support of organizations like the

British Council. It would appear that there is very little information about hockey, and I dare say, it could be the same for other sports to. Football of course, is the dominant sport, and for that there may be some records. Clearly, one of our failures in this country is inefficient record keeping and this fact has affected not only the recognition of senior citizens' contributions but even decisions on important policy issues.

## Time waits for no man

One of the most important reasons for our lack of progress in this country and in Africa generally is the lack of appreciation of time. We do not spend the time at our disposal profitably. We come late to work and leave early. If there is a function especially involving our traditional rulers, for example, a durbar which is scheduled to start at 10 o'clock in the morning, it may well be that by 2 o'clock some chiefs may still be arriving with large retinues, thus wasting everybody's time. We arrive late at Board meetings or sometimes fail to turn up at all. This may lead to lack of a quorum and the meeting having to be postponed. Sometimes too, because of our lateness, the meeting starts late and, therefore, there is not enough time to discuss important matters and decisions are therefore taken in a hasty manner.

Related to the above is the fact that we do not value time. We like too many holidays. We look for every opportunity to take a holiday. For example, I do feel that if an official holiday falls on a weekend day, say on Saturday or Sunday, it should be observed as a holiday all the same! But what happens is that when the holiday falls on a weekend, we take a weekday in order to compensate. All this adds up to time lost, and, therefore, productivity falls. I see no reason, also why Farmers' Day, which is celebrated on the first Friday of December every year should not be celebrated on a Saturday. Farmers are associated with hard work, and I do not know if the idea is that on that particular day, there should be a holiday so that they should rest together with the rest of the nation! I feel that it would have been more profitable if Farmers' Day was fixed for a Saturday. I do not think the country would lose anything. On the other hand, we would gain a whole working day, which, translated into cedis, could well be in billions! At the present time, we lose this huge amount because we remain idle on that Friday, when we should be working!

For a long time, our lack of punctuality has been termed "African time" or "African punctuality." Far from resenting it, we have learnt to accept it and, therefore, not to do anything about it. So we keep on losing time, all the time! If we were to add up the number of hours that we arrive late at work or functions over the years, it may well amount to several months of non-performance and, therefore, non-production!

## Indiscipline

Talking about productivity leads me on to the problem of indiscipline. Recently, the Vice-President started a campaign against indiscipline and I feel that it is an exercise that we should all support. Discipline is a quality which comes from within. At the same time, it has something to do with the way in which we are bought up, whether at home or at school. A proper education system should ensure that right from the start, there is a sense of discipline instilled into the child, so that by the time he/she leaves school, he/she has a proper understanding of what is right and what is wrong and learns, as a habit, to do the right thing always.

There are so many instances of indiscipline in our society, for example, the breach of traffic regulations, overspeeding, running against the red light, parking wrongly, and obstruction to the regular public traffic without good cause. The examples are countless. I was brought up in a puritanical atmosphere, and when I compare the discipline in our educational institutions in those days and what we have now, I feel a bit sad because I think it is possible, even now, for dedicated teachers and also well-meaning parents to make sure that right from the word go self-discipline becomes part and parcel of the nature and behaviour of the child. He will then grow up to become a responsible citizen. In our days, there was a subject on the curriculum called "Citizenship" and it was during that time that the pupil was taught about his rights, but, more importantly, his responsibilities in society and a sense of patriotism instilled in him at that age. He grew up with this. I grew up during the colonial days and at that time the national flag was the Union Jack. It saddens me to have to say this, but it looks as if in those days, Gold Coasters had a greater respect for the Union Jack than Ghanaians of today have for the Ghana flag!

## The Pull Him Down Syndrome

Related to the question of indiscipline and mediocrity is what has come to be known as the "pull him down syndrome" whereby Ghanaians, instead of working hard to get on and progress under their own steam, spend time undermining others who are doing well, in order to retard their progress and in order for them to be given posts which they do not deserve, and which, in any case, they cannot fill adequately! As a social phenomenon too, there was a time when it appeared that those in authority believed that in the interest of social justice and equity, the schools which were getting on should be brought down to the level of the schools which were not doing too well, a process of levelling down, instead of that of levelling up!

When I was young, there were no preparatory, private or international schools, the reason being that there was no need for them because the standard in the public schools was high. There were well-trained and dedicated teachers, and the mission or government schools were well endowed with good facilities. There was also a sense of mission regarding teaching as a calling, and, therefore, the standard of teaching in all schools was high. There was no need for expensive schools when quality education was ensured in public schools. These days the situation is different. The standard in our public schools is not as high as in the private schools where very high fees are charged and where there is better supervision and better facilities. I feel that this is a very important social problem which we must deal with. The problem is related to the whole question of funding which is also related to how affordable it would be to government, and which in turn depends on the health of the economy.

I have already implied that there was more discipline during the colonial period than in the post-independence period, and I think this has something to do with the introduction of party politics. I will give an example to illustrate the point. We all know that at independence the Convention People's Party, under the leadership of Kwame Nkrumah, won the elections and became the government of the day. They were in power for many years. It is a fact that during that time there was a good deal of political patronage.

Despite the unifying influence of the Convention People's Party which can be said to have introduced a sense of nationhood in the new country, Ghana, cadres of the party did things which tended to undermine discipline in the public service, especially. I recall that on one occasion, a female ward attendant, at the Kumasi Central Hospital (now Komfo Anokye Hospital), threatened to report an Indian gynecologist to the cadres of the CPP for some wrong she thought the doctor had done. When I looked into the matter, I found that the doctor was right. He was quite professional in what he did. This ward attendant was a staunch party girl but was highly incompetent. She did not like to be reprimanded because of the political connections she had with the ruling party. This example illustrates how discipline in the public service was undermined even at the early stage of our independence by cadres of the party. It is sad to say that this attitude which went down for some time with some governments, resurfaced in our recent past, to the extent that politics has made it impossible for us as a country to do certain things for ourselves. Political patronage has done a great deal to undermine discipline in our country. It is a problem which we are still grappling with and I do hope that the changes which we are experiencing today will take care of it!

I am a strong believer in multiparty democracy. I do not for one moment support a one party state. Unfortunately for Ghana, after starting on a good note, we went through a period of a one party state, which came in by legislation. A one party state can only be equated to a one party dictatorship. A small group of people, within the party organization concentrates power in their hands and they in turn cede absolute power to one man, who then, becomes the ultimate dictator. Unfortunately, we have had to go through such a period in our history. From the point of view of physical development, much happened at that time, but the restrictions on freedom of the individual were a negative aspect of that period. When you consider that the motto of Ghana is "Freedom and Justice", the whole situation appears rather incongruous!

Multiparty politics associated with freedom of speech and of expression is the greatest bulwark against dictatorship. However, such freedom may be abused to the extent of undermining that freedom itself, when almost every issue is subjected to partisan political treatment, even though issues of health, education, welfare, and foreign relations should be approached in a bipartisan manner.

## The *Aban* Mentality

Another issue which is of great concern to me is the attitude of Ghanaians towards Governant. "*Aban*", the Akan word for Government, is an entity looked upon by Ghanaians as something remote, and yet something to which Ghanaians look for everything to be done for them.

This dependency syndrome has for a long lime stifled local initiative, especially before the District Assembly arrangement was put in place. Even though there are well laid down channels of communication, working from the local level right to the top, there is a tendency for people to bypass constituted channels, and even try to get to the President. People address letters to the President, and on the radio, people call to make complaints which are clearly addressed to the President but which should, in the first place have been dealt with at the local level.

Another undesirable aspect of this *Aban* mentality is the manner in which citizens handle public property. People too often handle public property carelessly. Their attitude is one of nonchalance. "Well, it is government property, so if there is any damage, government will repair the damage or replace the item". In a situation where there is the tendency to evade or avoid taxes, and for the government to be robbed of much revenue which could be used in doing useful things, such an attitude is both unfair and irresponsible. I pity government for the demands made on it for subsidies, or for assistance in various forms. Requests for government to do this or to do that! People tend to forget that government gets its revenue from taxes, but when these wide-ranging demands are made and therefore taxes are increased or the tax net is widened, there is a complaint by the same people who want all manner of things done. Of course, I am fully aware that one of the greatest drawbacks in the economy at the moment is the inefficiency of revenue collection. It is important to cast the net of taxation as wide as possible, so that it would not be necessary to raise taxes unduly and thereby increase the burden of the same people who have been religiously paying their taxes. In a nutshell I feel that if the local assembly is efficiently run, it would help to gradually change the *Aban* mentality so that people will do things for themselves at the local level. *Aban* will come in where necessary, especially in areas which are less endowed, in order to supplement whatever has to be done, for reasons of equity!

## Religious Tolerance

I have been brought up as a christian, specifically, a Presbyterian, and I will hold on to my faith, whatever happens. The same thing goes for Moslems and people of other faiths in the community. Elsewhere, that is, in other countries, there have been clashes due to religious intolerance. I am happy to observe that on the whole, we do very well in Ghana in the area of religious tolerance. The cooperation between Moslems and Christians especially has always been excellent, with the exception of isolated minor clashes which have occurred from time to time in remote areas. I believe that this is an area where all well-meaning citizens should give their support, because without this religious tolerance it is possible for violence and unnecessary conflicts to erupt.

## The Fourth Estate of the Realm : A Double-Edged Sword?

I remember when I was a student at Achimota College in the 1930's; Dr. Nnamzi Azikiwe, who was the editor of the "African Morning Post," gave a lecture at the Palladium. The Palladium was a cinema house and is just across the road from the Wesley Cathedral, at Asafoatse Netty Road. In the absence of large public halls at that time, it was a popular place for public lectures. The lecture was titled "The Fourth Estate of the Realm." I was very much impressed by the lecture from which I learnt about the important role of the media. At that time, it was just press and radio, the latter being in its early stages in Ghana. Very few people had wireless sets and some people owned rediffusion boxes with programmemes relayed from station ZOY.

The lecturer, Dr. Azikiwe, stressed the important role of the media as the watch dog of society to see that there was good governance, and expose corruption and abuse of Human Rights. This was during the colonial days when there were stiff laws on sedition and one had to be careful with whatever one said. Azikiwe was a very courageous and powerful speaker. He was careful to emphasize that the power of the media should be used responsibly. I make this point to remind ourselves that what Azikiwe said at that time holds with even greater force today. The Constitution of Ghana places a heavy responsibility on the media regarding its watchdog role. The Constitution guards jealously freedom of speech and expression. In Ghana today, we have a very vibrant, vocal and vigorous media. We have the press (newspapers) and the electronic media in the form of radio and television. We have so many FM stations. There is freedom of speech, with people calling in freely into radio programmemes. After the law of Criminalisation of Speech was removed from the statute book, there has been even more freedom.

In such situations there are some who might abuse this freedom and turn it into licence. The comments which I would like to make relate to journalists. Over the years, we have had an increasing number of people who have undergone proper training in the journalistic profession. In the media today, we have some excellent people. In any profession you have competent people as well as quacks. There is a wide spectrum ranging from the mediocre to the excellent performers. I see the Fourth Estate of the Realm as a double-edged sword. It is a weapon which could be used positively or negatively. The role of the media is to inform, educate and entertain, and the media tries its best to do these three things with varying degrees of success. Those of us who read the newspapers regularly and also listen to radio programmemes and watch television can testify to the power that the media have in disseminating both truth and falsehood.

I think it is very important that the editor of a newspaper should be well educated. He should also be somebody who can be objective in seeking the truth. A person of high integrity. The same thing goes for the presenters on radio and television programmemes. They need to be well educated and competent and objective and men and women of integrity. They should perform their role bearing in mind the media's principal functions of information, education and entertainment. I regret to say that whereas there are some to whom one could award high marks in the performance of these functions, there are others who fall far short of expectation. For example, it is important that the newspapers, the radio and television are not used to try to destroy the reputation or character of individuals with baseless allegations and falsehood which once disseminated is often very difficult to retrieve.

It is important for a radio presenter also, for example, in reviewing newspapers or a particular topic, to be in a position to correct any caller who wants to peddle misinformation either intentionally, mischievously or out of ignorance. It is very important that the radio presenter himself should be in a position to correct any mistakes that may be made especially where he can do so authoritatively. Where he is not sure, it is always advisable for him to seek the help of experts who he may invite or call in to explain issues, so that mischievous misinformation, libellous allegation, ignorance or falsehood is not disseminated. If all media people will bear in mind the fact that what they should be after is the truth, and to speak the truth without fear or favour, and avoid the tendency, as we have now, of sometimes using half-truths to poison the public mind, they would be doing the public great service.

We have statutory constitutional bodies like the Media Commission and the Ghana Journalists Association, which play a regulatory role on the performance of journalists. When I hear, or read, or see some of the things in our media at the present moment, sometimes I become a bit worried, especially when the evidence shows quite clearly that the motive behind a publication is just to destroy an individual or discredit an organization. We cannot deny the fact that our society in Ghana today is highly polarized, politically. It is, therefore, incumbent on all well-meaning journalists and all well-informed people who use the media that they always seek the truth and do whatever it is in their power to educate the public and support any process of reconciliation which goes on.

I must end my story here for the time being. By the Grace of God I have led a full life and I can only count my blessings, and in doing so acknowledge the great things that he Lord has done in my life. Every morning when I wake up I give thanks to the Lord that He is still giving me a chance to serve Him. The Bible says that we must all work whilst it is day, for the night comes where we will no more be in a position to work (John 9:4). It is important that all of us realize that we are here for a purpose. We have been given an assignment to do within a short time of our transit in this world. In the Lord's own time, he will judge whatever we do and call us to account for our stewardship during the time that we were given the opportunity.

# APPENDIX A

# FAREWELL FATHER

## (A TRIBUTE TO DR. EVANS-ANFOM) BY DAVID TETTEH
## EDITOR OF 'FOCUS'

The greatest thing, perhaps, a simple Ghanaian can do [according to tradition] to show his respect to and admiration for someone is to spread his favourite cloth on the ground for his idol to walk on it; and this is-. exactly what I am doing, in my mind as I bid Dr. Emmanuel Evans-Anfom a soulful farewell.

Born on the 7th of October, 1919, Dr. Evans-Anfom was until he assumed duty as the Vice-Chancellor of Uni-versity of Science and Technology on 1st August, 1967, the Acting Medical Administrator of Korle Bu Teaching Hospital, Accra; and a Senior Lecturer in Surgery at the Ghana Medical School.

## HOT SEAT

It is not an easy thing to rule a society of people with questioning minds; but it is even more difficult for an administrator to define justice in a society where democracy' is at it's highest peak. It is therefore only natural for the seat of the Vice--Chancellor to be 'red hot'!

Yet, someone must sit on it and sit on it well too! There is no doubt, therefore, that that 'someone' must be a person of understanding, experience and self-control.

A record of Dr. Evans-Anfom's seven-year reign shows that he sat on the seat with considerable ease. No wonder one of the students who saw his reign from the beginning to the end described him as "the man who approached situations with the understanding of an affectionate father"

## STUDENTS' RIOTS

Perhaps his greatest achievement was his ability to calm down the an-gry student through negotiations. It is remarkable to note that with the exception of the demonstrations on the Engineering Lecturers'

*435*

resignation and the Loan Scheme (which were against the government, anyway), the comparatively few demonstrations on the campus were held in his absence. 'And even there, these demonstra-tions were not directly against his administration.

Throughout his reign, there were 3 major demonstrations by the stu-dents: the first was on the Engineering Lecturers' resignation, then on the loan scheme and finally on Mrs. Tackie's action (which was also against the hospital administration as a whole).

I wish to reiterate that throughout his reign, there was no occasion when Dr. Evans-Anfom's decision was received with heavy hearts by students

## DOUBTS

When Dr. Evans-Anfom was appointed the Vice-Chancellor of U.S.T., the Ghanaian public in genera, doubted his integrity since he was better known in the medical field. There was also some amount of disapproval since, at that time, the country need-ed doctors of his calibre.

On the part of the students, it was thought this appointment would provide a sort of relief because of his policy of non-committal. Happily, time has proved this right. He did not belong to any particular quarter of the University social groupings. Perhaps it is this policy that has won the hearts of U.S.T. students.

## CONTRIBUTIONS

His introduction of Matriculation into U.S.T., and his support for a students' Club house, coupled with a number of publications he has to his credit (which include "Intestinal Perforation - Some Observations on Aetiology and Management" and The Evidence for Transformation of Lymphocytes into Liver") and his enthusiasm in sports, as a whole prove that he is not only for the welfare of U.S.T. but also for the human society in general.

"When truth is evident, it speaks for itself." Dr. Emmanuel Evans-Anfom has proved to the 'doubtful Thomas' that his appointment as the Vice-Chancellor of University of Science and Technology was justified. And we can confidently say that he is easily one of the best, if not the best  Vice-Chancellors that we have had in the country.

*WE WISH HIM ALL THE BEST*

# ACCEPTANCE SPEECH*

*by*

### DR. EMMANUEL EVANS-ANFOM
### ON BEING ELECTED THE CHAIRMAN OF THE
### WEST AFRICAN EXAMINATIONS COUNCIL
### BANJUL, MARCH 22, 1991

Twenty-four years ago, in my capacity as Vice-Chancellor of the University of Science and Technology, Kumasi. I was one of the Ghana Government nominees on the West African Examinations Council. and served for a period of nearly seven years. Little did I dream then that I would one day, almost a quarter of a century later, be standing before you, nominated by my country and elected by you to the high office of Chairman of this Council. And yet, when I look back over the past 25 years it would seem that much of what I have done, or been asked to do, has directly or indirectly been preparing me for this day. My thanks first and foremost go to the Government of Ghana for honouring me by my nomination and, secondly, to you, my colleagues, for the confidence you have shown by electing me. I shall do my best always to justify that trust.

In accepting to serve as Chairman I am aware of the important role played, and the great contributions made by my illustrious predecessors in office towards building the West African Examinations Council into an organization widely respected interna-tionally and whose certificates and diplo-mas are greatly coveted in the sub-region. All my predecessors have been eminent persons, and I note with interest that I am the fourth medical doctor to wear the Chairman's mantle. The WAEC must indeed have an affinity for doctors!

My immediate predecessor, himself a surgeon, has maintained the high stan-dards set in the past and I hope as he leaves office today he does so with a feeling of satisfaction for a job well done. May I join others, Sir, in congratulating you warmly on your splendid performance in office. You handle both scalpel and pen with great dexterity and have also proved yourself a capable leader of men.

Mr. Chairman, the WAEC, which will be 40 next year, is a unique organization. Unlike other analogous regional organizations. e.g. The West African Currency Board, The West African Airways. The West African Cocoa Research Institute and The West Af-rican Court of

Appeal, which broke up at different times with the attainment of independence in the various member countries, it has displayed a wonderful capacity to survive. The strength intrinsic in its struc-tures has enabled it to withstand successfully the stresses and strains of time and change. It is to the credit of successive governments in the member countries that they have recognized the importance of the Council and resisted whatever temptation there might have been in the past to dis-member it.

Consequently not only has the Council survived but it has also grown and widened its scope of responsibilities and continued to receive the support of all member governments to realize the primary objectives in its establishment vlz: "to promote mutual understanding and coopera-tion and assist the harmonization of procedures and standards of prescribed examinations in member countries." The Coun-cil's role was aptly set forth by the Education Minister of a member country as "firstly, to assist in the development of sound education" secondly, "to ensure that educational standards are maintained" "thirdly, to give the people of West Africa a vision of the fertile land which lies beyond examinations".

The importance of education in the development of the individual into a good human being and a useful citizen cannot be over emphasized. At the end of the day, however, there will always be the need for assessment and evaluation of academic/vocational achievement and the search will continue for the best method or combination of methods for doing so in a way which would be fair to the candidate.

Alas, the need for that piece of paper testifying to achievement will be with us for a long time to come - if not, forever. The paper qualification syndrome will persist. The paper chase will continue, and fair or foul means will continue to be used by can-didates, friends and relatives to 'catch' that piece of paper - the certificate or diploma -and the attendant problems for the Council will continue and for which the Council has often quite unfairly in my opinion, been blamed.

Meanwhile research will continue to be an important function of the Council. The Educational Reforms taking place in member countries bring with them not only new opportunities but also new challenges which must be faced as well as pitfalls to be avoided, The WAEC has been, and will continue to be, actively involved in all problems attendant on the changes, especially in the area of assessment. The Council has already proved itself to be immensely ca-pable of adapting to change, and its rich experience will continue to benefit member countries that may be in need of it.

The Council's laudable and credit-able achievements so far have been made possible by a combination of factors : wise and capable leadership by past Chairmen, commitment and dedication of Council members, and the hardwork and integrity of successive Registrars and staff of the Council's international and national offices, who deserve high commendation. The 1990s promise to be years of challenge and excitement considering the education reforms taking place and the idea of widening membership to bring in Francophone coun-tries in the region.

It is clear, however, that if these de-velopments are to take place smoothly and efficiently the capability of WAEC needs to be strengthened, and this should be done by the member governments through both words and deeds. Let it not be said that whilst all over the world, countries and organizations are coming together to pool resources in order to survive and act effectively, WAEC is being slowly weakened in capability, influence, and prestige through neglect and starvation by member coun-tries. Let or member governments therefore reaffirm their trust and confidence in W AEC and provide the tools for doing the job, and let us therefore as councillors and Council staff resolve to re-dedicate ourselves anew to face the challenges of the future with greater commitment. and perform any tasks which we may be called upon to perform with greater zeal.

As your Chairman, all I ask of you is your cooperation and your prayers that God may grant me wisdom to lead by ex-ample. so that together we may march forward in the mission assigned us viz: of helping to develop the human resources in our region.

May the Almighty Himself bless our efforts ,and guide us as we take confident strides into the future.

*THANK YOU*

## APPENDIX C

# DR. EMMANUEL EVANS-ANFOM
### CITATION FOR HON. D.Sc. (Salford University) -
### JULY 4,1974

Emmanuel Evans-Anfom has a Welsh name, was educated at University in Scotland, has an America wife (who I'm glad to say is with us today) - but without question belongs to Ghana. Ghana, geographically, is a long way from Salford. When one visits West Africa first, it is the differences which strike you. The food is different. Fish and chips is replaced by pounded yam, gari, Do-Do, Fu-Fu, Ogusi or Ocra soup.

Here we have white women, who insist on lying in the sun trying to get brown. In Ghana, they have brown women, who apply in a skin whitener to try to become white.

Our women have straight hair and use curlers to try to kink it. In Ghana, they have kinked hair and they try their best to straighten it. So maybe our women are not so different really!

In Salford we would be surprised to see a car stop for a goat to cross the road, or a lizard scampering across the carpet, or a moth resting on a wall being suddenly snapped up by a Geco. Yes, Africa at first sight can appear another world.

But certain people have seen instinctively that these are only superficial differences. Basically, Ghanaians and Salfordians are brothers - for the simple reason that man is a brother to his fellow man, and a child of God. That has been the basic philosophy of Dr. Evans-Anfom throughout his eventful life. He has continually been building bridges, between black and white, privileged and under-privileged, the healthy and the sick. But there is one bridge we particularly value - and that is the one which stretches from Kumasi to Salford, the link between our two Chemistry Departments which now has been in existence more that 5 years.

Dr. Evans-Anfom was born on 7th October 1919, at Accra, and was brought up in a puritan Presbyterian atmosphere. His initial intention, after entering Achimota Secondary School, with the Cadbury Scholarship in 1935, was to become a Minister of Religion.

440

The motto *of* the school is *"Ut* Omnes Unum Sint," Aggrey famous motto, embossed on the school crest showing the black and white keys of the piano, indicating harmony between black and white. Obviously this exercised a profound influence on the young Evans-Anfom. His career throughout school was outstanding as a scholar and sportman, and it was no surprise that he won the coveted Gold Coast Government Medical scholarship to study medicine at Edinburgh University. This achievement coincided with the darkest hours *of* the war, and until the tide *of* war changed somewhat in 1942, he filled in the time as science master in his old school. Then he went North *of* the Border to University and started a distinguished career. He served on the Student Representative Council, numerous other College bodies and captained the Hockey 151 XI for 2 years. He captained also the Scottish Universities' XI. He also played in Scottish trials. Now *if* he had gone to Cardiff, with his Welsh name, he could have represented Wales, but the Scots arc not as catholic and they allow only Scotsmen to represent them. So they lost a potential match-winner.

Nevertheless, many other Scottish institutions took Evans-Anfom to their heart. The churches in particular did so, and he was in constant demand as a speaker at youth meetings throughout Scotland and Europe.

He did graduate with the M.B. Ch. B degree in 1947 - but thought he had not. When the results were announced, his fellow students commiserated with him when they found that he was not at the head *of* the list. But even then, he was prepared to share their triumph and accompanied them to the results board. Lo and behold - there was his name! Not under the A's where they had expected, but under the Evans.' How great was the rejoicing. It is the only time, I think, he has been sorry for his Welsh part-name.

Then began a very happy period at Dewsbury, which sir, is in a county we do not acknowledge by name in Salford! After very varied experience there he returned in 1950 to his beloved Gold cost, as it was then, where his services were badly needed. For 11 years he toiled in    hospitals all over the country: DUNKWA, TARKWA , SEKONDI, TAMALE, and finally reached the top as Surgical Specialist in charge *of* Kumasi Central Hospital, then the most advanced in west Africa.

But that time, you will recall, was not a happy time in Africa. The Congo crisis was raging, and it was Dr. Evans-Anfom who was the clinical leader of the team of Ghanaian doctors who went to the Congo. At that time there was not a single trained Congolese doctor, and the activities of the Ghanaian doctors, under Dr. Evans-Anfom, carried out momentous life-saving work.

In due course the Ghana Medical School was started, and Dr. Evans-Anfom joined as senior Lecturer. Then, in 1966, he became part-time Medical Superintendent, in addition to his position as premier surgeon. He had now reached the top of his profession in his country. Then in 1967 came the call to serve Ghana in another way, as Vice-Chancellor of the University of Science and Technology, Kumasi. It is here that I first came into contact with Dr. Evans-Anfom. In association with our own Vice-Chancellor at the time, Dr. Clifford Whitworth, they tried something new - a link between the Chemistry Departments 3,000 miles away from each other, but close in interests and objectives. Staff, technicians, students have been interchanged, so that it is quite normal to hear a Salford lecturer say, "Sorry, I can't play cricket next week, I have to pop to Kumasi". Research links have followed, and now we are eatlllg ice cream in Salford stabilized with gums from trees in Ghana. Could there possibly be greater intimacy?

It is natural, Sir, that we should here dwell on your role in bridging the miles between Kumasi and Salford, but we must not forget that you have bridged the gaps in your own country, too. Through the leadership of Dr. Evans-Anfom, the University at Kumasi came down from its ivory tower, and spread its expertise through the villages and townships of Ghana. Villagers were assisted with their technical problems and "Intermediate Technology" was born - before we in this country had even been able to devise the name.

Much could be said about Dr. Evans-Anfom's achievements at Kumasi - but it is not too much to summarize them by saying that, as a result, the University entered a new era of involvement and was given a new sense of purpose and direction. What is more, it was all achieved with dignity and tact.

Then, on St. David's Day this year, Dr Evans-Anfom was appointed Chairman of the National Council for Higher Educational in Ghana. This is the body which advises the Ghana Government on all higher education policy He is, therefore, now the Chief Adviser on Higher Education to the Government of Ghana.

The highest compliment that was ever paid to me in Africa was- "His face may be white but his heart is as black as ours." Dr Evans-Anfom is a surgeon who knows, and has lived the fact, that we all have the same red blood, and that our differences are only skin deep.

It is with pleasure and gratitude. therefore, that I present to you, sir, Dr Emmanuel Evans-Anfom, Bachelor of Medicine, Bachelor of Surgery, Fellow of the Royal College of Surgeons of Edinburgh, Fellow of the International Surgical Association, Fellow of the Ghana Academy of Arts and Sciences - a distinguished surgeon, scientist, educationalist, administrator, artist, Sportsman, but even more than them all, a great humanitarian

# THE UNIVERSITY OF EDINBURGH/
# ROYAL BANK OF SCOTIAND
## ALUMNUS OF THE YEAR AWARD 1996

Dr Emmanuel Evans-Anfom MBChB

Laureation Address - 7 December 1996

Mr Vice-Chancellor, Ladies and Gentlemen, I have pleasure in presenting to you,

The University of Edinburgh/Royal Bank of Scotland Alumnus of the Year 1996

### Dr Emmanuel Evans-Anfom

The Alumnus of the Year Award at The University of Edinburgh honours the outstanding achievement of the University's former students.

This is an unique and prestigious Award for achievements in the arts or sciences, or for distinction in business, public or academic life, or for exemplary service to the community. The Royal Bank of Scotland is proud to be associated with the Award and, as a graduate of the University, it gives me great pleasure to present it on behalf of the Royal Bank.

Dr. Emmanuel Evans-Anfom graduated MBChB from this University in 1947 and continued in Edinburgh *to* complete the post-graduate Diploma in Tropical Medicine and Hygiene. He was admitted a Fellow of the Royal College of Surgeons (Edinburgh) in 1955, a Fellow of the International College of Surgeons in 1960 and is a Fellow, and past-President, of the West African College of Surgeons.

Dr Evans-Anfom began his medical career at Dewsbury General Hospital as a House Physician. He returned to West Africa in 1950 and since then he has devoted all his working life to the continent of Africa. In 1960, during the early stages of the crisis in the Congo Dr

*443*

Evans-Anfom was appointed as a clinical leader of a team of Ghanaian doctors sent to the Congo under the auspices of the World Health Organization. There was not a single trained Congolese doctor in that country, at that time. These Ghanaian doctors had a seminal influence on the development of medicine in the Congo.

In his own country Dr Evans-Anfom became Senior Lecturer in Surgery at Ghana Medical School when it opened in 1964. In 1967 he was invited to become Vice--Chancellor of the University of Science and Technology in Kumasi. Although sad to leave academic medicine, he embraced the challenge to serve Ghana in a different capacity and did so with distinction. Dr Evans-Anfom has made a major contribution to higher education in Ghana, serving on many different bodies, including his Chairmanship of the National Education Commission.

Dr Evans-Anfom is a man of wide interests. While a student here at Edinburgh he took an active part in the life of the University. He became a member of the Students' Representative Council, President of the Edinburgh African Association, President of Edinburgh Colonial Students' Union and President of the Student Christian Movement. He was awarded a Hockey Blue each year from 1942 to 1947, was Captain of Edinburgh University XI and of the Scottish Universities' XI. Had he been a Scot he would certainly have been selected for the full Scottish national side. On return to Africa he captained the Ghanaian national team for four of his ten playing years.

Dr Evans-Anfom has retained his links with the University of Edinburgh and is President of the Edinburgh University Club of Ghana.

Throughout his long career Dr Evans-Anfom has remained dose to the Presbyterian Church and as well as serving as an Elder he has been involved in many youth, church and student organizations.

Ladies and Gentlemen, for over forty years Dr Emmanuel Evans-Anfom has made a distinguished contribution to the development of Ghana as a surgeon, scientist, educationalist, sportsman, staunch member of the Christian church and as a humanitarian. It gives me great pleasure to present, to him, the 1996 University of Edinburgh/ Royal Bank of Scotland Alumnus of the Year Award.

# INDEX

## A